The Captives

Volume Two

Descendants of
Sara dite Catherine Enneson or Hanson
and
Jean-Baptiste Sabourin

Gail Morin

© 2018

Introduction:

The second book in the Captives series is the descendants of the captive Sara Hanson and her husband Jean-Baptiste Sabourin. Sara, her mother Elisabeth Meador and two or three other children were taken captive by natives on August 7, 1724 at their home in Dover, New Hampshire and taken on a rigorous march to Quebec. Sara's mother and siblings were rescued by her father John Hanson in 1725, but Sara remained in Quebec.

Jean-Baptiste Sabourin and Sara dite Catherine Hanson dit Enneson were married at Oka, Quebec on on July 27, 1727. Ten children were born to this couple. Two daughters and one son married and had children. Six generations of their descendants are included in this book with many families recorded in Quebec in the 1850s. Their descendant Michel Hermenegilde Villenueve was in the 1835 Red River Settlement census.

Descendants of Sara dite Catherine Enneson or Hanson and Jean-Baptiste Sabourin

Generation One

1. **Sara dite Catherine Enneson or Hanson**, daughter of John Hanson or Enneson and Elisabeth Medor or Midar, was born circa 1710 Dover, New Hampshire *(Sara-Catherine Ennson (Hanson); Birthdate: November 13, 1708 (78); Birthplace: Dover, Strafford, New Hampshire)* (DGFQ Jette, Rene, *Dictionnaire Genealogique des Familles du Quebec des Origines a 1730* (Montreal, Quebec, Canada: University of Montreal Press, 1983), page 1028.). She was baptized on 21 Jul 1727 Oka, Quebec (Ibid.). A contract for the marriage to **Jean-Baptiste Sabourin**, son of **Pierre Sabourin** and **Madeleine Perrier,** was signed on 20 Jul 1727 *(Notary Raimbault fils)* (DGFQ, page 1028.). She married **Jean-Baptiste Sabourin**, son of **Pierre Sabourin** and **Madeleine Perrier,** on 27 Jul 1727 Lac-des-Deux-Montagnes, Oka, Quebec *(Jean Baptiste Sabourin, age 26, son of Pierre Sabourin and Madeleine Perrier both of Pointe-Claire, married, 27 Jul 1727, Catherine Ennson, origin: Village of Tomba, Boston, daughter of Jean Ennson and Elisabeth Midar both living in Village of Tomba, Boston, Present: Guillet, Pierre Parisien)* (DGFC Tanguay, Cyprien, *Dictionnaire Genealogique des Familles Canadiennes* (28 Felsmere Avenue, Pawtucket, Rhode Island 02861-2903: Quintin Publications, 1996 reprint), Volume 7, page 106.) (DGFQ, page 1028.) (PRDH online index, http://www.genealogic.umontreal.ca, No. 10026.). She died on 7 May 1787 Vaudreuil, Quebec (Ibid., No. 395123.). She was buried on 9 May 1787 Vaudreuil, Quebec *(age 76, wife of Paul Sabourin)* (PRDH online, No. 395123.).

"Feb 10, 1725, was Baptized francoise, aged about six months, of English father and mother. The godfather was francois de Coagnes and the godmother marie anne Lafayette.... who have signed. Mari anne lafayette, J. G. du Lescoat, priest." [This is probably Sara's infant sister.]

She witnessed the baptism of **Hyacinthe Pascal Seguin dit Laderoute** on 24 Mar 1742 Ste-Anne-de-Bellevue, Quebec *(Godfather: Hyacinthe St.Germain, Godmother: Catherine Henson, Leguer priest, missionary of Lac-des-Duex-Montagnes)* (DGFC, Volume 7, page 157.) (PRDH online, #116585.).

Jean-Baptiste Sabourin was born on 6 Oct 1701 (DGFQ, page 1027.). He was baptized on 8 Oct 1701 Lachine, Quebec (DGFC, Volume 7, page 105.) (DGFQ, page 1027.). He married according to the custom of the country **Marie-Josephe Ouatagamie (Amerindienne)** before 1719 (Ibid.). He died on 8 Oct 1781 Vaudreuil, Quebec, at age 80 (PRDH online, No. 378685.). He was buried on 9 Oct 1781 Vaudreuil, Quebec *(age 87)* (PRDH online, No. 378685.).

He witnessed the baptism of **Marie Madeleine Larocque** on 12 Apr 1725 Bellevue, Quebec *(Godfather: Jean Baptiste Sabourin, Godmother: Marie Madeleine Boyer of Ste-Anne-de-Bellevue, Deperet priest)* (DGFQ, page 281.) (PRDH online, No. 15161.).

He witnessed the baptism of **Reine Ursule Raizenne** on 11 Nov 1764 Oka, Quebec *(Godfather: Jean Baptiste Sabourin captain at Vaudreuil)* (PRDH online, #270259.).

Children of **Sara dite Catherine Enneson or Hanson** and **Jean-Baptiste Sabourin** were as follows:

2   i.   Paul Sabourin, b. 4 May 1731 Oka, Quebec; m. Marie Josephe Seguin dit Laderoute; d. 14 Mar 1798 Vaudreuil, Quebec; bur. 16 Mar 1798 Vaudreuil, Quebec.

    ii.   Jean Baptiste Sabourin was born on 1 Feb 1734 Seigneurie de Cavagnal, Quebec (Ibid., #116315.). He was baptized on 22 Mar 1734 Ste-Anne-de-Bellevue, Quebec *(Godfather: Jacques Charbonnier, Godmother: Marie Anne Crepin, J. Matis priest)* (PRDH online, #116315.). He died on 10 Mar 1735 Ste-Anne-de-Bellevue, Quebec, at age 1 (Ibid., #116967.). He was buried on 10 Mar 1735 Ste-Anne-de-Bellevue, Quebec *(Present: Jean Baptiste Laviolette, Jean Baptiste Lalonde, Michel Brebant, Antoine Lariviere, Deperet priest, missionary)* (PRDH online, #116967.).

    iii.   Marie Anne Reine Sabourin dit Saint-Barthelemy was baptized on 25 Dec 1735 Ste-Anne-de-Bellevue, Quebec *(Godmother: Marie Anne (Amerindienne), Ignace Soentakani (Amerindienne), Guen priest, missionary of Lac-des-Deux-Montagnes, Sartelon priest missionary)* (PRDH online, #116384.). She died on 14 Apr 1807 Notre-Dame-de-Montreal, Quebec, at age 71 (Ibid., #2390409.). She was buried on 16 Apr 1807 Notre-Dame-de-Montreal, Quebec *(age 71, Sister of the congregation of Notre Dame, a nun for 53 years and 7 months)* (PRDH online, #2390409.).

    iv.   Catherine Sabourin was born on 25 Sep 1737 Vaudreuil, Quebec (Ibid., #116430.). She was baptized on 25 Sep 1737 Quebec *(Godfather: Pierre Deschamps Jr., Godmother: Genevieve Dielle, Sartelon priest)* (PRDH online, #116430.). She was buried on 4 Oct 1737 Ste-Anne-de-Bellevue, Quebec *(of seigneurie de Vaudreuil, age 9 days, Present: Jacques St.Juien church warden, Sartelon priest)* (PRDH online, #116430.).

     v.   Catherine Laurette Sabourin was born on 20 Jul 1739 seigtneurie de Vaudreuil, Quebec (Ibid., #111575.).   She was baptized on 21 Jul 1739 Oka, Quebec *(Godfather: Louis Mallette, Godmother: Marie Josephe Fortin)* (PRDH online, #111575.).

3 vi. Marie Charlotte Sabourin, b. 15 Feb 1741; m. Jean Baptiste Jerome Raizenne.

    vii. Pierre Sabourin was baptized on 17 Mar 1743 Oka, Quebec *(father's occupation: captian of the militia, residence: seigneurie de Vaudreuil)* (PRDH online, #111598.). He was buried on 1 Oct 1743 Oka, Quebec *(age 7 months, residence: seigneurie de Vaudreuil)* (PRDH online, #111687.).

   viii. Elisabeth Sabourin was baptized on 26 Apr 1745 Oka, Quebec *(father's occupation: captian)* (PRDH online, #111615.).

4 ix. Therese Amable Sabourin, b. 16 Oct 1746 Oka, Quebec; m. Pierre Jean Villeneuve; d. 29 Sep 1810 Ste-Madeleine-de-Rigaud, Quebec; bur. 1 Oct 1810 Ste-Madeleine-de-Rigaud, Quebec.

    x. Jean Baptiste Guillaume Sabourin was baptized on 31 Jan 1752 Oka, Quebec (Ibid., #270064.).

Generation Two

2. Paul Sabourin was baptized on 4 May 1731 Oka, Quebec (DGFC, Volume 7, page 106.) (PRDH online, #148521.). He married **Marie Josephe Seguin dit Laderoute**, daughter of **Louis Seguin dit Laderoute** and **Marie Anne Raizenne dit Shoentakouani,** on 4 Nov 1752 Oka, Quebec *(Paul Sabourin, son of Sabourin a Captain in the militia, married 4 Nov 1752 Oka, Marie Josephte Seguin Laderoute, daughter of Louis Seguin Lieutenant in the militia)* (DGFC, Volume 7, page 106.) (PRDH online, #270300.). He died on 14 Mar 1798 Vaudreuil, Quebec, at age 66 (Ibid., No. 395236.). He was buried on 16 Mar 1798 Vaudreuil, Quebec *(age 67, a cultivator)* (PRDH online, No. 395236.).

He witnessed the baptism of **Marie Charlotte Sabourin** on 18 Feb 1741 Oka, Quebec *(Godfather: ___ DeBeauharnois chevalier, captain, represented by Paul Sabourin fils, Godmother: Catherine DeLaperelle, represented by Anastasie Raizinne)* (PRDH online, #111581.) (Ibid., #116546.).

He witnessed the baptism of **Paul Regis Villeneuve** on 18 Sep 1778 Vaudreuil, Quebec *(Godfather: Paul Sabourin his grandfather)* (PRDH online, #722386.).

Marie Josephe Seguin dit Laderoute was born circa 1738 (Ibid., #148522.). She died on 29 Dec 1814 Ste-Madeleine-de-Rigaud, Quebec (Ibid., #2681917.). She was buried on 31 Dec 1814 Ste-Madeleine-de-Rigaud, Quebec *(age 80, widow of Paul Sabourin)* (PRDH online, #2681917.).

Children of **Paul Sabourin** and **Marie Josephe Seguin dit Laderoute** were as follows:

    i. Jean Paul Sabourin was baptized on 19 Sep 1754 Oka, Quebec (Ibid., #270100.). He was buried on 25 Oct 1754 Oka, Quebec (Ibid., #270359.).

    ii. Marie Catherine Sabourin was baptized on 24 May 1757 Oka, Quebec *(baptized with the permission of the cure of Ste-Anne)* (PRDH online, #270132.).

   iii. Jean Baptiste Sabourin was born circa 13 Sep 1758 Ste-Anne-de-Bellevue, Quebec (Ibid., #276772.). He died on 18 Sep 1758 Ste-Anne-de-Bellevue, Quebec (Ibid.). He was buried on 19 Sep 1758 Ste-Anne-de-Bellevue, Quebec *(age 5 days, buried in the presence of Rene Riviere, Sartelon priest)* (PRDH online, #276772.).

5 iv. Marie Madeleine Sabourin, b. 7 Jan 1760 Oka, Quebec; m. Simon Villeneuve; m. Jean Toupin; d. 21 Nov 1824 Ste-Madeleine-de-Rigaud, Quebec; bur. 23 Nov 1824 Ste-Madeleine-de-Rigaud, Quebec.

    v. Paul Vincent Sabourin was baptized on 13 Apr 1761 Oka, Quebec (Ibid., #270178.).

6 vi. Hyacinthe Sabourin, b. 24 Oct 1762 Oka, Quebec; m. Marie Angelique Brasseur; d. 11 Mar 1824 Ste-Madeleine-de-Riguad, Quebec; bur. 13 Mar 1824 Ste-Madeleine-de-Riguad, Quebec.

   vii. Marie Elisabeth Sabourin was baptized on 20 Nov 1763 Oka, Quebec (Ibid., #270229.). She was buried on 23 Nov 1763 Oka, Quebec (Ibid., #270389.).

7 viii. Andre Paul Sabourin, b. 12 Mar 1765 Oka, Quebec; d. 19 May 1819 Ste-Madeleine-de-Riguad, Quebec; bur. 21 May 1819 Ste-Madeleine-de-Riguad, Quebec.

   ix. Jean Baptiste Sabourin was baptized on 13 Sep 1766 Oka, Quebec (Ibid., #738685.). He was buried on 26 Sep 1766 Oka, Quebec *(age 13 days)* (PRDH online, #415870.).

8 x. Marie Louise Amable Sabourin, b. 12 Nov 1767 Oka, Quebec; m. Pierre-Antoine Sauve; d. 15 Jun 1837 Ste-Madeleine-de-Rigaud, Quebec; bur. 17 Jun 1837 Ste-Madeleine-de-Rigaud, Quebec.

9 xi. Charles Sabourin, b. 22 Jan 1769 Oka, Quebec; m. Marie Anne Bedard; d. 18 Oct 1839 Ste-Madeleine-de-Riguad, Quebec; bur. 20 Oct 1839 Ste-Madeleine-de-Riguad, Quebec.

10 xii. Paul Sabourin, b. 24 Aug 1770 Oka, Quebec; m. Scholastique Sabourin; d. 8 Jul 1805 Ste-Madeleine-de-Riguad, Quebec; bur. 10 Jul 1805 Ste-Madeleine-de-Riguad, Quebec.

11 xiii. Antoine Sabourin, b. 10 Jun 1773 Oka, Quebec; m. Angelique Condon; d. 9 Feb 1820 Ste-Madeleine-de-Riguad, Quebec; bur. 11 Feb 1820 Ste-Madeleine-de-Riguad, Quebec.

xiv. Francois Sabourin was baptized on 4 Jul 1774 Oka, Quebec (Ibid., #738980.).

3. Marie Charlotte Sabourin was born on 15 Feb 1741 (Ibid., #116546.). She was baptized on 18 Feb 1741 Oka, Quebec *(Godfather: __ DeBeauharnois chevalier, captain, represented by Paul Sabourin fils, Godmother: Catherine DeLaperelle, represented by Anastasie Raizinne)* (PRDH online, #111581.) (Ibid., #116546.). She married **Jean Baptiste Jerome Raizenne**, son of **Josiah-Ignace Raizenne or Rising dit Shoentakouani** and **Marie-Elisabeth (Abagail) Nimbs dit Touatogouach,** on 15 Feb 1762 Oka, Quebec (Ibid., #270318.). A contract for the marriage to **Jean Baptiste Jerome Raizenne**, son of **Josiah-Ignace Raizenne or Rising dit Shoentakouani** and **Marie-Elisabeth (Abagail) Nimbs dit Touatogouach,** was signed on 19 Mar 1762 *(Notary Panet)* (PRDH online, #332998.).

Jean Baptiste Jerome Raizenne was baptized on 30 Sep 1740 Oka, Quebec (Ibid., #111580.). He died circa Jan 1795 Montreal, Quebec (Ibid., #3985011.). He was buried on 2 Feb 1795 Oka, Quebec *(He died at Montreal and his body was tranported to Oka for burial; age 54)* (PRDH online, #3985011.).

Children of **Marie Charlotte Sabourin** and **Jean Baptiste Jerome Raizenne** all born Oka, Quebec, were as follows:

i. Catherine Elisabeth Raizenne was baptized on 17 Nov 1762 (Ibid., #270204.).

ii. Reine Ursule Raizenne was baptized on 11 Nov 1764 *(Godfather: Jean Baptiste Sabourin captain at Vaudreuil)* (PRDH online, #270259.).

iii. Marie Clothilde Raizenne was baptized on 12 Apr 1766 (Ibid., #738672.).
She witnessed the baptism of Marie Angelique Raizenne on 20 Sep 1782 Oka, Quebec *(Godfather: Jerome Raizeen her brother, Godmother: Clothilde Raizenne her sister)* (PRDH online, #739071.).

iv. Joseph Jerome Raizenne was baptized on 19 Mar 1768 (Ibid., #738723.).
He witnessed the baptism of Marie Angelique Raizenne on 20 Sep 1782 Oka, Quebec *(Godfather: Jerome Raizeen her brother, Godmother: Clothilde Raizenne her sister)* (PRDH online, #739071.).

v. Scholastique Raizenne was baptized on 10 Feb 1770 (Ibid., #738796.).

12 vi. Ignace Raizenne, b. 8 Oct 1771; m. Clemence Marie Guindon; d. 23 Sep 1849; bur. 26 Sep 1849.

vii. Marie Charlotte Raizenne was baptized on 21 Feb 1773 (Ibid., #738937.).

13 viii. Marie Marguerite Raizenne dit Shoentakouani, b. 22 Oct 1775; m. Antoine Chevrier dit Lajeunesse; d. 18 Apr 1835; bur. 20 Apr 1835.

ix. Suzanne Raizenne was baptized on 6 Nov 1779 (Ibid., #739045.).

x. Marie Angelique Raizenne was baptized on 20 Sep 1782 *(Godfather: Jerome Raizeen her brother, Godmother: Clothilde Raizenne her sister)* (PRDH online, #739071.).

4. Therese Amable Sabourin was baptized on 16 Oct 1746 Oka, Quebec *(Amable Therese Sabourin, father's occupation: captian of the militia)* (PRDH online, #111631.). She married **Pierre Jean Villeneuve**, son of **Jean-Pierre Villeneuve** and **Marie Madeleine Bedard,** on 1 Aug 1768 Oka, Quebec (Ibid., #415837.). She died on 29 Sep 1810 Ste-Madeleine-de-Rigaud, Quebec, at age 63 (Ibid., #2681734.). She was buried on 1 Oct 1810 Ste-Madeleine-de-Rigaud, Quebec *(age 66, wife of Pierre Villeneuve, occupation: agriculture)* (PRDH online, #2681734.).

Pierre Jean Villeneuve was born on 19 Nov 1745 Charlesbourg, Quebec (Ibid., #173629.). He was baptized on 19 Nov 1745 Charlesbourg, Quebec *(Godfather: Jacques Villeneuve grandfather, Godmother: Marguerite Parens grandmother and wife of Bernard Bedard, Morisseaux vicar)* (PRDH online, #173629.). He died on 27 May 1815 Ste-Madeleine-de-Rigaud, Quebec, at age 69 (Ibid., #93348.). He was buried on 29 May 1815 Ste-Madeleine-de-Rigaud, Quebec (Ibid.).

He witnessed the marriage of **Simon Villeneuve** and **Marie Madeleine Sabourin** on 6 Nov 1775 Vaudreuil, Quebec *(Witnesses: Simon Villeneuve's brothers Pierre and Francois Villenevue)* (PRDH online, #227064.).

Children of **Therese Amable Sabourin** and **Pierre Jean Villeneuve** were as follows:

i. Andre Francois Xavier Villeneuve was baptized on 1 Dec 1770 Oka, Quebec (Ibid., #738841.).

14 ii. Angelique Amable Villeneuve, b. 14 Sep 1773 Oka, Quebec; m. Joseph Amable Sauve dit Laplante.

15 iii. Pantaleon Villeneuve, b. 27 Jul 1775 Oka, Quebec; m. Marie Francoise Lalonde; m. Genevieve Victoire Seguin; d. 18 Jul 1838 Ste-Madeleine-de-Rigaud, Quebec; bur. 20 Jul 1838 Ste-Madeleine-de-Rigaud, Quebec.

16   iv.   Francois Etienne Villeneuve, b. 5 Jan 1779 Vaudreuil, Quebec; m. Amable Marie Reine Gauthier; m. Angelique Daoust.

17   v.   Anastasie Villeneuve, b. 20 Jul 1781 Vaudreuil, Quebec; m. Francois Xavier Lemaire dit St.Germain; d. 29 Jan 1818 Ste-Madeleine-de-Rigaud, Quebec; bur. 30 Jan 1818 Ste-Madeleine-de-Rigaud, Quebec.

18   vi.   Paul Pierre Villeneuve, b. 8 Feb 1784 Vaudreuil, Quebec; m. Veronique Chevrier.

19   vii.   Vincent Xavier Villeneuve, b. 14 Oct 1786 Vaudreuil, Quebec; m. Euphrosine Marie Quesnel.

Generation Three

5. Marie Madeleine Sabourin was baptized on 7 Jan 1760 Oka, Quebec (DGFC, Volume 7, page 106.) (PRDH online, #270160.). She married **Simon Villeneuve**, son of **Jean-Pierre Villeneuve** and **Marie Madeleine Bedard,** on 6 Nov 1775 Vaudreuil, Quebec *(Witnesses: Simon Villeneuve's brothers Pierre and Francois Villenevue)* (PRDH online, #227064.). She married **Jean Toupin**, son of **Jean Toupin** and **Marie Fefeu,** on 26 Nov 1804 Ste-Madeleine-de-Rigaud, Quebec (Ibid., #54963.). She died on 21 Nov 1824 Ste-Madeleine-de-Rigaud, Quebec, at age 64 (Ibid., #2682440.). She was buried on 23 Nov 1824 Ste-Madeleine-de-Rigaud, Quebec *(age 67, wife of Jean Toupin)* (PRDH online, #2682440.).

Simon Villeneuve was baptized on 20 Feb 1751 Charlesbourg, Quebec *(Godfather: Simon Clapin sargent of the troops, Godmother: Marie Therese Thomas daughter of Jacques Thomas, Morisseaux priest, missionary)* (PRDH online, #260145.). He was born on 20 Feb 1751 Charlesbourg, Quebec (Ibid.). He died on 26 Apr 1801 Vaudreuil, Quebec, at age 50 (Ibid., #2592314.). He was buried on 27 Apr 1801 Vaudreuil, Quebec *(age 50)* (PRDH online, #2592314.).

Children of **Marie Madeleine Sabourin** and **Simon Villeneuve** were as follows:

20   i.   Regis Villeneuve, b. circa 1776; m. Ursule Seguin.

     ii.   Paul Regis Villeneuve was born on 17 Sep 1778 Vaudreuil, Quebec (Ibid., #722386.). He was baptized on 18 Sep 1778 Vaudreuil, Quebec *(Godfather: Paul Sabourin his grandfather)* (PRDH online, #722386.).

21   iii.   Marie Ostie Villeneuve, b. 17 Nov 1780 Vaudreuil, Quebec; m. Paul Francois Seguin dit Laderoute.

22   iv.   Xavier Louis Villeneuve, b. 19 Jun 1782 Vaudreuil, Quebec; m. Louise Veronique Seguin dit Laderoute.

23   v.   Pierre Anselme Seguin dit Asselin, b. 20 Apr 1785 Oka, Quebec; m. Louise Marie Seguin dit Laderoute.

24   vi.   Marie Theotiste Villeneuve, b. 9 Aug 1787 Vaudreuil, Quebec; m. Etienne Lefebvre or Lefaivre; d. 25 May 1839 Vaudreuil, Quebec; bur. 27 May 1839 Vaudreuil, Quebec.

25   vii.   Marie Judith Villeneuve, b. 14 Apr 1789 Oka, Quebec; m. Augustin Kemner dit Laflamme.

26   viii.   Marie Scholastique Villeneuve, b. 14 Apr 1789 Vaudreuil, Quebec; m. Francois Xavier Cadieux.

27   ix.   Marie Monique Villeneuve, b. 2 Jul 1792 Oka, Quebec; m. Hyacinthe Seguin dit Laderoute.

28   x.   Simon Benjamin Theodore Villeneuve, b. 2 May 1794 Oka, Quebec; m. Marie Angelique Chevrier dit Lajeunesse; m. Mary McDonell.

29   xi.   Michel Hermenegilde Villeneuve, b. 22 Jul 1795 Vaudreuil, Quebec; m. Josephte Genthon dit Dauphinais; d. before 1876.

30   xii.   Francois Jeremie Villeneuve, b. 14 Nov 1797 Vaudreuil, Quebec; m. Hippolyte Bedard.

     xiii.   Pierre Villeneuve was born on 7 Mar 1801 Oka, Quebec (Ibid., #2752197.). He was baptized on 7 Mar 1801 Oka, Quebec (Ibid.).

Jean Toupin was born on 1 Feb 1742 St-Benoit, Le Mans, Maine (Le Mans, Sarthe) (Ibid., #217588.). He married **Marie Angelique Demers dit Dumais**, daughter of **Francois Demers dit Dumais** and **Marie Suzanne Arel,** on 3 May 1773 Notre-Dame-de-Montreal, Quebec (Ibid.). He died on 30 Dec 1818 at age 76 (Ibid., #2593102.). He was buried on 1 Jan 1819 Vaudreuil, Quebec *(age 67 years and 10 months, husband of Marie Madeleine Sabourin)* (PRDH online, #2593102.).

6. Hyacinthe Sabourin was baptized on 24 Oct 1762 Oka, Quebec (Ibid., #270202.). He married **Marie Angelique Brasseur**, daughter of **Francois Brasseur** and **Marie Angelique Jerome dit Latour,** on 15 Feb 1790 Vaudreuil, Quebec *(Hyacinthe Sabourin, son of Paul Sabourin and Marie Josephe Seguin, married 15 Feb 1790, Marie Angelique Brasseux, daughter of Francois Brasseux dit Duamelle and Marie Angelique Jerome, Present: Andre, Pierre and Charles Sabourin brothers of the groom, Simon Villeneuve and Antoine Sauvey brother-in-laws of the groom, Jean Baptiste Razizenne uncle of the groom, Peirre Villeneuve uncle of the groom, Joseph and Francois Brasseux brothers* *of the bride, Mathias Jerome uncle of the bride)* (PRDH online, #358098.). He died on 11 Mar 1824 Ste-Madeleine-de-Riguad, Quebec, at age 61 (Ibid., #2682396.). He was buried on 13 Mar 1824 Ste-Madeleine-de-Riguad, Quebec *(age 64, occupation: cultivator, husband of Marie Angelique Brasseur)* (PRDH online, #2682396.).

Marie Angelique Brasseur was baptized on 23 Mar 1770 Oka, Quebec (Ibid., #216925.). She died on 17 Oct 1845 Ste-Madeleine-de-Riguad, Quebec, at age 75 (Ibid., #4624518.). She was buried on 18 Oct 1845 Ste-Madeleine-de-Riguad, Quebec *(age 74, widow of Hyacinthe Sabourin)* (PRDH online, #4624518.).

Children of **Hyacinthe Sabourin** and **Marie Angelique Brasseur** were as follows:

    i. Anonyme Sabourin was born on 24 Jan 1791 Vaudreuil, Quebec (Ibid., #586577.). He/she died on 24 Jan 1791 Vaudreuil, Quebec (Ibid.). He/she was buried on 24 Jan 1791 Vaudreuil, Quebec (Ibid.).

31 ii. Hyacinthe Sabourin, b. 2 Nov 1792 Vaudreuil, Quebec; m. Marie Reine Hurtubise; m. Marguerite Liboiron dit Bellefleur.

    iii. Andre Sabourin was born on 10 Sep 1796 Vaudreuil, Quebec (Ibid., #770838.). He was baptized on 11 Sep 1796 Vaudreuil, Quebec *(father's occupation: cultivator)* (PRDH online, #770838.). He died on 30 Mar 1813 Ste-Madeleine-de-Riguad, Quebec, at age 16 (Ibid., #2681821.). He was buried on 1 Apr 1813 Ste-Madeleine-de-Riguad, Quebec *(father's occupation: agriculture)* (PRDH online, #2681821.).

    iv. Marie Josephe Sabourin was born on 8 May 1798 Riviere de la Graisse, Quebec (Ibid., #642759.). She was baptized on 9 May 1798 Oka, Quebec (Ibid.). She died on 3 Jul 1798 Vaudreuil, Quebec (Ibid., #586887.). She was buried on 5 Jul 1798 Vaudreuil, Quebec *(father's occupation: cultivator)* (PRDH online, #586887.).

32 v. Marie Reine Sabourin, b. 13 Jul 1800 Vaudreuil, Quebec; m. Alexis Noel Cadieux.

    vi. Israel Sabourin was born on 16 Mar 1803 (Ibid., #2679145.). He was baptized on 22 Mar 1803 Ste-Madeleine-de-Riguad, Quebec (Ibid.).

    vii. Marie Josephe Sabourin was born on 20 May 1805 Ste-Madeleine-de-Riguad, Quebec (Ibid., #2679267.). She was baptized on 20 May 1805 Ste-Madeleine-de-Riguad, Quebec *(father's occupation: agriculture)* (PRDH online, #2679267.). She died on 20 May 1805 Ste-Madeleine-de-Riguad, Quebec (Ibid., #2681543.). She was buried on 21 May 1805 Ste-Madeleine-de-Riguad, Quebec *(father's occupation: agriculture)* (PRDH online, #2681543.).

33 viii. Marie Madeleine Rose Sabourin, b. 30 Aug 1806 Ste-Madeleine-de-Riguad, Quebec; m. Edouard Brouillard.

    ix. Pierre Simon Sabourin was born on 28 Oct 1811 Ste-Madeleine-de-Riguad, Quebec (Ibid., #2679823.). He was baptized on 28 Oct 1811 Ste-Madeleine-de-Riguad, Quebec *(father's occupation: agriculture)* (PRDH online, #2679823.).

7. Andre Paul Sabourin was baptized on 12 Mar 1765 Oka, Quebec *(father's occupation: lieutenant of the militia)* (PRDH online, #270271.). He married **Marie Madeleine Brasseur**, daughter of **Francois Brasseur** and **Marie Angelique Jerome dit Latour**, on 7 Mar 1791 Vaudreuil, Quebec *(Andre Sabourin, son of Paul Sabourin and Marie Josephe Seguin, married 7 Mar 1791, Madeleine Brasseur, daughter of Francois Brasseur and Angelique Jerome, Present: Hyaincthe, Charles and Antoine Sabourin brothers of the groom, Simon Villeneuve and Antoine Saver brother-in-laws of the groom, Francois Seguin, Pierre Villeneuve and Vital Bertrand uncles of the groom, Francois and Joseph Brasseur brothers of the bride, Marie Brasseur sister of the bride, Jean Marie Jerome and Louis Cote uncles of the bride)* (PRDH online, #358112.). He died on 19 May 1819 Ste-Madeleine-de-Riguad, Quebec, at age 54 (Ibid., #2682102.). He was buried on 21 May 1819 Ste-Madeleine-de-Riguad, Quebec *(age 56, occupation: agricuture, husband of Madeleine Brasseur)* (PRDH online, #2682102.).

Marie Madeleine Brasseur was born on 13 Feb 1774 Vaudreuil, Quebec (Ibid., #722091.). She was baptized on 14 Feb 1774 Vaudreuil, Quebec (Ibid.). She died on 29 Apr 1820 Ste-Madeleine-de-Riguad, Quebec, at age 46 (Ibid., #2682151.). She was buried on 1 May 1820 Ste-Madeleine-de-Riguad, Quebec *(age 47, wife of Andre Sabourin, cultivator)* (PRDH online, #2682151.).

Children of **Andre Paul Sabourin** and **Marie Madeleine Brasseur** were as follows:

    i. Andre Sabourin was born on 21 Dec 1791 Vaudreuil, Quebec (Ibid., #770352.). He was baptized on 22 Dec 1791 Vaudreuil, Quebec (Ibid.). He died on 15 Jun 1792 Vaudreuil, Quebec (Ibid., #586600.). He was buried on 17 Jun 1792 Vaudreuil, Quebec (Ibid.).

34 ii. Francois Sabourin, b. 20 Dec 1792 Oka, Quebec; m. Louise Seguin.

    iii. Anonyme Sabourin was born on 2 May 1796 Vaudreuil, Quebec (Ibid., #586748.). He died on 2 May 1796 Vaudreuil, Quebec (Ibid.). He was buried on 2 May 1796 Vaudreuil, Quebec (Ibid.).

        iv. Anonyme Sabourin was born on 2 May 1796 Vaudreuil, Quebec (Ibid., #586749.). He was buried on 12 May 1796 Vaudreuil, Quebec (Ibid.).

35   v. Antoine Sabourin, b. 6 Jun 1797 Vaudreuil, Quebec; m. Louise Chevrier.

36   vi. Magdelaine Rose Sabourin, b. 6 Feb 1801 Oka, Quebec; m. Paul Seguin dit Laderoute.

37 vii. Andre Sabourin, b. 4 Apr 1803; m. Marie Colombe Bedard.

38 viii. Marie Josephte Sabourin, b. 19 Oct 1804 Ste-Madeleine-de-Riguad, Quebec; m. Floribert Henri Hubert Seguin.

39   ix. Joseph Sabourin, b. 18 Sep 1807 Ste-Madeleine-de-Riguad, Quebec; m. Suzanne Portelance.

40   x. Adelaide Sabourin, b. circa 1809; m. Pierre Seguin.

        xi. Theodore Benjamin Sabourin was born on 8 Jan 1813 Ste-Madeleine-de-Riguad, Quebec (Ibid., #2679951.). He was baptized on 9 Jan 1813 Ste-Madeleine-de-Riguad, Quebec *(father's occupation: agriculture)* (PRDH online, #2679951.). He died on 10 Aug 1813 Ste-Madeleine-de-Riguad, Quebec (Ibid., #2681835.). He was buried on 11 Aug 1813 Ste-Madeleine-de-Riguad, Quebec (Ibid.).

       xii. Veronique Sabourin was born on 6 Apr 1815 Ste-Madeleine-de-Riguad, Quebec (Ibid., #2680171.). She was baptized on 7 Apr 1815 Ste-Madeleine-de-Riguad, Quebec (Ibid.).

8. **Marie Louise Amable Sabourin** was baptized on 12 Nov 1767 Oka, Quebec (Ibid., #738716.). She married **Pierre-Antoine Sauve**, son of **Marie-Antoine Sauve** and **Marie Anne Robillard,** on 25 Oct 1784 Vaudreuil, Quebec *(Antoine Sauvez Laplante, son of Antoine Sauvez Laplante and Marie Anne Robillard, married 25 Oct 1784 at Vaudreuil, Amable Sabourin, daughter of Paul Sabourin and Marie Josephe Seguin, Present: Jean Baptiste Sauvez, brother of the groom, Hippolyte Sauvez, sister of the groom, uncles of the groom: Jean Baptiste Robillard, Pierre Robillard, and Jacques Sagala, Joseph Robillard, brothers and sister of the bride: Hyacinthe Sabourin, Andre Sabourin, and Marie Madeleine Sabourin, Simon Villeneuve brother-in-law of the bride, uncles and aunt of the bride: Francois Seguin, Hyacinthe Seguin and Amable Sabourin)* (PRDH online, No. 227167.). She died on 15 Jun 1837 Ste-Madeleine-de-Riguad, Quebec, at age 69 (Ibid., #4623764.). She was buried on 17 Jun 1837 Ste-Madeleine-de-Riguad, Quebec *(age 70, wife of Antoine Sauve)* (PRDH online, #4623764.).

    Pierre-Antoine Sauve was born on 19 Feb 1762 Ste-Anne-de-Bellevue, Quebec (Ibid., No. 276152.). He was baptized on 20 Feb 1762 Ste-Anne-de-Bellevue, Quebec *(Godfather: Nicolas Robillard, grandfather of the infant, Godmother: Marie Josephte Gautier, wife of Jacques Legros, Sartelon ptre)* (PRDH online, No. 276152.) (DGFC, Volume 7, page 144.). He died on 9 Feb 1843 Ste-Madeleine-de-Riguad, Quebec, at age 80 (PRDH online, #4624306.). He was buried on 11 Feb 1843 Ste-Madeleine-de-Riguad, Quebec *(age 74, husband of Amable Sabourin)* (PRDH online, #4624306.). As of 25 Oct 1784, he was also known as **Antoine Sauve dit Laplante** (Ibid., No. 227167.).

He was *a voyageur* on 30 Sep 1807 Notre-Dame-de-Montreal, Quebec (Ibid., #2390611.).

Children of **Marie Louise Amable Sabourin** and **Pierre-Antoine Sauve** were as follows:

41   i. Antoine Frederic Sauve, b. 15 Jun 1786 Vaudreuil, Quebec; m. Marie Marguerite Tessier.

42   ii. Pascal Sauve, b. 30 Jul 1789 Vaudreuil, Quebec; m. Marie Angelique Larocque dit Rocbrune.

       iii. Hippolyte Sauve was born on 31 Mar 1791 Vaudreuil, Quebec (Ibid., #723579.). She was baptized on 3 Apr 1791 Vaudreuil, Quebec (Ibid.).

43   iv. Marie Euphrosine Sauve, b. 17 Dec 1793 Oka, Quebec; m. Pierre Louis Seguin.

44   v. Hyacinthe Sauve, b. 14 Apr 1796 Vaudreuil, Quebec; m. Josephe Larocque dit Rocbrune.

       vi. Anonyme Sauve was born on 18 Apr 1800 Vaudreuil, Quebec (Ibid., #2592245.). He died on 23 Apr 1800 Vaudreuil, Quebec (Ibid.). He was buried on 24 Apr 1800 Vaudreuil, Quebec (Ibid.).

      vii. Antoine Sauve was born on 4 Jun 1802 Vaudreuil, Quebec (Ibid., #2590045.). He was baptized on 5 Jun 1802 Vaudreuil, Quebec (Ibid.). He married Archange Bernesse, daughter of Guillaume Bernesse and Therese Partenait, on 7 Feb 1831 Ste-Madeleine-de-Riguad, Quebec (Ibid., #3461956.).

          Archange Bernesse was born circa 1810.

     viii. Benjamin Sauve was born on 9 Aug 1805 Vaudreuil, Quebec (Ibid., #2590349.). He was baptized on 9 Aug 1805 Vaudreuil, Quebec (Ibid.). He married Angelique Roy, daughter of Athanase Roy and Marie Cheffer, on 27 Oct 1828 Ste-Madeleine-de-Riguad, Quebec (Ibid., #3461021.).

          Angelique Roy was born on 24 Oct 1806 Ste-Madeleine-de-Riguad, Quebec (Ibid., #2679379.). She was baptized on 25 Oct 1806 Ste-Madeleine-de-Riguad, Quebec (Ibid.).

       ix. Antoine Sauve was born on 30 Sep 1807 Notre-Dame-de-Montreal, Quebec (Ibid., #2388449.). He was baptized on 30 Sep 1807 Notre-Dame-de-Montreal, Quebec *(father's occupation: voyageur)* (PRDH online, #2388449.). He died on 6 Oct 1807 Notre-Dame-de-Montreal, Quebec

(Ibid., #2390611.). He was buried on 8 Oct 1807 Notre-Dame-de-Montreal, Quebec *(father's occupation: voyageur)* (PRDH online, #2390611.).

    x. Adelaide Sauve was born on 23 May 1810 Vaudreuil, Quebec (Ibid., #2590780.). She was baptized on 23 May 1810 Vaudreuil, Quebec (Ibid.).

9. Charles Sabourin was baptized on 22 Jan 1769 Oka, Quebec (Ibid., #738759.). He married **Marie Anne Bedard**, daughter of **Antoine Bedard** and **Marie Charlotte Palin dit Dabonville,** on 13 Aug 1792 Vaudreuil, Quebec *(Charles Sabourin, son of Paul Sabourin and Josephe Seguin, married 13 Aug 1792, Marie Anne Bedard, daughter of Antoine Bedard and Charles Dabonville, Present: Hyacinthe, Paul, and Antoine Sabourin brothers of the groom, Pasca and Jean Bedard brothers of the bride, Jean and Joseph Bedard uncles of the bride, Isidore Vincent uncle of the bride)* (PRDH online, #358137.). He died on 18 Oct 1839 Ste-Madeleine-de-Riguad, Quebec, at age 70 (Ibid., #4623997.). He was buried on 20 Oct 1839 Ste-Madeleine-de-Riguad, Quebec *(age 70, husband of Marie Anne Bedard)* (PRDH online, #4623997.).

    Marie Anne Bedard was born on 15 Sep 1769 Pointe-Claire, Quebec (Ibid., #652792.). She was baptized on 15 Sep 1769 Pointe-Claire, Quebec (Ibid.).

    Children of **Charles Sabourin** and **Marie Anne Bedard** were as follows:

45   i. Charles Sabourin, b. 9 Sep 1793 Vaudreuil, Quebec; m. Madeleine Lalande dit Latreille or Lalonde.

46 ii. Marie Anne Sabourin, b. 11 Oct 1794 Quinchien, Riviere-a-la-Graisse, Quebec; m. Jacques Charbonneau; m. Louis Brunet.

    iii. Marie Angelique Sabourin was born on 13 Feb 1796 Rigaud, Quebec (Ibid., #642620.). She was baptized on 14 Feb 1796 Oka, Quebec *(conditional baptism)* (PRDH online, #642620.). She died on 30 Jan 1797 Vaudreuil, Quebec (Ibid., #586784.). She was buried on 1 Feb 1797 Vaudreuil, Quebec *(father's occupation: cultivator)* (PRDH online, #586784.).

47 iv. Paul Sabourin, b. 3 Jun 1797 Vaudreuil, Quebec; m. Marie Anne Leblanc.

48   v. Marie Sabourin, b. 24 Sep 1798 Oka, Quebec; m. Pierre Joseph Gabrion.

49 vi. Francois Xavier Sabourin, b. 12 Jan 1801 Oka, Quebec; m. Marie Anne Chantal Rocbrune; d. 26 Apr 1822; bur. 18 May 1822 Ste-Madeleine-de-Riguad, Quebec.

    vii. Marie Reine Sabourin was born on 26 Apr 1802 Ste-Madeleine-de-Riguad, Quebec (Ibid., #2679086.). She was baptized on 26 Apr 1802 Ste-Madeleine-de-Riguad, Quebec *(father's occupation: day laborer)* (PRDH online, #2679086.).

50 viii. Catherine Sabourin, b. 30 Oct 1805 Ste-Madeleine-de-Riguad, Quebec; m. Thomas Armstrong; d. 13 Feb 1845 Les Cedres, Quebec; bur. 15 Feb 1845 Les Cedres, Quebec.

    ix. Hyacinthe Sabourin was born on 6 Oct 1807 Ste-Madeleine-de-Riguad, Quebec (Ibid., #2679454.). He was baptized on 6 Oct 1807 Ste-Madeleine-de-Riguad, Quebec *(father's occupation: day laborer)* (PRDH online, #2679454.).

    x. Genevieve Hippolyte Sabourin was born on 3 Jan 1810 Ste-Madeleine-de-Riguad, Quebec (Ibid., #2679634.). She was baptized on 3 Jan 1810 Ste-Madeleine-de-Riguad, Quebec *(father's occupation: day laborer)* (PRDH online, #2679634.).

    xi. Veronique Sabourin was born on 12 Nov 1812 Ste-Madeleine-de-Riguad, Quebec (Ibid., #2679942.). She was baptized on 12 Nov 1812 Ste-Madeleine-de-Riguad, Quebec *(father's occupation: day laborer)* (PRDH online, #2679942.).

10. Paul Sabourin was baptized on 24 Aug 1770 Oka, Quebec (Ibid., #738832.). He married **Scholastique Sabourin**, daughter of **Jean Baptiste Sabourin** and **Marie Amable Brabant dit Lamothe,** on 20 Feb 1797 Vaudreuil, Quebec *(Paul Sabourin, cultivator, adult son of Paul Sabourin, cultivator, and Josephe Seguin, married 20 Feb 1797, Scholastique Sabourin, adult daughter of Jean Baptiste Sabourin, cultivator, and Amable Braban, Present: Hyacinthe, Charles and Antoine Sabourin brothers of the groom, Antoine Sauvey brother-in-law of the groom, Francois Seguin, uncle of the groom, Regis Villeneuve nephew of the groom, Pantaleon and Etienne Villeneuve cousins of the groom, Antoine Denis brother-in-law of the bride, Paul Sabourin stepfather of the bride, Francois Malette, Charles Braban and Jacques Sabourin uncles of the bride, Louis St.Aman cousin of the bride. Dispensation of 3rd degree relationship)* (PRDH online, #358240.) He died on 8 Jul 1805 Ste-Madeleine-de-Riguad, Quebec, at age 34 (Ibid., #2681546.). He was buried on 10 Jul 1805 Ste-Madeleine-de-Riguad, Quebec *(age 34, day laborer, killed by lightening, husband of Scholastique Sabourin)* (PRDH online, #2681546.).

    Scholastique Sabourin was baptized on 22 Mar 1771 Oka, Quebec (Ibid., #244660.). She married **Jean Baptiste Tessier dit Lavigne**, son of **Nicolas Tessier dit Lavigne** and **Marie Angelique Parent,** on 13 Feb 1809 Vaudreuil, Quebec (Ibid.).

    Children of **Paul Sabourin** and **Scholastique Sabourin** were as follows:

     i.   Paul Edouard Sabourin was born on 15 Oct 1798 Oka, Quebec (Ibid., #774136.). He was baptized on 16 Oct 1798 Oka, Quebec (Ibid.). He died on 21 May 1799 Vaudreuil, Quebec (Ibid., #586934.). He was buried on 22 May 1799 Vaudreuil, Quebec *(age 16 months, father's occupation: cultivator)* (PRDH online, #586934.).

51   ii.   Jean Baptiste Sabourin, b. 3 Oct 1804; m. Julie Eugenie Denomme.

  11. Antoine Sabourin was baptized on 10 Jun 1773 Oka, Quebec (Ibid., #738952.). He married **Angelique Condon**, daughter of **Georges Condon** and **Marie Sauve dit Laplante,** on 14 Oct 1799 Vaudreuil, Quebec *(Antoine Sabourin, cultivateur from Vaudreuil, adult son of Paul Sabourin, cultivateur from Vaudreuil, and Josephe Seguin, married 14 Oct 1799 at Vaudreuil, Angelique Condon minor daughter of Geroge Condon, cultivateur from Vaudreuil, and Marie Sauvez, Present: Charles Sabourin, brother of the groom, Antoine Sauvez, brother-in-law of the groom, Francois Seguin, maternal uncle, nephews of the groom: Francois Seguin, Regis Villeneuve, and Xavier Villeneuve, first cousins of the groom: Etienne Villeneuve and Theodre Seguin, Marie Anne Condon, sister of the bride, Antoine Sauve, maternal grandfather, paternal uncles: Louis Malette and Augustin Malette, maternal uncles of the bride: Antoine Sauvez and Hyacinthe Sauvez, Pierre Robillard, maternal grand-uncle of the bride, Eusebe Sabourin maternal uncle of the bride)* (PRDH online, No. 358287.). He died on 9 Feb 1820 Ste-Madeleine-de-Riguad, Quebec, at age 46 (Ibid., #2682141.). He was buried on 11 Feb 1820 Ste-Madeleine-de-Riguad, Quebec *(age 47, day laborer, husband of Angelique Condun)* (PRDH online, #2682141.).

  Angelique Condon was born on 13 Aug 1783 Vaudreuil, Quebec (Ibid., #250917.). She was baptized on 13 Aug 1783 Vaudreuil, Quebec (Ibid.). She married **Joseph Denomme**, son of **Joseph Denomme** and **Marie Anne Dubois,** on 1 Jun 1824 Ste-Madeleine-de-Riguad, Quebec (Ibid.).

Children of **Antoine Sabourin** and **Angelique Condon** were as follows:

     i.   Antoine Sabourin was born on 7 Oct 1801 Vaudreuil, Quebec (Ibid., #2589963.). He was baptized on 7 Oct 1801 Vaudreuil, Quebec (Ibid.). He died on 15 May 1802 Ste-Madeleine-de-Riguad, Quebec (Ibid., #2681450.). He was buried on 18 May 1802 Ste-Madeleine-de-Riguad, Quebec *(age 7 months and 7 days, father's occupation: cultivator)* (PRDH online, #2681450.).

52   ii.   Marie Sabourin, b. 28 Sep 1803 Vaudreuil, Quebec; m. Jean Baptiste Tessier dit Lavigne.

53   iii.   Francois Xavier Sabourin, b. 14 Dec 1806 Ste-Madeleine-de-Riguad, Quebec; m. Marie Mathilde Domitilde Thauvette; m. Sophie Gareau.

54   iv.   Marie Josephe Sabourin, b. 7 Sep 1808 Ste-Madeleine-de-Riguad, Quebec; m. Jean Baptiste Seguin.

    v.   Antoine Leandre Sabourin was born on 28 Feb 1815 Ste-Madeleine-de-Riguad, Quebec (Ibid., #2680152.). He was baptized on 28 Feb 1815 Ste-Madeleine-de-Riguad, Quebec *(father's occupation: day laborer)* (PRDH online, #2680152.). He died on 5 Mar 1817 Ste-Madeleine-de-Riguad, Quebec, at age 2 (Ibid., #2681998.). He was buried on 7 Mar 1817 Ste-Madeleine-de-Riguad, Quebec *(age 2 years and 5 days, father's occupation: day laborer)* (PRDH online, #2681998.).

55   vi.   Marie Sophie Sabourin, b. 17 Oct 1819 Ste-Madeleine-de-Riguad, Quebec; m. Benjamin Corneille Seguin dit Laderoute.

  12. Ignace Raizenne was baptized on 8 Oct 1771 Oka, Quebec (Ibid., #738877.). He married **Clemence Marie Guindon**, daughter of **Francois Guindon** and **Marie Francoise Guerin dit Bertrand,** on 22 Jan 1800 St-Eustache, Quebec (Ibid., #2226790.). He died on 23 Sep 1849 St-Benoit, Quebec, at age 77 (Ibid., #4674500.). He was buried on 26 Sep 1849 St-Benoit, Quebec *(age 78, husband of Marie Clemence Guindon)* (PRDH online, #4674500.).

  Clemence Marie Guindon was born on 5 Aug 1772 St-Eustache, Quebec (Ibid., #647376.). She was baptized on 8 Aug 1772 St-Eustache, Quebec (Ibid.).

Children of **Ignace Raizenne** and **Clemence Maric Guindon** were as follows:

     i.   Anonyme Raizenne was born on 14 Feb 1801 St-Benoit, Quebec (Ibid., #2517670.). He died on 14 Feb 1801 St-Benoit, Quebec (Ibid.). He was buried on 16 Feb 1801 St-Benoit, Quebec *(father's occupation: laborer)* (PRDH online, #2517670.).

    ii.   Marie Elisabeth Narsisse Raizenne was born on 10 Feb 1803 St-Benoit, Quebec (Ibid., #2512116.). She was baptized on 10 Feb 1803 St-Benoit, Quebec (Ibid.).

   iii.   Marie Marguerite Valerie Raizenne was born on 4 Aug 1804 St-Benoit, Quebec (Ibid., #2512373.). She was baptized on 4 Aug 1804 St-Benoit, Quebec *(father's occupation: laborer)* (PRDH online, #2512373.). She died on 23 Oct 1805 St-Eustache, Quebec, at age 1 (Ibid., #2832873.). She was buried on 24 Oct 1805 St-Eustache, Quebec *(age 14 months and 17 days)* (PRDH online, #2832873.).

56   iv.   Clet Raizenne, b. 28 Feb 1806 St-Eustache, Quebec; m. Rose Sophie Gauthier.

57   v.   Marie Antoinette Raizenne, b. 15 Feb 1809 St-Eustache, Quebec; m. Pierre Desrivieres dit Beaubien.

vi.   Marie Charles Anastasie Raizenne was born on 10 Dec 1812 St-Benoit, Quebec (Ibid., #2514195.). She was baptized on 12 Dec 1812 St-Benoit, Quebec *(conditional baptism, father's occupation: major of the militia)* (PRDH online, #2514195.). She died on 30 Apr 1837 Oka, Quebec, at age 24 (Ibid., #4722483.). She was buried on 2 May 1837 Oka, Quebec (Ibid.).

vii.   Xiste Thelesphore Raizenne was born on 27 May 1817 St-Benoit, Quebec (Ibid., #2515296.). He was baptized on 27 May 1817 St-Benoit, Quebec *(father's occupation: notary)* (PRDH online, #2515296.). He died on 23 Mar 1818 Oka, Quebec (Ibid., #2752565.). He was buried on 24 Mar 1818 Oka, Quebec *(age 10 months)* (PRDH online, #2752565.).

13. **Marie Marguerite Raizenne dit Shoentakouani** was baptized on 22 Oct 1775 Oka, Quebec (Ibid., #739020.). She married **Antoine Chevrier dit Lajeunesse**, son of **Joseph Chevrier dit Lajeunesse** and **Marie Madeleine Cholet dit Laviolette,** on 2 Feb 1796 Vaudreuil, Quebec (Ibid., #118673.). She died on 18 Apr 1835 Vaudreuil, Quebec, at age 59 (Ibid., #4181771.). She was buried on 20 Apr 1835 Vaudreuil, Quebec *(age 57, widow of Antoine Chevrier)* (PRDH online, #4181771.).

Antoine Chevrier dit Lajeunesse was baptized on 12 Jun 1770 Oka, Quebec (Ibid., #118663.). He died on 21 Mar 1826 Vaudreuil, Quebec, at age 55 (Ibid., #4181212.). He was buried on 22 Mar 1826 Vaudreuil, Quebec *(age 57, husband of Marie Marguerite Raisenne)* (PRDH online, #4181212.).

Children of **Marie Marguerite Raizenne dit Shoentakouani** and **Antoine Chevrier dit Lajeunesse** were as follows:

i.   Antoine Mathias Chevrier was born on 24 Feb 1798 Oka, Quebec (Ibid., #642738.). He was baptized on 24 Feb 1798 Oka, Quebec (Ibid.).

ii.   Joseph Cyrille Chevrier was baptized on 15 May 1799 Vaudreuil, Quebec *(father's occupaton: cultivator)* (PRDH online, #771133.). He died on 28 Aug 1799 Vaudreuil, Quebec (Ibid., #586955.). He was buried on 29 Aug 1799 Vaudreuil, Quebec *(age 3 months, father's occupaton: cultivator)* (PRDH online, #586955.).

58   iii.   Andre Cyrille Chevrier, b. 19 Jan 1801 Vaudreuil, Quebec; m. Flavie Leduc.

59   iv.   Joseph Jerome Chevrier, b. 16 Dec 1802 Vaudreuil, Quebec; m. Veronique Gauthier.

v.   Francois Cyprien Chevrier was born on 24 Feb 1805 Vaudreuil, Quebec (Ibid., #2590311.). He was baptized on 24 Feb 1805 Vaudreuil, Quebec *(father's occupaton: cultivator)* (PRDH online, #2590311.). He died on 25 Mar 1806 Vaudreuil, Quebec, at age 1 (Ibid., #2592556.). He was buried on 26 Mar 1806 Vaudreuil, Quebec *(father's occupaton: cultivator)* (PRDH online, #2592556.).

60   vi.   Jean Baptiste Chevrier, b. 16 Mar 1808 Vaudreuil, Quebec; m. Scholastique Gauthier.

61   vii.   Francois Pascal Chevrier, b. 8 Apr 1811 Oka, Quebec; m. Marie Agathe Leduc.

viii.   Marie Marguerite Charlotte Caroline Chevrier was born on 6 May 1814 Vaudreuil, Quebec (Ibid., #2591116.). She was baptized on 7 May 1814 Vaudreuil, Quebec *(father's occupaton: cultivator)* (PRDH online, #2591116.). She married Antoine Aubry, son of Audre Aubry dit Thecle and Marie Emerentienne Robineau dit Dumoulin, on 16 Jun 1834 Vaudreuil, Quebec (Ibid., #3474852.).

Antoine Aubry was born on 28 Jun 1802 (St-Laurent), Montreal, Quebec (Ibid., #2466062.). He was baptized on 28 Jun 1802 (St-Laurent), Montreal, Quebec (Ibid.).

ix.   Anonyme Chevrier was born on 2 Jun 1816 Vaudreuil, Quebec (Ibid., #2593002.). He died on 2 Jun 1816 Vaudreuil, Quebec (Ibid.). He was buried on 3 Jun 1816 Vaudreuil, Quebec (Ibid.).

x.   Marie Anatalie Chevrier was born on 18 Jan 1819 Vaudreuil, Quebec (Ibid., #2591565.). She was baptized on 19 Jan 1819 Vaudreuil, Quebec *(father's occupaton: cultivator)* (PRDH online, #2591565.).

14. **Angelique Amable Villeneuve** was baptized on 14 Sep 1773 Oka, Quebec (Ibid., #738957.). She married **Joseph Amable Sauve dit Laplante,** son of **Marie-Antoine Sauve** and **Marie Anne Robillard,** on 14 Oct 1793 Vaudreuil, Quebec *(Joseph Sauvey, son of Antone Sauvey and Marie Anne Robillard, married, 14 Oct 1793 at Vaudreuil, Angelique Villeneuve, daughter of Pierre Villeneuve and Amable Sabourin, Present: brothers of the groom: Antoine Sauvey and Jean Baptiste Sauvy, Pierre Robillard, uncle of the groom, uncles of the bride: Simon Villeneuve, Francois Villeneuve, Jean Marie Villeneuve, Paul Sabourin, and Jean Baptiste Raizenne, cousins of the bride: Paul Sabourin and Antoine Sabourin)* (PRDH online, No. 358165.).

She was in the census household of **Louis Cyprien Sauve** and **Marie Suzanne Leduc** in 1852 St.Michel, Vaudreuil, Vaudreuil, Quebec (Automated Genealogy 1852 Census Transcription Project and Census Images from the National Archives of Canada, http://www.automatedgenealogy.com, District 534, page 24d, 25a, (49), line 19-26.).

Joseph Amable Sauve dit Laplante was baptized on 29 Apr 1768 Oka, Quebec (PRDH online, #738730.). He died on 2 Jun 1845 Vaudreuil, Quebec, at age 77 (Ibid., #4182414.). He was buried on 4 Jun 1845 Vaudreuil, Quebec *(age 79, husband of Angelique Villeneuve)* (PRDH online, #4182414.).

Children of **Angelique Amable Villeneuve** and **Joseph Amable Sauve dit Laplante** were as follows:

    62   i.   Joseph Olivier Sauve, b. 31 Jul 1797 Vaudreuil, Quebec; m. Marie Adelaide Castonguay or Gastonguay.

    63   ii.   Marie Reine Sauve, b. circa 1799 Ste-Madeleine-de-Rigaud, Quebec; m. Paul Vachon.

          iii.   Marie Rose Sauve was born on 15 Jul 1800 Vaudreuil, Quebec (Ibid., #2589823.). She was baptized on 15 Jul 1800 Vaudreuil, Quebec *(father's occupation: cultivator)* (PRDH online, #2589823.).

          iv.   Pierre Sauve was born on 4 Aug 1802 Vaudreuil, Quebec (Ibid., #2590055.). He was baptized on 5 Aug 1802 Vaudreuil, Quebec *(father's occupation: cultivator)* (PRDH online, #2590055.). He married Suzanne Therese Lauzon, daughter of Andre Lauzon and Josephte Pilon, on 6 Feb 1832 Vaudreuil, Quebec (Ibid., #3474358.).

               Suzanne Therese Lauzon was born on 15 Oct 1809 Vaudreuil, Quebec (Ibid., #2590738.). She was baptized on 15 Oct 1809 Vaudreuil, Quebec *(father's occupation: cultivator)* (PRDH online, #2590738.).

    64   v.   Louis Cyprien Sauve, b. 9 Jan 1806 Vaudreuil, Quebec; m. Marie Suzanne Leduc.

    65   vi.   Angelique Amable Sauve, b. 27 May 1809 Vaudreuil, Quebec; m. Joseph Melchoir Baltazard Hurtubise.

    66   vii.   Eugenie Emilie Sauve, b. 29 Jul 1811 Vaudreuil, Quebec; m. Hyacinthe Denis dit St.Denis.

15. **Pantaleon Villeneuve** was baptized on 27 Jul 1775 Oka, Quebec (Ibid., #739008.). He married **Marie Francoise Lalonde**, daughter of **Antoine Lalonde** and **Marie Josephe Lefebvre dit Laciseray,** on 24 Sep 1798 Vaudreuil, Quebec *(Pantaleon Villeneuve, cultivator, adult son of Pierre Villeneuve, cultivator, and Therese Amable Sabourin, married 24 Sep 1798, Francoise Lalond, adult daughter of Antoine Lalonde, cultivator, and Marie Josephe Lefaivre, Present: Etienne Villeneuve brother of the groom, Simon, Francois, and Jean Marie Villeneuve uncles of the groom, Joseph Sauver brother-in-law of the groom, Regis and Xavier Villeneuve cousins of the groom, Antoine and Luc Lalonde brothers of the bride, Joseph, Charles and Francois Lalonde uncles of the bride, Eustache Ranger brother-in-law of the bride, Pierre and Vincent Gauthier brothers-in-law of the bride, Joseph Rapin cousin of the bride)* (PRDH online, #358262.). He married **Genevieve Victoire Seguin**, daughter of **Louis Amable Seguin dit Laderoute** and **Marie Pelagie Leger dit Parisien,** on 21 Jan 1823 Ste-Madeleine-de-Rigaud, Quebec (Ibid., #2220185.). He died on 18 Jul 1838 Ste-Madeleine-de-Rigaud, Quebec, at age 62 (Ibid., #4623861.). He was buried on 20 Jul 1838 Ste-Madeleine-de-Rigaud, Quebec *(age 61, husband of Victoire Seguin)* (PRDH online, #4623861.).

Marie Francoise Lalonde was born on 5 Oct 1774 Vaudreuil, Quebec (Ibid., #722111.). She was baptized on 5 Oct 1774 Vaudreuil, Quebec (Ibid.). She died on 3 Jun 1821 Ste-Madeleine-de-Rigaud, Quebec, at age 46 (Ibid., #2682227.). She was buried on 5 Jun 1821 Ste-Madeleine-de-Rigaud, Quebec *(age 42, wife of Pantaleon Villeneuve, cultivator)* (PRDH online, #2682227.).

Children of **Pantaleon Villeneuve** and **Marie Francoise Lalonde** were as follows:

          i.   Pierre Antoine Villeneuve was baptized on 26 Sep 1799 Vaudreuil, Quebec *(father's occupation: cultivator)* (PRDH online, #771180.). He died on 24 Oct 1799 Vaudreuil, Quebec (Ibid., #586965.). He was buried on 26 Oct 1799 Vaudreuil, Quebec *(age one month, father's occupation: cultivator)* (PRDH online, #586965.).

          ii.   Pierre Antoine Villeneuve was born on 14 Dec 1800 Vaudreuil, Quebec (Ibid., #2589880.). He was baptized on 14 Dec 1800 Vaudreuil, Quebec *(father's occupation: cultivator)* (PRDH online, #2589880.).

          iii.   Marie Josephte Amable Villeneuve was born on 20 Aug 1803 Ste-Madeleine-de-Rigaud, Quebec (Ibid., #2679177.). She was baptized on 21 Aug 1803 Ste-Madeleine-de-Rigaud, Quebec *(father's occupation: cultivator)* (PRDH online, #2679177.). She died on 4 Sep 1803 Ste-Madeleine-de-Rigaud, Quebec (Ibid., #2681493.). She was buried on 5 Sep 1803 Ste-Madeleine-de-Rigaud, Quebec *(Marie Catherine Amable Villeneuve, age 15 days, father's occupation: cultivator)* (PRDH online, #2681493.).

          iv.   Luc Amable Villeneuve was born on 11 Jan 1805 Ste-Madeleine-de-Rigaud, Quebec (Ibid., #2679249.). He was baptized on 11 Jan 1805 Ste-Madeleine-de-Rigaud, Quebec *(father's occupation: agriculture)* (PRDH online, #2679249.). He died on 4 Jun 1822 Ste-Madeleine-de-Rigaud, Quebec, at age 17 (Ibid., #2682286.). He was buried on 5 Jun 1822 Ste-Madeleine-de-Rigaud, Quebec *(father's occupation: cultivator)* (PRDH online, #2682286.).

    v.   Francois Xavier Villeneuve was born on 17 Sep 1807 Ste-Madeleine-de-Rigaud, Quebec (Ibid., #2679446.). He was baptized on 17 Sep 1807 Ste-Madeleine-de-Rigaud, Quebec *(father's occupation: agriculture)* (PRDH online, #2679446.). He died on 9 Nov 1833 Ste-Madeleine-de-Rigaud, Quebec, at age 26 (Ibid., #4623437.). He was buried on 11 Nov 1833 Ste-Madeleine-de-Rigaud, Quebec (Ibid.).

67   vi.   Marie Marguerite Villeneuve, b. 29 Apr 1810 Ste-Madeleine-de-Rigaud, Quebec; m. Andre Denis dit St.Denis.

    vii.   Pantaleon Emery Villeneuve was born on 18 May 1812 Ste-Madeleine-de-Rigaud, Quebec (Ibid., #2679872.). He was baptized on 18 May 1812 Ste-Madeleine-de-Rigaud, Quebec *(father's occupation: agriculture)* (PRDH online, #2679872.). He died on 27 Jul 1812 Ste-Madeleine-de-Rigaud, Quebec (Ibid., #2681798.). He was buried on 28 Jul 1812 Ste-Madeleine-de-Rigaud, Quebec *(age 2 months, father's occupation: agriculture)* (PRDH online, #2681798.).

    viii.   Victoire Emelie Villeneuve was born on 14 Sep 1813 Ste-Madeleine-de-Rigaud, Quebec (Ibid., #2680010.). She was baptized on 14 Sep 1813 Ste-Madeleine-de-Rigaud, Quebec *(father's occupation: agriculture)* (PRDH online, #2680010.). She died on 24 Sep 1813 Ste-Madeleine-de-Rigaud, Quebec (Ibid., #2681844.). She was buried on 26 Sep 1813 Ste-Madeleine-de-Rigaud, Quebec *(age 10 days, father's occupation: agriculture)* (PRDH online, #2681844.).

    ix.   Josephe Eugenie Villeneuve was born on 26 Sep 1815 Ste-Madeleine-de-Rigaud, Quebec (Ibid., #2680219.). She was baptized on 27 Sep 1815 Ste-Madeleine-de-Rigaud, Quebec *(father's occupation: agriculture)* (PRDH online, #2680219.).

68   x.   Marie Angelique Villeneuve, b. circa 1817; m. Antoine Boyer dit Germain.

    xi.   Xavier Marcel Villeneuve was born on 12 Jan 1818 Ste-Madeleine-de-Rigaud, Quebec (Ibid., #2680450.). He was baptized on 12 Jan 1818 Ste-Madeleine-de-Rigaud, Quebec *(father's occupation: agriculture)* (PRDH online, #2680450.). He died on 31 Jul 1818 Ste-Madeleine-de-Rigaud, Quebec (Ibid., #2682061.). He was buried on 1 Aug 1818 Ste-Madeleine-de-Rigaud, Quebec *(age 6 months and 17 days, father's occupation: agriculture)* (PRDH online, #2682061.).

Genevieve Victoire Seguin was born on 20 Oct 1775 Vaudreuil, Quebec (Ibid., #722134.). She was baptized on 20 Oct 1775 Vaudreuil, Quebec (Ibid.).

She was in the census household of **Francois Belanger** and **Marie Louise Seguin** in 1852 Ste.Madeleine, Rigaud, Vaudreuil, Quebec *(Bélanger, Frs, Journalier, St Vincent, Catholique, 62, M; Séguin, Marie, Rigaud, Catholique, 55, F; Bélanger, Jos, Voyageur, Rigaud, Catholique, 18, M; Bélanger, Gaspard, Voyageur, Rigaud, Catholique, 21, M; Bélanger, Vinc, Rigaud, Catholique, 13, M; Bélanger, Louise, Rigaud, Catholique, 20, F; Belange, Obeline, Rigaud, Catholique, 17, F; Bélanger, Caroline, Rigaud, Catholique, 15, F; Bélanger, Sélanie, Rigaud, Catholique, 9, F; Séguin, Vitctoire, Vaudreuil, Catholique, 75, F; Larocque, Louis, Cultivateur, Rigaud, Catholique, 65, M)* (1852C Cdn Transcription Project, District 536, page 57d, 58a, (115), line 20-29.).

16. Francois Etienne Villeneuve was born on 5 Jan 1779 Vaudreuil, Quebec (PRDH online, #722418.). He was baptized on 5 Jan 1779 Vaudreuil, Quebec (Ibid.). He married **Amable Marie Reine Gauthier**, daughter of **Jean Baptiste Gauthier** and **Marie Therese Seguin dit Laderoute,** on 21 Sep 1801 Vaudreuil, Quebec (Ibid., #2223723.). He married **Angelique Daoust**, daughter of **Francois Daoust** and **Francoise Amable Brunet dit Bourbonnais,** on 24 Oct 1808 Vaudreuil, Quebec (Ibid., #2224021.).

Amable Marie Reine Gauthier was born on 10 Sep 1778 Vaudreuil, Quebec (Ibid., #722383.). She was baptized on 11 Sep 1778 Vaudreuil, Quebec (Ibid.). She died on 10 Oct 1807 Ste-Madeleine-de-Rigaud, Quebec, at age 29 (Ibid., #2681622.). She was buried on 12 Oct 1807 Ste-Madeleine-de-Rigaud, Quebec *(age 29, wife of Etienne Villeneve, occupation: agriculture)* (PRDH online, #2681622.).

Children of **Francois Etienne Villeneuve** and **Amable Marie Reine Gauthier** both born Ste-Madeleine-de-Rigaud, Quebec, were as follows:

69   i.   Marie Reine Narcisse Villeneuve, b. 10 Mar 1803; m. Francois Xavier Berlinguet; m. Jean Baptiste Normand.

70   ii.   Marie Jeanne Dechantal Villeneuve, b. 30 Mar 1805; m. Francois Lauzon.

Angelique Daoust was born circa 1787.

Children of **Francois Etienne Villeneuve** and **Angelique Daoust** all born Ste-Madeleine-de-Rigaud, Quebec, were as follows:

71   i.   Angelique Louise Villeneuve, b. 22 Jun 1810; m. Gregoire Watier dit Lanoix.

      ii.   Pierre Etienne Villeneuve was born on 22 Jul 1811 (Ibid., #2679797.). He was baptized on 23 Jul 1811 Ste-Madeleine-de-Rigaud, Quebec *(father's occupation: agriculture)* (PRDH online, #2679797.).

72   iii.   Rose Emelie Villeneuve, b. 13 May 1815; m. Louis Goulet.

73   iv.   Francois Xavier Villeneuve, b. 29 Nov 1817; m. Angele Bourbonnais.

      v.   Rosalie Villeneuve was born on 10 Feb 1823 *(twin)* (PRDH online, #2681147.). She was baptized on 10 Feb 1823 Ste-Madeleine-de-Rigaud, Quebec *(father's occupation: cultivator)* (PRDH online, #2681147.). She died on 31 Jul 1823 Ste-Madeleine-de-Rigaud, Quebec (Ibid., #2682355.). She was buried on 1 Aug 1823 Ste-Madeleine-de-Rigaud, Quebec *(age 5 months and 20 days, father's occupation: cultivator)* (PRDH online, #2682355.).

      vi.   Anne Villeneuve was born on 10 Feb 1823 *(twin)* (PRDH online, #2681148.). She was baptized on 10 Feb 1823 Ste-Madeleine-de-Rigaud, Quebec *(father's occupation: cultivator)* (PRDH online, #2681148.). She married Francois Piette, son of Joseph Piette dit Lafreniere and Josephe Moreau dit St.Coeur, on 1 Feb 1847 Vaudreuil, Quebec (Ibid., #3477613.).

        Francois Piette was born on 29 Apr 1819 Pointe-Claire, Quebec (Ibid., #2801820.). He was baptized on 30 Apr 1819 Pointe-Claire, Quebec *(father's occupation: cultivator)* (PRDH online, #2801820.).

17. Anastasie Villeneuve was born on 20 Jul 1781 Vaudreuil, Quebec (Ibid., #722675.). She was baptized on 21 Jul 1781 Vaudreuil, Quebec (Ibid.). She married **Francois Xavier Lemaire dit St.Germain**, son of **Ignace Lemaire dit St.Germain** and **Marie Louise Rose Guay dit Castonguay,** on 22 Jan 1810 Ste-Madeleine-de-Rigaud, Quebec (Ibid., #2218808.). She died on 29 Jan 1818 Ste-Madeleine-de-Rigaud, Quebec, at age 36 (Ibid., #2682039.). She was buried on 30 Jan 1818 Ste-Madeleine-de-Rigaud, Quebec *(age 38, tavern owner, wife of Francois Xavier Lemaire dit St. Germain)* (PRDH online, #2682039.).

Francois Xavier Lemaire dit St.Germain was baptized on 18 Sep 1783 Oka, Quebec (Ibid., #739087.). He married **Louise Roy dit Lapensee,** daughter of **Francois Roy dit Lapensee** and **Marie Madeleine Bonhomme,** on 16 Feb 1819 (Sts-Anges-de-Lachine), Montreal, Quebec (Ibid., #2225630.). He died on 23 Jul 1832 Ste-Madeleine-de-Rigaud, Quebec, at age 48 (Ibid., #4623266.). He was buried on 24 Jul 1832 Ste-Madeleine-de-Rigaud, Quebec *(age 53, husband of Louise Lapensee)* (PRDH online, #4623266.).

Children of **Anastasie Villeneuve** and **Francois Xavier Lemaire dit St.Germain** were as follows:

      i.   Therese Amable Sophie Lemaire was born on 5 Dec 1810 Ste-Madeleine-de-Rigaud, Quebec (Ibid., #2679734.). She was baptized on 6 Dec 1810 Ste-Madeleine-de-Rigaud, Quebec (Ibid.). She died on 5 Oct 1811 Ste-Madeleine-de-Rigaud, Quebec (Ibid., #2681776.). She was buried on 6 Oct 1811 Ste-Madeleine-de-Rigaud, Quebec (Ibid.).

      ii.   Louise Sophie Lemaire dit St.Germain was born on 7 Feb 1812 Ste-Madeleine-de-Rigaud, Quebec (Ibid., #2679852.). She was baptized on 8 Feb 1812 Ste-Madeleine-de-Rigaud, Quebec *(father's occupation: merchant)* (PRDH online, #2679852.). She died on 30 Sep 1824 Ste-Madeleine-de-Rigaud, Quebec, at age 12 (Ibid., #2682433.). She was buried on 2 Oct 1824 Ste-Madeleine-de-Rigaud, Quebec *(father's occupation: merchant and farmer)* (PRDH online, #2682433.).

      iii.   Marie Louise Lemaire dit St.Germain was born on 14 Aug 1813 Vaudreuil, Quebec (Ibid., #2591055.). She was baptized on 14 Aug 1813 Vaudreuil, Quebec (Ibid.). She died on 1 Oct 1814 Vaudreuil, Quebec, at age 1 (Ibid., #2592950.). She was buried on 3 Oct 1814 Vaudreuil, Quebec (Ibid.).

      iv.   Patrice Alexandre Lemaire dit St.Germain was born on 17 Mar 1815 Oka, Quebec (Ibid., #2752382.). He was baptized on 17 Mar 1815 Oka, Quebec (Ibid.). He married Marie Emilie Jobin, daughter of Charles Jobin and Marie Sylvestre, on 8 Nov 1841 Notre-Dame-de-Montreal, Quebec *(no known children)* (PRDH online, #3544806.).

        He was *a day laborer* on 8 Nov 1841 (Ibid.).

        Marie Emilie Jobin was born circa 1819.

      v.   Ignace Lemaire dit St.Germain was born on 13 Jan 1818 Ste-Madeleine-de-Rigaud, Quebec (Ibid., #2680452.). He was baptized on 13 Jan 1818 Ste-Madeleine-de-Rigaud, Quebec *(father's occupation: tavern owner)* (PRDH online, #2680452.). He died on 12 May 1818 Oka, Quebec (Ibid., #2752566.). He was buried on 13 May 1818 Oka, Quebec (Ibid.).

      vi.   Leon Xavier Lemaire was born on 13 Jan 1818 Ste-Madeleine-de-Rigaud, Quebec (Ibid., #2680451.). He was baptized on 13 Jan 1818 Ste-Madeleine-de-Rigaud, Quebec *(father's occupation: tavern owner)* (PRDH online, #2680451.). He died on 27 Jan 1818 Ste-Madeleine-de-Rigaud, Quebec (Ibid., #2682038.). He was buried on 28 Jan 1818 Ste-Madeleine-de-Rigaud, Quebec *(father's occupation: tavern owner)* (PRDH online, #2682038.).

18. Paul Pierre Villeneuve was born on 8 Feb 1784 Vaudreuil, Quebec (Ibid., #722923.). He was baptized on 9 Feb 1784 Vaudreuil, Quebec (Ibid.). He married **Veronique Chevrier**, daughter of **Joseph Chevrier dit Lajeunesse** and **Josephte Charlebois**, on 17 Jan 1814 Ste-Madeleine-de-Rigaud, Quebec (Ibid., #3465663.).

He and **Veronique Chevrier** were enumerated in the census in 1852 Ste-Madeleine-de-Rigaud, Vaudreuil, Quebec. Also in the family: **Marie Josephte Villeneuve**, **Angelique Villeneuve**, **Pierre Paul Villeneuve**, and **Francois Xavier Villeneuve** *(Villeneuve, P. Paul, Cultivateur, Vaudreuil, Catholique, 73, M; Chevrier, Véronique, Rigaud, Catholique, 57, F; Villeneuve, Josephte, Rigaud Catholique, 22, F; Villeneuve, Angélique, Rigaud, Catholique, 28, F; Villeneuve, Pierre, Journalier, Rigaud, Catholique, 20, M; Villeneuve, Xavier, Journalier, Rigaud, Catholique, 18, M)* (1852C Cdn Transcription Project, District 536, page 30d, 31a, (61), line 6-11.).

Veronique Chevrier was baptized on 7 Oct 1794 Vaudreuil, Quebec (PRDH online, #770627.).

Children of **Paul Pierre Villeneuve** and **Veronique Chevrier** all born Ste-Madeleine-de-Rigaud, Quebec, were as follows:

74 i. Marie Veronique Villeneuve, b. 27 Sep 1814; m. Pierre Beaupre; m. Hyacinthe Daoust.

   ii. Amable Therese Villeneuve was born on 18 May 1816 (Ibid., #2680289.). She was baptized on 18 May 1816 Ste-Madeleine-de-Rigaud, Quebec *(father's occupation: laborer)* (PRDH online, #2680289.). She died on 10 Aug 1817 Ste-Madeleine-de-Rigaud, Quebec, at age 1 (Ibid., #2682020.). She was buried on 12 Aug 1817 Ste-Madeleine-de-Rigaud, Quebec *(age 14 months and 22 days, father's occupation: laborer)* (PRDH online, #2682020.).

75 iii. Joseph Benjamin Villeneuve, b. 12 Jan 1818; m. Rose Emelie Brunet dit Letang.

76 iv. Marie Louise Villeneuve, b. 21 Jul 1819; m. Joseph Seguin.

   v. Sophie Agnes Villeneuve was born on 30 Mar 1821 (Ibid., #2680856.). She was baptized on 31 Mar 1821 Ste-Madeleine-de-Rigaud, Quebec *(father's occupation: cultivator)* (PRDH online, #2680856.). She died on 3 Jun 1821 Ste-Madeleine-de-Rigaud, Quebec (Ibid., #2682226.). She was buried on 4 Jun 1821 Ste-Madeleine-de-Rigaud, Quebec *(age 3 months and 3 days, father's occupation: cultivator)* (PRDH online, #2682226.).

77 vi. Marie Sophie Villeneuve, b. 19 May 1822; m. Antoine Foubert.

   vii. Angelique Villeneuve was born on 21 Feb 1824 (Ibid., #2681312.). She was baptized on 21 Feb 1824 Ste-Madeleine-de-Rigaud, Quebec *(father's occupation: cultivator)* (PRDH online, #2681312.).

     She was in the census household of Paul Pierre Villeneuve and Veronique Chevrier in 1852 Ste-Madeleine-de-Rigaud, Vaudreuil, Quebec (1852C Cdn Transcription Project, District 536, page 30d, 31a, (61), line 6-11.).

   viii. Dorothee Villeneuve was born on 15 Oct 1825 (PRDH online, #4617271.). She was baptized on 15 Oct 1825 Ste-Madeleine-de-Rigaud, Quebec (Ibid.).

   ix. Joseph Theodore Villeneuve was born on 7 Aug 1827 (Ibid., #4617588.). He was baptized on 8 Aug 1827 Ste-Madeleine-de-Rigaud, Quebec (Ibid.).

   x. Marie Josephte Villeneuve was born on 7 Jul 1829 (Ibid., #4617971.). She was baptized on 8 Jul 1829 Ste-Madeleine-de-Rigaud, Quebec (Ibid.).

     She was in the census household of Paul Pierre Villeneuve and Veronique Chevrier in 1852 Ste-Madeleine-de-Rigaud, Vaudreuil, Quebec (1852C Cdn Transcription Project, District 536, page 30d, 31a, (61), line 6-11.).

   xi. Pierre Paul Villeneuve was born on 25 Jun 1831 (PRDH online, #4618388.). He was baptized on 25 Jun 1831 Ste-Madeleine-de-Rigaud, Quebec (Ibid.).

     He was in the census household of Paul Pierre Villeneuve and Veronique Chevrier in 1852 Ste-Madeleine-de-Rigaud, Vaudreuil, Quebec (1852C Cdn Transcription Project, District 536, page 30d, 31a, (61), line 6-11.).

   xii. Marie Virginie Villeneuve was born on 22 Jun 1833 (PRDH online, #4618910.). She was baptized on 23 Jun 1833 Ste-Madeleine-de-Rigaud, Quebec (Ibid.). She died on 8 Jul 1833 Ste-Madeleine-de-Rigaud, Quebec (Ibid., #4623412.). She was buried on 11 Jul 1833 Ste-Madeleine-de-Rigaud, Quebec *(age 18 days)* (PRDH online, #4623412.).

   xiii. Francois Xavier Villeneuve was born on 29 Jun 1834 (Ibid., #4619152.). He was baptized on 30 Jun 1834 Ste-Madeleine-de-Rigaud, Quebec (Ibid.).

He was in the census household of Paul Pierre Villeneuve and Veronique Chevrier in 1852 Ste-Madeleine-de-Rigaud, Vaudreuil, Quebec (1852C Cdn Transcription Project, District 536, page 30d, 31a, (61), line 6-11.).

19. Vincent Xavier Villeneuve was born on 14 Oct 1786 Vaudreuil, Quebec (PRDH online, #604870.). He was baptized on 15 Oct 1786 Vaudreuil, Quebec (Ibid.). He married **Euphrosine Marie Quesnel**, daughter of **Antoine Quesnel** and **Marguerite Eugenie Larocque dit Rocbrune**, on 6 Nov 1809 Vaudreuil, Quebec (Ibid.).

Euphrosine Marie Quesnel was born circa 1793 (Ibid., #68464.). As of 23 Nov 1835, she was also known as **Marie Anne Quesnel** (Ibid., #3463675.).

Children of **Vincent Xavier Villeneuve** and **Euphrosine Marie Quesnel** were as follows:

- i.   Amable Therese Villeneuve was born on 15 Oct 1810 Ste-Madeleine-de-Rigaud, Quebec (Ibid., #2679721.). She was baptized on 15 Oct 1810 Ste-Madeleine-de-Rigaud, Quebec *(father's occupation: agriculture)* (PRDH online, #2679721.). She died on 9 May 1811 Ste-Madeleine-de-Rigaud, Quebec (Ibid., #2681758.). She was buried on 10 May 1811 Ste-Madeleine-de-Rigaud, Quebec *(age 7 months, father's occupation: agriculture)* (PRDH online, #2681758.).
- ii. Birgitte Emelie Villeneuve was born on 8 Oct 1811 Ste-Madeleine-de-Rigaud, Quebec (Ibid., #2679819.). She was baptized on 8 Oct 1811 Ste-Madeleine-de-Rigaud, Quebec *(father's occupation: agriculture)* (PRDH online, #2679819.). She died on 6 Mar 1813 Ste-Madeleine-de-Rigaud, Quebec, at age 1 (Ibid., #2681817.). She was buried on 7 Mar 1813 Ste-Madeleine-de-Rigaud, Quebec *(father's occupation: agriculture)* (PRDH online, #2681817.).
- 78 iii. Vincent Xavier Villeneuve, b. 4 Apr 1813 Ste-Madeleine-de-Riguad, Quebec; m. Marie Sophie Cadieux.
- iv. Sylvestre Gelin Villeneuve was born on 31 Dec 1814 Ste-Madeleine-de-Rigaud, Quebec (Ibid., #2758353.). He was baptized on 1 Jan 1815 Ste-Madeleine-de-Rigaud, Quebec *(father's occupation: agriculture)* (PRDH online, #2758353.). He died on 2 Feb 1815 Ste-Madeleine-de-Rigaud, Quebec (Ibid., #2681922.). He was buried on 4 Feb 1815 Ste-Madeleine-de-Rigaud, Quebec *(father's occupation: agriculture)* (PRDH online, #2681922.).
- v.   Pierre Francois Villeneuve was born on 27 Feb 1816 Ste-Madeleine-de-Rigaud, Quebec (Ibid., #2680269.). He was baptized on 28 Feb 1816 Ste-Madeleine-de-Rigaud, Quebec *(father's occupation: agriculture)* (PRDH online, #2680269.).
- 79 vi. Clemence Villeneuve, b. 9 Sep 1817 Ste-Madeleine-de-Rigaud, Quebec; m. Michel Paul Amable St.Julien.
- 80 vii. Julienne Villeneuve, b. 4 Aug 1820 Ste-Madeleine-de-Riguad, Quebec; m. Jean Marie Cadieux.
- viii. Anastasie Villeneuve was born on 29 Oct 1822 Ste-Madeleine-de-Rigaud, Quebec (Ibid., #2681104.). She was baptized on 29 Oct 1822 Ste-Madeleine-de-Rigaud, Quebec (Ibid.). She married Pierre Evangeliste Leduc, son of Pierre Leduc and Marie Marguerite Brabant, on 23 Jul 1844 Ste-Madeleine-de-Rigaud, Quebec (Ibid., #3466007.).

  Pierre Evangeliste Leduc was born on 22 Feb 1818 Ste-Madeleine-de-Rigaud, Quebec (Ibid., #2680467.). He was baptized on 23 Feb 1818 Ste-Madeleine-de-Rigaud, Quebec (Ibid.).
- ix. Antoine Villeneuve was born on 15 Apr 1824 Ste-Madeleine-de-Rigaud, Quebec (Ibid., #2681342.). He was baptized on 15 Apr 1824 Ste-Madeleine-de-Rigaud, Quebec *(father's occupation: cultivator)* (PRDH online, #2681342.).

Generation Four

20. Regis Villeneuve was born circa 1776 (Ibid., #249454.). He married **Ursule Seguin**, daughter of **Francois de Sales Seguin dit Laderoute** and **Marie Angelique Quesnel**, on 28 Jan 1799 Vaudreuil, Quebec *(Regis Villenevue, cultivateur, adult son of Simon Villeneuve and Marie Madeleine Sabourin, married 28 January 1799, Ursule Seguin, adult daughter of Francois Seguin, cultivateur, and Marie Angelique Quenelle, Present: Francois Xavier Villeneuve brother of the groom, Francois Seguin, brother-in-law of the broom, Pierre Villeneuve paternal uncle, Hyacinthe, Andre, Charles, and Antoine Sabourin maternal uncles of the groom, Theodore Seguin brother of thebride, Michel Lalonde brother-in-law of the bride, Augustin Leduc brother-in-law of the bride, Louis Seguin paternal uncle, Jean Baptiste Quenel maternal uncle. Dispensation of 2nd and 3rd degree relationship)* (PRDH online, No. 358275.).

He and **Ursule Seguin** were enumerated in the census in 1852 Ste-Madeleine, Rigaud, Quebec. Also in the family: **Louise Villeneuve** *(Villeneuve, Regis, Bourgeois, Rigaud, Catholique, 72, M; Séguin, Ursule, Vaudreuil, Catholique, 73, F; Villeneuve, Louise, Rigaud, Catholique, 31, F)* (1852C Cdn Transcription Project, District 536, page 40d, 41a, (81), line 24-26.).

Ursule Seguin was born on 4 Jun 1778 Vaudreuil, Quebec (PRDH online, No. 722354.). She was baptized on 5 Jun 1778 Vaudreuil, Quebec (Ibid.).
Children of **Regis Villeneuve** and **Ursule Seguin** were as follows:

81   i.   Marie Rose Villeneuve, b. 30 Dec 1799 Oka, Quebec; m. Jean Baptiste Brazeau dit Brassault.

       ii.   Simon Regis Villeneuve was born on 26 Sep 1801 Oka, Quebec (Ibid., #2752214.). He was baptized on 27 Sep 1801 Oka, Quebec (Ibid.). He died on 24 Jul 1802 (Ibid., #2681453.). He was buried on 1 Aug 1802 Ste-Madeleine-de-Rigaud, Quebec *(age 10 months)* (PRDH online, #2681453.).

82   iii.   Simon Regis Villeneuve, b. 13 May 1803 Ste-Madeleine-de-Rigaud, Quebec; m. Marie Madeleine Belanger.

83   iv.   Antoine Theodore Villeneuve, b. 14 May 1805 Ste-Madeleine-de-Rigaud, Quebec; m. Veronique Emilie Chevrier dit Lajeunesse.

84   v.   Francois Xavier Villeneuve, b. 27 May 1807 Ste-Madeleine-de-Rigaud, Quebec; m. Marguerite Rachelle Ranger.

85   vi.   Marie Angelique Villeneuve, b. 7 May 1809 Vaudreuil, Quebec; m. Vincent Belanger.

86   vii.   Francois Villeneuve, b. 16 Feb 1812 Oka, Quebec; m. Marie Madeleine Lalonde.

87   viii.   Antoine Benjamin Villeneuve, b. 10 Jun 1814 Ste-Madeleine-de-Rigaud, Quebec; m. Marie Mathilde Thomas dit Tranchemontagne.

88   ix.   Veronique Villeneuve, b. 9 Nov 1816 Ste-Madeleine-de-Rigaud, Quebec; m. Francois Andre Sabourin.

       x.   Louise Villeneuve was born on 2 Sep 1819 Ste-Madeleine-de-Rigaud, Quebec (Ibid., #2680654.). She was baptized on 4 Sep 1819 Ste-Madeleine-de-Rigaud, Quebec *(father's occupation: cultivator)* (PRDH online, #2680654.).

           She was in the census household of Regis Villeneuve and Ursule Seguin in 1852 Ste-Madeleine, Rigaud, Quebec (1852C Cdn Transcription Project, District 536, page 40d, 41a, (81), line 24-26.).

21. Marie Ostie Villeneuve was born on 17 Nov 1780 Vaudreuil, Quebec (PRDH online, #243594.). She was baptized on 17 Nov 1780 Vaudreuil, Quebec (Ibid.). She married **Paul Francois Seguin dit Laderoute**, son of **Francois de Sales Seguin dit Laderoute** and **Marie Angelique Quesnel**, on 7 Nov 1796 Vaudreuil, Quebec *(Francois Seguin, cultivateur, adult son of Francois Seguin cultivateur and Angelique Quenelle, married 7 November 1796, Marie Ortie Villeneuve, minor daughter of Simon Villeneuve, cultivateur, and Marie Madeleine Sabourin, Present: Theodore Seguin brother of the groom, Albert Lalonde brother-in-law of the groom, Louis and Guillaume Laderoute uncles of the groom, Amable and Baptiste Quenelle uncles of the groom, Regis and Xavier Villeneuve brothers of the bride, Pierre, Francois, and Jean Baptiste Villeneuve uncles of the bride, Hyacinthe and Andre Abourin uncles of the bride. Dispensation of 2nd and 3rd degree relationship)* (PRDH online, No. 358233.).

She was also known as **Marie Lortie dit Villeneuve** (Ibid., #243594.). As of 7 Nov 1796, she was also known as **Marie dit Villeneuve** (Ibid., No. 358233.). As of 29 Jun 1801, she was also known as **Scholastique Villeneuve** (Ibid., #2752207.).

Paul Francois Seguin dit Laderoute was baptized on 10 Jul 1773 Oka, Quebec *(of Vaudreuil)* (PRDH online, No. 738954.). He died on 16 Aug 1832 Ste-Madeleine-de-Rigaud, Quebec, at age 59 (Ibid., #4623318.). He was buried on 16 Aug 1832 Ste-Madeleine-de-Rigaud, Quebec *(age 62, husband of Austie Villeneuve)* (PRDH online, #4623318.). He was also known as **Francois Seguin dit Laderoute** (Ibid., #3462197.). He was *a farmer* on 9 Oct 1797 (Ibid., No. 770957.).

Children of **Marie Ostie Villeneuve** and **Paul Francois Seguin dit Laderoute** were as follows:

89   i.   Francois Israel Seguin, b. 8 Oct 1797 Vaudreuil, Quebec; m. Marguerite Lecompte.

90   ii.   Antoine Seguin, b. 5 Oct 1798 Vaudreuil, Quebec; m. Theotiste St.Denis; m. Marie Lecompte.

       iii.   Antoine Seguin was baptized on 30 Nov 1799 Vaudreuil, Quebec (Ibid., No. 771198.). He died on 16 Feb 1801 at age 1 (Ibid., #2592297.). He was buried on 19 Feb 1801 Vaudreuil, Quebec *(age 15 months)* (PRDH online, #2592297.).

91   iv.   Theodore Seguin, b. 28 Jun 1801 Oka, Quebec; m. Marie Theotiste Brazeau.

92   v.   Marie Theotiste Seguin, b. 23 Apr 1803 Ste-Madeleine-de-Rigaud, Quebec; m. Michel Gelin St.Denis.

       vi.   Francois Xavier Seguin dit Laderoute was born circa May 1805 (Ibid., #2681580.). He died on 26 Jun 1806 Ste-Madeleine-de-Rigaud, Quebec (Ibid.). He was buried on 28 Jun 1806 Ste-Madeleine-de-Rigaud, Quebec *(age 14 months, father's occupation: agriculture)* (PRDH online, #2681580.).

       vii. Louis Xavier Seguin was born on 2 May 1805 Oka, Quebec (Ibid., #2752268.). He was baptized on 3 May 1805 Oka, Quebec *(father's occupation: cultivator)* (PRDH online, #2752268.).

      viii. Louis Xavier Seguin was born on 26 Apr 1807 Vaudreuil, Quebec (Ibid., #2590502.). He was baptized on 27 Apr 1807 Vaudreuil, Quebec (Ibid.).

93   ix. Marie Clothilde Cleophee Seguin dit Laderoute, b. 23 Mar 1809 Ste-Madeleine-de-Rigaud, Quebec; m. Joseph Vallee.

94   x. Jean Seguin dit Laderoute, b. 26 Mar 1811; m. Marie Louise Vallee.

      xi. Jeremie Seguin was born on 25 Feb 1813 Ste-Madeleine-de-Rigaud, Quebec (Ibid., #2679965.). He was baptized on 26 Feb 1813 Ste-Madeleine-de-Rigaud, Quebec *(father's occupation: agriculture)* (PRDH online, #2679765.). He died on 15 Jul 1814 Ste-Madeleine-de-Rigaud, Quebec, at age 1 (Ibid., #2681897.). He was buried on 16 Jul 1814 Ste-Madeleine-de-Rigaud, Quebec *(father's occupation: agriculture)* (PRDH online, #2681897.).

95   xii. Jeremie Seguin, b. 20 Jun 1816 Ste-Madeleine-de-Rigaud, Quebec; m. Josephte Rousselle.

96   xiii. Benjamin Seguin, b. 20 Sep 1818 Ste-Madeleine-de-Rigaud, Quebec; m. Flavie Dion.

97   xiv. Monique Seguin, b. 13 Mar 1820 Ste-Madeleine-de-Rigaud, Quebec; m. Alexandre Emery Rousselle.

      xv. Hilaire Dizier Seguin dit Laderoute was born on 25 Jan 1822 Ste-Madeleine-de-Rigaud, Quebec (Ibid., #2680971.). He was baptized on 26 Jan 1822 Ste-Madeleine-de-Rigaud, Quebec *(father's occupation: cultivator)* (PRDH online, #2680971.). He died on 18 Jun 1823 Ste-Madeleine-de-Rigaud, Quebec, at age 1 (Ibid., #2682344.). He was buried on 20 Jun 1823 Ste-Madeleine-de-Rigaud, Quebec *(father's occupation: cultivator)* (PRDH online, #2682344.).

22. Xavier Louis Villeneuve was born on 19 Jun 1782 Vaudreuil, Quebec (Ibid., #722771.). He was baptized on 20 Jun 1782 Vaudreuil, Quebec (Ibid.). He married **Louise Veronique Seguin dit Laderoute**, daughter of **Hyacinthe Seguin dit Laderoute** and **Marie Louise Rouleau,** on 15 Jun 1803 Ste-Madeleine-de-Rigaud, Quebec (Ibid., #52007.).

Louise Veronique Seguin dit Laderoute was born on 16 Dec 1785 (Ibid., #723127.). She was baptized on 17 Dec 1785 Vaudreuil, Quebec (Ibid.).

Children of **Xavier Louis Villeneuve** and **Louise Veronique Seguin dit Laderoute** all born Ste-Madeleine-de-Riguad, Quebec, were as follows:

98   i. Marie Elisabeth Sophie Villeneuve, b. 3 Oct 1805; m. Hyacinthe Seguin; d. 25 Jul 1843; bur. 27 Jul 1843.

      ii. Marie Theotiste Villeneuve was born on 7 Jan 1807 (Ibid., #2679391.). She was baptized on 7 Jan 1807 Ste-Madeleine-de-Riguad, Quebec (Ibid.). She died on 29 Mar 1807 Ste-Madeleine-de-Riguad, Quebec (Ibid., #2681599.). She was buried on 30 Mar 1807 Ste-Madeleine-de-Riguad, Quebec (Ibid.).

99   iii. Pierre Louis Xavier Villeneuve, b. 25 Feb 1808; m. Marie Sophie Sabourin.

      iv. Anonyme Villeneuve was born on 2 Dec 1808 (Ibid., #2681657.). He/she died on 2 Dec 1808 Ste-Madeleine-de-Riguad, Quebec (Ibid.). He/she was buried on 4 Dec 1808 Ste-Madeleine-de-Riguad, Quebec (Ibid.).

100   v. Pierre Emery Villeneuve, b. 19 Nov 1809; m. Marguerite Scholastique Lavallee.

101   vi. Marie Louise Madeleine Villeneuve, b. 2 Feb 1812; m. Jean Baptiste Bertrand.

102   vii. Vincent Hermenegilde Villeneuve, b. 22 Jan 1814; m. Marguerite Sophie Bertrand.

103   viii. Marie Luce Alice Villeneuve, b. 12 Dec 1815; m. Benjamin Patrice Belanger.

      ix. Josephte Domitilde Villeneuve was born on 19 Mar 1819 (Ibid., #2680603.). She was baptized on 19 Mar 1819 Ste-Madeleine-de-Rigaud, Quebec (Ibid.). She married Joseph Elie Leduc, son of Amable Leduc and Marie Madeleine Cholet, on 18 Nov 1839 Ste-Madeleine-de-Rigaud, Quebec (Ibid., #3464915.).

        Joseph Elie Leduc was born on 7 Mar 1803 (Ibid., #2679137.). He was baptized on 13 Mar 1803 Ste-Madeleine-de-Rigaud, Quebec (Ibid.). He married **Euphrosine Vallee**, daughter of **Pierre Vallee** and **Elisabeth Robillard,** on 18 Feb 1827 Ste-Anne-de-Bellevue, Quebec (Ibid., #3489752.).

      x. Marie Flavie Villeneuve was born on 6 May 1821 (Ibid., #2680873.). She was baptized on 7 May 1821 Ste-Madeleine-de-Riguad, Quebec (Ibid.).

      xi. Marie Josephe Villeneuve was born on 7 Mar 1823 (Ibid., #2681160.). She was baptized on 7 Mar 1823 Ste-Madeleine-de-Riguad, Quebec (Ibid.). She died on 4 Aug 1836 Ste-Madeleine-de-

Riguad, Quebec, at age 13 (Ibid., #4623698.). She was buried on 5 Aug 1836 Ste-Madeleine-de-Riguad, Quebec (Ibid.).

xii. Anonyme Villeneuve was born on 22 Feb 1827 (Ibid., #4622811.). She died on 22 Feb 1827 Ste-Madeleine-de-Riguad, Quebec (Ibid.). She was buried on 23 Feb 1827 Ste-Madeleine-de-Riguad, Quebec (Ibid.).

xiii. Veronique Villeneuve was born on 15 Sep 1829 (Ibid., #4618004.). She was baptized on 15 Sep 1829 Ste-Madeleine-de-Riguad, Quebec (Ibid.).

xiv. Marie Olympe Villeneuve was born on 23 Oct 1831 (Ibid., #4618458.). She was baptized on 23 Oct 1831 Ste-Madeleine-de-Riguad, Quebec (Ibid.).

23. Pierre Anselme Seguin dit Asselin was baptized on 20 Apr 1785 Oka, Quebec (Ibid., #739108.). He married **Louise Marie Seguin dit Laderoute**, daughter of **Hyacinthe Seguin dit Laderoute** and **Marie Louise Rouleau,** on 19 Feb 1810 Ste-Madeleine-de-Rigaud, Quebec (Ibid., #52007.).

Louise Marie Seguin dit Laderoute was born on 25 Nov 1789 Pointe-Claire, Quebec (Ibid., #606214.). She was baptized on 26 Nov 1789 Pointe-Claire, Quebec (Ibid.).

Children of **Pierre Anselme Seguin dit Asselin** and **Louise Marie Seguin dit Laderoute** all born Ste-Madeleine-de-Riguad, Quebec, were as follows:

i. Pierre Simon Seguin was born on 27 Jan 1811 (Ibid., #2679746.). He was baptized on 1 Feb 1811 Ste-Madeleine-de-Riguad, Quebec (Ibid.).

ii. Louise Seguin was born on 26 Aug 1812 (Ibid., #2679913.). She was baptized on 26 Aug 1812 Ste-Madeleine-de-Riguad, Quebec (Ibid.). She died on 18 Mar 1816 Ste-Madeleine-de-Riguad, Quebec, at age 3 (Ibid., #2681966.). She was buried on 19 Mar 1816 Ste-Madeleine-de-Riguad, Quebec *(father's occupation: farmer)* (PRDH online, #2681966.).

104 iii. Paul Regis Seguin, b. 30 Sep 1814; m. Julie Aurelie Tessier.

iv. Louise Seguin was born on 22 Aug 1816 (Ibid., #2680322.). She was baptized on 23 Aug 1816 Ste-Madeleine-de-Riguad, Quebec *(father's occupation: farmer)* (PRDH online, #2680322.).

v. Pierre Xavier Seguin was born on 3 Aug 1818 (Ibid., #2680524.). He was baptized on 4 Aug 1818 Ste-Madeleine-de-Riguad, Quebec *(father's occupation: farmer)* (PRDH online, #2680524.).

vi. Anonyme Seguin was born on 19 May 1820 (Ibid., #2682154.). She died on 19 May 1820 Ste-Madeleine-de-Riguad, Quebec (Ibid.). She was buried on 20 May 1820 Ste-Madeleine-de-Riguad, Quebec (Ibid.).

vii. Anonyme Seguin was born on 15 Aug 1821 (Ibid., #2682245.). She died on 15 Aug 1821 Ste-Madeleine-de-Riguad, Quebec (Ibid.). She was buried on 16 Aug 1821 Ste-Madeleine-de-Riguad, Quebec (Ibid.).

viii. Michel Etienne Seguin was born on 2 Aug 1822 (Ibid., #2681057.). He was baptized on 2 Aug 1822 Ste-Madeleine-de-Riguad, Quebec (Ibid.).

105 ix. Anthime Seguin, b. 14 Sep 1824; m. Marie Louise Seguin.

x. Marie Delphine Seguin was born on 28 Sep 1826 (Ibid., #4617426.). She was baptized on 28 Sep 1826 Ste-Madeleine-de-Riguad, Quebec (Ibid.). She died on 28 Jun 1831 Ste-Madeleine-de-Riguad, Quebec, at age 4 (Ibid., #4623122.). She was buried on 30 Jun 1831 Ste-Madeleine-de-Riguad, Quebec (Ibid.).

xi. Pierre Seguin was born on 5 Nov 1828 (Ibid., #4617830.). He was baptized on 5 Nov 1828 Ste-Madeleine-de-Riguad, Quebec (Ibid.).

xii. Anonyme Seguin was born on 25 Nov 1830 (Ibid., #4623074.). She died on 25 Nov 1830 Ste-Madeleine-de-Riguad, Quebec (Ibid.). She was buried on 26 Nov 1830 Ste-Madeleine-de-Riguad, Quebec (Ibid.).

xiii. Benjamin Seguin was born on 13 Nov 1832 (Ibid., #4618754.). He was baptized on 13 Nov 1832 Ste-Madeleine-de-Riguad, Quebec (Ibid.).

24. Marie Theotiste Villeneuve was born on 9 Aug 1787 Vaudreuil, Quebec (Ibid., #723285.). She was baptized on 10 Aug 1787 Vaudreuil, Quebec (Ibid.). She married **Etienne Lefebvre or Lefaivre**, son of **Louis Lefebvre dit Freve** and **Marie Rose Daussy dit Buisson,** on 20 Feb 1805 Vaudreuil, Quebec (Ibid., #52007.). She died on 25 May 1839 Vaudreuil, Quebec, at age 51 (Ibid., #4182029.). She was buried on 27 May 1839 Vaudreuil, Quebec (Ibid.).

Etienne Lefebvre or Lefaivre was born on 23 Jun 1778 Pointe-Claire, Quebec (Ibid., #589983.). He was baptized on 23 Jun 1778 Pointe-Claire, Quebec (Ibid.).

Children of **Marie Theotiste Villeneuve** and **Etienne Lefebvre or Lefaivre** were as follows:

      i.   Etienne Lefaivre was born on 29 May 1807 Vaudreuil, Quebec (Ibid., #2590510.). He was baptized on 30 May 1807 Vaudreuil, Quebec (Ibid.). He died on 3 Mar 1833 Vaudreuil, Quebec, at age 25 (Ibid., #4181604.). He was buried on 4 Mar 1833 Vaudreuil, Quebec (Ibid.).

      ii.   Marie Theotiste Lefaivre was born on 6 Nov 1808 Vaudreuil, Quebec (Ibid., #2590654.). She was baptized on 6 Nov 1808 Vaudreuil, Quebec (Ibid.).

106   iii.   Simon Francois Regis Lefaivre, b. 15 Jul 1810 Vaudreuil, Quebec; m. Sophie Robillard.

      iv.   Louis Lefebvre was born on 27 Oct 1811 Vaudreuil, Quebec (Ibid., #2590913.). He was baptized on 27 Oct 1811 Vaudreuil, Quebec (Ibid.). He died on 29 Apr 1835 at age 23 (Ibid., #4181781.). He was buried on 10 Jul 1835 Vaudreuil, Quebec (Ibid.).

      v.   Marie Victoire Lefaivre was born on 9 Jul 1814 Vaudreuil, Quebec (Ibid., #2591128.). She was baptized on 10 Jul 1814 Vaudreuil, Quebec (Ibid.).

      vi.   Francois Xavier Lefebvre was born on 12 Aug 1815 Vaudreuil, Quebec (Ibid., #2591256.). He was baptized on 13 Aug 1815 Vaudreuil, Quebec (Ibid.). He married Marie Hyppolite Aurelie Lefebvre, daughter of Michel Lefebvre and Hyppolyte Legault, on 24 Nov 1847 Vaudreuil, Quebec (Ibid., #3477955.).

         Marie Hyppolite Aurelie Lefebvre was born on 26 Oct 1829 Vaudreuil, Quebec (Ibid., #4178238.). She was baptized on 26 Oct 1829 Vaudreuil, Quebec (Ibid.).

107   vii.   Elisabeth Cecile Lefebvre, b. 11 Nov 1816 Vaudreuil, Quebec; m. Jean Evangeliste Gauthier.

108   viii.   Marie Ostie Lefebvre, b. 1 Apr 1819 Vaudreuil, Quebec; m. Jules Leger.

      ix.   Angele Lefebvre was born on 10 May 1820 Vaudreuil, Quebec (Ibid., #2591699.). She was baptized on 11 May 1820 Vaudreuil, Quebec (Ibid.).

109   x.   Marie Rose Lefaivre, b. 29 Jun 1822 Vaudreuil, Quebec; m. Cyprien Daout.

      xi.   Basile Lefaivre was born on 15 Nov 1823 Vaudreuil, Quebec (Ibid., #2592098.). He was baptized on 16 Nov 1823 Vaudreuil, Quebec (Ibid.). He died on 30 Aug 1825 Vaudreuil, Quebec, at age 1 (Ibid., #4181177.). He was buried on 2 Sep 1825 Vaudreuil, Quebec (Ibid.).

      xii.   Maxime Lefaivre was born on 4 Feb 1826 Vaudreuil, Quebec (Ibid., #4177821.). He was baptized on 5 Feb 1826 Vaudreuil, Quebec (Ibid.).

      xiii.   Anonyme Lefaivre was born on 16 Apr 1827 (Ibid., #4181259.). She died on 16 Apr 1827 (Ibid.). She was buried on 17 May 1827 Vaudreuil, Quebec (Ibid.).

      xiv.   Anonyme Lefaivre was born on 16 Apr 1827 (Ibid., #4181260.). She died on 16 Apr 1827 (Ibid.). She was buried on 17 May 1827 Vaudreuil, Quebec (Ibid.).

110   xv.   Marie Marine Lefaivre, b. circa 1828; m. Antoine Charlebois.

25. Marie Judith Villeneuve was born on 14 Apr 1789 Oka, Quebec (Ibid., #642319.). She was baptized on 16 Apr 1789 Oka, Quebec (Ibid.). She married **Augustin Kemner dit Laflamme**, son of **Pierre Kemner dit Lafamme** and **Julie Dumont**, on 26 Nov 1810 Vaudreuil, Quebec (Ibid., #52007.).

Augustin Kemner dit Laflamme was born on 15 May 1789 Boucherville, Quebec (Ibid., #638710.). He was baptized on 16 May 1789 Boucherville, Quebec (Ibid.). As of 26 Nov 1810, he was also known as **Augustin Timineur dit Laflamme** (Ibid., #2224097.).

Children of **Marie Judith Villeneuve** and **Augustin Kemner dit Laflamme** were as follows:

      i.   Marie Judith Timineur was born on 10 Oct 1811 Oka, Quebec (Ibid., #2752341.). She was baptized on 11 Oct 1811 Oka, Quebec *(father's occupation: agriculture)* (PRDH online, #2752341.).

         She was also known as **Marie Judith Kemner** (Ibid.).

111   ii.   Simon Timineur dit Laflamme, b. 13 Mar 1814 Ste-Madeleine-de-Riguad, Quebec; m. Mathilde St.Denis.

      iii.   Charlotte Clemence Thimineur dit Laflamme was born on 9 Nov 1815 Ste-Madeleine-de-Riguad, Quebec (Ibid., #2680230.). She was baptized on 10 Nov 1815 Ste-Madeleine-de-Riguad, Quebec *(father's occupation: day laborer)* (PRDH online, #2680230.).

         She was also known as **Charlotte Clemence Kemner** (Ibid.).

      iv.   Bibiane Thimineur dit Laflamme was born on 29 Nov 1819 Ste-Madeleine-de-Riguad, Quebec (Ibid., #2680686.). She was baptized on 29 Nov 1819 Ste-Madeleine-de-Riguad, Quebec *(father's occupation: day laborer)* (PRDH online, #2680686.). She died on 30 Nov 1819 Ste-Madeleine-de-Riguad, Quebec (Ibid., #2682133.). She was buried on 1 Dec 1819 Ste-Madeleine-de-Riguad, Quebec *(father's occupation: day laborer)* (PRDH online, #2682133.).

    v.   Marie Caroline Thimineur dit Laflamme was born on 5 Oct 1820 Ste-Madeleine-de-Riguad, Quebec (Ibid., #2680815.). She was baptized on 5 Oct 1820 Ste-Madeleine-de-Riguad, Quebec *(father's occupation: day laborer)* (PRDH online, #2680815.).

    vi.   Francois Regis Thimineur dit Laflamme was born on 29 Apr 1822 Ste-Madeleine-de-Riguad, Quebec (Ibid., #2681015.). He was baptized on 30 Apr 1822 Ste-Madeleine-de-Riguad, Quebec *(father's occupation: day laborer)* (PRDH online, #2681015.). He died on 10 Apr 1823 Ste-Madeleine-de-Riguad, Quebec (Ibid., #2682339.). He was buried on 11 Apr 1823 Ste-Madeleine-de-Riguad, Quebec *(age 11 months, father's occupation: day laborer)* (PRDH online, #2682339.).

    vii.   Marie Haustie Thimineur was born on 23 Jan 1824 Ste-Madeleine-de-Riguad, Quebec (Ibid., #2681291.). She was baptized on 23 Jan 1824 Ste-Madeleine-de-Riguad, Quebec *(father's occupation: carpenter)* (PRDH online, #2681291.).

    viii.   Marie Angelique Thimineur dit Laflamme was born on 30 Sep 1825 Ste-Madeleine-de-Riguad, Quebec (Ibid., #4617262.). She was baptized on 30 Sep 1825 Ste-Madeleine-de-Riguad, Quebec (Ibid.). She died on 12 Nov 1826 Ste-Madeleine-de-Riguad, Quebec, at age 1 (Ibid., #4622794.). She was buried on 13 Nov 1826 Ste-Madeleine-de-Riguad, Quebec *(age 16 months)* (PRDH online, #4622794.).

    ix.   Hilaire Timineur was born on 29 Apr 1827 Ste-Madeleine-de-Riguad, Quebec (Ibid., #4617529.). He was baptized on 30 Apr 1827 Ste-Madeleine-de-Riguad, Quebec (Ibid.). He died on 19 May 1827 Ste-Madeleine-de-Riguad, Quebec (Ibid., #4622825.). He was buried on 21 May 1827 Ste-Madeleine-de-Riguad, Quebec *(age 3 weeks)* (PRDH online, #4622825.).

    x.   Domitilde Timineur was born on 28 Mar 1828 Ste-Madeleine-de-Riguad, Quebec (Ibid., #4617714.). She was baptized on 28 Mar 1828 Ste-Madeleine-de-Riguad, Quebec (Ibid.). She died on 5 May 1828 Ste-Madeleine-de-Riguad, Quebec (Ibid., #4622903.). She was buried on 6 May 1828 Ste-Madeleine-de-Riguad, Quebec *(age one month)* (PRDH online, #4622903.).

    xi.   Marguerite Timineur was born on 19 Jun 1830 Ste-Madeleine-de-Riguad, Quebec (Ibid., #4618136.). She was baptized on 20 Jun 1830 Ste-Madeleine-de-Riguad, Quebec (Ibid.).

26. **Marie Scholastique Villeneuve** was born on 14 Apr 1789 Vaudreuil, Quebec (Ibid., #723582.). She was baptized on 15 Apr 1789 Vaudreuil, Quebec (Ibid.). She married **Francois Xavier Cadieux**, son of **Francois Cadieux** and **Marie Reine Rouleau**, on 4 Feb 1811 Ste-Madeleine-de-Rigaud, Quebec (Ibid., #52007.).

She was in the census household of **Michel Lefebvre** and **Josephte Caroline Cadieux** in 1852 Ste.Madeleine, Rigaud, Vaudreuil, Quebec (1852C Cdn Transcription Project, District 536, page 35d, 36a, (71), line 38-45.).

Francois Xavier Cadieux was born on 13 Mar 1790 Vaudreuil, Quebec (PRDH online, #609749.). He was baptized on 14 Mar 1790 Vaudreuil, Quebec (Ibid.). He died on 10 Aug 1834 Ste-Madeleine-de-Riguad, Quebec, at age 44 (Ibid., #4623527.). He was buried on 11 Aug 1834 Ste-Madeleine-de-Riguad, Quebec *(age 46, husband of Scholastique Villeneuve)* (PRDH online, #4623527.).

Children of **Marie Scholastique Villeneuve** and **Francois Xavier Cadieux** were as follows:

    i.   Francois Xavier Cadieux was born on 11 Nov 1811 Ste-Madeleine-de-Rigaud, Quebec (Ibid., #2679828.). He was baptized on 12 Nov 1811 Ste-Madeleine-de-Rigaud, Quebec *(father's occupation: agriculture)* (PRDH online, #2679828.). He died on 30 Sep 1814 Ste-Madeleine-de-Riguad, Quebec, at age 2 (Ibid., #2681905.). He was buried on 1 Oct 1814 Ste-Madeleine-de-Riguad, Quebec *(age 2 years, 7 months and 17 days)* (PRDH online, #2681905.).

    ii.   Louis Leandre Cadieux was born on 23 Feb 1813 Ste-Madeleine-de-Riguad, Quebec (Ibid., #2679964.). He was baptized on 26 Feb 1813 Ste-Madeleine-de-Riguad, Quebec *(father's occupation: agriculture)* (PRDH online, #2679964.). He died on 8 Oct 1813 Ste-Madeleine-de-Riguad, Quebec (Ibid., #2681845.). He was buried on 10 Oct 1813 Ste-Madeleine-de-Riguad, Quebec (Ibid.).

112   iii.   Marie Julienne Cadieux, b. 30 Jul 1814 Ste-Madeleine-de-Riguad, Quebec; m. Laurent Girouard.

113   iv.   Marie Sophie Cadieux, b. 18 Dec 1815 Ste-Madeleine-de-Riguad, Quebec; m. Vincent Xavier Villeneuve.

114   v.   Jean Marie Cadieux, b. 10 May 1817 Ste-Madeleine-de-Riguad, Quebec; m. Julienne Villeneuve.

    vi.   Marie Rose Cadieux was born on 31 Jul 1818 Ste-Madeleine-de-Riguad, Quebec (Ibid., #2680523.). She was baptized on 1 Aug 1818 Ste-Madeleine-de-Riguad, Quebec *(father's occupation: agriculture)* (PRDH online, #2680523.). She married Paul Lefebvre dit Lasiseraie, son of Hyacinthe Lefebvre dit Lasiseraie and Marie Madeleine Neveu dit Nepveu, on 16 Jan 1837 Ste-Madeleine-de-Rigaud, Quebec (Ibid., #3464177.). She married Paul Neveu, son of Joseph

Neveu and Marie Hyppolite Lefebvre, on 16 Feb 1846 Ste-Madeleine-de-Riguad, Quebec (Ibid., #3466622.).

Paul Lefebvre dit Lasiseraie was born on 31 Dec 1801 Pointe-Claire, Quebec (Ibid., #2800411.). He was baptized on 31 Dec 1801 Pointe-Claire, Quebec (Ibid.). He died on 16 Feb 1844 Ste-Madeleine-de-Riguad, Quebec, at age 42 (Ibid., #4624425.). He was buried on 19 Feb 1844 Ste-Madeleine-de-Riguad, Quebec *(age 40, husband of Rose Cadieux)* (PRDH online, #4624425.).

Paul Neveu was born on 16 Dec 1808 Pointe-Claire, Quebec (Ibid., #2801019.). He was baptized on 18 Dec 1808 Pointe-Claire, Quebec (Ibid.). He married **Elmire Pilon**, daughter of **Francois Pilon** and **Charlotte Sauve,** on 31 Jan 1842 Pointe-Claire, Quebec (Ibid., #3492780.).

115 vii. Josephte Caroline Cadieux, b. 19 Mar 1820 Ste-Madeleine-de-Riguad, Quebec; m. Michel Lefebvre.

 viii. Monique Angele Cadieux was born on 5 May 1821 Ste-Madeleine-de-Riguad, Quebec (Ibid., #2680872.). She was baptized on 6 May 1821 Ste-Madeleine-de-Riguad, Quebec (Ibid.). She died on 4 Oct 1838 Ste-Madeleine-de-Riguad, Quebec, at age 17 (Ibid., #4623890.). She was buried on 6 Oct 1838 Ste-Madeleine-de-Riguad, Quebec (Ibid.).

 ix. Clothilde Arline Adeline Cadieux was born on 26 Jan 1823 Ste-Madeleine-de-Riguad, Quebec (Ibid., #2681143.). She was baptized on 27 Jan 1823 Ste-Madeleine-de-Riguad, Quebec (Ibid.). She died on 12 Dec 1841 Ste-Madeleine-de-Riguad, Quebec, at age 18 (Ibid., #4624215.). She was buried on 14 Dec 1841 Ste-Madeleine-de-Riguad, Quebec (Ibid.).

 x. Michel Cadieux was born on 18 May 1824 Ste-Madeleine-de-Riguad, Quebec (Ibid., #2681352.). He was baptized on 19 May 1824 Ste-Madeleine-de-Riguad, Quebec (Ibid.). He died on 18 Feb 1831 Ste-Madeleine-de-Riguad, Quebec, at age 6 (Ibid., #4623093.). He was buried on 16 Feb 1831 Ste-Madeleine-de-Riguad, Quebec (Ibid.).

 xi. Francois Xavier Cadieux was born on 28 Jul 1825 Ste-Madeleine-de-Riguad, Quebec (Ibid., #4617234.). He was baptized on 28 Jul 1825 Ste-Madeleine-de-Riguad, Quebec (Ibid.). He married Eloise Rouleau, daughter of Joseph Rouleau and Marie Marguerite Gravel, on 29 Feb 1848 Ste-Madeleine-de-Riguad, Quebec (Ibid., #3467045.).

Eloise Rouleau was born on 15 Jun 1830 Vaudreuil, Quebec (Ibid., #4178305.). She was baptized on 16 Jun 1830 Vaudreuil, Quebec (Ibid.).

116 xii. Marie Denise Cadieux, b. 22 Dec 1826 Ste-Madeleine-de-Riguad, Quebec; m. Nicolas Emery Bertrand.

 xiii. Francois Barnabe Cadieux was born on 16 May 1828 Ste-Madeleine-de-Riguad, Quebec (Ibid., #4617734.). He was baptized on 16 May 1828 Ste-Madeleine-de-Riguad, Quebec (Ibid.).

 xiv. Marie Josephe Cadieux was born on 5 Jun 1830 Ste-Madeleine-de-Riguad, Quebec (Ibid., #4618126.). She was baptized on 5 Jun 1830 Ste-Madeleine-de-Riguad, Quebec (Ibid.).

 xv. Benjamin Cadieux was born on 8 Nov 1832 Ste-Madeleine-de-Riguad, Quebec (Ibid., #4618747.). He was baptized on 9 Nov 1832 Ste-Madeleine-de-Riguad, Quebec (Ibid.).

 xvi. Honore Cadieux was born circa 1851 (1852C Cdn Transcription Project, District 536, page 35d, 36a, (71), line 27-34.).

He was in the census household of Jean Marie Cadieux and Julienne Villeneuve in 1852 Ste.Madeleine, Rigaud, Vaudreuil, Quebec *(Cadieux, J. Marie, Cultivateur, Rigaud, Catholique, 35, M; Villeneuve, Julienne, Rigaud, Catholique, 31, F; Cadieux, Xavier, Rigaud, Catholique, 6, M; Cadieux, Napoléon, Rigaud, Catholique, 5, M; Cadieux, Sophie, Rigaud, Catholique, 2, F; Cadieux, Honoré, Rigaud, Catholique, 5 mois, M; Villeneuve, Marguerite, Servante, Rigaud, Catholique, 19, F; Cadieux, Benj, Voyageur, Rigaud, Catholique, 19, M)* (1852C Cdn Transcription Project, District 536, page 35d, 36a, (71), line 27-34.).

27. Marie Monique Villeneuve was born on 2 Jul 1792 Oka, Quebec (PRDH online, #642415.). She was baptized on 3 Jul 1792 Oka, Quebec (Ibid.). She married **Hyacinthe Seguin dit Laderoute**, son of **Hyacinthe Seguin dit Laderoute** and **Marie Louise Rouleau**, on 1 Feb 1813 Ste-Madeleine-de-Rigaud, Quebec (Ibid., #52007.).

She and **Hyacinthe Seguin dit Laderoute** were enumerated in the census in 1852 Notre-Dame, Petite Nation, Ottawa County, Ontario. Also in the family: **Alexandre Seguin**, **Francois Xavier Seguin**, and **Pierre Barnabe Seguin** *(Seguin, Hyacinthe Sr, Farmer, Canada East, Roman Catholic, 66, M; Seguin, Mad Hy, ditto, ditto, 60, F; Seguin, Alexandre, ditto, ditto, 25, M; Seguin, Francois, -----, ditto, ditto, 23, M; Seguin, Barnabe, ------, ditto, ditto, 21, M)* (1852C Cdn Transcription Project, District 274, page 39d, 30a, (79), line 37-42.).

Hyacinthe Seguin dit Laderoute was born circa 1786 (Ibid., District 294, page 39d, 30a, (79), line 37-42.).

Children of **Marie Monique Villeneuve** and **Hyacinthe Seguin dit Laderoute** all born Ste-Madeleine-de-Riguad, Quebec, were as follows:

    i.   Rosalie Seguin was born on 8 Jan 1814 (PRDH online, #2680043.). She was baptized on 9 Jan 1814 Ste-Madeleine-de-Riguad, Quebec *(father's occupation: day laborer)* (PRDH online, #2680043.). She died on 12 Jan 1814 Ste-Madeleine-de-Riguad, Quebec (Ibid., #2681857.). She was buried on 14 Jan 1814 Ste-Madeleine-de-Riguad, Quebec *(father's occupation: day laborer)* (PRDH online, #2681857.).

    ii.   Madeleine Monique Seguin was born on 21 Nov 1814 (Ibid., #2680127.). She was baptized on 22 Nov 1814 Ste-Madeleine-de-Riguad, Quebec *(father's occupation: day laborer)* (PRDH online, #2680127.). She died on 3 Sep 1815 Ste-Madeleine-de-Riguad, Quebec (Ibid., #2681952.). She was buried on 5 Sep 1815 Ste-Madeleine-de-Riguad, Quebec *(9 months, father's occupation: day laborer)* (PRDH online, #2681952.).

    iii.   Marie Noelette Seguin was born on 25 Dec 1815 (Ibid., #2680248.). She was baptized on 25 Dec 1815 Ste-Madeleine-de-Riguad, Quebec *(father's occupation: day laborer)* (PRDH online, #2680248.).

    iv.   Marie Clemence Seguin was born on 18 Feb 1817 (Ibid., #2680368.). She was baptized on 19 Feb 1817 Ste-Madeleine-de-Riguad, Quebec *(father's occupation: day laborer)* (PRDH online, #2680368.).

    v.   Marie Sophie Seguin was born on 25 Sep 1818 (Ibid., #2680540.). She was baptized on 26 Sep 1818 Ste-Madeleine-de-Riguad, Quebec (Ibid.).

    vi.   Marie Madeleine Seguin was born on 27 Mar 1820 (Ibid., #2680733.). She was baptized on 28 Mar 1820 Ste-Madeleine-de-Riguad, Quebec *(father's occupation: day laborer)* (PRDH online, #2680733.).

117   vii.   Hyacinthe Seguin, b. 16 Aug 1821; m. Marie Anne Charron.

    viii.   Marie Caroline Seguin was born on 30 Dec 1822 (Ibid., #2681137.). She was baptized on 30 Dec 1822 Ste-Madeleine-de-Riguad, Quebec *(father's occupation: day laborer)* (PRDH online, #2681137.). She died on 8 Aug 1823 Ste-Madeleine-de-Riguad, Quebec (Ibid., #2682358.). She was buried on 9 Aug 1823 Ste-Madeleine-de-Riguad, Quebec *(7 months, father's occupation: day laborer)* (PRDH online, #2682358.).

    ix.   Ursule Aurelie Seguin was born on 27 Jan 1824 (Ibid., #2681296.). She was baptized on 28 Jan 1824 Ste-Madeleine-de-Riguad, Quebec *(father's occupation: day laborer)* (PRDH online, #2681296.).

    x.   Alexandre Seguin was born on 14 Feb 1826 (Ibid., #4617309.). He was baptized on 14 Feb 1826 Ste-Madeleine-de-Riguad, Quebec (Ibid.).

       He was in the census household of Hyacinthe Seguin dit Laderoute and Marie Monique Villeneuve in 1852 Notre-Dame, Petite Nation, Ottawa County, Ontario (1852C Cdn Transcription Project, District 274, page 39d, 30a, (79), line 37-42.).

    xi.   Francois Xavier Seguin was born on 16 Sep 1827 (PRDH online, #4617619.). He was baptized on 17 Sep 1827 Ste-Madeleine-de-Riguad, Quebec (Ibid.).

       He was in the census household of Hyacinthe Seguin dit Laderoute and Marie Monique Villeneuve in 1852 Notre-Dame, Petite Nation, Ottawa County, Ontario (1852C Cdn Transcription Project, District 274, page 39d, 30a, (79), line 37-42.).

28. **Simon Benjamin Theodore Villeneuve** was born on 2 May 1794 Oka, Quebec (PRDH online, #642506.). He was baptized on 3 May 1794 Oka, Quebec (Ibid.). He married **Marie Angelique Chevrier dit Lajeunesse**, daughter of **Francois Chevrier dit Lajeunesse** and **Marguerite Rouleau**, on 12 Jan 1818 Ste-Madeleine-de-Rigaud, Quebec (Ibid., #52007.). He married **Mary McDonell**, daughter of **Alexandre McDonell** and **Marguerite McGillvray**, on 22 Sep 1834 Ste-Madeleine-de-Rigaud, Quebec (Ibid., #3463145.).

He and **Mary McDonell** were enumerated in the census in 1852 Ste.Madeleine, Rigaud, Vaudreuil, Quebec. Also in the family: **Marie Sophie Villeneuve, Francois Barnabe Villeneuve, Pierre Simon Villeneuve, Benjamin Villeneuve, Guillaume Villeneuve, Jean Michel Villeneuve, Marguerite Villeneuve**, and **Mary Villeneuve** *(Villeneuve, Benj, Cultivateur, Rigaud, Catholique, 58, M; Mc Donell, Mary, Haut-Cunada, Catholique, 44, F; Villeneuve, Sophie, Rigaud, Catholique, 21, F; Villeneuve, Barnabé, Rigaud, Catholique, 19, M; Villeneuve, Simon, Rigaud, Catholique, 30, M; Villeneuve, Benjamin, Rigaud, Catholique, 13, M; Villeneuve, William, Rigaud, Catholique, 11, M; Villeneuve, Michel, Rigaud, Catholique, 7, M; Villeneuve, Marguerite, Rigaud, Catholique, 10, F; Villeneuve, Mary, Rigaud, Catholique, 2, F)* (1852C Cdn Transcription Project, District 536, page 40d, 41a, (81), line 27-36.).

Marie Angelique Chevrier dit Lajeunesse was born on 10 Mar 1796 Vaudreuil, Quebec (PRDH online, #638735.). She was baptized on 12 Mar 1796 Vaudreuil, Quebec (Ibid.). She died on 30 Aug 1837 Ste-Madeleine-de-Riguad, Quebec, at age 41 (Ibid., #4623422.). She was buried on 31 Aug 1837 Ste-Madeleine-de-Riguad, Quebec *(age 37, wife of Benjamin Villeneuve)* (PRDH online, #4623422.).

Children of **Simon Benjamin Theodore Villeneuve** and **Marie Angelique Chevrier dit Lajeunesse** all born Ste-Madeleine-de-Riguad, Quebec, were as follows:

118   i.   Francois Regis Emilien Villeneuve, b. 10 Feb 1819; m. Marie Domitille Mathilde Cadieux.

    ii.   Marie Josephe Villeneuve was born on 12 Apr 1820 (Ibid., #2680742.). She was baptized on 12 Apr 1820 Ste-Madeleine-de-Riguad, Quebec (Ibid.). She married Alexandre Clement Goyet dit Julien, son of Alexis or Alexandre Goyette and Angelique Decoeur, on 11 Jun 1849 Ste-Madeleine-de-Riguad, Quebec (Ibid., #3467298.).

        Alexandre Clement Goyet dit Julien was born on 3 Mar 1825 Ste-Madeleine-de-Riguad, Quebec (Ibid., #4617170.). He was baptized on 3 Mar 1825 Ste-Madeleine-de-Riguad, Quebec (Ibid.).

    iii.   Francois Xavier Villeneuve was born on 24 May 1821 (Ibid., #2680879.). He was baptized on 24 May 1821 Ste-Madeleine-de-Riguad, Quebec *(father's occupation: cultivator)* (PRDH online, #2680879.). He died on 17 Aug 1821 Ste-Madeleine-de-Riguad, Quebec (Ibid., #2682246.). He was buried on 18 Aug 1821 Ste-Madeleine-de-Riguad, Quebec *(age 3 months, father's occupation: cultivator)* (PRDH online, #2682246.).

    iv.   Pierre Simon Villeneuve was born on 27 Jul 1822 (Ibid., #2681054.). He was baptized on 28 Jul 1822 Ste-Madeleine-de-Riguad, Quebec *(father's occupation: cultivator)* (PRDH online, #2681054.).

        He was in the census household of Simon Benjamin Theodore Villeneuve and Mary McDonell in 1852 Ste.Madeleine, Rigaud, Vaudreuil, Quebec (1852C Cdn Transcription Project, District 536, page 40d, 41a, (81), line 27-36.).

    v.   Angelique Villeneuve was born on 25 Oct 1823 (PRDH online, #2681257.). She was baptized on 26 Oct 1823 Ste-Madeleine-de-Riguad, Quebec *(father's occupation: cultivator)* (PRDH online, #2681257.). She married Joseph Robitaille, son of Joseph Robitaille and Marie Ricard, on 16 Apr 1849 Ste-Madeleine-de-Riguad, Quebec (Ibid., #3467262.).

    vi.   Francois Xavier Villeneuve was born on 9 Oct 1825 (Ibid., #4617174.). He was baptized on 10 Oct 1825 Ste-Madeleine-de-Riguad, Quebec *(father's occupation: cultivator)* (PRDH online, #4617174.). He died on 3 Sep 1826 Ste-Madeleine-de-Riguad, Quebec (Ibid., #4622781.). He was buried on 5 Sep 1826 Ste-Madeleine-de-Riguad, Quebec *(age 18 months)* (PRDH online, #4622781.).

    vii.   Hilaire Theodore Villeneuve was born on 16 Feb 1827 (Ibid., #4617483.). He was baptized on 16 Feb 1827 Ste-Madeleine-de-Riguad, Quebec (Ibid.). He married Marie Olympe Celanire Goyet, daughter of Alexis or Alexandre Goyette and Angelique Decoeur, on 6 Mar 1848 Ste-Madeleine-de-Riguad, Quebec (Ibid., #3467059.).

        Marie Olympe Celanire Goyet was born on 13 Jan 1829 Ste-Madeleine-de-Riguad, Quebec (Ibid., #4617865.). She was baptized on 14 Jan 1829 Ste-Madeleine-de-Riguad, Quebec (Ibid.).

    viii.   Marie Sophie Villeneuve was born on 25 Sep 1828 (Ibid., #4617817.). She was baptized on 28 Sep 1828 Ste-Madeleine-de-Riguad, Quebec (Ibid.).

        She was in the census household of Simon Benjamin Theodore Villeneuve and Mary McDonell in 1852 Ste.Madeleine, Rigaud, Vaudreuil, Quebec (1852C Cdn Transcription Project, District 536, page 40d, 41a, (81), line 27-36.).

    ix.   Francois Barnabe Villeneuve was born on 8 Nov 1829 (PRDH online, #4618024.). He was baptized on 9 Nov 1829 Ste-Madeleine-de-Riguad, Quebec (Ibid.).

        He was in the census household of Simon Benjamin Theodore Villeneuve and Mary McDonell in 1852 Ste.Madeleine, Rigaud, Vaudreuil, Quebec (1852C Cdn Transcription Project, District 536, page 40d, 41a, (81), line 27-36.).

    x.   Clement Villeneuve was born on 14 Jul 1831 (PRDH online, #4618403.). He was baptized on 14 Jul 1831 Ste-Madeleine-de-Riguad, Quebec (Ibid.). He died on 25 Apr 1834 Ste-Madeleine-de-Riguad, Quebec, at age 2 (Ibid., #4623485.). He was buried on 26 Apr 1834 Ste-Madeleine-de-Riguad, Quebec (Ibid.).

Mary McDonell was born circa 1808 Ontario (1852C Cdn Transcription Project, District 536, page 40d, 41a, (81), line 27-36.).

Children of **Simon Benjamin Theodore Villeneuve** and **Mary McDonell** were as follows:

    i.   Guillaume Villeneuve was born circa 1837 (PRDH online, #4623984.). He died on 25 Aug 1839 Ste-Madeleine-de-Riguad, Quebec (Ibid.). He was buried on 27 Aug 1839 Ste-Madeleine-de-Riguad, Quebec (Ibid.).

    ii.   Benjamin Villeneuve was born on 18 Mar 1839 Ste-Madeleine-de-Riguad, Quebec (Ibid., #4620360.). He was baptized on 18 Mar 1839 Ste-Madeleine-de-Riguad, Quebec (Ibid.).

       He was in the census household of Simon Benjamin Theodore Villeneuve and Mary McDonell in 1852 Ste.Madeleine, Rigaud, Vaudreuil, Quebec (1852C Cdn Transcription Project, District 536, page 40d, 41a, (81), line 27-36.).

    iii.   Guillaume Villeneuve was born on 9 Aug 1840 Ste-Madeleine-de-Riguad, Quebec (PRDH online, #4620691.). He was baptized on 9 Aug 1840 Ste-Madeleine-de-Riguad, Quebec (Ibid.).

       He was in the census household of Simon Benjamin Theodore Villeneuve and Mary McDonell in 1852 Ste.Madeleine, Rigaud, Vaudreuil, Quebec (1852C Cdn Transcription Project, District 536, page 40d, 41a, (81), line 27-36.).

    iv.   Marguerite Villeneuve was born circa 1842 (Ibid.).

       She was in the census household of Simon Benjamin Theodore Villeneuve and Mary McDonell in 1852 Ste.Madeleine, Rigaud, Vaudreuil, Quebec (1852C Cdn Transcription Project, District 536, page 40d, 41a, (81), line 27-36.).

    v.   Jean Michel Villeneuve was born on 9 Feb 1844 Ste-Madeleine-de-Riguad, Quebec (PRDH online, #4621528.). He was baptized on 9 Feb 1844 Ste-Madeleine-de-Riguad, Quebec (Ibid.).

       He was in the census household of Simon Benjamin Theodore Villeneuve and Mary McDonell in 1852 Ste.Madeleine, Rigaud, Vaudreuil, Quebec (1852C Cdn Transcription Project, District 536, page 40d, 41a, (81), line 27-36.).

    vi.   Alexandre Villeneuve was born on 26 Jun 1845 Ste-Madeleine-de-Riguad, Quebec (PRDH online, #4621849.). He was baptized on 26 Jun 1845 Ste-Madeleine-de-Riguad, Quebec (Ibid.). He died on 31 Jul 1845 Ste-Madeleine-de-Riguad, Quebec (Ibid., #4624501.). He was buried on 2 Aug 1845 Ste-Madeleine-de-Riguad, Quebec (Ibid.).

    vii.   Mary Villeneuve was born circa 1850 (1852C Cdn Transcription Project, District 536, page 40d, 41a, (81), line 27-36.).

       She was in the census household of Simon Benjamin Theodore Villeneuve and Mary McDonell in 1852 Ste.Madeleine, Rigaud, Vaudreuil, Quebec (1852C Cdn Transcription Project, District 536, page 40d, 41a, (81), line 27-36.).

29. Michel Hermenegilde Villeneuve was born on 22 Jul 1795 Vaudreuil, Quebec (PRDH online, #770724.). He was baptized on 23 Jul 1795 Vaudreuil, Quebec (Ibid.). He married **Josephte Genthon dit Dauphinais**, daughter of **Michel Genthon dit Dauphinais or Dauphine** and **Victoire Ouellette,** before 1838. He died before 1876.

He was enumerated in the census in 1835 Red River Settlement. *#526, Michl. Vallenneuve, age 40, Canada, Catholic, 1 unmarried man, 1 daughter (-15), 2 total inhabitants, 1 house, 2 oxen, 2 cows, 1 calf, 1 plough, 1 harrow, 1 cart, 5 acres. (1835 E.5/8) page 21* (1835C RRS HBCA E5/8 1835 Census of the Red River Settlement, HBCA E5/8, Hudson's Bay Company Archives, Provincial Archives, 200 Vaughan Street, Winnipeg, MB R3C 1T5, Canada., page 21.). As of 1835, he was also known as **Michel Villeneuve** (Ibid.).

Josephte Genthon dit Dauphinais was born in 1813 North West (MBS Scrip Applications, Original White Settlers & Halfbreeds residing in Manitoba on 15 July 1870, RG15-19, C-14934.). She died on 14 May 1885 St.Norbert, Manitoba *(age 70 years)* (Manitoba Vital Statistics online, http://web2.gov.mb.ca, Death Reg. #1885,002171.) (SN2 Catholic Parish Register of St.Norbert, S-14. Hereinafter cited as SN2.). She was buried on 16 May 1885 St.Norbert, Manitoba *(S-14, Josephte Dauphinais, buried 16 May 1885, died the day before yesterday, age around sixty-two years, widow of the deceased Michel Villeneuve, Present: Regis Perreault, Louis Delorme, Jean Baptiste Jolibois, N. J. Ritchot)* (SN2, S-14.).

She was enumerated in the census on 15 Jul 1870 St.Norbert, Manitoba. *#1072; Josephte Villeneuve, St.Norbert, born Red River, age 60, daughter of Michel Dauphinais, Metis, widow, British Subject, French Metis, Catholic. (page 35)* (1870C-MB 1870 Manitoba Census, National Archives of Canada, Ottawa, Ontario, Microfilm Reel Number C-2170., page 35, #1072.).

She witnessed the baptism of **Marie Jane Ouellette** on 16 Aug 1870 St.Norbert, Manitoba *(B-33, Marie Jeanne Ouellet, baptized 16 August 1870, born the day before yesterday, legitimate child of Moise Ouellet and Isabelle Dumas. Godparents: Augustin Ladouceur and Josephte Dauphinais, both who did not sign. N. J. Ritchot, priest. (page 133))* (SN1 Catholic Parish Register of St.Norbert 1857-1873, page 133, B-33. Hereinafter cited as SN1.).

She had a scrip application: on 7 Dec 1875 Ste.Agathe, Provencher, Manitoba *(Josephte Villeneuve; Ste.Agathe; Provencher; widow of Michel Velleneuve; farmer; HB Head: myself and children; Born: 1813; North West Territory; Father: Michel Dauphinais (French Canadian) [was]; Mother: Victoire Vallette (HB) [is]   French; 7 Dec 1875; Josephte Villeneuve (x); Rev. D. Samossette ptre; Baptiste Dupuis (x); farmer. C-14934)* (MBS, C-14934.).

Children of **Michel Hermenegilde Villeneuve** and **Josephte Genthon dit Dauphinais** were:

    119   i.   Judith Villeneuve, b. Aug 1838 St.Boniface, (Manitoba); m. Jean Baptiste Regis Perreault.

30. Francois Jeremie Villeneuve was baptized on 14 Nov 1797 Vaudreuil, Quebec *(father's occupation: cultivator)* (PRDH online, #770966.). He married **Hippolyte Bedard**, daughter of **Jean Bedard** and **Marie Hippolyte Sabourin,** on 25 Oct 1819 Ste-Madeleine-de-Rigaud, Quebec (Ibid., #2219858.).

Hippolyte Bedard was born on 14 Oct 1801 Vaudreuil, Quebec (Ibid., #647798.). She was baptized on 15 Oct 1801 Vaudreuil, Quebec (Ibid.).

Children of **Francois Jeremie Villeneuve** and **Hippolyte Bedard** were as follows:

    i.   Madelaine Rose Villeneuve was born on 15 Jun 1821 Ste-Madeleine-de-Riguad, Quebec (Ibid., #2680886.). She was baptized on 16 Jun 1821 Ste-Madeleine-de-Riguad, Quebec *(father's occupation: cultivator)* (PRDH online, #2680886.). She died on 2 Aug 1821 Ste-Madeleine-de-Riguad, Quebec (Ibid., #2682244.). She was buried on 3 Aug 1821 Ste-Madeleine-de-Riguad, Quebec *(one month and 17 days, father's occupation: cultivator)* (PRDH online, #2682244.).

    ii.   Simon Jeremie Villeneuve was born on 17 Mar 1823 Ste-Madeleine-de-Riguad, Quebec (Ibid., #2681167.). He was baptized on 18 Mar 1823 Ste-Madeleine-de-Riguad, Quebec *(father's occupation: cultivator)* (PRDH online, #2681167.).

    iii.   Marie Hypolite Villeneuve was born on 23 Mar 1825 (Ibid., #4617180.). She was baptized on 24 Mar 1825 Ste-Madeleine-de-Riguad, Quebec *(father's occupation: cultivator)* (PRDH online, #4617180.).

    iv.   Alexandre Villeneuve was born on 1 Mar 1827 Ste-Madeleine-de-Riguad, Quebec (Ibid., #4617490.). He was baptized on 1 Mar 1827 Ste-Madeleine-de-Riguad, Quebec (Ibid.).

    v.   Andre Villeneuve was born on 2 Jan 1829 Ste-Madeleine-de-Riguad, Quebec (Ibid., #4617860.). He was baptized on 3 Jan 1829 Ste-Madeleine-de-Riguad, Quebec (Ibid.). He died on 25 Jul 1849 Ste-Madeleine-de-Riguad, Quebec, at age 20 (Ibid., #4624737.). He was buried on 26 Jul 1849 Ste-Madeleine-de-Riguad, Quebec (Ibid.).

    vi.   Louise Veronique Villeneuve was born on 1 Jan 1830 Ste-Madeleine-de-Riguad, Quebec (Ibid., #4618048.). She was baptized on 1 Jan 1830 Ste-Madeleine-de-Riguad, Quebec (Ibid.). She died on 12 Jul 1830 Ste-Madeleine-de-Riguad, Quebec (Ibid., #4623029.). She was buried on 13 Jul 1830 Ste-Madeleine-de-Riguad, Quebec (Ibid.).

    vii.   Bazile Villeneuve was born on 16 Apr 1831 Ste-Madeleine-de-Riguad, Quebec (Ibid., #4618340.). He was baptized on 17 Apr 1831 Ste-Madeleine-de-Riguad, Quebec (Ibid.).

    viii.   Adelaide Villeneuve was born on 25 Apr 1832 Hawkesbury, Ontario (Ibid., #4618602.). She was baptized on 25 Apr 1832 Ste-Madeleine-de-Riguad, Quebec (Ibid.).

    ix.   Delphine Villeneuve was born on 11 Jan 1834 Ste-Madeleine-de-Riguad, Quebec (Ibid., #4619037.). She was baptized on 12 Jan 1834 Ste-Madeleine-de-Riguad, Quebec (Ibid.).

    x.   Marie Edesee Villeneuve was born on 9 Oct 1836 Ste-Madeleine-de-Riguad, Quebec (Ibid., #4619779.). She was baptized on 9 Oct 1836 Ste-Madeleine-de-Riguad, Quebec (Ibid.).

    xi.   Donat Benjamin Villeneuve was born on 6 Aug 1838 Ste-Madeleine-de-Riguad, Quebec (Ibid., #4620201.). He was baptized on 7 Aug 1838 Ste-Madeleine-de-Riguad, Quebec (Ibid.).

31. Hyacinthe Sabourin was baptized on 2 Nov 1792 Vaudreuil, Quebec (Ibid., #771617.). He married **Marie Reine Hurtubise**, daughter of **Gabriel Hurtubise** and **Marie Anne Leduc,** on 15 Feb 1819 Ste-Madeleine-de-Riguad, Quebec (Ibid., #2219816.). He married **Marguerite Liboiron dit Bellefleur**, daughter of **Louis Liboiron dit Bellefleur** and **Catherine Monpetit dit Potvin,** on 22 Apr 1823 Ste-Madeleine-de-Riguad, Quebec (Ibid., #2220215.).

He and **Marguerite Liboiron dit Bellefleur** were enumerated in the census in 1852 Ste.Madeleine, Rigaud, Vaudreuil, Quebec. Also in the family: **Marie Madeleine Eulalie Sabourin, Sophie Sabourin, Marie Gertrude Sabourin, Marie Justine Sabourin**, and **Louis Fabien Sabourin** *(Sabourin, Hythe, Cultivateur, Rigaud, Catholique romaine, 61, M; Biron, Marguerite, Vaudreuil, Catholique, 50, F; Sabourin, Eulalie, Rigaud, Catholique, 24, F; Sabourin, Sophie, Rigaud, Catholique, 21, F; Sabourin, Gertrude, Rigaud, Catholique, 12, F; Sabourin, Justine, Rigaud, Catholique, 8, F; Sabourin, Fabien, Rigaud, Catholique, 14, M)* (1852C Cdn Transcription Project, District 536, page 58d, 59a, (117), line 31-37.).

Marie Reine Hurtubise was born circa 1799 (PRDH online, #644508.). She died on 4 Jan 1822 Ste-Madeleine-de-Riguad, Quebec (Ibid., #2682267.). She was buried on 7 Jan 1822 Ste-Madeleine-de-Riguad, Quebec *(age 23, wife of Hyacinthe Sabourin cultivator)* (PRDH online, #2682267.).

Children of **Hyacinthe Sabourin** and **Marie Reine Hurtubise** were:

    120   i.   Marie Reine Sabourin, b. 5 May 1820 Ste-Madeleine-de-Riguad, Quebec; m. Hyacinthe Evangeliste Leduc.

Marguerite Liboiron dit Bellefleur was born on 10 Sep 1802 Vaudreuil, Quebec (Ibid., #666002.). She was baptized on 10 Sep 1802 Vaudreuil, Quebec (Ibid.).

Children of **Hyacinthe Sabourin** and **Marguerite Liboiron dit Bellefleur** were as follows:

    121   i.   Marie Scholastique Sabourin, b. 15 Jan 1824 Ste-Madeleine-de-Riguad, Quebec.

           ii.   Anonyme Sabourin was born on 2 Sep 1825 Ste-Madeleine-de-Riguad, Quebec (Ibid., #4622704.). He died on 2 Sep 1825 Ste-Madeleine-de-Riguad, Quebec (Ibid.). He was buried on 2 Sep 1825 Ste-Madeleine-de-Riguad, Quebec (Ibid.).

          iii.   Marie Madeleine Eulalie Sabourin was born on 5 Sep 1826 Ste-Madeleine-de-Riguad, Quebec (Ibid., #4617416.). She was baptized on 6 Sep 1826 Ste-Madeleine-de-Riguad, Quebec (Ibid.).

                She was in the census household of Hyacinthe Sabourin and Marguerite Liboiron dit Bellefleur in 1852 Ste.Madeleine, Rigaud, Vaudreuil, Quebec *(Sabourin, Hythe, Cultivateur, Rigaud, Catholique romaine, 61, M; Biron, Marguerite, Vaudreuil, Catholique, 50, F; Sabourin, Eulalie, Rigaud, Catholique, 24, F; Sabourin, Sophie, Rigaud, Catholique, 21, F; Sabourin, Gertrude, Rigaud, Catholique, 12, F; Sabourin, Justine, Rigaud, Catholique, 8, F; Sabourin, Fabien, Rigaud, Catholique, 14, M)* (1852C Cdn Transcription Project, District 536, page 58d, 59a, (117), line 31-37.).

          iv.   Marie Justine Sabourin was born on 5 Aug 1828 Ste-Madeleine-de-Riguad, Quebec (PRDH online, #4617781.). She was baptized on 6 Aug 1828 Ste-Madeleine-de-Riguad, Quebec (Ibid.).

          v.   Sophie Sabourin was born on 6 Aug 1830 Ste-Madeleine-de-Riguad, Quebec (Ibid., #4618166.). She was baptized on 7 Aug 1830 Ste-Madeleine-de-Riguad, Quebec (Ibid.).

                She was in the census household of Hyacinthe Sabourin and Marguerite Liboiron dit Bellefleur in 1852 Ste.Madeleine, Rigaud, Vaudreuil, Quebec *(Sabourin, Hythe, Cultivateur, Rigaud, Catholique romaine, 61, M; Biron, Marguerite, Vaudreuil, Catholique, 50, F; Sabourin, Eulalie, Rigaud, Catholique, 24, F; Sabourin, Sophie, Rigaud, Catholique, 21, F; Sabourin, Gertrude, Rigaud, Catholique, 12, F; Sabourin, Justine, Rigaud, Catholique, 8, F; Sabourin, Fabien, Rigaud, Catholique, 14, M)* (1852C Cdn Transcription Project, District 536, page 58d, 59a, (117), line 31-37.).

          vi.   Marguerite Sabourin was born circa 1833 (PRDH online, #4621310.). She died on 24 Apr 1846 Ste-Madeleine-de-Riguad, Quebec (Ibid.). She was buried on 26 Apr 1846 Ste-Madeleine-de-Riguad, Quebec *(age 13)* (PRDH online, #4621310.).

         vii.   Justine Leocadie Sabourin was born on 21 Aug 1835 Ste-Madeleine-de-Riguad, Quebec (Ibid., #4619445.). She was baptized on 21 Aug 1835 Ste-Madeleine-de-Riguad, Quebec (Ibid.). She died on 15 Jul 1836 Ste-Madeleine-de-Riguad, Quebec (Ibid., #4623695.). She was buried on 17 Jul 1836 Ste-Madeleine-de-Riguad, Quebec (Ibid.).

       viii.   Louis Fabien Sabourin was born on 5 Jul 1837 Ste-Madeleine-de-Riguad, Quebec (Ibid., #4619964.). He was baptized on 5 Jul 1837 Ste-Madeleine-de-Riguad, Quebec (Ibid.).

                He was in the census household of Hyacinthe Sabourin and Marguerite Liboiron dit Bellefleur in 1852 Ste.Madeleine, Rigaud, Vaudreuil, Quebec *(Sabourin, Hythe, Cultivateur, Rigaud, Catholique romaine, 61, M; Biron, Marguerite, Vaudreuil, Catholique, 50, F; Sabourin, Eulalie, Rigaud, Catholique, 24, F; Sabourin, Sophie, Rigaud, Catholique, 21, F; Sabourin, Gertrude, Rigaud, Catholique, 12, F; Sabourin, Justine, Rigaud, Catholique, 8, F; Sabourin, Fabien, Rigaud, Catholique, 14, M)* (1852C Cdn Transcription Project, District 536, page 58d, 59a, (117), line 31-37.).

          ix.   Marie Gertrude Sabourin was born on 15 Sep 1839 Ste-Madeleine-de-Riguad, Quebec (PRDH online, #4620480.). She was baptized on 15 Sep 1839 Ste-Madeleine-de-Riguad, Quebec (Ibid.).

                She was in the census household of Hyacinthe Sabourin and Marguerite Liboiron dit Bellefleur in 1852 Ste.Madeleine, Rigaud, Vaudreuil, Quebec *(Sabourin, Hythe, Cultivateur, Rigaud, Catholique romaine, 61, M; Biron, Marguerite, Vaudreuil, Catholique, 50, F; Sabourin, Eulalie, Rigaud, Catholique, 24, F; Sabourin, Sophie, Rigaud, Catholique, 21, F; Sabourin, Gertrude, Rigaud, Catholique, 12, F; Sabourin, Justine, Rigaud, Catholique, 8, F; Sabourin, Fabien,*

Rigaud, Catholique, 14, M) (1852C Cdn Transcription Project, District 536, page 58d, 59a, (117), line 31-37.).

x. Marie Justine Sabourin was born on 29 Jan 1843 Ste-Madeleine-de-Riguad, Quebec (PRDH online, #4621310.). She was baptized on 1 Feb 1843 Ste-Madeleine-de-Riguad, Quebec (Ibid.).
She was in the census household of Hyacinthe Sabourin and Marguerite Liboiron dit Bellefleur in 1852 Ste.Madeleine, Rigaud, Vaudreuil, Quebec *(Sabourin, Hythe, Cultivateur, Rigaud, Catholique romaine, 61, M; Biron, Marguerite, Vaudreuil, Catholique, 50, F; Sabourin, Eulalie, Rigaud, Catholique, 24, F; Sabourin, Sophie, Rigaud, Catholique, 21, F; Sabourin, Gertrude, Rigaud, Catholique, 12, F; Sabourin, Justine, Rigaud, Catholique, 8, F; Sabourin, Fabien, Rigaud, Catholique, 14, M)* (1852C Cdn Transcription Project, District 536, page 58d, 59a, (117), line 31-37.).

32. **Marie Reine Sabourin** was born on 13 Jul 1800 Vaudreuil, Quebec (PRDH online, #2589821.). She was baptized on 13 Jul 1800 Vaudreuil, Quebec (Ibid.). She married **Alexis Noel Cadieux**, son of **Francois Cadieux** and **Marie Reine Rouleau,** on 14 Sep 1829 Ste-Madeleine-de-Riguad, Quebec (Ibid., #3461234.).

Alexis Noel Cadieux was baptized on 7 Jun 1799 Vaudreuil, Quebec *(father's occupation: cultivator)* (PRDH online, #771142.).

Children of **Marie Reine Sabourin** and **Alexis Noel Cadieux** were as follows:

i. Joseph Alexandre Cadieux was born on 21 Nov 1831 Ontario (Ibid., #4618476.). He was baptized on 21 Nov 1831 Ste-Madeleine-de-Riguad, Quebec (Ibid.). He died on 29 Jun 1844 Ste-Madeleine-de-Riguad, Quebec, at age 12 (Ibid., #4624454.). He was buried on 1 Jul 1844 Ste-Madeleine-de-Riguad, Quebec (Ibid.).

ii. Francois Dosithee Cadieux was born on 11 Apr 1843 Ste-Madeleine-de-Riguad, Quebec (Ibid., #4621344.). He was baptized on 12 Apr 1843 Ste-Madeleine-de-Riguad, Quebec (Ibid.). He died on 12 Apr 1843 Ste-Madeleine-de-Riguad, Quebec (Ibid., #4624324.). He was buried on 14 Apr 1843 Ste-Madeleine-de-Riguad, Quebec (Ibid.).

33. **Marie Madeleine Rose Sabourin** was born on 30 Aug 1806 Ste-Madeleine-de-Riguad, Quebec (Ibid., #2679368.). She was baptized on 30 Aug 1806 Ste-Madeleine-de-Riguad, Quebec *(father's occupation: agriculture)* (PRDH online, #2679368.). She married **Edouard Brouillard**, son of **Pierre Brouillard** and **Josephe Marie Henault dit Deschamps or Huneau,** on 19 Feb 1844 Ste-Madeleine-de-Riguad, Quebec (Ibid., #3465929.).

Edouard Brouillard was born on 13 Apr 1808 Pointe-Claire, Quebec (Ibid., #700090.). He was baptized on 13 Apr 1808 Pointe-Claire, Quebec (Ibid.). He married **Esther Perrier**, daughter of **Hyacinthe Perrier** and **Genevieve Jolive,** on 12 Jan 1829 St-Benoit, Quebec (Ibid., #3484675.).

Children of **Marie Madeleine Rose Sabourin** and **Edouard Brouillard** both born Ste-Madeleine-de-Riguad, Quebec, were as follows:

i. Marie Onesime Brouillard was born on 15 Sep 1845 (Ibid., #4621902.). She was baptized on 16 Sep 1845 Ste-Madeleine-de-Riguad, Quebec (Ibid.).

ii. Elie Napoleon Brouillard was born on 4 Feb 1847 (Ibid., #4727863.). He was baptized on 5 Feb 1847 Ste-Madeleine-de-Riguad, Quebec (Ibid.). He died on 3 Apr 1848 Ste-Madeleine-de-Riguad, Quebec, at age 1 (Ibid., #4728166.). He was buried on 5 Apr 1848 Ste-Madeleine-de-Riguad, Quebec (Ibid.).

34. Francois Sabourin was born on 20 Dec 1792 Oka, Quebec (Ibid., #631647.). He was baptized on 21 Dec 1792 Oka, Quebec (Ibid.). He married **Louise Seguin**, daughter of **Joseph Marie Seguin dit Laderoute** and **Marie Josephe Larocque dit Rocbrune,** on 26 Feb 1816 Ste-Madeleine-de-Riguad, Quebec (Ibid., #631648.).

He and **Louise Seguin** were enumerated in the census circa 1852 Ste.Madeleine, Rigaud, Vaudreuil, Quebec. Also in the family: **Paul Sabourin, Marie Angelique Brazeau dit Brassault, Marie Aurelie Sabourin, Sophie Sabourin, Marie Rose Christine Sabourin, Antoine Ubalde Sabourin**, and **Treffle Sabourin** *(Sabourin, François, Cultivateur, Rigaud, Catholique, 59, M; Séguin, Louise, Rigaud, Catholique, 54, F; Sabourin, Paul, Cultivateur, Rigaud, Catholique, 29, M; Brazeau, Angèle, Rigaud, Catholique, 28, F; Sabourin, Aurelie, Rigaud, Catholique, 22, F; Sabourin, Sophie, Rigaud, Catholique, 18, F; Sabourin, Christine, Rigaud, Catholique, 15, F; Sabourin, Antoine, Rigaud, Catholique, 13, M; Sabourin, Trefflé, Rigaud, Catholique, 7 mois, M)* (1852C Cdn Transcription Project, District 536, page 8d, 9a, (17), line 19-27.).

Louise Seguin was born on 10 Sep 1797 Oka, Quebec (PRDH online, #631648.). She was baptized on 11 Sep 1797 Oka, Quebec (Ibid.).

Children of **Francois Sabourin** and **Louise Seguin** were as follows:

122　i. Francois Andre Sabourin, b. 15 Dec 1816 Ste-Madeleine-de-Rigaud, Quebec; m. Marie Agnes Edesse Vallee; m. Veronique Villeneuve.

      ii.   Marie Louise Sabourin was born on 10 Sep 1818 Ste-Madeleine-de-Riguad, Quebec (Ibid., #2680534.). She was baptized on 11 Sep 1818 Ste-Madeleine-de-Riguad, Quebec (Ibid.). She died on 27 Aug 1819 Ste-Madeleine-de-Riguad, Quebec (Ibid., #2682124.). She was buried on 29 Aug 1819 Ste-Madeleine-de-Riguad, Quebec *(age 11 months, father's occupation: cultivator)* (PRDH online, #2682124.).

123 iii. Madeleine Sabourin, b. 25 Jun 1820 Ste-Madeleine-de-Riguad, Quebec; m. Pierre Portelance.

124 iv. Paul Sabourin, b. 4 Aug 1822 Ste-Madeleine-de-Rigaud, Quebec; m. Marie Angelique Brazeau dit Brassault.

125 v. Justine Sabourin, b. 17 May 1824 Ste-Madeleine-de-Riguad, Quebec; m. Joseph Vallee.

126 vi. Joseph Sabourin, b. 8 May 1826 Ste-Madeleine-de-Riguad, Quebec; m. Marie Louise Brazeau.

      vii. Marcien Sabourin was born on 2 Mar 1828 Ste-Madeleine-de-Riguad, Quebec (Ibid., #4617690.). He was baptized on 3 Mar 1828 Ste-Madeleine-de-Riguad, Quebec (Ibid.). He died on 30 Apr 1828 Ste-Madeleine-de-Riguad, Quebec (Ibid., #4622902.). He was buried on 1 May 1828 Ste-Madeleine-de-Riguad, Quebec *(age 2 months)* (PRDH online, #4622902.).

      viii. Marie Aurelie Sabourin was born on 24 Aug 1829 Ste-Madeleine-de-Riguad, Quebec (Ibid., #4617994.). She was baptized on 24 Aug 1829 Ste-Madeleine-de-Riguad, Quebec (Ibid.).

        She was in the census household of Francois Sabourin and Louise Seguin circa 1852 Ste.Madeleine, Rigaud, Vaudreuil, Quebec (1852C Cdn Transcription Project, District 536, page 8d, 9a, (17), line 19-27.).

      ix. Antoine Sabourin was born on 4 Jun 1831 Ste-Madeleine-de-Riguad, Quebec (PRDH online, #4618377.). He was baptized on 5 Jun 1831 Ste-Madeleine-de-Riguad, Quebec (Ibid.). He died on 29 Mar 1832 Ste-Madeleine-de-Riguad, Quebec (Ibid., #4623197.). He was buried on 30 Mar 1832 Ste-Madeleine-de-Riguad, Quebec (Ibid.).

      x. Sophie Sabourin was born on 4 Sep 1833 Ste-Madeleine-de-Riguad, Quebec (Ibid., #4618961.). She was baptized on 4 Sep 1833 Ste-Madeleine-de-Riguad, Quebec (Ibid.).

        She was in the census household of Francois Sabourin and Louise Seguin circa 1852 Ste.Madeleine, Rigaud, Vaudreuil, Quebec (1852C Cdn Transcription Project, District 536, page 8d, 9a, (17), line 19-27.).

      xi. Marie Rose Christine Sabourin was born on 29 Mar 1836 Ste-Madeleine-de-Riguad, Quebec (PRDH online, #4619748.). She was baptized on 30 Mar 1836 Ste-Madeleine-de-Riguad, Quebec (Ibid.).

        She was in the census household of Francois Sabourin and Louise Seguin circa 1852 Ste.Madeleine, Rigaud, Vaudreuil, Quebec (1852C Cdn Transcription Project, District 536, page 8d, 9a, (17), line 19-27.).

      xii. Antoine Ubalde Sabourin was born on 26 Aug 1838 Ste-Madeleine-de-Riguad, Quebec (PRDH online, #4620212.). He was baptized on 27 Aug 1838 Ste-Madeleine-de-Riguad, Quebec (Ibid.).

        He was in the census household of Francois Sabourin and Louise Seguin circa 1852 Ste.Madeleine, Rigaud, Vaudreuil, Quebec (1852C Cdn Transcription Project, District 536, page 8d, 9a, (17), line 19-27.).

35. Antoine Sabourin was born on 6 Jun 1797 Vaudreuil, Quebec (PRDH online, #770914.). He was baptized on 7 Jun 1797 Vaudreuil, Quebec *(father's occupation: cultivator)* (PRDH online, #770914.). He married **Louise Chevrier**, daughter of **Joseph Chevrier dit Lajeunesse** and **Josephte Charlebois**, on 28 Jan 1823 Ste-Madeleine-de-Riguad, Quebec (Ibid., #2220188.).

He and **Louise Chevrier** were enumerated in the census in 1852 Ste.Madeleine, Rigaud, Vaudreuil, Quebec. Also in the family: **Marie Olympe Sabourin, Eulalie Sabourin, Antoine Alexandre Sabourin, Joseph Sabourin,** and **Francis Amedee Sabourin** *(Sabourin, Ant, Cultivateur, Rigaud, Catholique, 54, M; Chevrier, Louise, Rigaud, Catholique, 51, F; Sabourin, Olympe, Rigaud, Catholique, 20, F; Sabourin, Eulalie, Rigaud, Catholique, 17, F; Sabourin, Ant., Rigaud, Catholique, 22, M; Sabourin, Joseph, Rigaud, Catholique, 15, M; Sabourin, Amédée, Rigaud, Catholique, 13, M)* (1852C Cdn Transcription Project, District 536, page 24d, 25a, (49), line 35-41.).

Louise Chevrier was baptized on 29 Jul 1799 Vaudreuil, Quebec (PRDH online, #771157.)

Children of **Antoine Sabourin** and **Louise Chevrier** were as follows:

      i. Joseph Antoine Sabourin was born on 9 Jul 1824 Ste-Madeleine-de-Riguad, Quebec (Ibid., #2681371.). He was baptized on 10 Jul 1824 Ste-Madeleine-de-Riguad, Quebec *(father's occupation: cultivator)* (PRDH online, #2681371.). He died on 24 Jul 1824 Ste-Madeleine-de-Riguad, Quebec (Ibid., #2682416.). He was buried on 25 Jul 1824 Ste-Madeleine-de-Riguad, Quebec *(father's occupation: cultivator)* (PRDH online, #2682416.).

     ii.   Marie Louise Sabourin was born on 10 Jul 1824 Ste-Madeleine-de-Riguad, Quebec (Ibid., #2681372.). She was baptized on 10 Jul 1824 Ste-Madeleine-de-Riguad, Quebec *(father's occupation: cultivator)* (PRDH online, #2681372.). She died on 29 Jul 1824 Ste-Madeleine-de-Riguad, Quebec (Ibid., #2682417.). She was buried on 30 Jul 1824 Ste-Madeleine-de-Riguad, Quebec *(father's occupation: cultivator)* (PRDH online, #2682417.).

127 iii. Louise Justine Sabourin, b. 18 Jul 1825 Ste-Madeleine-de-Riguad, Quebec; m. Louis Seguin.

    iv. Marie Marine Sabourin was born on 24 Jul 1827 Ste-Madeleine-de-Riguad, Quebec (Ibid., #4617572.). She was baptized on 24 Jul 1827 Ste-Madeleine-de-Riguad, Quebec (Ibid.). She died on 15 Oct 1829 Ste-Madeleine-de-Riguad, Quebec, at age 2 (Ibid., #4622994.). She was buried on 17 Oct 1829 Ste-Madeleine-de-Riguad, Quebec (Ibid.).

    v. Antoine Alexandre Sabourin was born on 2 Sep 1829 Ste-Madeleine-de-Riguad, Quebec (Ibid., #4618000.). He was baptized on 6 Sep 1829 Ste-Madeleine-de-Riguad, Quebec (Ibid.).
He was in the census household of Antoine Sabourin and Louise Chevrier in 1852 Ste.Madeleine, Rigaud, Vaudreuil, Quebec (1852C Cdn Transcription Project, District 536, page 24d, 25a, (49), line 35-41.).

    vi. Marie Olympe Sabourin was born on 18 Dec 1831 Ste-Madeleine-de-Riguad, Quebec (PRDH online, #4618494.). She was baptized on 18 Dec 1831 Ste-Madeleine-de-Riguad, Quebec (Ibid.).
She was in the census household of Antoine Sabourin and Louise Chevrier in 1852 Ste.Madeleine, Rigaud, Vaudreuil, Quebec (1852C Cdn Transcription Project, District 536, page 24d, 25a, (49), line 35-41.).

    vii. Eulalie Sabourin was born on 13 Feb 1834 Ste-Madeleine-de-Riguad, Quebec (PRDH online, #4619057.). She was baptized on 14 Feb 1834 Ste-Madeleine-de-Riguad, Quebec (Ibid.).
She was in the census household of Antoine Sabourin and Louise Chevrier in 1852 Ste.Madeleine, Rigaud, Vaudreuil, Quebec (1852C Cdn Transcription Project, District 536, page 24d, 25a, (49), line 35-41.).

    viii. Joseph Sabourin was born circa 1836 (Ibid.).
He was in the census household of Antoine Sabourin and Louise Chevrier in 1852 Ste.Madeleine, Rigaud, Vaudreuil, Quebec (1852C Cdn Transcription Project, District 536, page 24d, 25a, (49), line 35-41.).

    ix. Francis Amedee Sabourin was born on 3 Apr 1838 Ste-Madeleine-de-Riguad, Quebec (PRDH online, #4620108.). He was baptized on 4 Apr 1838 Ste-Madeleine-de-Riguad, Quebec (Ibid.).
He was in the census household of Antoine Sabourin and Louise Chevrier in 1852 Ste.Madeleine, Rigaud, Vaudreuil, Quebec (1852C Cdn Transcription Project, District 536, page 24d, 25a, (49), line 35-41.).

    x. Anonyme Sabourin was born on 19 Apr 1840 Ste-Madeleine-de-Riguad, Quebec (PRDH online, #4624033.). He/she died on 19 Apr 1840 Ste-Madeleine-de-Riguad, Quebec (Ibid.). He/she was buried on 20 Apr 1840 Ste-Madeleine-de-Riguad, Quebec (Ibid.).

    xi. Marguerite Alphonsine Sabourin was born on 14 May 1842 Ste-Madeleine-de-Riguad, Quebec (Ibid., #4621127.). She was baptized on 14 May 1842 Ste-Madeleine-de-Riguad, Quebec (Ibid.). She died on 5 Jun 1842 Ste-Madeleine-de-Riguad, Quebec (Ibid., #4624257.). She was buried on 7 Jun 1842 Ste-Madeleine-de-Riguad, Quebec (Ibid.).

36. **Magdelaine Rose Sabourin** was born on 6 Feb 1801 Oka, Quebec (Ibid., #2752194.). She was baptized on 6 Feb 1801 Oka, Quebec *(father's occupation: cultivator)* (PRDH online, #2752194.). She married **Paul Seguin dit Laderoute**, son of **Joseph Marie Seguin dit Laderoute** and **Marie Josephe Larocque dit Rocbrune,** on 23 Oct 1820 Ste-Madeleine-de-Riguad, Quebec *(Consanguinity)* (PRDH online, #2219982.).
Paul Seguin dit Laderoute was baptized on 4 Aug 1795 Oka, Quebec (Ibid., #652819.).
Children of **Magdelaine Rose Sabourin** and **Paul Seguin dit Laderoute** were:
    128 i. Joseph Paul Seguin, b. 11 Oct 1821 Ste-Madeleine-de-Riguad, Quebec; m. Marie Rachel Denys.

37. **Andre Sabourin** was born on 4 Apr 1803 (Ibid., #2679149.). He was baptized on 9 Apr 1803 Ste-Madeleine-de-Riguad, Quebec (Ibid.). He married **Marie Colombe Bedard**, daughter of **Jean Bedard** and **Marie Colombe Seguin dit Laderoute,** on 18 Feb 1827 Ste-Madeleine-de-Riguad, Quebec (Ibid., #3460453.).
He was enumerated in the census in 1852 Ste.Madeleine, Rigaud, Vaudreuil, Quebec. Also in the family: **Andre Sabourin, Paul Sabourin, Dosithee Sabourin, Hubert Sabourin, Hilaire Sabourin, Marie Rose Sabourin, Philomene Sabourin, Magdeleine Sabourin,** and **Marie Antoinette Sabourin** *(Sabourin, André, Cultivateur, Rigaud, Catholique, 50, M; Sabourin, André, Rigaud, Catholique, 21, M; Sabourin, Paul, Rigaud, Catholique, 16, M; Sabourin, Dosithé, Rigaud, Catholique, 12, M; Sabourin, Hubert, Rigaud, Catholique, 10, M; Sabourin, Hilaire,*

Rigaud, Catholique, 8, M; Sabourin, Rose, Rigaud, Catholique, 18, F; Sabourin, Philomène, Rigaud, Catholique, 14, F; Sabourin, Magdeleine, Rigaud, Catholique, 13, F; Sabourin, Antoinette, Rigaud, Catholique, 7, F) (1852C Cdn Transcription Project, District 536, page 28d, 29a, (57), line 12-21.).

Marie Colombe Bedard was born on 22 Nov 1808 Ste-Madeleine-de-Riguad, Quebec (PRDH online, #2679548.). She was baptized on 22 Nov 1808 Ste-Madeleine-de-Riguad, Quebec *(father's occupation: agriculture)* (PRDH online, #2679548.).

Children of **Andre Sabourin** and **Marie Colombe Bedard** all born Ste-Madeleine-de-Riguad, Quebec, were as follows:

    i. Sophie Sabourin was born on 26 Aug 1827 (Ibid., #4617605.). She was baptized on 26 Aug 1827 Ste-Madeleine-de-Riguad, Quebec (Ibid.). She died on 31 Oct 1827 Ste-Madeleine-de-Riguad, Quebec (Ibid., #4622860.). She was buried on 3 Nov 1827 Ste-Madeleine-de-Riguad, Quebec *(age 2 months)* (PRDH online, #4622860.).

    ii. Virginie Sabourin was born on 18 Jun 1829 (Ibid., #4617959.). She was baptized on 18 Jun 1829 Ste-Madeleine-de-Riguad, Quebec (Ibid.). She died on 8 Sep 1829 Ste-Madeleine-de-Riguad, Quebec (Ibid., #4622988.). She was buried on 11 Sep 1829 Ste-Madeleine-de-Riguad, Quebec *(age 2 months)* (PRDH online, #4622988.).

    iii. Andre Sabourin was born on 14 Nov 1830 (Ibid., #4618223.). He was baptized on 15 Nov 1830 Ste-Madeleine-de-Riguad, Quebec (Ibid.).

      He was in the census household of Andre Sabourin in 1852 Ste.Madeleine, Rigaud, Vaudreuil, Quebec (1852C Cdn Transcription Project, District 536, page 28d, 29a, (57), line 12-21.).

    iv. Julie Sabourin was born on 29 Mar 1832 (PRDH online, #4618584.). She was baptized on 30 Mar 1832 Ste-Madeleine-de-Riguad, Quebec (Ibid.). She died on 31 Mar 1832 Ste-Madeleine-de-Riguad, Quebec (Ibid., #4623198.). She was buried on 2 Apr 1832 Ste-Madeleine-de-Riguad, Quebec *(age 2 days)* (PRDH online, #4623198.).

    v. Marie Rose Sabourin was born on 9 Sep 1833 (Ibid., #4618963.). She was baptized on 9 Sep 1833 Ste-Madeleine-de-Riguad, Quebec (Ibid.).

      She was in the census household of Andre Sabourin in 1852 Ste.Madeleine, Rigaud, Vaudreuil, Quebec (1852C Cdn Transcription Project, District 536, page 28d, 29a, (57), line 12-21.).

    vi. Paul Sabourin was born on 23 Apr 1835 (PRDH online, #4619346.). He was baptized on 23 Apr 1835 Ste-Madeleine-de-Riguad, Quebec (Ibid.).

      He was in the census household of Andre Sabourin in 1852 Ste.Madeleine, Rigaud, Vaudreuil, Quebec (1852C Cdn Transcription Project, District 536, page 28d, 29a, (57), line 12-21.).

    vii. Joseph Hilaire Sabourin was born on 28 Sep 1836 (PRDH online, #4619767.). He was baptized on 29 Sep 1836 Ste-Madeleine-de-Riguad, Quebec (Ibid.). He died on 22 Sep 1837 Ste-Madeleine-de-Riguad, Quebec (Ibid., #4623790.). He was buried on 23 Sep 1837 Ste-Madeleine-de-Riguad, Quebec (Ibid.).

    viii. Philomene Sabourin was born on 8 Feb 1838 (Ibid., #4620077.). She was baptized on 9 Feb 1838 Ste-Madeleine-de-Riguad, Quebec (Ibid.).

      She was in the census household of Andre Sabourin in 1852 Ste.Madeleine, Rigaud, Vaudreuil, Quebec (1852C Cdn Transcription Project, District 536, page 28d, 29a, (57), line 12-21.).

    ix. Magdeleine Sabourin was born on 15 Jun 1839 (PRDH online, #4620425.). She was baptized on 16 Jun 1839 Ste-Madeleine-de-Riguad, Quebec (Ibid.).

      She was in the census household of Andre Sabourin in 1852 Ste.Madeleine, Rigaud, Vaudreuil, Quebec (1852C Cdn Transcription Project, District 536, page 28d, 29a, (57), line 12-21.).

    x. Dosithee Sabourin was born on 14 Jun 1840 (PRDH online, #4620657.). He was baptized on 15 Jun 1840 Ste-Madeleine-de-Riguad, Quebec (Ibid.).

      He was in the census household of Andre Sabourin in 1852 Ste.Madeleine, Rigaud, Vaudreuil, Quebec (1852C Cdn Transcription Project, District 536, page 28d, 29a, (57), line 12-21.).

    xi. Hubert Sabourin was born on 5 Nov 1841 (PRDH online, #4620998.). He was baptized on 6 Nov 1841 Ste-Madeleine-de-Riguad, Quebec (Ibid.).

      He was in the census household of Andre Sabourin in 1852 Ste.Madeleine, Rigaud, Vaudreuil, Quebec (1852C Cdn Transcription Project, District 536, page 28d, 29a, (57), line 12-21.).

    xii. Hilaire Sabourin was born on 20 Dec 1842 (PRDH online, #4621273.). He was baptized on 21 Dec 1842 Ste-Madeleine-de-Riguad, Quebec (Ibid.).

      He was in the census household of Andre Sabourin in 1852 Ste.Madeleine, Rigaud, Vaudreuil, Quebec (1852C Cdn Transcription Project, District 536, page 28d, 29a, (57), line 12-21.).

xiii. Marie Antoinette Sabourin was born on 17 Feb 1845 (PRDH online, #4621767.). She was baptized on 17 Feb 1845 Ste-Madeleine-de-Riguad, Quebec (Ibid.).
  She was in the census household of Andre Sabourin in 1852 Ste.Madeleine, Rigaud, Vaudreuil, Quebec (1852C Cdn Transcription Project, District 536, page 28d, 29a, (57), line 12-21.).

xiv. Emelie Sabourin was born on 12 Jul 1846 (PRDH online, #4622076.). She was baptized on 12 Jul 1846 Ste-Madeleine-de-Riguad, Quebec (Ibid.). She died on 26 Jul 1846 Ste-Madeleine-de-Riguad, Quebec (Ibid., #4624572.). She was buried on 27 Jul 1846 Ste-Madeleine-de-Riguad, Quebec *(age 15 days)* (PRDH online, #4624572.).

xv. Joseph Dorsineau Sabourin was born on 12 Mar 1848 (Ibid., #4622373.). He was baptized on 13 Mar 1848 Ste-Madeleine-de-Riguad, Quebec (Ibid.). He died on 14 Jun 1848 Ste-Madeleine-de-Riguad, Quebec (Ibid., #4624679.). He was buried on 15 Jun 1848 Ste-Madeleine-de-Riguad, Quebec *(age 3 months)* (PRDH online, #4624679.).

38. **Marie Josephte Sabourin** was born on 19 Oct 1804 Ste-Madeleine-de-Riguad, Quebec (Ibid., #2679235.). She was baptized on 20 Oct 1804 Ste-Madeleine-de-Riguad, Quebec *(father's occupation: agriculture)* (PRDH online, #2679235.). She married **Floribert Henri Hubert Seguin**, son of **Jean Antoine Seguin dit Laderoute** and **Marie Rose Brabant dit Lamothe,** on 16 Oct 1820 Ste-Madeleine-de-Riguad, Quebec (Ibid., #2219964.).

Floribert Henri Hubert Seguin was born on 10 Jul 1791 Oka, Quebec (Ibid., No. 642378.). He was baptized on 10 Jul 1791 Oka, Quebec *([no godparents])* (PRDH online, No. 642378.).

Children of **Marie Josephte Sabourin** and **Floribert Henri Hubert Seguin** were as follows:

i. Madeleine Rose Seguin was born on 22 Sep 1821 Ste-Madeleine-de-Riguad, Quebec (Ibid., #2680928.). She was baptized on 22 Sep 1821 Ste-Madeleine-de-Riguad, Quebec (Ibid.). She died on 25 Jul 1822 Ste-Madeleine-de-Riguad, Quebec *(age 10 months)* (PRDH online, #2682297.). She was buried on 26 Jul 1822 Ste-Madeleine-de-Riguad, Quebec (Ibid.).

ii. Damase Hubert Seguin was born on 24 Aug 1830 Montebello, Quebec (Ibid., #4088243.). He was baptized on 24 Aug 1830 Montebello, Quebec (Ibid.).

39. **Joseph Sabourin** was born on 18 Sep 1807 Ste-Madeleine-de-Riguad, Quebec (Ibid., #2679447.). He was baptized on 18 Sep 1807 Ste-Madeleine-de-Riguad, Quebec *(father's occupation: agriculture)* (PRDH online, #2679447.). He married **Suzanne Portelance**, daughter of **Henry Portelance** and **Suzanne Vachon,** on 15 Jan 1830 Ste-Madeleine-de-Riguad, Quebec (Ibid., #3461646.).

He and **Suzanne Portelance** were enumerated in the census in 1852 Ste.Madeleine, Rigaud, Vaudreuil, Quebec. Also in the family: **Joseph Damase Sabourin**, **Andre Sabourin**, **Francois Amedee Sabourin**, **Telesphore Sabourin**, **Marie Genevieve Philomene Sabourin**, **Paul Alphonse Sabourin**, **Antoine Sabourin**, **Pierre Sabourin**, and **Marie Magdalene Sabourin** *(Sabourin, Joseph, Cultivateur, Rigaud, Catholique, 40, M; Portelance, Suzanne, Rigaud, Catholique, 38, F; Sabourin, Damase, Rigaud, Catholique, 18, M; Sabourin, André, Rigaud, Catholique, 17, M; Sabourin, Amedee, Rigaud, Catholique, 14, M; Sabourin, Télesphore, Rigaud, Catholique, 12, M; Sabourin, Philomène, Rigaud, Catholique, 10, F; Sabourin, Alphonse, Rigaud, Catholique, 9, M; Sabourin, Antoine, Rigaud, Catholique, 5, M; Sabourin, Pierre, Rigaud, Catholique, 3, M; Sabourin, Magdeleine, Rigaud, Catholique, 2, F)* (1852C Cdn Transcription Project, District 536, page 24d, 25a, (49).).

Suzanne Portelance was born on 7 Oct 1812 Ste-Madeleine-de-Riguad, Quebec (PRDH online, #706192.). She was baptized on 11 Oct 1812 Ste-Madeleine-de-Riguad, Quebec (Ibid.).

Children of **Joseph Sabourin** and **Suzanne Portelance** all born Ste-Madeleine-de-Riguad, Quebec, were as follows:

i. Joseph Damase Sabourin was born on 29 Mar 1832 (Ibid., #4618585.). He was baptized on 30 Mar 1832 Ste-Madeleine-de-Riguad, Quebec (Ibid.).
  He was in the census household of Joseph Sabourin and Suzanne Portelance in 1852 Ste.Madeleine, Rigaud, Vaudreuil, Quebec (1852C Cdn Transcription Project, District 536, page 24d, 25a, (49).).

ii. Antoine Aime Sabourin was born on 13 Sep 1833 (PRDH online, #4618964.). He was baptized on 13 Sep 1833 Ste-Madeleine-de-Riguad, Quebec (Ibid.). He died on 14 Apr 1834 Ste-Madeleine-de-Riguad, Quebec (Ibid., #4623483.). He was buried on 15 Apr 1834 Ste-Madeleine-de-Riguad, Quebec *(age 7 months)* (PRDH online, #4623483.).

iii. Andre Sabourin was born on 17 Mar 1835 (Ibid., #4619325.). He was baptized on 17 Mar 1835 Ste-Madeleine-de-Riguad, Quebec (Ibid.).
  He was in the census household of Joseph Sabourin and Suzanne Portelance in 1852 Ste.Madeleine, Rigaud, Vaudreuil, Quebec (1852C Cdn Transcription Project, District 536, page 24d, 25a, (49).).

    iv.   Marie Magdeleine Philomene Sabourin was born on 22 Jul 1836 (PRDH online, #4619714.). She was baptized on 23 Jul 1836 Ste-Madeleine-de-Riguad, Quebec (Ibid.). She died on 24 May 1837 Ste-Madeleine-de-Riguad, Quebec (Ibid., #4623757.). She was buried on 26 May 1837 Ste-Madeleine-de-Riguad, Quebec (Ibid.).

    v.   Francois Amedee Sabourin was born on 9 Mar 1838 (Ibid., #4620097.). He was baptized on 10 Mar 1838 Ste-Madeleine-de-Riguad, Quebec (Ibid.).

       He was in the census household of Joseph Sabourin and Suzanne Portelance in 1852 Ste.Madeleine, Rigaud, Vaudreuil, Quebec (1852C Cdn Transcription Project, District 536, page 24d, 25a, (49).).

    vi.   Telesphore Sabourin was born on 16 Nov 1839 (PRDH online, #4620515.). He was baptized on 17 Nov 1839 Ste-Madeleine-de-Riguad, Quebec (Ibid.).

       He was in the census household of Joseph Sabourin and Suzanne Portelance in 1852 Ste.Madeleine, Rigaud, Vaudreuil, Quebec (1852C Cdn Transcription Project, District 536, page 24d, 25a, (49).).

    vii.   Marie Genevieve Philomene Sabourin was born on 12 Jul 1841 (PRDH online, #4620933.). She was baptized on 12 Jul 1841 Ste-Madeleine-de-Riguad, Quebec (Ibid.).

       She was in the census household of Joseph Sabourin and Suzanne Portelance in 1852 Ste.Madeleine, Rigaud, Vaudreuil, Quebec (1852C Cdn Transcription Project, District 536, page 24d, 25a, (49).).

    viii.   Paul Alphonse Sabourin was born on 25 Apr 1843 (PRDH online, #4621359.). He was baptized on 26 Apr 1843 Ste-Madeleine-de-Riguad, Quebec (Ibid.).

       He was in the census household of Joseph Sabourin and Suzanne Portelance in 1852 Ste.Madeleine, Rigaud, Vaudreuil, Quebec (1852C Cdn Transcription Project, District 536, page 24d, 25a, (49).).

    ix.   Antoine Sabourin was born on 25 Sep 1845 (PRDH online, #4621909.). He was baptized on 29 Sep 1845 Ste-Madeleine-de-Riguad, Quebec (Ibid.).

       He was in the census household of Joseph Sabourin and Suzanne Portelance in 1852 Ste.Madeleine, Rigaud, Vaudreuil, Quebec (1852C Cdn Transcription Project, District 536, page 24d, 25a, (49).).

    x.   Pierre Sabourin was born on 28 Nov 1847 (PRDH online, #4622320.). He was baptized on 29 Nov 1847 Ste-Madeleine-de-Riguad, Quebec (Ibid.).

       He was in the census household of Joseph Sabourin and Suzanne Portelance in 1852 Ste.Madeleine, Rigaud, Vaudreuil, Quebec (1852C Cdn Transcription Project, District 536, page 24d, 25a, (49).).

    xi.   Marie Magdalene Sabourin was born on 21 Aug 1849 (PRDH online, #4728089.). She was baptized on 22 Aug 1849 Ste-Madeleine-de-Riguad, Quebec (Ibid.).

       She was in the census household of Joseph Sabourin and Suzanne Portelance in 1852 Ste.Madeleine, Rigaud, Vaudreuil, Quebec (1852C Cdn Transcription Project, District 536, page 24d, 25a, (49).).

40. Adelaide Sabourin was born circa 1809 (PRDH online, #3460496.) (1852C Cdn Transcription Project, District 536, page 1a, (1).). She married **Pierre Seguin**, son of **Joseph Marie Seguin dit Laderoute** and **Marie Josephe Larocque dit Rocbrune,** on 26 Feb 1827 Ste-Madeleine-de-Riguad, Quebec (PRDH online, #3460496.).

She and **Pierre Seguin** were enumerated in the census in 1852 Ste.Madeleine, Rigaud, Vaudreuil, Quebec. Also in the family: **Emelie Seguin, Marie Judith Seguin, Antoinette Seguin, Marie Philomene Seguin, Marie Sophie Seguin, Marie Reine Clorinthe Seguin, Andre Seguin, Benjamin Seguin, Alphonse Seguin**, and **Telesphore Seguin** *(Séguin, Pierre, Cultivateur, Rigaud, Catholique, 48, M; Sabourin, Denise, Rigaud, Catholique, 43, F; Séguin, Emilie, Rigaud, Catholique, 22, F; Séguin, Julie, Rigaud, Catholique, 21, F; Séguin, Antoinette, Rigaud, Catholique, 15, F; Séguin, Philomene, Rigaud, Catholique, 11, F; Séguin, Sophie, Rigaud, Catholique, 8, F; Séguin, Clorinette, Rigaud, Catholique, 6, F; Séguin, Andre, Rigaud, Catholique, 17, M; Séguin, Benjamin, Rigaud, Catholique, 12, M; Séguin, Alphonse, Rigaud, Catholique, 9, M; Séguin, Telesphore, Rigaud, Catholique, 19M, M)* (1852C Cdn Transcription Project, District 536, page 1a, (1).).

Pierre Seguin was born on 21 Jul 1803 Ste-Madeleine-de-Riguad, Quebec (PRDH online, #2679175.). He was baptized on 21 Jul 1803 Ste-Madeleine-de-Riguad, Quebec *(father's occupation: cultivator)* (PRDH online, #2679175.).

Children of **Adelaide Sabourin** and **Pierre Seguin** were as follows:

i. Joseph Seguin was born on 13 Dec 1827 Ste-Madeleine-de-Riguad, Quebec (Ibid., #4617651.). He was baptized on 15 Dec 1827 Ste-Madeleine-de-Riguad, Quebec (Ibid.).

ii. Emelie Seguin was born on 5 Oct 1829 Ste-Madeleine-de-Riguad, Quebec (Ibid., #4618016.). She was baptized on 5 Oct 1829 Ste-Madeleine-de-Riguad, Quebec (Ibid.).
  She was in the census household of Pierre Seguin and Adelaide Sabourin in 1852 Ste.Madeleine, Rigaud, Vaudreuil, Quebec (1852C Cdn Transcription Project, District 536, page 1a, (1).).

iii. Marie Judith Seguin was born on 6 Dec 1830 Ste-Madeleine-de-Riguad, Quebec (PRDH online, #4618239.). She was baptized on 7 Dec 1830 Ste-Madeleine-de-Riguad, Quebec (Ibid.).
  She was in the census household of Pierre Seguin and Adelaide Sabourin in 1852 Ste.Madeleine, Rigaud, Vaudreuil, Quebec (1852C Cdn Transcription Project, District 536, page 1a, (1).).

iv. Pierre Seguin was born on 28 Jun 1832 Ste-Madeleine-de-Riguad, Quebec (PRDH online, #4618664.). He was baptized on 28 Jun 1832 Ste-Madeleine-de-Riguad, Quebec (Ibid.). He died on 7 May 1833 Ste-Madeleine-de-Riguad, Quebec (Ibid., #4623398.). He was buried on 8 May 1833 Ste-Madeleine-de-Riguad, Quebec *(age 10 months)* (PRDH online, #4623398.).

v. Andre Seguin was born on 9 Jun 1834 Ste-Madeleine-de-Riguad, Quebec (Ibid., #4619133.). He was baptized on 10 Jun 1834 Ste-Madeleine-de-Riguad, Quebec (Ibid.).
  He was in the census household of Pierre Seguin and Adelaide Sabourin in 1852 Ste.Madeleine, Rigaud, Vaudreuil, Quebec (1852C Cdn Transcription Project, District 536, page 1a, (1).).

vi. Antoinette Seguin was born on 3 Mar 1836 Ste-Madeleine-de-Riguad, Quebec (PRDH online, #4619583.). She was baptized on 4 Mar 1836 Ste-Madeleine-de-Riguad, Quebec (Ibid.).
  She was in the census household of Pierre Seguin and Adelaide Sabourin in 1852 Ste.Madeleine, Rigaud, Vaudreuil, Quebec (1852C Cdn Transcription Project, District 536, page 1a, (1).).

vii. Francois Xavier Seguin was born on 4 Oct 1838 Ste-Madeleine-de-Riguad, Quebec (PRDH online, #4620240.). He was baptized on 4 Oct 1838 Ste-Madeleine-de-Riguad, Quebec (Ibid.). He died on 5 Oct 1838 Ste-Madeleine-de-Riguad, Quebec (Ibid., #4623889.). He was buried on 5 Oct 1838 Ste-Madeleine-de-Riguad, Quebec (Ibid.).

viii. Benjamin Seguin was born on 24 Sep 1839 Ste-Madeleine-de-Riguad, Quebec (Ibid., #4620493.). He was baptized on 25 Sep 1839 Ste-Madeleine-de-Riguad, Quebec (Ibid.).
  He was in the census household of Pierre Seguin and Adelaide Sabourin in 1852 Ste.Madeleine, Rigaud, Vaudreuil, Quebec (1852C Cdn Transcription Project, District 536, page 1a, (1).).

ix. Marie Philomene Seguin was born on 1 May 1841 Ste-Madeleine-de-Riguad, Quebec (PRDH online, #4620886.). She was baptized on 2 May 1841 Ste-Madeleine-de-Riguad, Quebec (Ibid.).
  She was in the census household of Pierre Seguin and Adelaide Sabourin in 1852 Ste.Madeleine, Rigaud, Vaudreuil, Quebec (1852C Cdn Transcription Project, District 536, page 1a, (1).).

x. Alphonse Seguin was born on 28 Oct 1842 Ste-Madeleine-de-Riguad, Quebec (PRDH online, #4621231.). He was baptized on 28 Oct 1842 Ste-Madeleine-de-Riguad, Quebec (Ibid.).
  He was in the census household of Pierre Seguin and Adelaide Sabourin in 1852 Ste.Madeleine, Rigaud, Vaudreuil, Quebec (1852C Cdn Transcription Project, District 536, page 1a, (1).).

xi. Marie Sophie Seguin was born on 18 Mar 1844 Ste-Madeleine-de-Riguad, Quebec (PRDH online, #4621549.). She was baptized on 18 Mar 1844 Ste-Madeleine-de-Riguad, Quebec (Ibid.).
  She was in the census household of Pierre Seguin and Adelaide Sabourin in 1852 Ste.Madeleine, Rigaud, Vaudreuil, Quebec (1852C Cdn Transcription Project, District 536, page 1a, (1).).

xii. Marie Reine Clorinthe Seguin was born on 6 Jan 1846 Ste-Madeleine-de-Riguad, Quebec (PRDH online, #4621965.). She was baptized on 7 Jan 1846 Ste-Madeleine-de-Riguad, Quebec (Ibid.).
  She was in the census household of Pierre Seguin and Adelaide Sabourin in 1852 Ste.Madeleine, Rigaud, Vaudreuil, Quebec (1852C Cdn Transcription Project, District 536, page 1a, (1).).

xiii. Marie Seguin was born on 24 Jun 1848 Ste-Madeleine-de-Riguad, Quebec (PRDH online, #4622418.). She was baptized on 24 Jun 1848 Ste-Madeleine-de-Riguad, Quebec (Ibid.). She died on 26 Jun 1848 Ste-Madeleine-de-Riguad, Quebec (Ibid., #4624681.). She was buried on 27 Jun 1848 Ste-Madeleine-de-Riguad, Quebec *(age 2 days)* (PRDH online, #4624681.).

xiv. Antoine Napoleon Seguin was born on 28 Apr 1849 Ste-Madeleine-de-Riguad, Quebec (Ibid., #4622546.). He was baptized on 28 Apr 1849 Ste-Madeleine-de-Riguad, Quebec (Ibid.).

xv. Telesphore Seguin was born circa 1850 (1852C Cdn Transcription Project, District 536, page 1a, (1).).
  He was in the census household of Pierre Seguin and Adelaide Sabourin in 1852 Ste.Madeleine, Rigaud, Vaudreuil, Quebec (1852C Cdn Transcription Project, District 536, page 1a, (1).).

41. **Antoine Frederic Sauve** was born on 15 Jun 1786 Vaudreuil, Quebec (PRDH online, #723173.). He was baptized on 16 Jun 1786 Vaudreuil, Quebec (Ibid.). He married **Marie Marguerite Tessier**, daughter of **Jean Baptiste Tessier dit Lavigne** and **Marie Archange Picard,** on 24 Apr 1809 Vaudreuil, Quebec (Ibid., #2224040.).
 Marie Marguerite Tessier was born on 31 May 1786 Notre-Dame-de-Montreal, Quebec (Ibid., #624734.). She was baptized on 1 Jun 1786 Notre-Dame-de-Montreal, Quebec (Ibid.).
Children of **Antoine Frederic Sauve** and **Marie Marguerite Tessier** were as follows:

     129   i.   Marie Ostie Sauve, b. 19 Feb 1810 Vaudreuil, Quebec; m. Pierre Francois Sauve dit Laplante.
     130   ii.   Archange Sauve, b. 4 Apr 1812 Vaudreuil, Quebec; m. Joachim Ranger.
            iii. Louis Sauve was born on 20 Jun 1814 Ste-Madeleine-de-Riguad, Quebec (Ibid., #2680083.). He was baptized on 21 Jun 1814 Ste-Madeleine-de-Riguad, Quebec *(father's occupation: agriculture)* (PRDH online, #2680083.). He died on 10 May 1815 Ste-Madeleine-de-Riguad, Quebec (Ibid., #2681940.). He was buried on 11 May 1815 Ste-Madeleine-de-Riguad, Quebec *(age 10 months and 20 days, father's occupation: agriculture)* (PRDH online, #2681940.).
            iv. Pierre Casimir Sauve was born on 5 Mar 1816 Ste-Madeleine-de-Riguad, Quebec (Ibid., #2680272.). He was baptized on 6 Mar 1816 Ste-Madeleine-de-Riguad, Quebec *(father's occupation: laborer)* (PRDH online, #2680272.). He married Rosalie Barbary dit Grandmaison, daughter of Pierre Barbary dit Grandmaison and Marie Louise Morin, on 22 Jun 1840 Ste-Madeleine-de-Riguad, Quebec (Ibid., #3465084.).

               Rosalie Barbary dit Grandmaison was born on 17 Mar 1816 St-Eustache, Quebec (Ibid., #2829843.). She was baptized on 18 Mar 1816 St-Eustache, Quebec (Ibid.).
             v. Angelique Sauve was born on 17 Sep 1817 Ste-Madeleine-de-Riguad, Quebec (Ibid., #2680418.). She was baptized on 18 Sep 1817 Ste-Madeleine-de-Riguad *(father's occupation: agriculture)* (PRDH online, #2680418.). She died on 8 Apr 1819 Ste-Madeleine-de-Riguad, Quebec, at age 1 (Ibid., #2682097.). She was buried on 9 Apr 1819 Ste-Madeleine-de-Riguad, Quebec *(age 18 months, father's occupation: agriculture)* (PRDH online, #2682097.).
            vi. Marie Adelaide Sauve was born on 1 Sep 1819 Ste-Madeleine-de-Riguad, Quebec (Ibid., #2680655.). She was baptized on 4 Sep 1819 Ste-Madeleine-de-Riguad, Quebec *(father's occupation: cultivator)* (PRDH online, #2680655.). She died on 28 Sep 1820 Ste-Madeleine-de-Riguad, Quebec, at age 1 (Ibid., #2682178.). She was buried on 29 Sep 1820 Ste-Madeleine-de-Riguad, Quebec *(age 26 days, father's occupation: cultivator)* (PRDH online, #2682178.).
           vii. Edouard Sauve was born on 26 Aug 1821 Ste-Madeleine-de-Riguad, Quebec (Ibid., #2680915.). He was baptized on 27 Aug 1821 Ste-Madeleine-de-Riguad, Quebec *(father's occupation: cultivator)* (PRDH online, #2680915.).
          viii. Antoine Israel Sauve was born on 20 Jul 1823 Ste-Madeleine-de-Riguad, Quebec (Ibid., #2681215.). He was baptized on 21 Jul 1823 Ste-Madeleine-de-Riguad, Quebec *(father's occupation: cultivator)* (PRDH online, #2681215.).
            ix. Joseph Sauve was born on 20 May 1825 Ste-Madeleine-de-Riguad, Quebec (Ibid., #4617200.). He was baptized on 20 May 1825 Ste-Madeleine-de-Riguad, Quebec (Ibid.).
             x. Elise Sauve was born on 30 Sep 1827 Ste-Madeleine-de-Riguad, Quebec (Ibid., #4617629.). She was baptized on 3 Oct 1827 Ste-Madeleine-de-Riguad, Quebec (Ibid.).

42. **Pascal Sauve** was born on 30 Jul 1789 Vaudreuil, Quebec (Ibid., #723441.). He was baptized on 31 Jul 1789 Vaudreuil, Quebec (Ibid.). He married **Marie Angelique Larocque dit Rocbrune**, daughter of **Charles Amable Larocque** and **Marie Anne Zacharie,** on 21 Feb 1814 Vaudreuil, Quebec (Ibid., #2224212.).
 Marie Angelique Larocque dit Rocbrune was born on 12 May 1789 Riviere du Nord, Quebec (Ibid., No. 642321.). She was baptized on 21 May 1789 Oka, Quebec *(conditional baptism)* (PRDH online, No. 642321.).
Children of **Pascal Sauve** and **Marie Angelique Larocque dit Rocbrune** were as follows:

             i. Francois Xavier Hygin Sauve was born on 8 Jan 1815 Vaudreuil, Quebec (Ibid., #2591183.). He was baptized on 9 Jan 1815 Vaudreuil, Quebec (Ibid.).
            ii. Antoine Frederic Sauve was born on 6 Mar 1817 Ste-Madeleine-de-Riguad, Quebec (Ibid., #2680375.). He was baptized on 9 Mar 1817 Ste-Madeleine-de-Riguad, Quebec *(father's occupation: cultivator)* (PRDH online, #2680375.).
           iii. Rose Sauve was born on 29 Aug 1818 Ste-Madeleine-de-Riguad, Quebec (Ibid., #2680528.). She was baptized on 30 Aug 1818 Ste-Madeleine-de-Riguad, Quebec *(father's occupation: cultivator)* (PRDH online, #2680528.).

    iv. Joseph Alexandre Sauve was born on 23 Jan 1820 Ste-Madeleine-de-Riguad, Quebec (Ibid., #2680703.). He was baptized on 24 Jan 1820 Ste-Madeleine-de-Riguad, Quebec *(father's occupation: cultivator)* (PRDH online, #2680703.).

    v. Anne Sauve was born on 18 Sep 1821 Ste-Madeleine-de-Riguad, Quebec (Ibid., #2680925.). She was baptized on 19 Sep 1821 Ste-Madeleine-de-Riguad, Quebec *(father's occupation: cultivator)* (PRDH online, #2680925.).

    vi. Jean Baptiste Pascal Sauve was born on 2 Jun 1825 Ste-Madeleine-de-Riguad, Quebec (Ibid., #4617207.). He was baptized on 3 Jun 1825 Ste-Madeleine-de-Riguad, Quebec (Ibid.).

    vii. Marie Henriette Sauve was born on 12 Sep 1826 Ste-Madeleine-de-Riguad, Quebec (Ibid., #4617420.). She was baptized on 14 Sep 1826 Ste-Madeleine-de-Riguad, Quebec (Ibid.).

    viii. Marie Therese Sauve was born on 22 Mar 1829 Montebello, Quebec (Ibid., #4088063.). She was baptized on 25 Mar 1829 Montebello, Quebec (Ibid.).

43. **Marie Euphrosine Sauve** was born on 17 Dec 1793 Oka, Quebec (Ibid., #642489.). She was baptized on 18 Dec 1793 Oka, Quebec (Ibid.). She married **Pierre Louis Seguin**, son of **Hyacinthe Seguin dit Laderoute** and **Marie Louise Rouleau,** on 26 Feb 1816 Ste-Madeleine-de-Riguad, Quebec (Ibid., #2219439.).

  Pierre Louis Seguin was born on 24 Aug 1793 Ste-Anne-de-Bellevue, Quebec (Ibid., #662683.). He was baptized on 25 Aug 1793 Ste-Anne-de-Bellevue, Quebec (Ibid.).

  Children of **Marie Euphrosine Sauve** and **Pierre Louis Seguin** all born Ste-Madeleine-de-Riguad, Quebec, were as follows:

    i. Marie Caroline Seguin was born on 11 Dec 1818 (Ibid., #2680568.). She was baptized on 11 Dec 1818 Ste-Madeleine-de-Riguad, Quebec *(father's occupation: cultivator)* (PRDH online, #2680568.). She died on 9 Jul 1819 Ste-Madeleine-de-Riguad, Quebec (Ibid., #2682109.). She was buried on 10 Jul 1819 Ste-Madeleine-de-Riguad, Quebec *(age 7 months, father's occupation: cultivator)* (PRDH online, #2682109.).

    ii. Marcelline Domitilde Seguin was born on 26 May 1822 (Ibid., #2681032.). She was baptized on 27 May 1822 Ste-Madeleine-de-Riguad, Quebec *(father's occupation: cultivator)* (PRDH online, #2681032.).

    iii. Marie Adelaide Seguin was born on 17 Apr 1824 (Ibid., #2681343.). She was baptized on 18 Apr 1824 Ste-Madeleine-de-Riguad, Quebec *(father's occupation: day laborer)* (PRDH online, #2681343.).

    iv. Marie Edesse Louise Seguin was born on 28 Oct 1826 (Ibid., #4617438.). She was baptized on 29 Oct 1826 Ste-Madeleine-de-Riguad, Quebec (Ibid.). She died on 28 May 1829 Ste-Madeleine-de-Riguad, Quebec, at age 2 (Ibid., #4622963.). She was buried on 31 May 1829 Ste-Madeleine-de-Riguad, Quebec (Ibid.).

    v. Pierre Barnabe Seguin was born on 30 Mar 1829 (Ibid., #4617911.). He was baptized on 30 Mar 1829 Ste-Madeleine-de-Riguad, Quebec (Ibid.). He married Emilie Vesina, daughter of Vincent Vesina and Agathe Demers, on 16 Jan 1849 Ste-Madeleine-de-Riguad, Quebec (Ibid., #3467130.).

    He was in the census household of Hyacinthe Seguin dit Laderoute and Marie Monique Villeneuve in 1852 Notre-Dame, Petite Nation, Ottawa County, Ontario (1852C Cdn Transcription Project, District 274, page 39d, 30a, (79), line 37-42.).

    Emilie Vesina was born on 10 May 1825 (Pierrefonds), Ste-Genevieve, Quebec (PRDH online, #4503003.). She was baptized on 10 May 1825 (Pierrefonds), Ste-Genevieve, Quebec (Ibid.).

    vi. Benjamin Seguin was born on 7 Nov 1834 (Ibid., #4619240.). He was baptized on 8 Nov 1834 Ste-Madeleine-de-Riguad, Quebec (Ibid.).

44. **Hyacinthe Sauve** was baptized on 14 Apr 1796 Vaudreuil, Quebec *(father's occupation: cultivator)* (PRDH online, No. 770788.). He married **Josephe Larocque dit Rocbrune**, daughter of **Charles Amable Larocque** and **Marie Anne Zacharie,** on 16 Nov 1818 Ste-Madeleine-de-Riguad, Quebec (Ibid., #2219761.).

  Josephe Larocque dit Rocbrune was born on 29 Nov 1792 (Ibid., No. 770445.). She was baptized on 1 Dec 1792 Vaudreuil, Quebec (Ibid.).

  Children of **Hyacinthe Sauve** and **Josephe Larocque dit Rocbrune** all born Ste-Madeleine-de-Riguad, Quebec, were as follows:

    i. Hyacinthe Sauve was born on 11 Oct 1820 (Ibid., #2680817.). He was baptized on 12 Oct 1820 Ste-Madeleine-de-Riguad, Quebec *(father's occupation: cultivator)* (PRDH online, #2680817.). He died on 26 Feb 1822 Ste-Madeleine-de-Riguad, Quebec, at age 1 (Ibid., #2682273.). He was buried on 27 Feb 1822 Ste-Madeleine-de-Riguad, Quebec *(age 16 months and 15 days, father's occupation: cultivator)* (PRDH online, #2682273.).

    ii.   Edmond Sauve was born on 26 Oct 1822 (Ibid., #2681102.). He was baptized on 26 Oct 1822 Ste-Madeleine-de-Riguad, Quebec *(father's occupation: cultivator)* (PRDH online, #2681102.).

    iii.   Guillaume Sauve was born on 5 Aug 1824 (Ibid., #2681379.). He was baptized on 5 Aug 1824 Ste-Madeleine-de-Riguad, Quebec *(father's occupation: cultivator)* (PRDH online, #2681379.).

    iv.   Edesse Denise Sauve was born on 1 Jan 1827 (Ibid., #4617464.). She was baptized on 4 Jan 1827 Ste-Madeleine-de-Riguad, Quebec (Ibid.).

    v.   Marie Josephte Sauve was born on 15 Apr 1829 (Ibid., #4617922.). She was baptized on 16 Apr 1829 Ste-Madeleine-de-Riguad, Quebec (Ibid.).

45. **Charles Sabourin** was born on 9 Sep 1793 Vaudreuil, Quebec (Ibid., #770527.). He was baptized on 11 Sep 1793 Vaudreuil, Quebec *(conditional baptism)* (PRDH online, #770527.). He married **Madeleine Lalande dit Latreille or Lalonde**, daughter of **Francois Lalande** and **Marie Anne Cardinal,** on 18 Jul 1814 Ste-Madeleine-de-Riguad, Quebec (Ibid., #2219150.).

He and **Madeleine Lalande dit Latreille or Lalonde** were enumerated in the census in 1852 Ste.Madeleine, Rigaud, Vaudreuil, Quebec. Also in the family: **Marie Mathilde Sabourin** *(Sabourin, Charles, Journalier/ Dayworker, Vaudreuil, Lower Canada, Catholic, 50, M; Lalande, Magdeleine, St. Eustache, Lower Canada, Catholic, 60, F; Sabourin, Mathilde, Rigaud, Lower Canada, Catholic, 25, F)* (1852C Cdn Transcription Project, District 536, page 2d, 3a, (5), line 31-33.).

Madeleine Lalande dit Latreille or Lalonde was born circa 1793 St-Eustache, Quebec (Ibid.).

Children of **Charles Sabourin** and **Madeleine Lalande dit Latreille or Lalonde** all born Ste-Madeleine-de-Riguad, Quebec, were as follows:

    131   i.   Charles Norbert Sabourin, b. 21 Jun 1816; m. Marguerite Jeanne Franche.

    ii.   Hyacinthe Venant Sabourin was born on 18 May 1818 (PRDH online, #2680492.). He was baptized on 19 May 1818 Ste-Madeleine-de-Riguad, Quebec *(father's occupation: day laborer)* (PRDH online, #2680492.). He died on 24 Mar 1821 Ste-Madeleine-de-Riguad, Quebec, at age 2 (Ibid., #2682214.). He was buried on 25 Mar 1821 Ste-Madeleine-de-Riguad, Quebec *(father's occupation: day laborer)* (PRDH online, #2682214.).

    132   iii.   Arsene Clement Sabourin, b. 14 Aug 1821; m. Mare Adelaide Patry or Patrice.

    iv.   Clemence Tarsile Sabourin was born on 22 Sep 1824 (Ibid., #2681410.). She was baptized on 22 Sep 1824 Ste-Madeleine-de-Riguad, Quebec *(father's occupation: day laborer)* (PRDH online, #2681410.). She died on 2 Jun 1840 Ste-Madeleine-de-Riguad, Quebec, at age 15 (Ibid., #4624041.). She was buried on 4 Jun 1840 Ste-Madeleine-de-Riguad, Quebec (Ibid.).

    v.   Marie Mathilde Sabourin was born on 5 Nov 1826 (Ibid., #4617442.). She was baptized on 6 Nov 1826 Ste-Madeleine-de-Riguad, Quebec (Ibid.).

        She was in the census household of Charles Sabourin and Madeleine Lalande dit Latreille or Lalonde in 1852 Ste.Madeleine, Rigaud, Vaudreuil, Quebec (1852C Cdn Transcription Project, District 536, page 2d, 3a, (5), line 31-33.).

    vi.   Hyacinthe Sabourin was born on 29 Jan 1829 (PRDH online, #4617875.). He was baptized on 30 Jan 1829 Ste-Madeleine-de-Riguad, Quebec (Ibid.).

    vii.   Antoine Severe Sabourin was born on 12 May 1831 (Ibid., #4618362.). He was baptized on 13 May 1831 Ste-Madeleine-de-Riguad, Quebec (Ibid.).

46. **Marie Anne Sabourin** was born on 11 Oct 1794 Quinchien, Riviere-a-la-Graisse, Quebec (Ibid., #642546.). She was baptized on 12 Oct 1794 Oka, Quebec (Ibid.). She married **Jacques Charbonneau**, son of **Joseph Charbonneau** and **Marguerite Proulx,** on 12 Jun 1815 Ste-Madeleine-de-Riguad, Quebec (Ibid., #2219255.). She married **Louis Brunet**, son of **Michel Brunet** and **Genevieve Jerome dit Latour,** on 30 Sep 1833 (Mirabel), Ste-Scholastique, Quebec (Ibid., #3477455.).

She was in the census household of **Benjamin Luc Charbonneau** in 1852 Ste.Madeleine, Rigaud, Vaudreuil, Quebec (1852C Cdn Transcription Project, District 536, page 9d, 10a, (19), line 31-33.).

Jacques Charbonneau was born on 29 May 1792 St-Eustache, Quebec (PRDH online, #627825.) He was baptized on 29 May 1792 St-Eustache, Quebec (Ibid.). He died on 11 Aug 1832 (Mirabel), Ste-Scholastique, Quebec, at age 40 (Ibid., #4560948.). He was buried on 12 Aug 1832 (Mirabel), Ste-Scholastique, Quebec *(age 42, husband of Marie Anne Sabourin)* (PRDH online, #4560948.).

Children of **Marie Anne Sabourin** and **Jacques Charbonneau** were as follows:

      i.   Joseph Charbonneau was born on 26 Apr 1816 St-Benoit, Quebec (Ibid., #2515057.). He was baptized on 26 Apr 1816 St-Benoit, Quebec *(father's occupation: laborer)* (PRDH online, #2515057.).

     ii.   Marie Sophie Charbonneau was born on 22 Jan 1818 St-Benoit, Quebec (Ibid., #2515453.). She was baptized on 22 Jan 1818 St-Benoit, Quebec *(father's occupation: laborer)* (PRDH online, #2515453.).

   iii.   Marie Victoire Charbonneau was born on 24 Mar 1819 St-Benoit, Quebec (Ibid., #2515799.). She was baptized on 24 Mar 1819 St-Benoit, Quebec *(father's occupation: laborer)* (PRDH online, #2515799.). She died on 6 Aug 1819 Ste-Madeleine-de-Riguad, Quebec (Ibid., #2682117.). She was buried on 7 Aug 1819 Ste-Madeleine-de-Riguad, Quebec *(age 4 months, father's occupation: carpenter)* (PRDH online, #2682117.).

   iv.   Marie Victoire Charbonneau was born on 3 Jun 1820 Ste-Madeleine-de-Riguad, Quebec (Ibid., #2680766.). She was baptized on 4 Jun 1820 Ste-Madeleine-de-Riguad, Quebec *(father's occupation: day laborer)* (PRDH online, #2680766.). She died on 13 Jun 1821 Ste-Madeleine-de-Riguad, Quebec, at age 1 (Ibid., #2682229.). She was buried on 14 Jun 1821 Ste-Madeleine-de-Riguad, Quebec *(father's occupation: day laborer)* (PRDH online, #2682229.).

133   v.   Benjamin Luc Charbonneau, b. 24 Apr 1822 St-Benoit, Quebec; m. Virginie Belec.

    vi.   Angele Charbonneau was born on 9 Feb 1824 St-Benoit, Quebec (Ibid., #2517334.). She was baptized on 9 Feb 1824 St-Benoit, Quebec *(father's occupation: laborer)* (PRDH online, #2517334.). She died on 31 Jul 1825 St-Benoit, Quebec, at age 1 (Ibid., #4671855.). She was buried on 2 Aug 1825 St-Benoit, Quebec *(age 18 months)* (PRDH online, #4671855.).

   vii.   Ester Charbonneau was born on 17 Oct 1825 (Mirabel), Ste-Scholastique, Quebec (Ibid., #4666508.). She was baptized on 18 Oct 1825 St-Benoit, Quebec (Ibid.).

  viii.   Josephte Charbonneau was born on 2 Jun 1827 (Mirabel), Ste-Scholastique, Quebec (Ibid., #4554478.). She was baptized on 3 Jun 1827 (Mirabel), Ste-Scholastique, Quebec (Ibid.).

134   ix.   Virginie Charbonneau, b. 12 Oct 1829 (Mirabel), Ste-Scholastique, Quebec; m. Francois Xavier Rouleau; d. 2 Jan 1849 Ste-Anne-du-Grand-Calumet, Quebec; bur. 4 Jan 1849 Ste-Anne-du-Grand-Calumet, Quebec.

    x.   Alexandre Charbonneau was born on 17 Aug 1831 (Mirabel), Ste-Scholastique, Quebec (Ibid., #4555514.). He was baptized on 18 Aug 1831 (Mirabel), Ste-Scholastique, Quebec (Ibid.). He died on 17 Aug 1832 (Mirabel), Ste-Scholastique, Quebec, at age 1 (Ibid., #4560980.). He was buried on 18 Aug 1832 (Mirabel), Ste-Scholastique, Quebec *(age 11 months)* (PRDH online, #4560980.).

Louis Brunet was baptized on 17 Jul 1780 (Pierrefonds), Ste-Genevieve, Quebec (Ibid., #660716.). He was born on 17 Jul 1780 (Pierrefonds), Ste-Genevieve, Quebec (Ibid.). He married **Marguerite Massy**, daughter of **Francois Massy** and **Marie Celeste Daragon,** on 15 Feb 1802 (Pierrefonds), Ste-Genevieve, Quebec (Ibid., #2225137.). He married **Therese Laperle** on 22 Feb 1830 (Mirabel), Ste-Scholastique, Quebec (Ibid., #3475808.).

Children of **Marie Anne Sabourin** and **Louis Brunet** were:

      i.   Alexandre Brunet was born on 30 Jun 1834 (Mirabel), Ste-Scholastique, Quebec (Ibid., #4556479.). He was baptized on 1 Jul 1834 (Mirabel), Ste-Scholastique, Quebec (Ibid.). He died on 26 Apr 1838 (Mirabel), Ste-Scholastique, Quebec, at age 3 (Ibid., #4561670.). He was buried on 28 Apr 1838 (Mirabel), Ste-Scholastique, Quebec (Ibid.).

47. Paul Sabourin was born on 3 Jun 1797 Vaudreuil, Quebec (Ibid., #642709.). He was baptized on 4 Jun 1797 Oka, Quebec (Ibid.). He married **Marie Anne Leblanc**, daughter of **Jean Baptiste Leblanc dit Lacombe** and **Marie Charlotte Deloge dit Poirier,** on 22 Nov 1819 Ste-Madeleine-de-Riguad, Quebec (Ibid., #2219868.).

He and **Marie Anne Leblanc** were enumerated in the census in 1852 Ste.Madeleine, Rigaud, Vaudreuil, Quebec. Also in the family: **Paul Desire Sabourin, Marie Julie Brunet, Noel Sabourin, Virginie Sabourin, Mathilde Sabourin, Marie Melina Sabourin, Marie Angele Sabourin, Napoleon Sabourin, Theophile Sabourin, Julie Sabourin,** and **Josephine Sabourin** *(Sabourin, Paul, Journalier, Rigaud, Catholique, 55, M; Leblanc, Marie, Vaudreuil, Catholique, 52, F; Sabourin, Désire, Rigaud, Catholique, 31, M; Brunet, Julie, Rigaud, Catholique, 23, F; Sabourin, Noël, Rigaud, Catholique, 20, M; Sabourin, Virginie, Rigaud, Catholique, 23, F; Sabourin, Mathilde, Rigaud, Catholique, 22, F; Sabourin, Mélina, Rigaud, Catholique, 17, F; Sabourin, Angèle, Rigaud, Catholique, 13, F; Sabourin, Napoléon, Rigaud, Catholique, 8, M; Sabourin, Théophile, Rigaud, Catholique, 5, M; Sabourin, Julie, Rigaud, Catholique, 3, F; Sabourin, Josephine, Rigaud, Catholique, 1, F)* (1852C Cdn Transcription Project, District 536, page 50d, 51a, (101), line 5-17.).

Marie Anne Leblanc was born on 20 Apr 1801 Vaudreuil, Quebec (PRDH online, #2589911.). She was baptized on 20 Apr 1801 Vaudreuil, Quebec (Ibid.).

Children of **Paul Sabourin** and **Marie Anne Leblanc** all born Ste-Madeleine-de-Riguad, Quebec, were as follows:

135   i.   Marie Julienne Sabourin, b. 21 Jul 1820; m. Antoine Gagnon.

136   ii.   Paul Desire Sabourin, b. 21 Jul 1821; m. Marie Julie Brunet.

137   iii.   Edouard Sabourin, b. 6 Feb 1823; m. Marie Arline Brunet dit Letang.

138   iv.   Marie Rose Adele Sabourin, b. 21 Mar 1825.

       v.   Barnabe Sabourin was born on 7 Sep 1826 (Ibid., #4617417.). He was baptized on 8 Sep 1826 Ste-Madeleine-de-Riguad, Quebec (Ibid.).

       vi.   Virginie Sabourin was born on 6 May 1828 (Ibid., #4617729.). She was baptized on 7 May 1828 Ste-Madeleine-de-Riguad, Quebec (Ibid.).

           She was in the census household of Paul Sabourin and Marie Anne Leblanc in 1852 Ste.Madeleine, Rigaud, Vaudreuil, Quebec (1852C Cdn Transcription Project, District 536, page 50d, 51a, (101), line 5-17.).

       vii.   Mathilde Sabourin was born on 18 Mar 1830 (PRDH online, #4618087.). She was baptized on 18 Mar 1830 Ste-Madeleine-de-Riguad, Quebec (Ibid.).

           She was in the census household of Paul Sabourin and Marie Anne Leblanc in 1852 Ste.Madeleine, Rigaud, Vaudreuil, Quebec (1852C Cdn Transcription Project, District 536, page 50d, 51a, (101), line 5-17.).

       viii.   Noel Sabourin was born on 25 Dec 1831 (PRDH online, #4618503.). He was baptized on 26 Dec 1831 Ste-Madeleine-de-Riguad, Quebec (Ibid.).

           He was in the census household of Paul Sabourin and Marie Anne Leblanc in 1852 Ste.Madeleine, Rigaud, Vaudreuil, Quebec (1852C Cdn Transcription Project, District 536, page 50d, 51a, (101), line 5-17.).

       ix.   Francois Anthyme Sabourin was born on 20 Aug 1833 (PRDH online, #4618952.). He was baptized on 21 Aug 1833 Ste-Madeleine-de-Riguad, Quebec (Ibid.). He died on 20 Nov 1834 Ste-Madeleine-de-Riguad, Quebec, at age 1 (Ibid., #4623560.). He was buried on 21 Nov 1834 Ste-Madeleine-de-Riguad, Quebec *(age 15 months)* (PRDH online, #4623560.).

       x.   Marie Melina Sabourin was born on 30 Apr 1835 (Ibid., #4619352.). She was baptized on 30 Apr 1835 Ste-Madeleine-de-Riguad, Quebec (Ibid.).

           She was in the census household of Paul Sabourin and Marie Anne Leblanc in 1852 Ste.Madeleine, Rigaud, Vaudreuil, Quebec (1852C Cdn Transcription Project, District 536, page 50d, 51a, (101), line 5-17.).

       xi.   Marie Angele Sabourin was born on 20 Feb 1838 (PRDH online, #4620083.). She was baptized on 22 Feb 1838 Ste-Madeleine-de-Riguad, Quebec (Ibid.).

           She was in the census household of Paul Sabourin and Marie Anne Leblanc in 1852 Ste.Madeleine, Rigaud, Vaudreuil, Quebec (1852C Cdn Transcription Project, District 536, page 50d, 51a, (101), line 5-17.).

       xii.   Gilbert Sabourin was born on 10 Oct 1839 (PRDH online, #4620511.). He was baptized on 11 Oct 1839 Ste-Madeleine-de-Riguad, Quebec (Ibid.).

       xiii.   Andre Paul Sabourin was born on 28 Nov 1841 (Ibid., #4621017.). He was baptized on 28 Nov 1841 Ste-Madeleine-de-Riguad, Quebec (Ibid.).

       xiv.   Napoleon Sabourin was born on 28 Aug 1843 (Ibid., #4621440.). He was baptized on 28 Aug 1843 Ste-Madeleine-de-Riguad, Quebec (Ibid.).

           He was in the census household of Paul Sabourin and Marie Anne Leblanc in 1852 Ste.Madeleine, Rigaud, Vaudreuil, Quebec (1852C Cdn Transcription Project, District 536, page 50d, 51a, (101), line 5-17.).

48. **Marie Sabourin** was born on 24 Sep 1798 Oka, Quebec (PRDH online, #774126.). She was baptized on 24 Sep 1798 Oka, Quebec (Ibid.). She married **Pierre Joseph Gabrion**, son of **Joseph Gabrion dit St.Laurent** and **Marie Angelique Therese Cerat dit Coquillard,** on 22 Feb 1819 Ste-Madeleine-de-Riguad, Quebec (Ibid., #2219832.).

Pierre Joseph Gabrion was born on 24 Mar 1785 Les Cedres, Quebec (Ibid., #609478.). He was baptized on 24 Mar 1785 Les Cedres, Quebec (Ibid.). He married **Charlotte Picard dit Noiret**, daughter of **Louis Alexandre Picard dit Noiret** and **Marie Josephe Martin dit St.Jean,** on 21 Jan 1811 Les Cedres, Quebec (Ibid.).

Children of **Marie Sabourin** and **Pierre Joseph Gabrion** were as follows:

i. Marie Clemence Clothilde Gabrion was born on 11 Dec 1819 Vaudreuil, Quebec (Ibid., #2591656.). She was baptized on 13 Dec 1819 Vaudreuil, Quebec (Ibid.). She died on 27 Nov 1820 Ste-Madeleine-de-Riguad, Quebec (Ibid., #2682189.). She was buried on 29 Nov 1820 Ste-Madeleine-de-Riguad, Quebec *(age 11 months, father's occupation: usher)* (PRDH online, #2682189.).

ii. Pierre Joseph Alexandre Philippe Gabrion was born on 30 Jan 1821 Ste-Madeleine-de-Riguad, Quebec (Ibid., #2680842.). He was baptized on 30 Jan 1821 Ste-Madeleine-de-Riguad, Quebec *(father's occupation: usher)* (PRDH online, #2680842.). He married Marie Angele Bray, daughter of Guillaume Bray and Marie Josephe Lalonde, on 14 Jun 1842 Les Cedres, Quebec (Ibid., #3459828.). He married Henriette Henault dit Deschamps, daughter of Louis Henault dit Deschamps and Marie Josephe Leger dit Parisien, on 9 Nov 1846 St-Polycarpe, Quebec (Ibid., #3468563.).

   Marie Angele Bray was born on 3 Jun 1821 Les Cedres, Quebec (Ibid., #2676026.). She was baptized on 3 Jun 1821 Les Cedres, Quebec (Ibid.). She died on 21 Nov 1845 Les Cedres, Quebec, at age 24 (Ibid., #4414619.). She was buried on 24 Nov 1845 Les Cedres, Quebec *(age 20, wife of Alex Gabrion)* (PRDH online, #4414619.).

   Henriette Henault dit Deschamps was born on 29 May 1818 Les Cedres, Quebec (Ibid., #756519.). She was baptized on 30 May 1818 Les Cedres, Quebec (Ibid.). She married **Francois Benoit dit Laguerre**, son of **Francois Benoit** and **Marie Louise Tenasse dit Poulin,** on 25 Oct 1836 St-Polycarpe, Quebec (Ibid., #3464312.).

iii. Amedee Gabrion was born on 15 May 1822 Les Cedres, Quebec (Ibid., #2676196.). He was baptized on 16 May 1822 Les Cedres, Quebec *(father's occupation: usher)* (PRDH online, #2676196.). He died on 30 Aug 1823 Les Cedres, Quebec, at age 1 (Ibid., #2678622.). He was buried on 1 Sep 1823 Les Cedres, Quebec *(He was called Pierre Julien, age 16 months)* (PRDH online, #2678622.).

iv. Marie Clemence Elmire Gabrion was born on 20 Dec 1823 Les Cedres, Quebec (Ibid., #2676515.). She was baptized on 21 Dec 1823 Les Cedres, Quebec *(father's occupation: usher)* (PRDH online, #2676515.). She died on 26 Dec 1824 Les Cedres, Quebec, at age 1 (Ibid., #2678728.). She was buried on 27 Dec 1824 Les Cedres, Quebec *(father's occupation: usher)* (PRDH online, #2678728.).

v. Marie Clemence Leocadie Gabrion was born on 31 May 1825 Les Cedres, Quebec (Ibid., #4410001.). She was baptized on 31 May 1825 Les Cedres, Quebec (Ibid.). She died on 11 Oct 1826 Les Cedres, Quebec, at age 1 (Ibid., #4413380.). She was buried on 13 Oct 1826 Les Cedres, Quebec (Ibid.).

vi. Marie Gabrion was born on 14 Jan 1827 Les Cedres, Quebec (Ibid., #4410325.). She was baptized on 15 Jan 1827 Les Cedres, Quebec (Ibid.). She died on 15 Aug 1828 Les Cedres, Quebec, at age 1 (Ibid., #4413525.). She was buried on 18 Aug 1828 Les Cedres, Quebec *(age 19 months)* (PRDH online, #4413525.).

vii. Anonyme Gabrion was born on 22 Jan 1829 Les Cedres, Quebec (Ibid., #4413543.). He/she died on 22 Jan 1829 Les Cedres, Quebec (Ibid.). He/she was buried on 22 Jan 1829 Les Cedres, Quebec (Ibid.).

viii. Marie Virginie Gabrion was born on 26 Dec 1829 Les Cedres, Quebec (Ibid., #4410900.). She was baptized on 27 Dec 1829 Les Cedres, Quebec (Ibid.). She died on 8 Jan 1831 Les Cedres, Quebec, at age 1 (Ibid., #4413678.). She was buried on 10 Jan 1831 Les Cedres, Quebec (Ibid.).

ix. Pierre Joseph Gabrion was born on 24 Jul 1831 Les Cedres, Quebec (Ibid., #4411207.). He was baptized on 25 Jul 1831 Les Cedres, Quebec (Ibid.). He died on 5 Aug 1832 Les Cedres, Quebec, at age 1 (Ibid., #4413926.). He was buried on 7 Aug 1832 Les Cedres, Quebec (Ibid.).

x. Pierre Joseph Gabrion was born on 28 Dec 1832 Les Cedres, Quebec (Ibid., #4411512.). He was baptized on 28 Dec 1832 Les Cedres, Quebec (Ibid.). He died on 23 Dec 1835 Les Cedres, Quebec, at age 2 (Ibid., #4414174.). He was buried on 24 Dec 1835 Les Cedres, Quebec (Ibid.).

xi. Pierre Joseph Marc Aurelle Gabrion was born on 5 Aug 1836 Les Cedres, Quebec (Ibid., #4411916.). He was baptized on 5 Aug 1836 Les Cedres, Quebec (Ibid.). He died on 17 Nov 1848 St-Polycarpe, Quebec, at age 12 (Ibid., #4459731.). He was buried on 20 Nov 1848 St-Polycarpe, Quebec (Ibid.).

xii. Marie Elmire Leocadie Gabrion was born on 14 Nov 1838 Les Cedres, Quebec (Ibid., #4412133.). She was baptized on 14 Nov 1838 Les Cedres, Quebec (Ibid.).

49. **Francois Xavier Sabourin** was born on 12 Jan 1801 Oka, Quebec (Ibid., #2752191.). He was baptized on 12 Jan 1801 Oka, Quebec (Ibid.). He married **Marie Anne Chantal Rocbrune**, daughter of **Pierre Couillaud dit Larocque or Larocquebrune** and **Marie Anne Servant,** on 11 Jan 1819 Ste-Madeleine-de-Riguad, Quebec (Ibid., #2219775.). He died on 26 Apr 1822 at age 21 (Ibid., #2682283.). He was buried on 18 May 1822 Ste-Madeleine-de-Riguad, Quebec *(drowned, a carpenter, husband of Marie Rocbrune)* (PRDH online, #2682283.).

Marie Anne Chantal Rocbrune was baptized on 30 May 1794 Oka, Quebec (Ibid., #642516.). She married **Pierre Henault** on 18 Jun 1827 Ste-Madeleine-de-Riguad, Quebec (Ibid., #3460527.).

Children of **Francois Xavier Sabourin** and **Marie Anne Chantal Rocbrune** both born Ste-Madeleine-de-Riguad, Quebec, were as follows:

  139 i. Francois Charles Sabourin, b. 27 Sep 1819; m. Marie Marguerite Hamelin.
  140 ii. Pierre Clement Sabourin, b. 16 Apr 1821; m. Marguerite Deguire.

50. **Catherine Sabourin** was born on 30 Oct 1805 Ste-Madeleine-de-Riguad, Quebec (Ibid., #2679307.). She was baptized on 30 Oct 1805 Ste-Madeleine-de-Riguad, Quebec *(father's occupation: day laborer)* (PRDH online, #2679307.). She married **Thomas Armstrong**, son of **Thomas Armstrong** and **Hypollite Veldun,** on 24 Jan 1825 Ste-Madeleine-de-Riguad, Quebec (Ibid., #3459587.). She died on 13 Feb 1845 Les Cedres, Quebec, at age 39 (Ibid., #4414586.). She was buried on 15 Feb 1845 Les Cedres, Quebec *(age 38, wife of Thomas Armstrong)* (PRDH online, #4414586.).

Thomas Armstrong was born circa 1800.

Children of **Catherine Sabourin** and **Thomas Armstrong** all born Les Cedres, Quebec, were as follows:

  i. Louis Thomas Armstrong was born on 18 Nov 1825 (Ibid., #4410107.). He was baptized on 18 Nov 1825 Les Cedres, Quebec (Ibid.). He died on 19 Aug 1826 Les Cedres, Quebec (Ibid., #4413367.). He was buried on 20 Aug 1826 Les Cedres, Quebec *(age 9 months)* (PRDH online, #4413367.).

  ii. Francois Thomas Armstrong was born on 16 May 1827 (Ibid., #4410399.). He was baptized on 17 May 1827 Les Cedres, Quebec (Ibid.). He died on 18 Jan 1829 Les Cedres, Quebec, at age 1 (Ibid., #4413541.). He was buried on 20 Jan 1829 Les Cedres, Quebec *(age 20 months)* (PRDH online, #4413541.).

  iii. Marie Catherine Armstrong was born on 29 Oct 1828 (Ibid., #4410705.). She was baptized on 29 Oct 1828 Les Cedres, Quebec (Ibid.). She died on 28 Aug 1830 Les Cedres, Quebec, at age 1 (Ibid., #4413649.). She was buried on 30 Aug 1830 Les Cedres, Quebec (Ibid.).

  iv. Marie Marguerite Armstrong was born on 26 Feb 1830 (Ibid., #4410934.). She was baptized on 26 Feb 1830 Les Cedres, Quebec (Ibid.). She died on 16 Aug 1830 Les Cedres, Quebec (Ibid., #4413641.). She was buried on 17 Aug 1830 Les Cedres, Quebec (Ibid.).

  v. Marie Josephte Armstrong was born on 6 Jun 1831 (Ibid., #4411185.). She was baptized on 6 Jun 1831 Les Cedres, Quebec (Ibid.).

  vi. Louis Thomas Armstrong was born on 9 Mar 1835 (Ibid., #4411770.). He was baptized on 10 Mar 1835 Les Cedres, Quebec (Ibid.). He died on 21 Jul 1836 Les Cedres, Quebec, at age 1 (Ibid., #4414196.). He was buried on 22 Jul 1836 Les Cedres, Quebec *(age 16 months)* (PRDH online, #4414196.).

  vii. Marie Louise Armstrong was born on 16 May 1837 (Ibid., #4411996.). She was baptized on 16 May 1837 Les Cedres, Quebec (Ibid.).

  viii. Mathilde Armstrong was born on 26 Jan 1839 (Ibid., #4412166.). She was baptized on 26 Jan 1839 Les Cedres, Quebec (Ibid.).

  ix. Jean Narcisse Armstrong was born on 23 Feb 1841 (Ibid., #4412366.). He was baptized on 23 Feb 1841 Les Cedres, Quebec (Ibid.).

  x. Adelaide Armstrong was born on 25 Feb 1843 (Ibid., #4412571.). She was baptized on 25 Feb 1843 Les Cedres, Quebec (Ibid.). She died on 24 Dec 1843 Les Cedres, Quebec (Ibid., #4414542.). She was buried on 26 Dec 1843 Les Cedres, Quebec *(age 10 months)* (PRDH online, #4414542.).

  xi. Joseph Armstrong was born on 11 Feb 1845 (Ibid., #4414585.). He died on 11 Feb 1845 Les Cedres, Quebec (Ibid.). He was buried on 12 Feb 1845 Les Cedres, Quebec (Ibid.).

51. **Jean Baptiste Sabourin** was born on 3 Oct 1804 (Ibid., #2679236.). He was baptized on 24 Oct 1804 Ste-Madeleine-de-Riguad, Quebec (Ibid.). He married **Julie Eugenie Denomme**, daughter of **Joseph Denomme** and **Eugenie Robillard,** on 7 Feb 1831 Ste-Madeleine-de-Riguad, Quebec (Ibid., #3461946.).

Julie Eugenie Denomme was born on 25 Dec 1811 Ste-Madeleine-de-Riguad, Quebec (Ibid., #2679835.). She was baptized on 25 Dec 1811 Ste-Madeleine-de-Riguad, Quebec *(father's occupation: agriculture)* (PRDH online, #2679835.).

Children of **Jean Baptiste Sabourin** and **Julie Eugenie Denomme** were as follows:

    i. Jean Baptiste Sabourin was born on 26 Dec 1831 Ste-Madeleine-de-Riguad, Quebec (Ibid., #4618502.). He was baptized on 26 Dec 1831 Ste-Madeleine-de-Riguad, Quebec (Ibid.). He died on 10 Jan 1832 Ste-Madeleine-de-Riguad, Quebec (Ibid., #4623180.). He was buried on 11 Jan 1832 Ste-Madeleine-de-Riguad, Quebec *(age 15 days)* (PRDH online, #4623180.).

    ii. Emelie Sabourin was born on 10 Nov 1834 Ste-Madeleine-de-Riguad, Quebec (Ibid., #4619244.). She was baptized on 10 Nov 1834 Ste-Madeleine-de-Riguad, Quebec (Ibid.).

    iii. Paul Sabourin was born on 30 Mar 1837 Ste-Madeleine-de-Riguad, Quebec (Ibid., #4619904.). He was baptized on 31 Mar 1837 Ste-Madeleine-de-Riguad, Quebec (Ibid.). He died on 24 Mar 1838 Ste-Madeleine-de-Riguad, Quebec (Ibid., #4623832.). He was buried on 26 Mar 1838 Ste-Madeleine-de-Riguad, Quebec (Ibid.).

    iv. Jean Baptiste Sabourin was born on 4 Apr 1839 Ste-Madeleine-de-Riguad, Quebec (Ibid., #4620380.). He was baptized on 5 Apr 1839 Ste-Madeleine-de-Riguad, Quebec (Ibid.).

    v. Isidore Sabourin was born on 9 Apr 1841 Ste-Madeleine-de-Riguad, Quebec (Ibid., #4620872.). He was baptized on 10 Apr 1841 Ste-Madeleine-de-Riguad, Quebec (Ibid.). He died on 14 Mar 1842 Ste-Madeleine-de-Riguad, Quebec (Ibid., #4624235.). He was buried on 17 Mar 1842 Ste-Madeleine-de-Riguad, Quebec *(age 11 months)* (PRDH online, #4624235.).

    vi. Marie Philomene Sabourin was born on 22 Apr 1843 Ste-Madeleine-de-Riguad, Quebec (Ibid., #4621351.). She was baptized on 22 Apr 1843 Ste-Madeleine-de-Riguad, Quebec (Ibid.).

    vii. George Sabourin was born on 27 Oct 1844 Ste-Marthe, Quebec (Ibid., #4723617.). He was baptized on 27 Oct 1844 Ste-Marthe, Quebec (Ibid.).

52. Marie Sabourin was born on 28 Sep 1803 Vaudreuil, Quebec (Ibid., #2590181.). She was baptized on 28 Sep 1803 Vaudreuil, Quebec (Ibid.). She married **Jean Baptiste Tessier dit Lavigne**, son of **Jean Baptiste Tessier dit Lavigne** and **Marie Archange Picard,** on 26 Feb 1827 Ste-Madeleine-de-Riguad, Quebec (Ibid., #3460488.).

Jean Baptiste Tessier dit Lavigne was born on 17 Apr 1801 Notre-Dame-de-Montreal, Quebec (Ibid., #2453599.). He was baptized on 17 Apr 1801 Notre-Dame-de-Montreal, Quebec *(father's occupation: tanner)* (PRDH online, #2453599.).

Children of **Marie Sabourin** and **Jean Baptiste Tessier dit Lavigne** all born Ste-Madeleine-de-Riguad, Quebec, were as follows:

    i. Anonyme Tessier was born on 30 Dec 1827 (Ibid., #4622870.). She died on 30 Dec 1827 Ste-Madeleine-de-Riguad, Quebec (Ibid.). She was buried on 31 Dec 1827 Ste-Madeleine-de-Riguad, Quebec (Ibid.).

    ii. Scholastique Tessier was born on 12 Jun 1830 (Ibid., #4618128.). She was baptized on 12 Jun 1830 Ste-Madeleine-de-Riguad, Quebec (Ibid.).

    iii. Marie Theophile Adelphine Tessier was born on 14 Feb 1832 (Ibid., #4618543.). She was baptized on 14 Feb 1832 Ste-Madeleine-de-Riguad, Quebec (Ibid.). She died on 13 May 1849 Ste-Madeleine-de-Riguad, Quebec, at age 17 (Ibid., #4624726.). She was buried on 15 May 1849 Ste-Madeleine-de-Riguad, Quebec (Ibid.).

    iv. Emelie Tessier was born on 9 Nov 1834 (Ibid., #4619242.). She was baptized on 9 Nov 1834 Ste-Madeleine-de-Riguad, Quebec (Ibid.).

    v. Marie Philomene Tessier dit Lavigne was born on 3 Apr 1837 (Ibid., #4619907.). She was baptized on 4 Apr 1837 Ste-Madeleine-de-Riguad, Quebec (Ibid.).

    vi. Moyse Tessier was born on 24 Feb 1839 (Ibid., #4620343.). He was baptized on 25 Feb 1839 Ste-Madeleine-de-Riguad, Quebec (Ibid.).

    vii. Marie Onesime Tessier dit Lavigne was born on 14 Jan 1841 (Ibid., #4620793.). She was baptized on 14 Jan 1841 Ste-Madeleine-de-Riguad, Quebec (Ibid.). She died on 18 Mar 1842 Ste-Madeleine-de-Riguad, Quebec, at age 1 (Ibid., #4624237.). She was buried on 20 Mar 1842 Ste-Madeleine-de-Riguad, Quebec *(age 14 months)* (PRDH online, #4624237.).

    viii. Janvier Alzire Tessier was born on 8 Aug 1845 (Ibid., #4621878.). He was baptized on 9 Aug 1845 Ste-Madeleine-de-Riguad, Quebec (Ibid.).

53. Francois Xavier Sabourin was born on 14 Dec 1806 Ste-Madeleine-de-Riguad, Quebec (Ibid., #2679386.). He was baptized on 14 Dec 1806 Ste-Madeleine-de-Riguad, Quebec *(father's occupation: agriculture)* (PRDH online, #2679386.). He married **Marie Mathilde Domitilde Thauvette**, daughter of **Joseph Thauvette dit Sansoucy** and

Josephe Seguin, on 12 Jan 1835 Ste-Madeleine-de-Riguad, Quebec (Ibid., #3463261.). He married **Sophie Gareau**, daughter of **Antoine Gareau** and **Marie Berlinguet,** on 19 Feb 1844 Ste-Madeleine-de-Riguad, Quebec (Ibid., #3465936.).

 He and **Sophie Gareau** were enumerated in the census in 1852 Ste.Madeleine, Rigaud, Vaudreuil, Quebec. Also in the family: **Domithilde Sabourin**, **Sophie Sabourin**, **Josephine Sabourin**, **Darsino Sabourin**, and **Xavier Sabourin** *(Sabourin, Xavier, Cultivateur, Rigaud, Catholique, 45, M; Gareau, Sophie, Rigaud, Catholique, 36, F; Sabourin, Domithilde, Rigaud, Catholique, 13, F; Sabourin, Sophie, Rigaud, Catholique, 12, F; Sabourin, Joséphine, Rigaud, Catholique, 3, F; Sabourin, Darsino, Rigaud, Catholique, 2, M; Sabourin, Xavier, Rigaud, Catholique, 15 jours, M)* (1852C Cdn Transcription Project, District 536, page 27d, 28a, (55), line 18-24.).

 Marie Mathilde Domitilde Thauvette was born on 21 Feb 1818 Ste-Madeleine-de-Riguad, Quebec (PRDH online, #2680466.). She was baptized on 21 Feb 1818 Ste-Madeleine-de-Riguad, Quebec *(father's occupation: cultivator)* (PRDH online, #2680466.). She died on 22 Jun 1841 Ste-Madeleine-de-Riguad, Quebec, at age 23 (Ibid., #4624158.). She was buried on 24 Jun 1841 Ste-Madeleine-de-Riguad, Quebec *(age 22, wife of Francois Sabourin)* (PRDH online, #4624158.).

 Children of **Francois Xavier Sabourin** and **Marie Mathilde Domitilde Thauvette** both born Ste-Madeleine-de-Riguad, Quebec, were as follows:

> i. Domithilde Sabourin was born on 21 Dec 1838 (Ibid., #4620290.). She was baptized on 22 Dec 1838 Ste-Madeleine-de-Riguad, Quebec (Ibid.).
>
> She was in the census household of Francois Xavier Sabourin and Sophie Gareau in 1852 Ste.Madeleine, Rigaud, Vaudreuil, Quebec (1852C Cdn Transcription Project, District 536, page 27d, 28a, (55), line 18-24.).
>
> ii. Sophie Sabourin was born on 17 Apr 1840 (PRDH online, #4620616.). She was baptized on 17 Apr 1840 Ste-Madeleine-de-Riguad, Quebec (Ibid.).
>
> She was in the census household of Francois Xavier Sabourin and Sophie Gareau in 1852 Ste.Madeleine, Rigaud, Vaudreuil, Quebec (1852C Cdn Transcription Project, District 536, page 27d, 28a, (55), line 18-24.).

 Sophie Gareau was born on 31 Mar 1816 Vaudreuil, Quebec (Ibid.) (PRDH online, #2591305.). She was baptized on 31 Mar 1816 Vaudreuil, Quebec (Ibid.).

 Children of **Francois Xavier Sabourin** and **Sophie Gareau** were as follows:

> i. Marie Julie Sabourin was born on 14 Dec 1844 Ste-Madeleine-de-Riguad, Quebec (Ibid., #4621724.). She was baptized on 16 Dec 1844 Ste-Madeleine-de-Riguad, Quebec (Ibid.). She died on 25 Aug 1845 Ste-Madeleine-de-Riguad, Quebec (Ibid., #4624510.). She was buried on 26 Aug 1845 Ste-Madeleine-de-Riguad, Quebec *(age 8 months)* (PRDH online, #4624510.).
>
> ii. Francois Xavier Alphonse Sabourin was born on 29 Dec 1845 Ste-Madeleine-de-Riguad, Quebec (Ibid., #4621960.). He was baptized on 29 Dec 1845 Ste-Madeleine-de-Riguad, Quebec (Ibid.). He died on 9 May 1847 Ste-Madeleine-de-Riguad, Quebec, at age 1 (Ibid., #4624607.). He was buried on 10 May 1847 Ste-Madeleine-de-Riguad, Quebec *(age 17 months)* (PRDH online, #4624607.).
>
> iii. Julie Sabourin was born on 10 Feb 1847 Ste-Madeleine-de-Riguad, Quebec (Ibid., #4622183.). She was baptized on 11 Feb 1847 Ste-Madeleine-de-Riguad, Quebec (Ibid.). She died on 25 Sep 1847 Ste-Madeleine-de-Riguad, Quebec (Ibid., #4624650.). She was buried on 27 Sep 1847 Ste-Madeleine-de-Riguad, Quebec *(age 7 months)* (PRDH online, #4624650.).
>
> iv. Josephine Sabourin was born on 6 Oct 1848 Ste-Marthe, Quebec (Ibid., #4728010.). She was baptized on 7 Oct 1848 Ste-Marthe, Quebec (Ibid.).
>
> She was in the census household of Francois Xavier Sabourin and Sophie Gareau in 1852 Ste.Madeleine, Rigaud, Vaudreuil, Quebec (1852C Cdn Transcription Project, District 536, page 27d, 28a, (55), line 18-24.).
>
> v. Darsino Sabourin was born circa 1850 (Ibid.).
>
> He was in the census household of Francois Xavier Sabourin and Sophie Gareau in 1852 Ste.Madeleine, Rigaud, Vaudreuil, Quebec (1852C Cdn Transcription Project, District 536, page 27d, 28a, (55), line 18-24.).
>
> vi. Xavier Sabourin was born circa 1852 (Ibid.).
>
> He was in the census household of Francois Xavier Sabourin and Sophie Gareau in 1852 Ste.Madeleine, Rigaud, Vaudreuil, Quebec (1852C Cdn Transcription Project, District 536, page 27d, 28a, (55), line 18-24.).

54. Marie Josephe Sabourin was born on 7 Sep 1808 Ste-Madeleine-de-Riguad, Quebec (PRDH online, #2679530.). She was baptized on 7 Sep 1808 Ste-Madeleine-de-Riguad, Quebec *(father's occupation: day laborer)* (PRDH online, #2679530.). She married **Jean Baptiste Seguin**, son of **Jean Noel Seguin** and **Marie Rocbrune,** on 18 Oct 1824 Ste-Madeleine-de-Riguad, Quebec *(Present: George Condon grandfather of the bride)* (PRDH online, #2220386.).

Jean Baptiste Seguin was born on 16 Nov 1802 Ste-Madeleine-de-Riguad, Quebec (Ibid., #2679126.). He was baptized on 16 Nov 1802 Ste-Madeleine-de-Riguad, Quebec *(father's occupation: cultivator)* (PRDH online, #2679126.).

Children of **Marie Josephe Sabourin** and **Jean Baptiste Seguin** all born Ste-Madeleine-de-Riguad, Quebec, were as follows:

    i.   Anonyme Seguin was born on 28 Jul 1825 (Ibid., #4622687.). She died on 28 Jul 1825 Ste-Madeleine-de-Riguad, Quebec (Ibid.). She was buried on 29 Jul 1825 Ste-Madeleine-de-Riguad, Quebec (Ibid.).

    ii.   Jean Baptiste Seguin was born on 23 Sep 1826 (Ibid., #4617424.). He was baptized on 23 Sep 1826 Ste-Madeleine-de-Riguad, Quebec (Ibid.). He died on 10 Jul 1827 Ste-Madeleine-de-Riguad, Quebec (Ibid., #4622830.). He was buried on 12 Jul 1827 Ste-Madeleine-de-Riguad, Quebec *(age 10 months)* (PRDH online, #4622830.).

141   iii.   Josephte Seguin, b. 2 Aug 1828; m. Pierre Poitras.

    iv.   Emery Seguin was born on 31 May 1830 (Ibid., #4618124.). He was baptized on 31 May 1830 Ste-Madeleine-de-Riguad, Quebec (Ibid.).

    v.   Gregoire Seguin was born on 20 Jan 1832 (Ibid., #4618522.). He was baptized on 20 Jan 1832 Ste-Madeleine-de-Riguad, Quebec (Ibid.). He died on 23 Jan 1832 Ste-Madeleine-de-Riguad, Quebec (Ibid., #4623184.). He was buried on 27 Jan 1832 Ste-Madeleine-de-Riguad, Quebec *(age 9 days)* (PRDH online, #4623184.).

    vi.   Joseph Seguin was born on 4 Jan 1833 (Ibid., #4618780.). He was baptized on 4 Jan 1833 Ste-Madeleine-de-Riguad, Quebec (Ibid.).

    vii.   Pierre Seguin was born on 3 May 1834 (Ibid., #4619115.). He was baptized on 3 May 1834 Ste-Madeleine-de-Riguad, Quebec (Ibid.). He died on 31 Mar 1838 Ste-Madeleine-de-Riguad, Quebec, at age 3 (Ibid., #4623835.). He was buried on 2 Apr 1838 Ste-Madeleine-de-Riguad, Quebec (Ibid.).

    viii.   Marguerite Seguin was born on 11 Jun 1835 (Ibid., #4619387.). She was baptized on 12 Jun 1835 Ste-Madeleine-de-Riguad, Quebec (Ibid.). She died on 8 Nov 1838 Ste-Madeleine-de-Riguad, Quebec, at age 3 (Ibid., #4623906.). She was buried on 10 Nov 1838 Ste-Madeleine-de-Riguad, Quebec (Ibid.).

    ix.   Henriette Seguin was born on 26 Aug 1836 (Ibid., #4619745.). She was baptized on 28 Aug 1836 Ste-Madeleine-de-Riguad, Quebec (Ibid.).

    x.   Rose Seguin was born on 17 Nov 1839 (Ibid., #4620516.). She was baptized on 18 Nov 1839 Ste-Madeleine-de-Riguad, Quebec (Ibid.).

    xi.   Marguerite Seguin was born on 9 Apr 1841 (Ibid., #4620873.). She was baptized on 10 Apr 1841 Ste-Madeleine-de-Riguad, Quebec (Ibid.).

    xii.   Joseph Alphonse Seguin was born on 22 Jan 1845 (Ibid., #4621746.). He was baptized on 23 Jan 1845 Ste-Madeleine-de-Riguad, Quebec (Ibid.).

    xiii.   Joseph Napoleon Seguin was born on 28 Jan 1847 (Ibid., #4622176.). He was baptized on 30 Jan 1847 Ste-Madeleine-de-Riguad, Quebec (Ibid.).

    xiv.   Jean Baptiste Seguin was born on 10 Nov 1848 (Ibid., #4622476.). He was baptized on 11 Nov 1848 Ste-Madeleine-de-Riguad, Quebec (Ibid.).

55. Marie Sophie Sabourin was born on 17 Oct 1819 Ste-Madeleine-de-Riguad, Quebec (Ibid., #2680675.). She was baptized on 18 Oct 1819 Ste-Madeleine-de-Riguad, Quebec *(father's occupation: day laborer)* (PRDH online, #2680675.). She married **Benjamin Corneille Seguin dit Laderoute**, son of **Jean Noel Seguin** and **Marie Rocbrune,** on 24 Nov 1834 Ste-Madeleine-de-Riguad, Quebec (Ibid., #3463229.).

She and **Benjamin Corneille Seguin dit Laderoute** were enumerated in the census in 1852 Ste.Madeleine, Rigaud, Vaudreuil, Quebec. Also in the family: **Cyprien Seguin, Francois Amedee Seguin, Luce Seguin, Moyse Seguin, Octavie Seguin, Francois Napoleon Seguin**, and **Victorine Seguin** *(Séguin, Benj., Journalier, Rigaud, Catholique, 44, M; Sabourin, Sophia, Rigaud, Catholique, 34, F; Séguin, Cyprien, Rigaud, Catholique, 15, M; Séguin, Amèdee, Rigaud, Catholique, 13, M; Séguin, Luce, Rigaud, Catholique, 11, F; Séguin, Moyse, Rigaud, Catholique, 8, M;*

Séguin, Octavie, Rigaud, Catholique, 5, F; Séguin, Napoleon, Rigaud, Catholique, 2, M; Séguin, Victorine, Rigaud, Catholique, 6M, F) (1852C Cdn Transcription Project, District 536, page 1a, (1), line 33-41.).

Benjamin Corneille Seguin dit Laderoute was born on 16 Sep 1809 Ste-Madeleine-de-Riguad, Quebec (PRDH online, #2679622.). He was baptized on 16 Sep 1809 Ste-Madeleine-de-Riguad, Quebec *(father's occupation: agriculture)* (PRDH online, #2679622.).

Children of **Marie Sophie Sabourin** and **Benjamin Corneille Seguin dit Laderoute** were as follows:

- i. Cyprien Seguin was born on 8 Jun 1836 Ste-Madeleine-de-Riguad, Quebec (Ibid., #4619665.). He was baptized on 9 Jun 1836 Ste-Madeleine-de-Riguad, Quebec (Ibid.).

   He was in the census household of Benjamin Corneille Seguin dit Laderoute and Marie Sophie Sabourin in 1852 Ste.Madeleine, Rigaud, Vaudreuil, Quebec (1852C Cdn Transcription Project, District 536, page 1a, (1), line 33-41.).

- ii. Francois Amedee Seguin was born on 18 Sep 1838 Ste-Madeleine-de-Riguad, Quebec (PRDH online, #4620227.). He was baptized on 19 Sep 1838 Ste-Madeleine-de-Riguad, Quebec (Ibid.).

   He was in the census household of Benjamin Corneille Seguin dit Laderoute and Marie Sophie Sabourin in 1852 Ste.Madeleine, Rigaud, Vaudreuil, Quebec (1852C Cdn Transcription Project, District 536, page 1a, (1), line 33-41.).

- iii. Luce Seguin was born on 13 Dec 1840 Ste-Madeleine-de-Riguad, Quebec (PRDH online, #4620769.). She was baptized on 14 Dec 1840 Ste-Madeleine-de-Riguad, Quebec (Ibid.).

   She was in the census household of Benjamin Corneille Seguin dit Laderoute and Marie Sophie Sabourin in 1852 Ste.Madeleine, Rigaud, Vaudreuil, Quebec (1852C Cdn Transcription Project, District 536, page 1a, (1), line 33-41.).

- iv. Moyse Seguin was born on 25 Apr 1843 Ste-Madeleine-de-Riguad, Quebec (PRDH online, #4621356.). He was baptized on 25 Apr 1843 Ste-Madeleine-de-Riguad, Quebec (Ibid.).

   He was in the census household of Benjamin Corneille Seguin dit Laderoute and Marie Sophie Sabourin in 1852 Ste.Madeleine, Rigaud, Vaudreuil, Quebec (1852C Cdn Transcription Project, District 536, page 1a, (1), line 33-41.).

- v. Octavie Seguin was born on 13 Oct 1846 Ste-Marthe, Quebec (PRDH online, #4727839.). She was baptized on 13 Oct 1846 Ste-Marthe, Quebec (Ibid.).

   She was in the census household of Benjamin Corneille Seguin dit Laderoute and Marie Sophie Sabourin in 1852 Ste.Madeleine, Rigaud, Vaudreuil, Quebec (1852C Cdn Transcription Project, District 536, page 1a, (1), line 33-41.).

- vi. Francois Napoleon Seguin was born on 24 May 1849 Ste-Madeleine-de-Riguad, Quebec (PRDH online, #4622554.). He was baptized on 25 May 1849 Ste-Madeleine-de-Riguad, Quebec (Ibid.).

   He was in the census household of Benjamin Corneille Seguin dit Laderoute and Marie Sophie Sabourin in 1852 Ste.Madeleine, Rigaud, Vaudreuil, Quebec (1852C Cdn Transcription Project, District 536, page 1a, (1), line 33-41.).

- vii. Victorine Seguin was born circa 1851 (Ibid.).

   She was in the census household of Benjamin Corneille Seguin dit Laderoute and Marie Sophie Sabourin in 1852 Ste.Madeleine, Rigaud, Vaudreuil, Quebec (1852C Cdn Transcription Project, District 536, page 1a, (1), line 33-41.).

56. Clet Raizenne was born on 28 Feb 1806 St-Eustache, Quebec (PRDH online, #2827740.). He was baptized on 28 Feb 1806 St-Eustache, Quebec (Ibid.). He married **Rose Sophie Gauthier**, daughter of **Hyacinthe Gauthier** and **Marie Rose Lalonde,** on 7 Feb 1831 Ste-Madeleine-de-Rigaud, Quebec *(Present: Hyacinthe Gauther grandfather of the bride, both Clet and Sophie signed)* (PRDH online, #3461986.).

He and **Rose Sophie Gauthier** were enumerated in the census in 1852 Ste.Madeleine, Rigaud, Vaudreuil, Quebec. Also in the family: **Marie Antoinette Raizenne, Marie Arice Philomene Raizenne, Jean Baptiste Ignace Paschal Raizenne, Marie Rose Raizenne, Ignace Procule Raizenne, Marie Norberine Raizenne, Adrien Raizenne,** and **Guillelmine Raizenne** *(Raizenne, Clet, Notaire, St Eustache, Catholique, 45, M; Gauthier, Sophie, Rigaud, Catholique, 37, F; Raizenne, Valburge, Institutrice, Lac D. Montagne, Catholique, 17, F; Raizenne, Philomène, Cornwell, Catholique, 10, F, Raizenne, JB, Lac D. Montagne, Catholique, 13, M, Raizenne, Sophie, Lac D. Montagne, Catholique, 10, F; Raizenne, Procul, Coteau du Lac, Catholique, 8, M; Raizenne, Narbérine, Rigaud, Catholique, 6, F; Raizenne, Adrien, Rigaud, Catholique, 1, M; Raizenne, Guillelmine, Rigaud, Catholique, 4 mois, F)* (1852C Cdn Transcription Project, District 536, page 62d, 63a, (125), line 37-46.).

He was *a notary* in 1852 Ste-Madeleine-de-Rigaud, Quebec (Ibid.).

Rose Sophie Gauthier was born on 23 Sep 1814 Ste-Madeleine-de-Rigaud, Quebec (PRDH online, #2680109.). She was baptized on 24 Sep 1814 Ste-Madeleine-de-Rigaud, Quebec *(father's occupation: agriculture)* (PRDH online, #2680109.).

Children of **Clet Raizenne** and **Rose Sophie Gauthier** were as follows:

    i. Sophie Claudomire Raizenne was born on 24 Dec 1831 Oka, Quebec (Ibid., #4722176.). She was baptized on 24 Dec 1831 Oka, Quebec (Ibid.). She died on 15 Sep 1832 Oka, Quebec (Ibid., #4722460.). She was buried on 16 Sep 1832 Oka, Quebec *(age 9 months)* (PRDH online, #4722460.).

    ii. Marie Antoinette Raizenne was born on 25 Feb 1834 Oka, Quebec (Ibid., #4722197.). She was baptized on 26 Feb 1834 Oka, Quebec (Ibid.).

      She was in the census household of Clet Raizenne and Rose Sophie Gauthier in 1852 Ste.Madeleine, Rigaud, Vaudreuil, Quebec (1852C Cdn Transcription Project, District 536, page 62d, 63a, (125), line 37-46.).

    iii. Marie Arice Philomene Raizenne was born on 13 Jan 1836 Cornwall, Ontario (PRDH online, #4669241.). She was baptized on 2 Apr 1836 St-Benoit, Quebec (Ibid.).

      She was in the census household of Clet Raizenne and Rose Sophie Gauthier in 1852 Ste.Madeleine, Rigaud, Vaudreuil, Quebec (1852C Cdn Transcription Project, District 536, page 62d, 63a, (125), line 37-46.).

    iv. Jean Baptiste Ignace Paschal Raizenne was born on 30 Mar 1839 Oka, Quebec (PRDH online, #4722263.). He was baptized on 31 Mar 1839 Oka, Quebec (Ibid.).

      He was in the census household of Clet Raizenne and Rose Sophie Gauthier in 1852 Ste.Madeleine, Rigaud, Vaudreuil, Quebec (1852C Cdn Transcription Project, District 536, page 62d, 63a, (125), line 37-46.).

    v. Marie Rose Raizenne was born on 15 May 1841 Oka, Quebec (PRDH online, #4722311.). She was baptized on 16 May 1841 Oka, Quebec (Ibid.).

      She was in the census household of Clet Raizenne and Rose Sophie Gauthier in 1852 Ste.Madeleine, Rigaud, Vaudreuil, Quebec (1852C Cdn Transcription Project, District 536, page 62d, 63a, (125), line 37-46.).

    vi. Ignace Procule Raizenne was born on 3 Apr 1843 St-Ignace-de-Coteau-du-Lac, Quebec (PRDH online, #3272686.). He was baptized on 4 Apr 1843 St-Ignace-de-Coteau-du-Lac, Quebec (Ibid.).

      He was in the census household of Clet Raizenne and Rose Sophie Gauthier in 1852 Ste.Madeleine, Rigaud, Vaudreuil, Quebec (1852C Cdn Transcription Project, District 536, page 62d, 63a, (125), line 37-46.).

    vii. Marie Norberine Raizenne was born on 7 Jun 1845 Ste-Madeleine-de-Rigaud, Quebec (PRDH online, #4621833.). She was baptized on 8 Jun 1845 Ste-Madeleine-de-Rigaud, Quebec (Ibid.).

      She was in the census household of Clet Raizenne and Rose Sophie Gauthier in 1852 Ste.Madeleine, Rigaud, Vaudreuil, Quebec (1852C Cdn Transcription Project, District 536, page 62d, 63a, (125), line 37-46.).

    viii. Adrien Raizenne was born circa 1850 (Ibid.).

      He was in the census household of Clet Raizenne and Rose Sophie Gauthier in 1852 Ste.Madeleine, Rigaud, Vaudreuil, Quebec (1852C Cdn Transcription Project, District 536, page 62d, 63a, (125), line 37-46.).

    ix. Guillelmine Raizenne was born circa 1851 (Ibid.).

      She was in the census household of Clet Raizenne and Rose Sophie Gauthier in 1852 Ste.Madeleine, Rigaud, Vaudreuil, Quebec (1852C Cdn Transcription Project, District 536, page 62d, 63a, (125), line 37-46.).

57. Marie Antoinette Raizenne was born on 15 Feb 1809 St-Eustache, Quebec (PRDH online, #5682232.). She was baptized on 16 Feb 1809 St-Eustache, Quebec (Ibid.). She married **Pierre Desrivieres dit Beaubien**, son of **Pierre Robert Trottier dit Beaubien or Desrivieres** and **Henriette Pilet,** on 24 Feb 1840 St-Benoit, Quebec (Ibid., #3489280.).

She and **Pierre Desrivieres dit Beaubien** were enumerated in the census in 1852 St-Benoit, Deux Montagnes, Quebec. Also in the family: **Marie Charles Anastasie Desrivieres dit Beaubien, Pierre Francois Xavier Rodolph Desrivieres dit Beaubien, Marie Elisabeth Henriette Desrivieres dit Beaubien**, and **Marie Louise Antoinette Desrivieres** *(Des Rivières Beaubien, P. Notaire, Canada F, Catholique romaine, 41, M; Raizenne, Antoinette, Canada F, Catholique romaine, 42, F; Des Rivières, Caroline, Canada F, Catholique romaine, 11, F; Des Rivières, Adolphe, Canada F, Catholique romaine, 9, M; Des Rivières, Eliza, Canada F, Catholique romaine, 7, F; Des Rivières, Marie,*

Canada F, Catholique romaine, 4, F; Crochetière, Zoë, Canada F, Catholique romaine, 16, F) (1852C Cdn Transcription Project, District 516, page 20d, 21a, (41), line 25-31.).

Pierre Desrivieres dit Beaubien was born on 23 May 1810 Oka, Quebec (PRDH online, #2752326.). He was baptized on 24 May 1810 Oka, Quebec (Ibid.).

Children of **Marie Antoinette Raizenne** and **Pierre Desrivieres dit Beaubien** all born St-Benoit, Quebec, were as follows:

i. Marie Charles Anastasie Desrivieres dit Beaubien was born on 30 Apr 1841 (Ibid., #4670116.). She was baptized on 1 May 1841 St-Benoit, Quebec *(father's occupation: notary)* (PRDH online, #4670116.).

   She was in the census household of Pierre Desrivieres dit Beaubien and Marie Antoinette Raizenne in 1852 St-Benoit, Deux Montagnes, Quebec (1852C Cdn Transcription Project, District 516, page 20d, 21a, (41), line 25-31.).

ii. Pierre Francois Xavier Rodolph Desrivieres dit Beaubien was born on 2 Dec 1842 (PRDH online, #4670385.). He was baptized on 3 Dec 1842 St-Benoit, Quebec *(father's occupation: notary)* (PRDH online, #4670385.).

   He was in the census household of Pierre Desrivieres dit Beaubien and Marie Antoinette Raizenne in 1852 St-Benoit, Deux Montagnes, Quebec (1852C Cdn Transcription Project, District 516, page 20d, 21a, (41), line 25-31.).

iii. Marie Elisabeth Henriette Desrivieres dit Beaubien was born on 8 Jul 1844 (PRDH online, #4670663.). She was baptized on 8 Jul 1844 St-Benoit, Quebec *(father's occupation: notary public)* (PRDH online, #4670663.).

   She was in the census household of Pierre Desrivieres dit Beaubien and Marie Antoinette Raizenne in 1852 St-Benoit, Deux Montagnes, Quebec (1852C Cdn Transcription Project, District 516, page 20d, 21a, (41), line 25-31.).

iv. Marie Louise Antoinette Desrivieres was born on 18 Jun 1848 (PRDH online, #4671378.). She was baptized on 19 Jun 1848 St-Benoit, Quebec *(father's occupation: notary public)* (PRDH online, #4671378.).

   She was in the census household of Pierre Desrivieres dit Beaubien and Marie Antoinette Raizenne in 1852 St-Benoit, Deux Montagnes, Quebec (1852C Cdn Transcription Project, District 516, page 20d, 21a, (41), line 25-31.).

58. Andre Cyrille Chevrier was born on 19 Jan 1801 Vaudreuil, Quebec (PRDH online, #2589886.). He was baptized on 19 Jan 1801 Vaudreuil, Quebec *(father's occupaton: cultivator)* (PRDH online, #2589886.). He married **Flavie Leduc**, daughter of **Augustin Leduc** and **Eugenie Seguin,** on 16 Oct 1826 Vaudreuil, Quebec (Ibid., #3473189.).

He and **Flavie Leduc** were enumerated in the census in 1852 St-Polycarpe, Vaudreuil, Quebec. Also in the family: **Christine Chevrier, Joseph Chevrier, Zephirine Chevrier**, and **Antoine Chevrier** *(Chevrier, Sérile, Cultivateur St Polycarpe F, Catholique, 49, M; Leduc, Flavie, St Polycarpe F, Catholique, 45, F; Chevrier, Christine, St Polycarpe F, Catholique, 17, F; Chevrier, Joseph, St Polycarpe F, Catholique, 14, M; Chevrier, Zéphirine, St Polycarpe F, Catholique, 11, F; Chevrier, Antoine, St Polycarpe F, Catholique, 23, M)* (1852C Cdn Transcription Project, District 538, page 26d, 27a, (53), line 16-21.).

Flavie Leduc was born on 4 Jul 1804 Vaudreuil, Quebec (PRDH online, #2590257.). She was baptized on 4 Jul 1804 Vaudreuil, Quebec (Ibid.).

Children of **Andre Cyrille Chevrier** and **Flavie Leduc** were as follows:

i. Antoine Chevrier was born on 9 Feb 1828 St-Polycarpe, Quebec (Ibid., #4454063.). He was baptized on 10 Feb 1828 St-Polycarpe, Quebec (Ibid.).

   He was in the census household of Andre Cyrille Chevrier and Flavie Leduc in 1852 St-Polycarpe, Vaudreuil, Quebec (1852C Cdn Transcription Project, District 538, page 26d, 27a, (53), line 16-21.).

ii. Augustin Chevrier was born on 20 Apr 1829 St-Polycarpe, Quebec (PRDH online, #4454234.). He was baptized on 20 Apr 1829 St-Polycarpe, Quebec (Ibid.). He died on 15 Dec 1834 St Polycarpe, Quebec, at age 5 (Ibid., #4458800.). He was buried on 17 Dec 1834 St-Polycarpe, Quebec (Ibid.).

iii. Cyrille Chevrier was born circa 1831 (Ibid., #4459700.). He died on 17 Jun 1848 St-Polycarpe, Quebec (Ibid.). He was buried on 20 Jun 1848 St-Polycarpe, Quebec (Ibid.).

iv. Christine Chevrier was born on 6 Nov 1833 St-Polycarpe, Quebec (Ibid., #4455074.). She was baptized on 6 Nov 1833 St-Polycarpe, Quebec (Ibid.).

She was in the census household of Andre Cyrille Chevrier and Flavie Leduc in 1852 St-Polycarpe, Vaudreuil, Quebec (1852C Cdn Transcription Project, District 538, page 26d, 27a, (53), line 16-21.).

v. Virginie Chevrier was born on 28 Aug 1835 St-Polycarpe, Quebec *(twin)* (PRDH online, #4455374.). She was baptized on 29 Aug 1835 St-Polycarpe, Quebec (Ibid.).

vi. Anselme Chevrier was born on 28 Aug 1835 St-Polycarpe, Quebec *(twin)* (PRDH online, #4455375.). He was baptized on 29 Aug 1835 St-Polycarpe, Quebec (Ibid.). He died on 24 Sep 1835 St-Polycarpe, Quebec (Ibid., #4458847.). He was buried on 26 Sep 1835 St-Polycarpe, Quebec *(age 3 weeks)* (PRDH online, #4458847.).

vii. Joseph Chevrier was born circa 1838 (1852C Cdn Transcription Project, District 538, page 26d, 27a, (53), line 16-21.).

He was in the census household of Andre Cyrille Chevrier and Flavie Leduc in 1852 St-Polycarpe, Vaudreuil, Quebec (1852C Cdn Transcription Project, District 538, page 26d, 27a, (53), line 16-21.).

viii. Zephirine Chevrier was born circa 1841 (Ibid.).

She was in the census household of Andre Cyrille Chevrier and Flavie Leduc in 1852 St-Polycarpe, Vaudreuil, Quebec (1852C Cdn Transcription Project, District 538, page 26d, 27a, (53), line 16-21.).

ix. Flavie Chevrier was born on 27 Dec 1842 St-Polycarpe, Quebec (PRDH online, #4456639.). She was baptized on 27 Dec 1842 St-Polycarpe, Quebec (Ibid.). She died on 13 May 1848 St-Polycarpe, Quebec, at age 5 (Ibid., #4459688.). She was buried on 14 May 1848 St-Polycarpe, Quebec (Ibid.).

59. Joseph Jerome Chevrier was born on 16 Dec 1802 Vaudreuil, Quebec (Ibid., #2590102.). He was baptized on 16 Dec 1802 Vaudreuil, Quebec *(father's occupaton: cultivator)* (PRDH online, #2590102.). He married **Veronique Gauthier**, daughter of **Hyacinthe Gauthier** and **Josephe Charlebois,** on 2 May 1831 Ste-Madeleine-de-Rigaud, Quebec (Ibid., #3462022.).

Veronique Gauthier was born on 4 Sep 1804 (Ibid., #2679226.). She was baptized on 9 Sep 1804 Ste-Madeleine-de-Rigaud, Quebec *(father's occupation: cultivator)* (PRDH online, #2679226.).

Children of **Joseph Jerome Chevrier** and **Veronique Gauthier** were as follows:

i. Joseph Maxime Chevrier was born on 14 Feb 1832 Ste-Madeleine-de-Rigaud, Quebec (Ibid., #4618542.). He was baptized on 14 Feb 1832 Ste-Madeleine-de-Rigaud, Quebec (Ibid.).

ii. Emelie Cornelie Chevrier was born on 23 Mar 1834 Ste-Madeleine-de-Rigaud, Quebec (Ibid., #4619082.). She was baptized on 24 Mar 1834 Ste-Madeleine-de-Rigaud, Quebec (Ibid.).

iii. Philomene Chevrier was born on 14 Jul 1836 Ste-Madeleine-de-Rigaud, Quebec (Ibid., #4619706.). She was baptized on 15 Jul 1836 Ste-Madeleine-de-Rigaud, Quebec (Ibid.).

iv. Marie Celine Chevrier was born on 2 Jun 1839 Ste-Madeleine-de-Rigaud, Quebec (Ibid., #4620414.). She was baptized on 2 Jun 1839 Ste-Madeleine-de-Rigaud, Quebec (Ibid.).

v. Antoine Evaneliste Chevrier was born on 13 Sep 1841 Ste-Madeleine-de-Rigaud, Quebec (Ibid., #4620972.). He was baptized on 14 Sep 1841 Ste-Madeleine-de-Rigaud, Quebec (Ibid.).

vi. Joseph Noel Chevrier was born on 23 Dec 1844 Grand Chantier (Ibid., #4621728.). He was baptized on 23 Dec 1844 Ste-Madeleine-de-Rigaud, Quebec (Ibid.).

60. Jean Baptiste Chevrier was born on 16 Mar 1808 Vaudreuil, Quebec (Ibid., #2590578.). He was baptized on 17 Mar 1808 Vaudreuil *(father's occupaton: cultivator)* (PRDH online, #2590578.). He married **Scholastique Gauthier**, daughter of **Hyacinthe Gauthier** and **Veronique Amable Charlebois,** on 12 Oct 1829 Vaudreuil, Quebec (Ibid., #3473896.).

He and **Scholastique Gauthier** were enumerated in the census in 1852 Vaudreuil, Vaudreuil, Quebec. Also in the family: **Marie Marguerite Tharsille Chevrier, Marie Sophie Glaudinil Chevrier, Marie Philomene Chevrier, Marie Victoire Chevrier, Francois Jean Baptiste Adolphis Chevrier, Marie Caroline Chevrier, Francois Xavier Honore Chevrier,** and **Alphonsine Chevrier** (1852C Cdn Transcription Project, District 534, page 24d, 25a, (49), line 6-16.).

Scholastique Gauthier was born on 18 May 1811 Vaudreuil, Quebec (PRDH online, #3590871.). She was baptized on 18 May 1811 Vaudreuil, Quebec *(father's occupaton: cultivator)* (PRDH online, #3590871.).

Children of **Jean Baptiste Chevrier** and **Scholastique Gauthier** were as follows:

i. Marie Marguerite Tharsille Chevrier was born on 14 Nov 1830 Vaudreuil, Quebec (Ibid., #4178352.). She was baptized on 15 Nov 1830 Vaudreuil, Quebec (Ibid.).

      She was in the census household of Jean Baptiste Chevrier and Scholastique Gauthier in 1852 Vaudreuil, Vaudreuil, Quebec (1852C Cdn Transcription Project, District 534, page 24d, 25a, (49), line 6-16.).

ii. Joseph Antoine Clovis Chevrier was born on 10 Feb 1832 Vaudreuil, Quebec (PRDH online, #4178533.). He was baptized on 11 Feb 1832 Vaudreuil, Quebec (Ibid.). He died on 2 Feb 1834 Vaudreuil, Quebec, at age 1 (Ibid., #4181677.). He was buried on 3 Feb 1834 Vaudreuil, Quebec (Ibid.).

iii. Marie Marcelle Chevrier was born on 22 Sep 1833 Vaudreuil, Quebec (Ibid., #4178800.). She was baptized on 23 Sep 1833 Vaudreuil, Quebec (Ibid.). She died on 12 Jan 1836 Vaudreuil, Quebec, at age 2 (Ibid., #4181827.). She was buried on 14 Jan 1836 Vaudreuil, Quebec (Ibid.).

iv. Marie Sophie Glaudinil Chevrier was born on 18 Jul 1835 Vaudreuil, Quebec (Ibid., #4179081.). She was baptized on 18 Jul 1835 Vaudreuil, Quebec (Ibid.).

      She was in the census household of Jean Baptiste Chevrier and Scholastique Gauthier in 1852 Vaudreuil, Vaudreuil, Quebec (1852C Cdn Transcription Project, District 534, page 24d, 25a, (49), line 6-16.).

v. Marie Philomene Chevrier was born on 30 Jul 1837 Vaudreuil, Quebec (PRDH online, #4179357.). She was baptized on 31 Jul 1837 Vaudreuil, Quebec (Ibid.).

      She was in the census household of Jean Baptiste Chevrier and Scholastique Gauthier in 1852 Vaudreuil, Vaudreuil, Quebec (1852C Cdn Transcription Project, District 534, page 24d, 25a, (49), line 6-16.).

vi. Marie Victoire Chevrier was born on 23 Apr 1839 Vaudreuil, Quebec (PRDH online, #4179591.). She was baptized on 24 Apr 1839 Vaudreuil, Quebec (Ibid.).

      She was in the census household of Jean Baptiste Chevrier and Scholastique Gauthier in 1852 Vaudreuil, Vaudreuil, (1852C Cdn Transcription Project, District 534, page 24d, 25a, (49), line 6-16.).

vii. Francois Jean Baptiste Adolphis Chevrier was born on 22 Jun 1841 Vaudreuil, Quebec (PRDH online, #4179875.). He was baptized on 22 Jun 1841 Vaudreuil, Quebec (Ibid.).

      He was in the census household of Jean Baptiste Chevrier and Scholastique Gauthier in 1852 Vaudreuil, Vaudreuil, Quebec (1852C Cdn Transcription Project, District 534, page 24d, 25a, (49), line 6-16.).

viii. Marie Caroline Chevrier was born on 6 Jul 1843 Vaudreuil, Quebec (PRDH online, #4180172.). She was baptized on 7 Jul 1843 Vaudreuil, Quebec (Ibid.). She died on 25 Jul 1843 Vaudreuil, Quebec (Ibid., #4182313.). She was buried on 26 Jul 1843 Vaudreuil, Quebec (Ibid.).

      She was in the census household of Jean Baptiste Chevrier and Scholastique Gauthier in 1852 Vaudreuil, Vaudreuil, Quebec (1852C Cdn Transcription Project, District 534, page 24d, 25a, (49), line 6-16.).

ix. Francois Xavier Honore Chevrier was born on 14 Nov 1846 Vaudreuil, Quebec (PRDH online, #4180650.).

      She was in the census household of Jean Baptiste Chevrier and Scholastique Gauthier in 1852 Vaudreuil, Vaudreuil, Quebec (1852C Cdn Transcription Project, District 534, page 24d, 25a, (49), line 6-16.).

x. Marie Angelique Caroline Chevrier was born on 13 Nov 1848 Vaudreuil, Quebec (PRDH online, #4180968.). She was baptized on 14 Nov 1848 Vaudreuil, Quebec (Ibid.).

xi. Alphonsine Chevrier was born circa 1850 (1852C Cdn Transcription Project, District 534, page 24d, 25a, (49), line 6-16.).

      She was in the census household of Jean Baptiste Chevrier and Scholastique Gauthier in 1852 Vaudreuil, Vaudreuil, Quebec (1852C Cdn Transcription Project, District 534, page 24d, 25a, (49), line 6-16.).

61. Francois Pascal Chevrier was born on 8 Apr 1811 Oka, Quebec (PRDH online, #2752337.). He was baptized on 8 Apr 1811 Oka, Quebec *(father's occupation: cultivator)* (PRDH online, #2752337.). He married **Marie Agathe Leduc**, daughter of **Antoine Nicolas Leduc** and **Marie Angelique Prudhomme,** on 4 Feb 1839 (St-Laurent), Montreal, Quebec (Ibid., #3509756.).

He and **Marie Agathe Leduc** were enumerated in the census in 1852 St-Jerome, Terrebonne, Quebec. Also in the family: **Marie Joseph Desire Chevrier** and **Marie Agathe Philomene Chevrier** *(Chevrier, François, Cultivateur, Bas-Canada, Catholique, 41, M; Leduc, Agathe, Bas-Canada, Catholique, 41, F; Chevrier, Désiré, Bas-Canada,*

Catholique, 8, M; Chevrier, Philomène, Bas-Canada, Catholique, 4, F) (1852C Cdn Transcription Project, District 506, page 37d, 38a, (75), line 25-28.).

Marie Agathe Leduc was born on 20 Feb 1809 (St-Laurent), Montreal, Quebec (PRDH online, #2466626.). She was baptized on 20 Feb 1809 (St-Laurent), Montreal, Quebec (Ibid.).

Children of **Francois Pascal Chevrier** and **Marie Agathe Leduc** all born St-Benoit, Quebec, were as follows:

    i.   Marie Francois Alphonse Deligori Chevrier was born on 2 Nov 1840 (Ibid., #4670042.). He was baptized on 3 Nov 1840 St-Benoit, Quebec (Ibid.).

    ii. Marie Antoine Maxime Chevrier was born on 3 Feb 1842 (Ibid., #4428973.). He was baptized on 3 Feb 1842 (Deux-Montagnes), St-Hermas, Quebec (Ibid.). He died on 29 May 1842 St-Benoit, Quebec (Ibid., #4673935.). He was buried on 30 May 1842 St-Benoit, Quebec (Ibid.).

    iii. Marie Joseph Desire Chevrier was born on 1 Feb 1845 (Ibid., #4670750.). He was baptized on 2 Feb 1845 St-Benoit, Quebec (Ibid.).

       He was in the census household of Francois Pascal Chevrier and Marie Agathe Leduc in 1852 St-Jerome, Terrebonne, Quebec (1852C Cdn Transcription Project, District 506, page 37d, 38a, (75), line 25-28.).

    iv. Marie Agathe Philomene Chevrier was born on 20 Jul 1848 (PRDH online, #4671396.). She was baptized on 21 Jul 1848 St-Benoit, Quebec (Ibid.).

       She was in the census household of Francois Pascal Chevrier and Marie Agathe Leduc in 1852 St-Jerome, Terrebonne, Quebec (1852C Cdn Transcription Project, District 506, page 37d, 38a, (75), line 25-28.).

62. Joseph Olivier Sauve was baptized on 31 Jul 1797 Vaudreuil, Quebec *(father's occupation: cultivator)* (PRDH online, #770933.). He married **Marie Adelaide Castonguay or Gastonguay**, daughter of **Pierre Castonguay or Gastonguay** and **Pelagie Gauthier,** on 4 Jul 1820 Vaudreuil, Quebec (Ibid., #2224454.).

He and **Marie Adelaide Castonguay or Gastonguay** were enumerated in the census in 1852 Ste-Madeleine-de-Rigaud, Vaudreuil, Quebec. Also in the family: **Joseph Arsene Sauve, Angelle Sauve**, and **Etienne Jean Baptiste Sauve** *(Sauvé, Olivier, Cultivateur, Vaudreuil, Catholique, 58, M; Castonguay, Adélaïde, Vaudreuil, Catholique, 48, F; Sauvé, Arsenne, Rigaud, Catholique, 26, M; Sauvé, Angèle, Rigaud, Catholique, 18, F; Sauvé, J B, Rigaud, Catholique, 7, M)* (1852C Cdn Transcription Project, District 536, page 7d, 8a, (15), line 46-50.).

Marie Adelaide Castonguay or Gastonguay was born on 27 Aug 1802 Vaudreuil, Quebec (PRDH online, #2590061.). She was baptized on 27 Aug 1802 Vaudreuil, Quebec *(father's occupation: blacksmith)* (PRDH online, #2590061.).

Children of **Joseph Olivier Sauve** and **Marie Adelaide Castonguay or Gastonguay** were as follows:

    i.   Marguerite Stanislas Sauve was born on 24 Oct 1820 Vaudreuil, Quebec (Ibid., #2591742.). She was baptized on 24 Oct 1820 Vaudreuil, Quebec *(father's occupation: cultivator)* (PRDH online, #2591742.).

142 ii. Joseph Edouard Sauve, b. 16 Oct 1822 Vaudreuil, Quebec; m. Marcelline Denys dit St.Denys.

    iii. Joseph Arsene Sauve was born on 15 Aug 1824 Ste-Madeleine-de-Rigaud, Quebec (Ibid., #2681388.). He was baptized on 16 Aug 1824 Ste-Madeleine-de-Rigaud, Quebec *(father's occupation: cultivator)* (PRDH online, #2681388.).

       He was in the census household of Joseph Olivier Sauve and Marie Adelaide Castonguay or Gastonguay in 1852 Ste-Madeleine-de-Rigaud, Vaudreuil, Quebec (1852C Cdn Transcription Project, District 536, page 7d, 8a, (15), line 46-50.).

    iv. Paul Sauve was born on 26 Nov 1826 Ste-Madeleine-de-Rigaud, Quebec (PRDH online, #4617451.). He was baptized on 26 Nov 1826 Ste-Madeleine-de-Rigaud, Quebec (Ibid.). He died on 4 Jul 1827 Ste-Madeleine-de-Rigaud, Quebec (Ibid., #4622829.). He was buried on 5 Jul 1827 Ste-Madeleine-de-Rigaud, Quebec *(age 8 months)* (PRDH online, #4622829.).

    v. Henriette Sauve was born on 9 Jul 1828 Ste-Madeleine-de-Rigaud, Quebec (Ibid., #4617765.). She was baptized on 10 Jul 1828 Ste-Madeleine-de-Rigaud, Quebec (Ibid.). She died on 21 Aug 1832 Ste-Madeleine-de-Rigaud, Quebec, at age 4 (Ibid., #4623327.). She was buried on 21 Aug 1832 Ste-Madeleine-de-Rigaud, Quebec (Ibid.).

    vi. Emilie Sauve was born on 31 Jul 1830 Ste-Madeleine-de-Rigaud, Quebec (Ibid., #4618160.). She was baptized on 31 Jul 1830 Ste-Madeleine-de-Rigaud, Quebec (Ibid.).

    vii. Angelle Sauve was born on 19 May 1832 Ste-Madeleine-de-Rigaud, Quebec (Ibid., #4618625.). She was baptized on 19 May 1832 Ste-Madeleine-de-Rigaud, Quebec (Ibid.).

She was in the census household of Joseph Olivier Sauve and Marie Adelaide Castonguay or Gastonguay in 1852 Ste-Madeleine-de-Rigaud, Vaudreuil, Quebec (1852C Cdn Transcription Project, District 536, page 7d, 8a, (15), line 46-50.).

viii. Joseph Olivier Sauve was born on 2 May 1834 Ste-Madeleine-de-Rigaud, Quebec (PRDH online, #4619113.). He was baptized on 3 May 1834 Ste-Madeleine-de-Rigaud, Quebec (Ibid.). He died on 28 Feb 1835 Ste-Madeleine-de-Rigaud, Quebec (Ibid., #4623573.). He was buried on 2 Mar 1835 Ste-Madeleine-de-Rigaud, Quebec *(age 10 months)* (PRDH online, #4623573.).

ix. Virginie Sauve was born on 30 Apr 1835 Ste-Madeleine-de-Rigaud, Quebec (Ibid., #4619353.). She was baptized on 1 May 1835 Ste-Madeleine-de-Rigaud, Quebec (Ibid.). She died on 8 Sep 1835 Ste-Madeleine-de-Rigaud, Quebec (Ibid., #4623627.). She was buried on 12 Sep 1835 Ste-Madeleine-de-Rigaud, Quebec *(age 4 months)* (PRDH online, #4623627.).

x. Veronique Sauve was born on 6 May 1836 Ste-Madeleine-de-Rigaud, Quebec (Ibid., #4619639.). She was baptized on 8 May 1836 Ste-Madeleine-de-Rigaud, Quebec (Ibid.). She died on 24 Sep 1836 Ste-Madeleine-de-Rigaud, Quebec (Ibid., #4623711.). She was buried on 26 Sep 1836 Ste-Madeleine-de-Rigaud, Quebec *(age 5 months)* (PRDH online, #4623711.).

xi. Onesime Philomene Sauve was born on 30 May 1837 Ste-Madeleine-de-Rigaud, Quebec (Ibid., #4619945.). She was baptized on 4 Jun 1837 Ste-Madeleine-de-Rigaud, Quebec (Ibid.). She died on 4 Nov 1837 Ste-Madeleine-de-Rigaud, Quebec (Ibid., #4623801.). She was buried on 6 Nov 1837 Ste-Madeleine-de-Rigaud, Quebec *(age 5 months)* (PRDH online, #4623801.).

xii. Marie Eleonore Sauve was born on 28 Jun 1838 Ste-Madeleine-de-Rigaud, Quebec (Ibid., #4620170.). She was baptized on 28 Jun 1838 Ste-Madeleine-de-Rigaud, Quebec (Ibid.). She died on 11 Aug 1838 Ste-Madeleine-de-Rigaud, Quebec (Ibid., #4623872.). She was buried on 13 Aug 1838 Ste-Madeleine-de-Rigaud, Quebec (Ibid.).

xiii. Henriette Virginie Sauve was born on 7 Aug 1839 Ste-Madeleine-de-Rigaud, Quebec (Ibid., #4620459.). She was baptized on 9 Aug 1839 Ste-Madeleine-de-Rigaud, Quebec (Ibid.). She died on 21 Aug 1839 Ste-Madeleine-de-Rigaud, Quebec (Ibid., #4623982.). She was buried on 23 Aug 1839 Ste-Madeleine-de-Rigaud, Quebec (Ibid.).

xiv. Pierre Sauve was born on 1 Sep 1840 Ste-Madeleine-de-Rigaud, Quebec (Ibid., #4620702.). He was baptized on 2 Sep 1840 Ste-Madeleine-de-Rigaud, Quebec (Ibid.). He died on 12 May 1841 Ste-Madeleine-de-Rigaud, Quebec (Ibid., #4624129.). He was buried on 14 May 1841 Ste-Madeleine-de-Rigaud, Quebec *(age 8 months)* (PRDH online, #4624129.).

xv. Joseph Sauve was born on 2 May 1842 Ste-Madeleine-de-Rigaud, Quebec (Ibid., #4621114.). He was baptized on 3 May 1842 Ste-Madeleine-de-Rigaud, Quebec (Ibid.). He died on 10 May 1842 Ste-Madeleine-de-Rigaud, Quebec (Ibid., #4624252.). He was buried on 11 May 1842 Ste-Madeleine-de-Rigaud, Quebec (Ibid.).

xvi. Benjamin Sauve was born on 21 May 1843 Ste-Madeleine-de-Rigaud, Quebec (Ibid., #4621376.). He was baptized on 22 May 1843 Ste-Madeleine-de-Rigaud, Quebec (Ibid.). He died on 19 Aug 1843 Ste-Madeleine-de-Rigaud, Quebec (Ibid., #4624374.). He was buried on 21 Aug 1843 Ste-Madeleine-de-Rigaud, Quebec (Ibid.).

xvii. Etienne Jean Baptiste Sauve was born on 24 Oct 1844 Vaudreuil, Quebec (Ibid., #4621690.). He was baptized on 25 Oct 1844 Vaudreuil, Quebec (Ibid.).

He was in the census household of Joseph Olivier Sauve and Marie Adelaide Castonguay or Gastonguay in 1852 Ste-Madeleine-de-Rigaud, Vaudreuil, Quebec (1852C Cdn Transcription Project, District 536, page 7d, 8a, (15), line 46-50.).

xviii. Pierre Joseph Sauve was born on 10 Aug 1847 Rigaud, Quebec (PRDH online, #4727911.). He was baptized on 11 Aug 1847 Ste-Marthe, Quebec (Ibid.). He died on 19 Sep 1847 Ste-Madeleine-de-Rigaud, Quebec (Ibid., #4624646.). He was buried on 21 Sep 1847 Ste-Madeleine-de-Rigaud, Quebec (Ibid.).

xix. Hugh Sauve was born on 15 Sep 1849 Ste-Madeleine-de-Rigaud, Quebec (Ibid., #4622601.). He was baptized on 15 Sep 1849 Ste-Madeleine-de-Rigaud, Quebec (Ibid.).

63. **Marie Reine Sauve** was born circa 1799 Ste-Madeleine-de-Rigaud, Quebec (1852C Cdn Transcription Project, District 536, page 28d, 29a, (57), line 47-50.). She married **Paul Vachon**, son of **Jean Baptiste Vachon** and **Suzanne Pretaboire dit Besner**, on 18 Feb 1822 Vaudreuil, Quebec (PRDH online, #2224517.).

She and **Paul Vachon** were enumerated in the census in 1852 Ste-Madeleine-de-Rigaud, Vaudreuil, Quebec. Also in the family: **Marie Reine Vachon**, **Marie Virginie Vachon**, **Philomene Vachon**, and **Hypolite Sauve** *(Vachon, Paul, Cultivateur, Rigaud, Catholique, 52, M; Sauvé, Marie, Rigaud, Catholique, 52, F; Vachon, Reine, Rigaud,*

Catholique, 22, F; Vachon, Virginie, Rigaud, Catholique, 17, F; Vachon, Philomene, Rigaud, Catholique, 8, F; Vachon, Pierre, Rigaud, Catholique, 18, M; Vachon, Paul, Rigaud, Catholique, 15, M; Vachon, Emery, Rigaud, Catholique, 15, M; Vachon, Cyprien, Rigaud, Catholique, 13, M; Sauvé, Hypolite, Rigaud, Catholique, 61, F) (1852C Cdn Transcription Project, District 536, page 28d, 29a, (57), line 47-50; page 24d, 25a, (49), line 1-6.).

Paul Vachon was baptized on 21 Oct 1799 Oka, Quebec (PRDH online, #774035.).

Children of **Marie Reine Sauve** and **Paul Vachon** all born Ste-Madeleine-de-Rigaud, Quebec, were as follows:

143   i.   Suzanne Vachon, b. 1 Dec 1822; m. Felix Duchesne; d. 4 Feb 1842; bur. 6 Feb 1842.

144   ii.   Jean Baptiste Vachon, b. 5 Sep 1824; m. Marie Elisabeth Cardinal.

     iii.   Marie Angelique Vachon was born on 22 Aug 1826 (Ibid., #4617414.). She was baptized on 23 Aug 1826 Ste-Madeleine-de-Rigaud, Quebec (Ibid.). She died on 14 Jul 1827 Ste-Madeleine-de-Rigaud, Quebec (Ibid., #4622832.). She was buried on 15 Jul 1827 Ste-Madeleine-de-Rigaud, Quebec *(age 11 months)* (PRDH online, #4622832.).

     iv.   Virginie Vachon was born on 22 Feb 1828 (Ibid., #4617684.). She was baptized on 23 Feb 1828 Ste-Madeleine-de-Rigaud, Quebec (Ibid.). She died on 2 Aug 1832 Ste-Madeleine-de-Rigaud, Quebec, at age 4 (Ibid., #4623283.). She was buried on 3 Aug 1832 Ste-Madeleine-de-Rigaud, Quebec (Ibid.).

     v.   Marie Reine Vachon was born on 7 Jan 1830 (Ibid., #4618051.). She was baptized on 7 Jan 1830 Ste-Madeleine-de-Rigaud, Quebec (Ibid.).

       She was in the census household of Paul Vachon and Marie Reine Sauve in 1852 Ste-Madeleine-de-Rigaud, Vaudreuil, Quebec (1852C Cdn Transcription Project, District 536, page 28d, 29a, (57), line 47-50; page 24d, 25a, (49), line 1-6.).

     vi.   Paul Jude Vachon was born on 16 Oct 1831 (PRDH online, #4618452.). He was baptized on 17 Oct 1831 Ste-Madeleine-de-Rigaud, Quebec (Ibid.). He died on 6 Aug 1832 Ste-Madeleine-de-Rigaud, Quebec (Ibid., #4623296.). He was buried on 7 Aug 1832 Ste-Madeleine-de-Rigaud, Quebec *(age 9 months)* (PRDH online, #4623296.).

     vii.   Pierre Vachon was born on 19 Aug 1833 (Ibid., #4618951.). He was baptized on 20 Aug 1833 Ste-Madeleine-de-Rigaud, Quebec (Ibid.).

     viii.   Marie Virginie Vachon was born on 18 Feb 1835 (Ibid., #4619302.). She was baptized on 18 Feb 1835 Ste-Madeleine-de-Rigaud, Quebec (Ibid.).

       She was in the census household of Paul Vachon and Marie Reine Sauve in 1852 Ste-Madeleine-de-Rigaud, Vaudreuil, Quebec (1852C Cdn Transcription Project, District 536, page 28d, 29a, (57), line 47-50; page 24d, 25a, (49), line 1-6.).

     ix.   Emery Vachon was born on 3 Nov 1836 *(twin)* (PRDH online, #4619789.). He was baptized on 3 Nov 1836 Ste-Madeleine-de-Rigaud, Quebec (Ibid.).

     x.   Paul Jude Vachon was born on 3 Nov 1836 *(twin)* (PRDH online, #4619790.). He was baptized on 3 Nov 1836 Ste-Madeleine-de-Rigaud, Quebec (Ibid.).

     xi.   Joseph Cyprien Vachon was born on 9 Nov 1838 (Ibid., #4620259.). He was baptized on 9 Nov 1838 Ste-Madeleine-de-Rigaud, Quebec (Ibid.).

     xii.   Andre Damase Vachon was born on 16 Mar 1841 (Ibid., #4620848.). He was baptized on 16 Mar 1841 Ste-Madeleine-de-Rigaud, Quebec (Ibid.). He died on 26 Jan 1842 Ste-Madeleine-de-Rigaud, Quebec (Ibid., #4624225.). He was buried on 28 Jan 1842 Ste-Madeleine-de-Rigaud, Quebec *(age 10 months)* (PRDH online, #4624225.).

     xiii.   Philomene Vachon was born on 12 Sep 1843 (Ibid., #4621452.). She was baptized on 12 Sep 1843 Ste-Madeleine-de-Rigaud, Quebec (Ibid.).

       She was in the census household of Paul Vachon and Marie Reine Sauve in 1852 Ste-Madeleine-de-Rigaud, Vaudreuil, Quebec (1852C Cdn Transcription Project, District 536, page 28d, 29a, (57), line 47-50; page 24d, 25a, (49), line 1-6.).

     xiv.   Octave Vachon was born on 25 Oct 1845 (PRDH online, #4621926.). He was baptized on 27 Oct 1845 Ste-Madeleine-de-Rigaud, Quebec (Ibid.). He died on 4 Apr 1846 Ste-Madeleine-de-Rigaud, Quebec (Ibid., #4624543.). He was buried on 6 Apr 1846 Ste-Madeleine-de-Rigaud, Quebec (Ibid.).

64. Louis Cyprien Sauve was born on 9 Jan 1806 Vaudreuil, Quebec (Ibid., #2590381.). He was baptized on 9 Jan 1806 Vaudreuil, Quebec *(father's occupation: cultivator)* (PRDH online, #2590381.). He married **Marie Suzanne Leduc**, daughter of **Augustin Leduc** and **Eugenie Seguin,** on 12 Feb 1827 Vaudreuil, Quebec (Ibid., #3473334.).

He and **Marie Suzanne Leduc** were enumerated in the census in 1852 St.Michel, Vaudreuil, Vaudreuil, Quebec.

Also in the family: **Antoine Cyprien Sauve, Eugene Emelie Sauve, Roch Theophile Sauve, Jean Baptiste Clovis**

Sauve, **Andre Hilaire Sauve**, and **Angelique Amable Villeneuve** *(Sauvé, Suprien, Cultivateur, Vaudreuil F, Catholique romaine, 46, M; Leduc, Suzanne, Vaudreuil F, Catholique romaine, 54, F; Sauvé, Antoine, voyageur, Vaudreuil F, Catholique romaine, 25, M; Sauvé, Suprien R., Vaudreuil F, Catholique romaine, 20, M; Sauvé, Emelie, Vaudreuil F, Catholique romaine, 21, F; Sauvé, Clovis, Vaudreuil F, Catholique romaine, 18, M; Sauvé, Hilaire, Vaudreuil F, Catholique romaine, 15, M; Villeneuve, Angelique, Mission du Lac F Catholique romaine, 78, F; Sauvé, M. L., Domestique, Vaudreuil F, Catholique romaine, 29, F)* (1852C Cdn Transcription Project, District 534, page 24d, 25a, (49), line 19-26.).

Marie Suzanne Leduc was born on 11 Sep 1797 Vaudreuil, Quebec (PRDH online, No. 774060.). She was baptized on 11 Sep 1797 Oka, Quebec (Ibid.).

Children of **Louis Cyprien Sauve** and **Marie Suzanne Leduc** all born Vaudreuil, Quebec, were as follows:

      i. Antoine Cyprien Sauve was born on 5 May 1828 (Ibid., #4178071.). He was baptized on 5 May 1828 Vaudreuil, Quebec (Ibid.).

          He was in the census household of Louis Cyprien Sauve and Marie Suzanne Leduc in 1852 St.Michel, Vaudreuil, Vaudreuil, Quebec (1852C Cdn Transcription Project, District 534, page 24d, 25a, (49), line 19-26.).

     ii. Eugene Emelie Sauve was born on 10 Aug 1830 (PRDH online, #4178330.). She was baptized on 10 Aug 1830 Vaudreuil, Quebec (Ibid.).

          She was in the census household of Louis Cyprien Sauve and Marie Suzanne Leduc in 1852 St.Michel, Vaudreuil, Vaudreuil, Quebec (1852C Cdn Transcription Project, District 534, page 24d, 25a, (49), line 19-26.).

    iii. Roch Theophile Sauve was born on 25 Jun 1832 (PRDH online, #4178597.). He was baptized on 25 Jun 1832 Vaudreuil, Quebec (Ibid.).

          He was in the census household of Louis Cyprien Sauve and Marie Suzanne Leduc in 1852 St.Michel, Vaudreuil, Vaudreuil, Quebec (1852C Cdn Transcription Project, District 534, page 24d, 25a, (49), line 19-26.).

     iv. Jean Baptiste Clovis Sauve was born on 4 Jul 1835 (PRDH online, #4179073.). He was baptized on 4 Jul 1835 Vaudreuil, Quebec (Ibid.).

          He was in the census household of Louis Cyprien Sauve and Marie Suzanne Leduc in 1852 St.Michel, Vaudreuil, Vaudreuil, Quebec (1852C Cdn Transcription Project, District 534, page 24d, 25a, (49), line 19-26.).

      v. Andre Hilaire Sauve was born on 26 May 1838 (PRDH online, #4179455.). He was baptized on 27 May 1838 Vaudreuil, Quebec (Ibid.).

          He was in the census household of Louis Cyprien Sauve and Marie Suzanne Leduc in 1852 St.Michel, Vaudreuil, Vaudreuil, Quebec (1852C Cdn Transcription Project, District 534, page 24d, 25a, (49), line 19-26.).

65. Angelique Amable Sauve was born on 27 May 1809 Vaudreuil, Quebec (PRDH online, #2590708.). She was baptized on 27 May 1809 Vaudreuil, Quebec *(father's occupation: cultivator)* (PRDH online, #2590708.). She married **Joseph Melchoir Baltazard Hurtubise**, son of **Gabriel Hurtubise** and **Marie Anne Leduc,** on 7 Feb 1825 Vaudreuil, Quebec (Ibid., #3472922.).

She and **Joseph Melchoir Baltazard Hurtubise** were enumerated in the census in 1852 Ste-Madeleine-de-Rigaud, Vaudreuil, Quebec. Also in the family: **Emelie Hurtubise**, **Louise Hurtubise**, **Marcelline Hurtubise**, **Andre Hurtubise**, **Prosper Hurtubise**, **Octave Hurtubise**, and **Joseph Hurtubise** *(Hurtubise, Joseph, Cultivateur, Rigaud, Catholique, 53, M; Sauvé, Angélique, Vaudreuil, Catholique, 44, F; Hurtubise, Josephte, Rigaud, Catholique, 23, F; Brasseur, Marguerite, Rigaud, Catholique, 19, F; Hurtubise, Milie, Rigaud, Catholique, 14, F; Hurtubise, Louise, Rigaud, Catholique, 8, F; Hurtubise, Marceline, Rigaud, Catholique, 6, F; Hurtubise, André, Rigaud, Catholique, 11, M; Hurtubise, Prospère, Rigaud, Catholique, 9, M; Hurtubise, Octave, Rigaud, Catholique, 1, M; Hurtubise, Joseph, Rigaud, Catholique, 4 mois, M)* (1852C Cdn Transcription Project, District 536, page 27d, 28a, (55), line 29-39.).

Joseph Melchoir Baltazard Hurtubise was born on 8 Jan 1798 Vaudreuil, Quebec (PRDH online, #642722.). He was baptized on 8 Jan 1798 Oka, Quebec *(conditional baptism)* (PRDH online, #642722.).

Children of **Angelique Amable Sauve** and **Joseph Melchoir Baltazard Hurtubise** were as follows:

      i. Marguerite Hurtubise was born on 30 Jan 1826 Ste-Madeleine-de-Rigaud, Quebec (Ibid., #4617306.). She was baptized on 30 Jan 1826 Ste-Madeleine-de-Rigaud, Quebec (Ibid.). She was buried on 7 Dec 1826 Ste-Madeleine-de-Rigaud, Quebec *(age 8 days)* (PRDH online, #4622726.).

ii. Anonyme Hurtubise was born on 23 Sep 1826 Ste-Madeleine-de-Rigaud, Quebec (Ibid., #4622790.). He/she died on 23 Sep 1826 Ste-Madeleine-de-Rigaud, Quebec (Ibid.). He/she was buried on 25 Sep 1826 Ste-Madeleine-de-Rigaud, Quebec (Ibid.).

iii. Marie Anne Hurtubise was born on 28 Sep 1827 Ste-Madeleine-de-Rigaud, Quebec (Ibid., #4617626.). She was baptized on 28 Sep 1827 Ste-Madeleine-de-Rigaud, Quebec (Ibid.). She died on 29 Sep 1827 Ste-Madeleine-de-Rigaud, Quebec (Ibid., #4622854.). She was buried on 1 Oct 1827 Ste-Madeleine-de-Rigaud, Quebec *(age 2 days)* (PRDH online, #4622854.).

iv. Joseph Jean Marie Hurtubise was born on 11 Aug 1828 Ste-Madeleine-de-Rigaud, Quebec (Ibid., #4617786.). He was baptized on 11 Aug 1828 Ste-Madeleine-de-Rigaud, Quebec (Ibid.).

v. Eulalie Hurtubise was born on 21 Jun 1830 Ste-Madeleine-de-Rigaud, Quebec (Ibid., #4618137.). She was baptized on 21 Jun 1830 Ste-Madeleine-de-Rigaud, Quebec (Ibid.). She died on 6 Feb 1834 Ste-Madeleine-de-Rigaud, Quebec, at age 3 (Ibid., #4623458.). She was buried on 8 Feb 1834 Ste-Madeleine-de-Rigaud, Quebec (Ibid.).

vi. Louis Hurtubise was born on 26 Jun 1832 Ste-Madeleine-de-Rigaud, Quebec (Ibid., #4618663.). He was baptized on 27 Jun 1832 Ste-Madeleine-de-Rigaud, Quebec (Ibid.). He died on 2 Sep 1837 Ste-Madeleine-de-Rigaud, Quebec, at age 5 (Ibid., #4623784.). He was buried on 3 Sep 1837 Ste-Madeleine-de-Rigaud, Quebec (Ibid.).

vii. Antoine Hurtubise was born on 27 Jun 1834 Ste-Madeleine-de-Rigaud, Quebec (Ibid., #4619143.). He was baptized on 27 Jun 1834 Ste-Madeleine-de-Rigaud, Quebec (Ibid.). He died on 18 Feb 1836 Ste-Madeleine-de-Rigaud, Quebec, at age 1 (Ibid., #4623665.). He was buried on 20 Feb 1836 Ste-Madeleine-de-Rigaud, Quebec *(age 19 months)* (PRDH online, #4623665.).

viii. Marie Rose Hurtubise was born on 11 Aug 1836 Ste-Madeleine-de-Rigaud, Quebec (Ibid., #4619729.). She was baptized on 13 Aug 1836 Ste-Madeleine-de-Rigaud, Quebec (Ibid.). She died on 27 Aug 1837 Ste-Madeleine-de-Rigaud, Quebec, at age 1 (Ibid., #4623777.). She was buried on 28 Aug 1837 Ste-Madeleine-de-Rigaud, Quebec (Ibid.).

ix. Emelie Hurtubise was born on 30 Aug 1838 Ste-Madeleine-de-Rigaud, Quebec (Ibid., #4620213.). She was baptized on 30 Aug 1838 Ste-Madeleine-de-Rigaud, Quebec (Ibid.).
   She was in the census household of Joseph Melchoir Baltazard Hurtubise and Angelique Amable Sauve in 1852 Ste-Madeleine-de-Rigaud, Vaudreuil, Quebec (1852C Cdn Transcription Project, District 536, page 27d, 28a, (55), line 29-39.).

x. Andre Hurtubise was born on 19 Sep 1840 Ste-Madeleine-de-Rigaud, Quebec (PRDH online, #4620715.). He was baptized on 20 Sep 1840 Ste-Madeleine-de-Rigaud, Quebec (Ibid.).
   He was in the census household of Joseph Melchoir Baltazard Hurtubise and Angelique Amable Sauve in 1852 Ste-Madeleine-de-Rigaud, Vaudreuil, Quebec (1852C Cdn Transcription Project, District 536, page 27d, 28a, (55), line 29-39.).

xi. Prosper Hurtubise was born on 2 May 1842 Ste-Madeleine-de-Rigaud, Quebec (PRDH online, #4621113.). He was baptized on 3 May 1842 Ste-Madeleine-de-Rigaud, Quebec (Ibid.).
   He was in the census household of Joseph Melchoir Baltazard Hurtubise and Angelique Amable Sauve in 1852 Ste-Madeleine-de-Rigaud, Vaudreuil, Quebec (1852C Cdn Transcription Project, District 536, page 27d, 28a, (55), line 29-39.).

xii. Louise Hurtubise was born circa 1844 (Ibid.).
   She was in the census household of Joseph Melchoir Baltazard Hurtubise and Angelique Amable Sauve in 1852 Ste-Madeleine-de-Rigaud, Vaudreuil, Quebec (1852C Cdn Transcription Project, District 536, page 27d, 28a, (55), line 29-39.).

xiii. Marcelline Hurtubise was born on 6 Sep 1846 Ste-Madeleine-de-Rigaud, Quebec (PRDH online, #4622115.). She was baptized on 6 Sep 1846 Ste-Madeleine-de-Rigaud, Quebec (Ibid.).
   She was in the census household of Joseph Melchoir Baltazard Hurtubise and Angelique Amable Sauve in 1852 Ste-Madeleine-de-Rigaud, Vaudreuil, Quebec (1852C Cdn Transcription Project, District 536, page 27d, 28a, (55), line 29-39.).

xiv. Cyprien Hurtubise was born on 4 Sep 1848 Ste-Madeleine-de-Rigaud, Quebec (PRDH online, #4622444.). He was baptized on 5 Sep 1848 Ste-Madeleine-de-Rigaud, Quebec (Ibid.).

xv. Octave Hurtubise was born circa 1850 (1852C Cdn Transcription Project, District 536, page 27d, 28a, (55), line 29-39.).
   He was in the census household of Joseph Melchoir Baltazard Hurtubise and Angelique Amable Sauve in 1852 Ste-Madeleine-de-Rigaud, Vaudreuil, Quebec (1852C Cdn Transcription Project, District 536, page 27d, 28a, (55), line 29-39.).

xvi.   Joseph Hurtubise was born circa 1851 (Ibid.).

He was in the census household of Joseph Melchoir Baltazard Hurtubise and Angelique Amable Sauve in 1852 Ste-Madeleine-de-Rigaud, Vaudreuil, Quebec (1852C Cdn Transcription Project, District 536, page 27d, 28a, (55), line 29-39.).

66. Eugenie Emilie Sauve was born on 29 Jul 1811 Vaudreuil, Quebec (PRDH online, #2590893.). She was baptized on 29 Jul 1811 Vaudreuil, Quebec *(father's occupation: cultivator)* (PRDH online, #2590893.). She married **Hyacinthe Denis dit St.Denis**, son of **Hyacinthe Denis dit St.Denis** and **Marie Rose Cholet,** on 23 Feb 1829 Vaudreuil, Quebec (Ibid., #3473702.).

She and **Hyacinthe Denis dit St.Denis** were enumerated in the census in 1852 St.Polycarpe, Vaudreuil, Quebec. Also in the family: **Henriette St.Denis**, **Marie Brazelle St.Denis**, **Hyacinthe Denis**, **Joseph St.Denis**, **Louis Denis**, **Joseph Morice St.Denis**, **Pierre Supplie St.Denis**, **Pierre St.Denis**, and **Jean Baptiste St.Denis** *(St Denis, Hyacinthe, Cultivateur, St. Polycarpe F, Catholique, 52, M; Sauvé, Emilie, St. Polycarpe F, Catholique, 45, F; St Denis, Henriette, St. Polycarpe F, Catholique, 7, F; St Denis, Grasille, St. Polycarpe F, Catholique, 5, F; St Denis, Hyacinthe, St. Polycarpe F, Catholique, 23, M; St Denis, Joseph, Forgeron, St. Polycarpe F, Catholique, St Eustache, 19, M; St Denis, Louis, St. Polycarpe F, Catholique, 15, M; St Denis, Morile, St. Polycarpe F, Catholique, 13, M; St Denis, Pierre, St. Polycarpe F, Catholique, 11, M; St Denis, JBt, St. Polycarpe F, Catholique, 9, M; St Denis, Souplien?, St. Polycarpe F, Catholique, 10, M)* (1852C Cdn Transcription Project, District 538, page 63d, 64a, (127), line 10-20.).

Hyacinthe Denis dit St.Denis was born on 12 Aug 1801 Vaudreuil, Quebec (PRDH online, #2589945.). He was baptized on 13 Aug 1801 Vaudreuil, Quebec *(father's occupation: cultivator)* (PRDH online, #2589945.).

Children of **Eugenie Emilie Sauve** and **Hyacinthe Denis dit St.Denis** all born St.Polycarpe, Quebec, were as follows:

i.   Hyacinthe Denis was born on 16 Nov 1829 (Ibid., #4454333.). He was baptized on 17 Nov 1829 St.Polycarpe, Quebec (Ibid.).

He was in the census household of Hyacinthe Denis dit St.Denis and Eugenie Emilie Sauve in 1852 St.Polycarpe, Vaudreuil, Quebec (1852C Cdn Transcription Project, District 538, page 63d, 64a, (127), line 10-20.).

ii.   Emilie Denis was born on 15 Jan 1831 (PRDH online, #4454510.). She was baptized on 16 Jan 1831 St.Polycarpe, Quebec (Ibid.). She died on 21 Feb 1831 St.Polycarpe, Quebec (Ibid., #4181447.). She was buried on 22 Feb 1831 St.Polycarpe, Quebec *(age 6 weeks)* (PRDH online, #4181447.).

iii.   Joseph St.Denis was born on 8 Mar 1832 (Ibid., #4454738.). He was baptized on 8 Mar 1832 St.Polycarpe, Quebec (Ibid.).

He was in the census household of Hyacinthe Denis dit St.Denis and Eugenie Emilie Sauve in 1852 St.Polycarpe, Vaudreuil, Quebec (1852C Cdn Transcription Project, District 538, page 63d, 64a, (127), line 10-20.).

iv.   Louis Denis was born on 15 Oct 1833 (PRDH online, #4455064.). He was baptized on 16 Oct 1833 St.Polycarpe, Quebec (Ibid.).

He was in the census household of Hyacinthe Denis dit St.Denis and Eugenie Emilie Sauve in 1852 St.Polycarpe, Vaudreuil, Quebec (1852C Cdn Transcription Project, District 538, page 63d, 64a, (127), line 10-20.).

v.   Joseph Morice St.Denis was born on 22 Jul 1835 (PRDH online, #4455350.). He was baptized on 23 Jul 1835 St.Polycarpe, Quebec (Ibid.).

He was in the census household of Hyacinthe Denis dit St.Denis and Eugenie Emilie Sauve in 1852 St.Polycarpe, Vaudreuil, Quebec (1852C Cdn Transcription Project, District 538, page 63d, 64a, (127), line 10-20.).

vi.   Pierre St.Denis was born on 30 Sep 1837 (PRDH online, #4455704.). He was baptized on 30 Sep 1837 St.Polycarpe, Quebec (Ibid.).

He was in the census household of Hyacinthe Denis dit St.Denis and Eugenie Emilie Sauve in 1852 St.Polycarpe, Vaudreuil, Quebec (1852C Cdn Transcription Project, District 538, page 63d, 64a, (127), line 10-20.).

vii.   Jean Baptiste St.Denis was born on 7 Jun 1839 (PRDH online, #4455982.). He was baptized on 7 Jun 1839 St.Polycarpe, Quebec (Ibid.).

He was in the census household of Hyacinthe Denis dit St.Denis and Eugenie Emilie Sauve in 1852 St.Polycarpe, Vaudreuil, Quebec (1852C Cdn Transcription Project, District 538, page 63d, 64a, (127), line 10-20.).

    viii.   Anonyme St.Denis was born on 1 Sep 1841 (PRDH online, #4459177.). He/she died on 1 Sep 1841 St.Polycarpe, Quebec (Ibid.). He/she was buried on 3 Sep 1841 St.Polycarpe, Quebec (Ibid.).

    ix.   Pierre Supplie St.Denis was born on 13 Nov 1842 (Ibid., #4456618.). He was baptized on 14 Nov 1842 St.Polycarpe, Quebec (Ibid.).
      He was in the census household of Hyacinthe Denis dit St.Denis and Eugenie Emilie Sauve in 1852 St.Polycarpe, Vaudreuil, Quebec (1852C Cdn Transcription Project, District 538, page 63d, 64a, (127), line 10-20.).

    x.   Henriette St.Denis was born on 8 Sep 1844 (PRDH online, #4456975.). She was baptized on 8 Sep 1844 St.Polycarpe, Quebec (Ibid.).
      She was in the census household of Hyacinthe Denis dit St.Denis and Eugenie Emilie Sauve in 1852 St.Polycarpe, Vaudreuil, Quebec (1852C Cdn Transcription Project, District 538, page 63d, 64a, (127), line 10-20.).

    xi.   Marie Brazelle St.Denis was born on 15 Mar 1847 (PRDH online, #4457512.). She was baptized on 15 Mar 1847 St.Polycarpe, Quebec (Ibid.).
      She was in the census household of Hyacinthe Denis dit St.Denis and Eugenie Emilie Sauve in 1852 St.Polycarpe, Vaudreuil, Quebec (1852C Cdn Transcription Project, District 538, page 63d, 64a, (127), line 10-20.).

67. Marie Marguerite Villeneuve was born on 29 Apr 1810 Ste-Madeleine-de-Rigaud, Quebec (PRDH online, #2679671.). She was baptized on 29 Apr 1810 Ste-Madeleine-de-Rigaud, Quebec *(father's occupation: agriculture)* (PRDH online, #2679671.). She married **Andre Denis dit St.Denis**, son of **Amable Denis dit St.Denis** and **Pelagie Felicite Normand,** on 3 May 1830 Ste-Madeleine-de-Rigaud, Quebec *(Consanguinity: 4)* (PRDH online, #3461798.).
Andre Denis dit St.Denis was born on 7 Jun 1805 Vaudreuil, Quebec (Ibid., #2590334.). He was baptized on 8 Jun 1805 Vaudreuil, Quebec *(father's occupation: cultivator)* (PRDH online, #2590334.).
Children of **Marie Marguerite Villeneuve** and **Andre Denis dit St.Denis** were:

    i.   Mathilde St.Denis was born on 28 Mar 1831 Ste-Madeleine-de-Rigaud, Quebec (Ibid., #4618329.). She was baptized on 28 Mar 1831 Ste-Madeleine-de-Rigaud, Quebec (Ibid.). She died on 16 Oct 1832 Ste-Madeleine-de-Rigaud, Quebec, at age 1 (Ibid., #4623363.). She was buried on 18 Oct 1832 Ste-Madeleine-de-Rigaud, Quebec *(age 16 months)* (PRDH online, #4623363.).

68. Marie Angelique Villeneuve was born circa 1817 (Ibid., #3463947.). She married **Antoine Boyer dit Germain**, son of **Pierre Boyer dit Fontaine** and **Marie Josephe Leduc,** on 8 Aug 1836 Ste-Madeleine-de-Rigaud, Quebec (Ibid.).
Antoine Boyer dit Germain was born on 30 Nov 1804 (Ste-Jeanne-de-Chantal), L'Ile Perrot, Quebec (Ibid., #2873124.). He was baptized on 1 Dec 1804 (Ste-Jeanne-de-Chantal), L'Ile Perrot, Quebec *(father's occupation: voyageur)* (PRDH online, #2873124.).
Children of **Marie Angelique Villeneuve** and **Antoine Boyer dit Germain** were as follows:

    i.   Marguerite Caroline Boyer was born on 16 Aug 1837 Rigaud, Quebec (Ibid., #4681706.). She was baptized on 16 Aug 1837 St-Andre-d'Argenteuil, Quebec (Ibid.).

    ii.   Sarah Anne Boyer was born on 13 Feb 1840 Pointe Fortune, Quebec (Ibid., #4681961.). She was baptized on 14 Feb 1840 St-Andre-d'Argenteuil, Quebec (Ibid.).

    iii.   Philomene Boyer was born on 6 Oct 1843 Pointe Fortune, Quebec (Ibid., #4682271.). She was baptized on 8 Oct 1843 St-Andre-d'Argenteuil, Quebec (Ibid.).

    iv.   Narcisse Godfroi Boyer was born on 6 Dec 1845 (Ibid., #4682526.). He was baptized on 7 Dec 1845 St-Andre-d'Argenteuil, Quebec (Ibid.).

    v.   Julie Boyer was born on 28 Dec 1847 (Ibid., #4682768.). She was baptized on 1 Jan 1848 St-Andre-d'Argenteuil, Quebec (Ibid.). She died on 12 Jan 1848 (Ibid., #4683350.). She was buried on 14 Jan 1848 St-Andre-d'Argenteuil, Quebec (Ibid.).

    vi.   Antoine Marcel Boyer was born on 10 Apr 1849 (Ibid., #4682924.). He was baptized on 11 Apr 1849 St-Andre-d'Argenteuil, Quebec (Ibid.).

69. Marie Reine Narcisse Villeneuve was born on 10 Mar 1803 Ste-Madeleine-de-Rigaud, Quebec (Ibid., #2679143.). She was baptized on 12 Mar 1803 Ste-Madeleine-de-Rigaud, Quebec (Ibid.). She married **Francois Xavier Berlinguet**, son of **Francois Xavier Berlinguet** and **Marie Genevieve Ranger,** on 31 Jan 1820 Ste-Madeleine-de-Rigaud, Quebec (Ibid., #2219903.). She married **Jean Baptiste Normand**, son of **Jean Baptiste Normand** and **Marguerite Poirier dit Desloges,** on 1 Oct 1839 Vaudreuil, Quebec (Ibid., #3476124.).

She was in the census household of **Leandre Legault dit Deslauriers** and **Marie Angelique Berlinguet** in 1852 St.Michel, Vaudreuil, Vaudreuil, Quebec (1852C Cdn Transcription Project, District 534, page 25d, 26a, (51), line 43-47.).

Francois Xavier Berlinguet was born on 11 May 1793 Vaudreuil, Quebec (PRDH online, #770489.). He was baptized on 12 May 1793 Vaudreuil, Quebec (Ibid.). He died on 17 Jul 1832 Ste-Madeleine-de-Rigaud, Quebec, at age 39 (Ibid., #4623247.). He was buried on 18 Jul 1832 Ste-Madeleine-de-Rigaud, Quebec *(age 39, husband of Reine Villeneuve)* (PRDH online, #4623247.).

Children of **Marie Reine Narcisse Villeneuve** and **Francois Xavier Berlinguet** all born Ste-Madeleine-de-Rigaud, Quebec, were as follows:

        i.   Francois Xavier Berlinguet was born on 17 Jul 1824 (Ibid., #2681211.). He was baptized on 18 Jul 1824 Ste-Madeleine-de-Rigaud, Quebec *(father's occupation: cultivator)* (PRDH online, #2681211.). He died on 22 Jul 1824 Ste-Madeleine-de-Rigaud, Quebec (Ibid., #2682353.). He was buried on 23 Jul 1824 Ste-Madeleine-de-Rigaud, Quebec *(age 4 days, father's occupation: cultivator)* (PRDH online, #2682353.).

145   ii.   Joseph Alexandre Berlinguet, b. 19 Jun 1825; m. Justine Normand.

146   iii. Marie Angelique Berlinguet, b. 21 Jul 1827; m. Leandre Legault dit Deslauriers.

       iv.   Henriette Berlinguet was born on 28 Oct 1830 (Ibid., #4618211.). She was baptized on 29 Oct 1830 Ste-Madeleine-de-Rigaud, Quebec (Ibid.). She died on 8 Feb 1842 St-Ignace-de-Coteau-du-Lac, Quebec, at age 11 (Ibid., #3274256.). She was buried on 10 Feb 1842 St-Ignace-de-Coteau-du-Lac, Quebec *(age 11 years and 3 months)* (PRDH online, #3274256.).

Jean Baptiste Normand was baptized on 3 Jul 1794 Vaudreuil, Quebec (Ibid., #637304.). He married **Genevieve Marie Poirier dit Desloges**, daughter of **Pierre Joseph Poirier dit Desloges** and **Marie Genevieve Cadieux,** on 22 Sep 1817 Vaudreuil, Quebec (Ibid., #605882.).

Children of **Marie Reine Narcisse Villeneuve** and **Jean Baptiste Normand** were as follows:

        i.   Jean Baptiste Normand was born circa 1 Jul 1840 St-Ignace-de-Coteau-du-Lac, Quebec (Ibid., #3272254.). He was baptized on 1 Aug 1840 St-Ignace-de-Coteau-du-Lac, Quebec (Ibid.). He died on 13 Feb 1841 St-Ignace-de-Coteau-du-Lac, Quebec (Ibid., #3274189.). He was buried on 15 Feb 1841 St-Ignace-de-Coteau-du-Lac, Quebec (Ibid.).

       ii.   Adolphe Normand was born on 5 Dec 1842 Vaudreuil, Quebec (Ibid., #4180084.). He was baptized on 6 Dec 1842 Vaudreuil, Quebec (Ibid.). He died on 4 Jan 1843 Vaudreuil, Quebec (Ibid., #4182273.). He was buried on 5 Jan 1843 Vaudreuil, Quebec (Ibid.).

70. Marie Jeanne Dechantal Villeneuve was born on 30 Mar 1805 Ste-Madeleine-de-Rigaud, Quebec (Ibid., #2679260.). She was baptized on 30 Mar 1805 Ste-Madeleine-de-Rigaud, Quebec *(father's occupation: agriculture)* (PRDH online, #2679260.). She married **Francois Lauzon**, son of **Joseph Lauzon** and **Scholastique Beauchamp,** on 26 Feb 1827 Ste-Madeleine-de-Rigaud, Quebec (Ibid., #3460493.).

Francois Lauzon was born on 16 Mar 1807 St.Henry, Lauzon, Quebec (Ibid., #2776998.). He was baptized on 17 Mar 1807 Lachenaie, Quebec *(father's occupation: laborer)* (PRDH online, #2776998.).

Children of **Marie Jeanne Dechantal Villeneuve** and **Francois Lauzon** all born Ste-Madeleine-de-Rigaud, Quebec, were as follows:

        i.   Marie Adele Lauzon was born on 25 Dec 1829 (Ibid., #4618043.). She was baptized on 26 Dec 1829 Ste-Madeleine-de-Rigaud, Quebec (Ibid.). She died on 25 Aug 1831 Ste-Madeleine-de-Rigaud, Quebec, at age 1 (Ibid., #4623146.). She was buried on 26 Aug 1831 Ste-Madeleine-de-Rigaud, Quebec (Ibid.).

       ii.   Marie Adelaide Lauzon was born on 23 Dec 1831 (Ibid., #4618496.). She was baptized on 24 Dec 1831 Ste-Madeleine-de-Rigaud, Quebec (Ibid.).

      iii.   Anonyme Lauzon was born on 23 Dec 1831 (Ibid., #4623175.). He died on 23 Dec 1831 Ste-Madeleine-de-Rigaud, Quebec (Ibid.). He was buried on 24 Dec 1831 Ste-Madeleine-de-Rigaud, Quebec (Ibid.).

71. Angelique Louise Villeneuve was born on 22 Jun 1810 Ste-Madeleine-de-Rigaud, Quebec (Ibid., #2679686.). She was baptized on 22 Jun 1810 Ste-Madeleine-de-Rigaud, Quebec *(father's occupation: agriculture)* (PRDH online, #2679686.). She married **Gregoire Watier dit Lanoix**, son of **Antoine Watier dit Lanoix** and **Josephe Dubois,** on 17 Apr 1837 St-Ignace-de-Coteau-du-Lac, Quebec (Ibid., #3448563.).

She and **Gregoire Watier dit Lanoix** were enumerated in the census in 1852 St.Clet, Vaudreuil, Quebec. Also in the family: **Calixte Watier, Gilbert Watier, Gergroire Watier, Samuel Watier, Antoine Watier dit Lanoix**, and **Josephe Dubois** *(Watier, Grégoire, Cultivateur, Vaudreuil F, Catholique, 42, M; Vilneuve, Angelique, Rigaud F, Catholique, 42, F; Watier, Calis, St. Ignace F, Catholique, 10, M; Watier, Gilbert, St. Ignace F, Catholique, 9, M;*

Watier, Gregoire, St. Ignace F, Catholique, 6, M; Watier, Samuel, St. Ignace F, Catholique, 3, M; Watier, Antoine, Soulanges F, Catholique, 86, M; Dubois, Josephte, Vaudreuil F, Catholique, 80, F) (1852C Cdn Transcription Project, District 541, page 19d, 20a, (39), line 11-18.).

Gregoire Watier dit Lanoix was born on 9 Aug 1810 Vaudreuil, Quebec (PRDH online, #2590778.). He was baptized on 9 Aug 1810 Vaudreuil, Quebec *(father's occupation: laborer)* (PRDH online, #2590778.).

Children of **Angelique Louise Villeneuve** and **Gregoire Watier dit Lanoix** were as follows:

i. Fereole Watier was born on 23 Jan 1838 St-Polycarpe, Quebec (Ibid., #4455740.). He was baptized on 24 Jan 1838 St-Polycarpe, Quebec (Ibid.). He died on 18 Jun 1838 (Ibid., #4414287.). He was buried on 20 Jun 1838 Les Cedres, Quebec *(age 5 months)* (PRDH online, #4414287.).

ii. Odile Watier was born on 15 May 1839 St-Ignace, Quebec (Ibid., #4412202.). She was baptized on 16 May 1839 Les Cedres, Quebec (Ibid.). She died on 15 Aug 1842 St-Ignace-de-Coteau-du-Lac, Quebec, at age 3 (Ibid., #3274319.). She was buried on 16 Aug 1842 St-Ignace-de-Coteau-du-Lac, Quebec (Ibid.).

iii. Calixte Watier was born on 5 Jul 1841 St-Ignace-de-Coteau-du-Lac, Quebec (Ibid., #3272395.). He was baptized on 6 Jul 1841 St-Ignace-de-Coteau-du-Lac, Quebec (Ibid.).
He was in the census household of Gregoire Watier dit Lanoix and Angelique Louise Villeneuve in 1852 St.Clet, Vaudreuil, Quebec (1852C Cdn Transcription Project, District 541, page 19d, 20a, (39), line 11-18.).

iv. Gilbert Watier was born on 30 Dec 1843 St-Ignace-de-Coteau-du-Lac, Quebec (PRDH online, #3272817.). He was baptized on 30 Dec 1843 St-Ignace-de-Coteau-du-Lac, Quebec (Ibid.).
He was in the census household of Gregoire Watier dit Lanoix and Angelique Louise Villeneuve in 1852 St.Clet, Vaudreuil, Quebec (1852C Cdn Transcription Project, District 541, page 19d, 20a, (39), line 11-18.).

v. Gergroire Watier was born on 13 Jul 1846 St-Ignace-de-Coteau-du-Lac, Quebec (PRDH online, #3273275.). He was baptized on 13 Jul 1846 St-Ignace-de-Coteau-du-Lac, Quebec (Ibid.).
He was in the census household of Gregoire Watier dit Lanoix and Angelique Louise Villeneuve in 1852 St.Clet, Vaudreuil, Quebec (1852C Cdn Transcription Project, District 541, page 19d, 20a, (39), line 11-18.).

vi. Samuel Watier was born on 23 Nov 1848 St-Ignace-de-Coteau-du-Lac, Quebec (PRDH online, #3273716.). He was baptized on 23 Nov 1848 St-Ignace-de-Coteau-du-Lac, Quebec (Ibid.).
He was in the census household of Gregoire Watier dit Lanoix and Angelique Louise Villeneuve in 1852 St.Clet, Vaudreuil, Quebec (1852C Cdn Transcription Project, District 541, page 19d, 20a, (39), line 11-18.).

72. Rose Emelie Villeneuve was born on 13 May 1815 Ste-Madeleine-de-Rigaud, Quebec (PRDH online, #2680181.). She was baptized on 14 May 1815 Ste-Madeleine-de-Rigaud, Quebec *(father's occupation: agriculture)* (PRDH online, #2680181.). She married **Louis Goulet**, son of **Francois Goulet** and **Josephe Poudrette dit Caluchon or Lavigne,** on 27 Sep 1842 Les Cedres, Quebec (Ibid., #3459858.).

She and **Louis Goulet** were enumerated in the census in 1852 St.Clet, Vaudreuil, Quebec. Also in the family: **Hilaire Goulet, Louis Alfred Goulet, Moyse Goulet, Joseph Goulet, Alexandre Goulet, Adele Goulet, Gelas Goulet, Delina Goulet,** and **Priscille Goulet** *(Goulet, Louis, Cultivateur, Soulanges F, Catholique, 43, M; Vilneuve, Emilie, Rigaud F, Catholique, 36, F; Goulet, Hilaire, Journalier, St. Ignace F, Catholique, 13, M; Goulet, Alfred, Soulanges F, Catholique, 16, M; Goulet, Moïse, St. Ignace F, Catholique, 14, M; Goulet, Joseph, St. Ignace F, Catholique, 8, M; Goulet, Alexandre, St. Ignace F, Catholique, 6, M; Goulet, Adèle, St. Ignace F, Catholique, 4, F; Goulet, Gélas, St. Ignace F, Catholique, 2, M; Goulet, Délina, St. Clet F, Catholique, 1 mois, F; Goulet, Précile, St. Clet F, Catholique, 1 mois, F)* (1852C Cdn Transcription Project, District 541, page 22d, 23a, (45), line 9-19.).

Louis Goulet was born on 27 Jun 1810 Vaudreuil, Quebec (PRDH online, #2590784.). He was baptized on 28 Jun 1810 Vaudreuil, Quebec *(father's occupation: day laborer)* (PRDH online, #2590784.). He married **Angelique Sabourin,** daughter of **Louis Sabourin** and **Rose Ranger,** on 22 Apr 1833 Vaudreuil, Quebec (Ibid., #3474635.).

Children of **Rose Emelie Villeneuve** and **Louis Goulet** were as follows:

i. Joseph Goulet was born on 26 Oct 1843 St-Ignace-de-Coteau-du-Lac, Quebec (Ibid., #3272786.). He was baptized on 26 Oct 1843 St-Ignace-de-Coteau-du-Lac, Quebec (Ibid.).
He was in the census household of Louis Goulet and Rose Emelie Villeneuve in 1852 St.Clet, Vaudreuil, Quebec (1852C Cdn Transcription Project, District 541, page 22d, 23a, (45), line 9-19.).

ii. Alexandre Goulet was born on 18 Oct 1845 St-Ignace-de-Coteau-du-Lac, Quebec (PRDH online, #3273146.). He was baptized on 18 Oct 1845 St-Ignace-de-Coteau-du-Lac, Quebec (Ibid.).

He was in the census household of Louis Goulet and Rose Emelie Villeneuve in 1852 St.Clet, Vaudreuil, Quebec (1852C Cdn Transcription Project, District 541, page 22d, 23a, (45), line 9-19.).

    iii.   Louis Goulet was born on 13 Sep 1847 St-Ignace-de-Coteau-du-Lac, Quebec *(twin)* (PRDH online, #3273487.). He was baptized on 14 Sep 1847 St-Ignace-de-Coteau-du-Lac, Quebec (Ibid.). He died on 21 May 1848 St-Ignace-de-Coteau-du-Lac, Quebec (Ibid., #3274654.). He was buried on 23 May 1848 St-Ignace-de-Coteau-du-Lac, Quebec *(age 8 months)* (PRDH online, #3274654.).

    iv.   Adele Goulet was born on 13 Sep 1847 St-Ignace-de-Coteau-du-Lac, Quebec *(twin)* (PRDH online, #3273488.). She was baptized on 14 Sep 1847 St-Ignace-de-Coteau-du-Lac, Quebec (Ibid.).

    She was in the census household of Louis Goulet and Rose Emelie Villeneuve in 1852 St.Clet, Vaudreuil, Quebec (1852C Cdn Transcription Project, District 541, page 22d, 23a, (45), line 9-19.).

    v.   Gelas Goulet was born circa 1849 (Ibid.).

    He was in the census household of Louis Goulet and Rose Emelie Villeneuve in 1852 St.Clet, Vaudreuil, Quebec (1852C Cdn Transcription Project, District 541, page 22d, 23a, (45), line 9-19.).

    vi.   Delina Goulet was born circa 1851 *(twin)* (1852C Cdn Transcription Project, District 541, page 22d, 23a, (45), line 9-19.).

    She was in the census household of Louis Goulet and Rose Emelie Villeneuve in 1852 St.Clet, Vaudreuil, Quebec (1852C Cdn Transcription Project, District 541, page 22d, 23a, (45), line 9-19.).

    vii.   Priscille Goulet was born circa 1851 *(twin)* (1852C Cdn Transcription Project, District 541, page 22d, 23a, (45), line 9-19.).

    She was in the census household of Louis Goulet and Rose Emelie Villeneuve in 1852 St.Clet, Vaudreuil, Quebec (1852C Cdn Transcription Project, District 541, page 22d, 23a, (45), line 9-19.).

73. Francois Xavier Villeneuve was born on 29 Nov 1817 Ste-Madeleine-de-Rigaud, Quebec (PRDH online, #2680436.). He was baptized on 29 Nov 1817 Ste-Madeleine-de-Rigaud, Quebec *(father's occupation: agriculture)* (PRDH online, #2680436.). He married **Angele Bourbonnais**, daughter of **Jean Baptiste Brunet dit Bourbonnais or Payant** and **Genevieve Daoust,** on 31 Oct 1842 St-Ignace-de-Coteau-du-Lac, Quebec (Ibid., #3450113.).

Angele Bourbonnais was born on 17 Aug 1823 Les Cedres, Quebec (Ibid., #2676461.). She was baptized on 17 Aug 1823 Les Cedres, Quebec *(father's occupation: cultivator)* (PRDH online, #2676461.).

Children of **Francois Xavier Villeneuve** and **Angele Bourbonnais** all born St-Ignace-de-Coteau-du-Lac, Quebec, were as follows:

    i.   Francois Xavier Villeneuve was born on 2 Oct 1843 (Ibid., #3272772.). He was baptized on 2 Oct 1843 St-Ignace-de-Coteau-du-Lac, Quebec (Ibid.).

    ii.   Mathilde Villeneuve was born on 4 May 1845 (Ibid., #3273073.). She was baptized on 4 May 1845 St-Ignace-de-Coteau-du-Lac, Quebec (Ibid.). She died on 18 May 1848 St-Ignace-de-Coteau-du-Lac, Quebec, at age 3 (Ibid., #3274653.). She was buried on 19 May 1848 St-Ignace-de-Coteau-du-Lac, Quebec (Ibid.).

    iii.   Joseph Villeneuve was born on 7 Mar 1848 (Ibid., #3273567.). He was baptized on 7 Mar 1848 St-Ignace-de-Coteau-du-Lac, Quebec (Ibid.).

74. Marie Veronique Villeneuve was born on 27 Sep 1814 Ste-Madeleine-de-Rigaud, Quebec (Ibid., #2680110.). She was baptized on 27 Sep 1814 Ste-Madeleine-de-Rigaud, Quebec *(father's occupation: agriculture)* (PRDH online, #2680110.). She married **Pierre Beaupre**, son of **Pierre Beaupre** and **Marguerite Bellefeuille,** on 15 Feb 1830 Ste-Madeleine-de-Rigaud, Quebec (Ibid., #3461669.). She married **Hyacinthe Daoust**, son of **Jacques Daoust** and **Marie Josephe Amable Jamme dit Carrier or James,** on 4 May 1846 Ste-Madeleine-de-Rigaud, Quebec (Ibid., #3466697.).

Pierre Beaupre was born circa 1790 (Ibid., #4624178.). He died on 15 Aug 1841 Ste-Madeleine-de-Rigaud, Quebec (Ibid.). He was buried on 17 Aug 1841 Ste-Madeleine-de-Rigaud, Quebec *(age 51, husband of Veronique Villeneuve)* (PRDH online, #4624178.).

Children of **Marie Veronique Villeneuve** and **Pierre Beaupre** all born Ste-Madeleine-de-Rigaud, Quebec, were as follows:

     i.   Joseph Beaupre was born on 8 Dec 1833 (Ibid., #4619014.). He was baptized on 9 Dec 1833 Ste-Madeleine-de-Rigaud, Quebec (Ibid.).

    ii.   Julienne Beaupre was born on 19 Feb 1836 (Ibid., #4619571.). She was baptized on 20 Feb 1836 Ste-Madeleine-de-Rigaud, Quebec (Ibid.). She died on 4 May 1842 Ste-Madeleine-de-Rigaud, Quebec, at age 6 (Ibid., #4624251.). She was buried on 6 May 1842 Ste-Madeleine-de-Rigaud, Quebec (Ibid.).

    iii.   Francois Xavier Beaupre was born on 2 Jul 1837 (Ibid., #4619961.). He was baptized on 3 Jul 1837 Ste-Madeleine-de-Rigaud, Quebec (Ibid.).

    iv.   Marie Marcelline Beaupre was born on 22 Aug 1839 (Ibid., #4620464.). She was baptized on 25 Aug 1839 Ste-Madeleine-de-Rigaud, Quebec (Ibid.).

Hyacinthe Daoust was baptized on 4 Mar 1792 (Pierrefonds), Ste-Genevieve, Quebec (Ibid., #634242.). He married **Marie Proulx**, daughter of **Louis Proulx** and **Marie Angelique Vinet dit Larente,** on 25 Nov 1816 (Pierrefonds), Ste-Genevieve, Quebec (Ibid., #634243.). He married **Adelaide Marie Demers dit Dumais**, daughter of **Michel Demers** and **Genevieve Larocque,** on 31 Jul 1820 (Pierrefonds), Ste-Genevieve, Quebec (Ibid., #2228128.).

Children of **Marie Veronique Villeneuve** and **Hyacinthe Daoust** both born Ste-Madeleine-de-Rigaud, Quebec, were as follows:

     i.   Marie Justine Daoust was born on 5 Feb 1847 (Ibid., #4622181.). She was baptized on 7 Feb 1847 Ste-Madeleine-de-Rigaud, Quebec (Ibid.).

    ii.   Marie Louise Daoust was born on 18 Sep 1848 (Ibid., #4622449.). She was baptized on 18 Sep 1848 Ste-Madeleine-de-Rigaud, Quebec (Ibid.).

75. Joseph Benjamin Villeneuve was born on 12 Jan 1818 Ste-Madeleine-de-Rigaud, Quebec (Ibid., #2680449.). He was baptized on 12 Jan 1818 Ste-Madeleine-de-Rigaud, Quebec *(father's occupation: agriculture)* (PRDH online, #2680449.). He married **Rose Emelie Brunet dit Letang**, daughter of **Jean Baptiste Brunet dit Letang** and **Marie Rose Bedard,** on 19 Nov 1839 Ste-Madeleine-de-Rigaud, Quebec (Ibid., #3464927.).

Rose Emelie Brunet dit Letang was born on 6 Sep 1820 Ste-Madeleine-de-Rigaud, Quebec (Ibid., #2680804.). She was baptized on 6 Sep 1820 Ste-Madeleine-de-Rigaud, Quebec *(father's occupation: cultivator)* (PRDH online, #2680804.).

Children of **Joseph Benjamin Villeneuve** and **Rose Emelie Brunet dit Letang** all born Ste-Madeleine-de-Rigaud, Quebec, were as follows:

     i.   Joseph Amedee Villeneuve was born on 9 Dec 1840 (Ibid., #4620766.). He was baptized on 12 Dec 1840 Ste-Madeleine-de-Rigaud, Quebec (Ibid.).

    ii.   Emilie Villeneuve was born on 9 Aug 1842 (Ibid., #4621184.). She was baptized on 12 Aug 1842 Ste-Madeleine-de-Rigaud, Quebec (Ibid.).

    iii.   Julie Villeneuve was born on 1 Aug 1844 (Ibid., #4621644.). She was baptized on 3 Aug 1844 Ste-Madeleine-de-Rigaud, Quebec (Ibid.).

    iv.   Joseph Napoleon Villeneuve was born on 21 Sep 1846 (Ibid., #4622126.). He was baptized on 21 Sep 1846 Ste-Madeleine-de-Rigaud, Quebec (Ibid.). He died on 30 Mar 1847 Ste-Madeleine-de-Rigaud, Quebec (Ibid., #4624600.). He was buried on 1 Apr 1847 Ste-Madeleine-de-Rigaud, Quebec *(age 6 months)* (PRDH online, #4624600.).

    v.   Joseph Napoleon Villeneuve was born on 20 Dec 1847 (Ibid., #4622334.). He was baptized on 21 Dec 1847 Ste-Madeleine-de-Rigaud, Quebec (Ibid.). He died on 17 Jan 1848 Ste-Madeleine-de-Rigaud, Quebec (Ibid., #4624658.). He was buried on 18 Jan 1848 Ste-Madeleine-de-Rigaud, Quebec *(age 4 weeks)* (PRDH online, #4624658.).

76. Marie Louise Villeneuve was born on 21 Jul 1819 Ste-Madeleine-de-Rigaud, Quebec (Ibid., #2680646.). She was baptized on 22 Jul 1819 Ste-Madeleine-de-Rigaud, Quebec *(father's occupation: cultivator)* (PRDH online, #2680646.). She married **Joseph Seguin**, son of **Joseph Charles Seguin** and **Marie Augustine Ruth Kingsley,** on 23 Jan 1843 Ste-Madeleine-de-Rigaud, Quebec (Ibid., #3465663.).

As of 22 Jul 1819, she was also known as **Madelaine Louise Villeneuve** (Ibid., #2680646.).

Joseph Seguin was born on 24 May 1820 Ste-Madeleine-de-Rigaud, Quebec (Ibid., #2680761.). He was baptized on 24 May 1820 Ste-Madeleine-de-Rigaud, Quebec (Ibid.).

Children of **Marie Louise Villeneuve** and **Joseph Seguin** all born Ste-Madeleine-de-Rigaud, Quebec, were as follows:

     i.   Marie Louise Seguin was born on 30 Nov 1843 (Ibid., #4621491.). She was baptized on 1 Dec 1843 Ste-Madeleine-de-Rigaud, Quebec (Ibid.). She died on 5 Mar 1849 Ste-Madeleine-de-Rigaud, Quebec, at age 5 (Ibid., #4624711.). She was buried on 7 Mar 1849 Ste-Madeleine-de-Rigaud, Quebec (Ibid.).

      ii. Joseph Alphonse Seguin was born on 21 Jun 1845 (Ibid., #4621848.). He was baptized on 23 Jun 1845 Ste-Madeleine-de-Rigaud, Quebec (Ibid.).

      iii. Louis Napoleon Seguin was born on 17 May 1847 (Ibid., #4622239.). He was baptized on 20 May 1847 Ste-Madeleine-de-Rigaud, Quebec (Ibid.).

77. Marie Sophie Villeneuve was born on 19 May 1822 Ste-Madeleine-de-Rigaud, Quebec (Ibid., #2681024.). She was baptized on 19 May 1822 Ste-Madeleine-de-Rigaud, Quebec *(father's occupation: cultivator)* (PRDH online, #2681024.). She married **Antoine Foubert**, son of **Michel Foubert** and **Marie Rose Gastonguay,** on 24 Nov 1840 Ste-Madeleine-de-Rigaud, Quebec (Ibid., #3465178.).

Antoine Foubert was born on 16 Apr 1816 Ste-Madeleine-de-Rigaud, Quebec (Ibid., #2680279.). He was baptized on 16 Apr 1816 Ste-Madeleine-de-Rigaud, Quebec *(father's occupation: cultivator)* (PRDH online, #2680279.).

Children of **Marie Sophie Villeneuve** and **Antoine Foubert** both born Ste-Madeleine-de-Rigaud, Quebec, were as follows:

      i. Michel Foubert was born on 3 Sep 1842 (Ibid., #4621196.). He was baptized on 4 Sep 1842 Ste-Madeleine-de-Rigaud, Quebec (Ibid.). He died on 16 Oct 1842 (Ibid., #4624285.). He was buried on 20 Oct 1842 Ste-Madeleine-de-Rigaud, Quebec *(age 6 weeks)* (PRDH online, #4624285.).

      ii. Marie Hermine Foubert was born on 15 Jan 1844 (Ibid., #4621519.). She was baptized on 16 Jan 1844 Ste-Madeleine-de-Rigaud, Quebec (Ibid.).

78. Vincent Xavier Villeneuve was born on 4 Apr 1813 Ste-Madeleine-de-Riguad, Quebec (Ibid., #2679976.). He was baptized on 4 Apr 1813 Ste-Madeleine-de-Riguad, Quebec (Ibid.). He married **Marie Sophie Cadieux,** daughter of **Francois Xavier Cadieux** and **Marie Scholastique Villeneuve,** on 23 Nov 1835 Ste-Madeleine-de-Riguad, Quebec *(Consanguinity: 4)* (PRDH online, #3463675.).

As of 23 Nov 1835, he was also known as **Francois Xavier Villeneuve** (Ibid.).

Marie Sophie Cadieux was born on 18 Dec 1815 Ste-Madeleine-de-Riguad, Quebec (Ibid., #2680247.). She was baptized on 19 Dec 1815 Ste-Madeleine-de-Riguad, Quebec *(father's occupation: agriculture)* (PRDH online, #2680247.).

Children of **Vincent Xavier Villeneuve** and **Marie Sophie Cadieux** all born Ste-Madeleine-de-Riguad, Quebec, were as follows:

      i. Francois Barnabe Villeneuve was born on 31 Aug 1836 (Ibid., #4619749.). He was baptized on 31 Aug 1836 Ste-Madeleine-de-Riguad, Quebec (Ibid.).

      ii. Antoine Villeneuve was born on 20 Apr 1838 (Ibid., #4620124.). He was baptized on 20 Apr 1838 Ste-Madeleine-de-Riguad, Quebec (Ibid.).

      iii. Alphonse Villeneuve was born on 23 Dec 1839 (Ibid., #4620533.). He was baptized on 23 Dec 1839 Ste-Madeleine-de-Riguad, Quebec (Ibid.).

      iv. Joseph Michel Villeneuve was born on 2 Jun 1841 (Ibid., #4620906.). He was baptized on 2 Jun 1841 Ste-Madeleine-de-Riguad, Quebec (Ibid.). He died on 27 Oct 1844 Ste-Madeleine-de-Riguad, Quebec, at age 3 (Ibid., #4624472.). He was buried on 30 Oct 1844 Ste-Madeleine-de-Riguad, Quebec (Ibid.).

      v. Paul Villeneuve was born on 28 May 1842 (Ibid., #4621143.). He was baptized on 29 May 1842 Ste-Madeleine-de-Riguad, Quebec (Ibid.). He died on 1 Mar 1844 Ste-Madeleine-de-Riguad, Quebec, at age 1 (Ibid., #4624427.). He was buried on 3 Mar 1844 Ste-Madeleine-de-Riguad, Quebec (Ibid.).

      vi. Anastasie Villeneuve was born on 26 Aug 1843 (Ibid., #4621437.). She was baptized on 27 Aug 1843 Ste-Madeleine-de-Riguad, Quebec (Ibid.).

      vii. Joseph Edmond Villeneuve was born on 19 Apr 1845 (Ibid., #4621800.). He was baptized on 20 Apr 1845 Ste-Madeleine-de-Riguad, Quebec (Ibid.).

      viii. Marie Louise Villeneuve was born on 12 Nov 1846 (Ibid., #4622148.). She was baptized on 13 Nov 1846 Ste-Madeleine-de-Riguad, Quebec (Ibid.).

      ix. Eleonore Villeneuve was born on 19 Sep 1848 (Ibid., #4622455.). She was baptized on 20 Sep 1848 Ste-Madeleine-de-Riguad, Quebec (Ibid.). She died on 1 Aug 1849 Ste-Madeleine-de-Riguad, Quebec (Ibid., #4624744.). She was buried on 2 Aug 1849 Ste-Madeleine-de-Riguad, Quebec (Ibid.).

79. Clemence Villeneuve was born on 9 Sep 1817 Ste-Madeleine-de-Rigaud, Quebec (Ibid., #2680414.). She was baptized on 9 Sep 1817 Ste-Madeleine-de-Rigaud, Quebec *(father's occupation: agriculture)* (PRDH online, #2680414.). She married **Michel Paul Amable St.Julien**, son of **Michel St.Julien** and **Marguerite Cadieux,** on 7 May 1838 Ste-Madeleine-de-Rigaud, Quebec (Ibid., #3464495.).

She and **Michel Paul Amable St.Julien** were enumerated in the census in 1852 Ste-Madeleine-de-Rigaud, Vaudreuil, Quebec. Also in the family: **Michel St.Julien, Francois Xavier St.Julien, David St.Julien, Evangeliste St.Julien, Pierre St.Julien, Edouard St.Julien**, and **Eleonard St.Julien** *(St Julien, Paul, Voyageur, Rigaud, Catholique, 38, M; Villeneuve, Clémence, Rigaud, Catholique, 36, F; St Julien, Michel, Voyageur, Rigaud, Catholique, 13, M; St Julien, Xavier, Rigaud, Catholique, 12, M; St Julien, David, Rigaud, Catholique, 9, M; St Julien, Evangeliste, Rigaud, Catholique, 8, M; St Julien, Pierre, Rigaud, Catholique, 5, M; St Julien, Edouard, Rigaud, Catholique, 3, M; St Julien, Eléonard, Rigaud, Catholique, 1, F)* (1852C Cdn Transcription Project, District 536, page 35d, 36a, (71), line 18-26.).

Michel Paul Amable St.Julien was born on 15 Jan 1816 Ste-Madeleine-de-Rigaud, Quebec (PRDH online, #2680256.). He was baptized on 15 Jan 1816 Ste-Madeleine-de-Rigaud, Quebec *(father's occupation: agriculture)* (PRDH online, #2680256.).

Children of **Clemence Villeneuve** and **Michel Paul Amable St.Julien** all born Ste-Madeleine-de-Rigaud, Quebec, were as follows:

  i. Michel St.Julien was born on 30 Oct 1838 (Ibid., #4620252.). He was baptized on 31 Oct 1838 Ste-Madeleine-de-Rigaud, Quebec (Ibid.).
   He was in the census household of Michel Paul Amable St.Julien and Clemence Villeneuve in 1852 Ste-Madeleine-de-Rigaud, Vaudreuil, Quebec (1852C Cdn Transcription Project, District 536, page 35d, 36a, (71), line 18-26.).

  ii. Francois Xavier St.Julien was born on 23 Sep 1840 (PRDH online, #4620717.). He was baptized on 24 Sep 1840 Ste-Madeleine-de-Rigaud, Quebec (Ibid.).
   He was in the census household of Michel Paul Amable St.Julien and Clemence Villeneuve in 1852 Ste-Madeleine-de-Rigaud, Vaudreuil, Quebec (1852C Cdn Transcription Project, District 536, page 35d, 36a, (71), line 18-26.).

  iii. David St.Julien was born on 2 Jan 1843 (PRDH online, #4621283.). He was baptized on 4 Jan 1843 Ste-Madeleine-de-Rigaud, Quebec (Ibid.).
   His telephone number was *Quebec Metis.* He was in the census household of Michel Paul Amable St.Julien and Clemence Villeneuve in 1852 Ste-Madeleine-de-Rigaud, Vaudreuil, Quebec (1852C Cdn Transcription Project, District 536, page 35d, 36a, (71), line 18-26.).

  iv. Evangeliste St.Julien was born on 19 Jan 1845 (PRDH online, #4621744.). He was baptized on 19 Jan 1845 Ste-Madeleine-de-Rigaud, Quebec (Ibid.).
   He was in the census household of Michel Paul Amable St.Julien and Clemence Villeneuve in 1852 Ste-Madeleine-de-Rigaud, Vaudreuil, Quebec (1852C Cdn Transcription Project, District 536, page 35d, 36a, (71), line 18-26.).

  v. Pierre St.Julien was born on 4 Jan 1847 (PRDH online, #4622166.). He was baptized on 4 Jan 1847 Ste-Madeleine-de-Rigaud, Quebec (Ibid.).
   He was in the census household of Michel Paul Amable St.Julien and Clemence Villeneuve in 1852 Ste-Madeleine-de-Rigaud, Vaudreuil, Quebec (1852C Cdn Transcription Project, District 536, page 35d, 36a, (71), line 18-26.).

  vi. Edouard St.Julien was born on 11 Oct 1848 (PRDH online, #4622464.). He was baptized on 12 Oct 1848 Ste-Madeleine-de-Rigaud, Quebec (Ibid.).
   He was in the census household of Michel Paul Amable St.Julien and Clemence Villeneuve in 1852 Ste-Madeleine-de-Rigaud, Vaudreuil, Quebec (1852C Cdn Transcription Project, District 536, page 35d, 36a, (71), line 18-26.).

  vii. Eleonard St.Julien was born circa 1851 (Ibid.).
   She was in the census household of Michel Paul Amable St.Julien and Clemence Villeneuve in 1852 Ste-Madeleine-de-Rigaud, Vaudreuil, Quebec (1852C Cdn Transcription Project, District 536, page 35d, 36a, (71), line 18-26.).

80. Julienne Villeneuve was born on 4 Aug 1820 Ste-Madeleine-de-Riguad, Quebec (PRDH online, #2680784.). She was baptized on 4 Aug 1820 Ste-Madeleine-de-Riguad, Quebec (Ibid.). She married **Jean Marie Cadieux**, son of **Francois Xavier Cadieux** and **Marie Scholastique Villeneuve,** on 13 Feb 1844 Ste-Madeleine-de-Riguad, Quebec *(Consanguinity: 4)* (PRDH online, #3465916.).

She and **Jean Marie Cadieux** were enumerated in the census in 1852 Ste.Madeleine, Rigaud, Vaudreuil, Quebec. Also in the family: **Francois Xavier Cadieux, Napoleon Cadieux, Marie Sophie Cadieux, Honore Cadieux**, and **Marguerite Villeneuve** *(Cadieux, J. Marie, Cultivateur, Rigaud, Catholique, 35, M; Villeneuve, Julienne, Rigaud, Catholique, 31, F; Cadieux, Xavier, Rigaud, Catholique, 6, M; Cadieux, Napoléon, Rigaud, Catholique, 5, M; Cadieux, Sophie, Rigaud, Catholique, 2, F; Cadieux, Honoré, Rigaud, Catholique, 5 mois, M; Villeneuve, Marguerite,*

Servante, Rigaud, Catholique, 19, F; Cadieux, Benj, Voyageur, Rigaud, Catholique, 19, M) (1852C Cdn Transcription Project, District 536, page 35d, 36a, (71), line 27-34.).

Jean Marie Cadieux was born on 10 May 1817 Ste-Madeleine-de-Riguad, Quebec (PRDH online, #2680393.). He was baptized on 11 May 1817 Ste-Madeleine-de-Riguad, Quebec *(father's occupation: agriculture)* (PRDH online, #2680393.).

Children of **Julienne Villeneuve** and **Jean Marie Cadieux** all born Ste-Madeleine-de-Riguad, Quebec, were as follows:

    i. Francois Xavier Cadieux was born on 20 Apr 1845 (Ibid., #4621797.). He was baptized on 20 Apr 1845 Ste-Madeleine-de-Riguad, Quebec (Ibid.).

      He was in the census household of Jean Marie Cadieux and Julienne Villeneuve in 1852 Ste.Madeleine, Rigaud, Vaudreuil, Quebec (1852C Cdn Transcription Project, District 536, page 35d, 36a, (71), line 27-34.).

    ii. Napoleon Cadieux was born on 9 Aug 1846 (PRDH online, #4622091.). He was baptized on 10 Aug 1846 Ste-Madeleine-de-Riguad, Quebec (Ibid.).

      He was in the census household of Jean Marie Cadieux and Julienne Villeneuve in 1852 Ste.Madeleine, Rigaud, Vaudreuil, Quebec (1852C Cdn Transcription Project, District 536, page 35d, 36a, (71), line 27-34.).

    iii. Marie Eleonore Cadieux was born on 9 Jun 1848 (PRDH online, #4622341.). She was baptized on 9 Jun 1848 Ste-Madeleine-de-Riguad, Quebec (Ibid.).

    iv. Marie Sophie Cadieux was born on 22 Nov 1849 (Ibid., #4622633.). She was baptized on 22 Nov 1849 Ste-Madeleine-de-Riguad, Quebec (Ibid.).

      She was in the census household of Jean Marie Cadieux and Julienne Villeneuve in 1852 Ste.Madeleine, Rigaud, Vaudreuil, Quebec (1852C Cdn Transcription Project, District 536, page 35d, 36a, (71), line 27-34.).

Generation Five

81. **Marie Rose Villeneuve** was born on 30 Dec 1799 Oka, Quebec (PRDH online, No. 774040.). She was baptized on 30 Dec 1799 Oka, Quebec (Ibid.). She married **Jean Baptiste Brazeau dit Brassault**, son of **Jean-Baptiste Brazeau** and **Archange Campeau**, on 20 Nov 1820 Ste-Madeleine-de-Rigaud, Quebec (Ibid., #2220009.).

She and **Jean Baptiste Brazeau dit Brassault** were enumerated in the census in 1852 Ste-Madeleine, Rigaud, Quebec. Also in the family: **Marie Sophie Brazeau**, **Marie Edesse Brazeau**, **Emily Rose Brazeau**, **Marie Josephine Brazeau**, **Rose Gertrude Brazeau**, **Jean Baptiste Brazeau**, **Francois Xavier Brazeau**, and **Bernard Benjamin Treffle Brazeau** *(Brazeau, J B, Cultivateur, Rigaud, Catholique, 59, M; Villeneuve, M. Rose, Rigaud, Catholique, 52, F; Brazeau, Sophie, Rigaud, Catholique, 22, F; Brazeau, Edesse, Rigaud, Catholique, 19, F; Brazeau, Mélie, Rigaud, Catholique, 11, F; Brazeau, Josephine, Rigaud, Catholique, 9, F; Brazeau, Gertrude, Rigaud, Catholique, 8, F; Brazeau, J. B., Rigaud, Catholique, 17, M; Brazeau, Xavier, Rigaud, Catholique, 16, M; Brazeau, Trefflé, Rigaud, Catholique, 14, M)* (1852C Cdn Transcription Project, District 536, page 7d, 8a, (15), line 20-29.).

Jean Baptiste Brazeau dit Brassault was baptized on 16 Mar 1793 Vaudreuil, Quebec (PRDH online, #653354.).

Children of **Marie Rose Villeneuve** and **Jean Baptiste Brazeau dit Brassault** all born Ste-Madeleine-de-Rigaud, Quebec, were as follows:

    i. Marie Elisabeth Brassault was born on 12 Sep 1821 (Ibid., #2680921.). She was baptized on 12 Sep 1821 Ste-Madeleine-de-Rigaud, Quebec *(father's occupation: cultivator)* (PRDH online, #2680921.). She died on 20 Dec 1821 Ste-Madeleine-de-Rigaud, Quebec (Ibid., #2682266.). She was buried on 21 Dec 1821 Ste-Madeleine-de-Rigaud, Quebec *(age 3 months and 8 days, father's occupation: cultivator)* (PRDH online, #2682266.).

    ii. Jean Baptiste Brassault was born on 29 Oct 1822 (Ibid., #2681105.). He was baptized on 30 Oct 1822 Ste-Madeleine-de-Rigaud, Quebec *(father's occupation: cultivator)* (PRDH online, #2681105.). He died on 20 Nov 1822 Ste-Madeleine-de-Rigaud, Quebec (Ibid., #2682322.). He was buried on 21 Nov 1822 Ste-Madeleine-de-Rigaud, Quebec *(age 20 days, father's occupation: cultivator)* (PRDH online, #2682322.).

147   iii. Marie Angelique Brazeau dit Brassault, b. 5 Dec 1823; m. Paul Sabourin.

    iv. Marie Sophie Brazault was born on 26 Jun 1826 (Ibid., #4617377.). She was baptized on 27 Jun 1826 Ste-Madeleine-de-Rigaud, Quebec (Ibid.). She died on 29 Aug 1827 Ste-Madeleine-de-Rigaud, Quebec, at age 1 (Ibid., #4622846.). She was buried on 1 Sep 1827 Ste-Madeleine-de-Rigaud, Quebec *(age 10 months)* (PRDH online, #4622846.).

148   v.   Marie Louise Brazeau, b. 30 Jul 1827; m. Joseph Sabourin.

     vi.   Marie Sophie Brazeau was born on 3 Oct 1829 (Ibid., #4618013.). She was baptized on 4 Oct 1829 Ste-Madeleine-de-Rigaud, Quebec (Ibid.).

         She was in the census household of Jean Baptiste Brazeau dit Brassault and Marie Rose Villeneuve in 1852 Ste-Madeleine, Rigaud, Quebec (1852C Cdn Transcription Project, District 536, page 7d, 8a, (15), line 20-29.).

     vii.   Marie Helene Brazeau was born on 1 Apr 1831 (PRDH online, #4618331.). She was baptized on 2 Apr 1831 Ste-Madeleine-de-Rigaud, Quebec (Ibid.). She died on 21 Aug 1832 Ste-Madeleine-de-Rigaud, Quebec, at age 1 (Ibid., #4623326.). She was buried on 21 Aug 1832 Ste-Madeleine-de-Rigaud, Quebec (Ibid.).

     viii.   Marie Edesse Brazeau was born on 17 Jun 1832 (Ibid., #4618653.). She was baptized on 17 Jun 1832 Ste-Madeleine-de-Rigaud, Quebec (Ibid.).

         She was in the census household of Jean Baptiste Brazeau dit Brassault and Marie Rose Villeneuve in 1852 Ste-Madeleine, Rigaud, Quebec (1852C Cdn Transcription Project, District 536, page 7d, 8a, (15), line 20-29.).

     ix.   Jean Baptiste Brazeau was born on 22 Jul 1834 (PRDH online, #4619164.). He was baptized on 23 Jul 1834 Ste-Madeleine-de-Rigaud, Quebec (Ibid.).

         He was in the census household of Jean Baptiste Brazeau dit Brassault and Marie Rose Villeneuve in 1852 Ste-Madeleine, Rigaud, Quebec (1852C Cdn Transcription Project, District 536, page 7d, 8a, (15), line 20-29.).

     x.   Francois Xavier Brazeau was born on 13 Jan 1836 (PRDH online, #4619546.). He was baptized on 15 Jan 1836 Ste-Madeleine-de-Rigaud, Quebec (Ibid.).

         He was in the census household of Jean Baptiste Brazeau dit Brassault and Marie Rose Villeneuve in 1852 Ste-Madeleine, Rigaud, Quebec (1852C Cdn Transcription Project, District 536, page 7d, 8a, (15), line 20-29.).

     xi.   Bernard Benjamin Treffle Brazeau was born on 19 Aug 1838 (PRDH online, #4620207.). He was baptized on 20 Aug 1838 Ste-Madeleine-de-Rigaud, Quebec (Ibid.).

         He was in the census household of Jean Baptiste Brazeau dit Brassault and Marie Rose Villeneuve in 1852 Ste-Madeleine, Rigaud, Quebec (1852C Cdn Transcription Project, District 536, page 7d, 8a, (15), line 20-29.).

     xii.   Emily Rose Brazeau was born on 15 Apr 1840 (PRDH online, #4620615.). She was baptized on 16 Apr 1840 Ste-Madeleine-de-Rigaud, Quebec (Ibid.).

         She was in the census household of Jean Baptiste Brazeau dit Brassault and Marie Rose Villeneuve in 1852 Ste-Madeleine, Rigaud, Quebec (1852C Cdn Transcription Project, District 536, page 7d, 8a, (15), line 20-29.).

     xiii.   Marie Josephine Brazeau was born on 12 Jun 1842 (PRDH online, #4621154.). She was baptized on 13 Jun 1842 Ste-Madeleine-de-Rigaud, Quebec (Ibid.).

         She was in the census household of Jean Baptiste Brazeau dit Brassault and Marie Rose Villeneuve in 1852 Ste-Madeleine, Rigaud, Quebec (1852C Cdn Transcription Project, District 536, page 7d, 8a, (15), line 20-29.).

     xiv.   Rose Gertrude Brazeau was born on 11 Dec 1843 (PRDH online, #4621502.). She was baptized on 12 Dec 1843 Ste-Madeleine-de-Rigaud, Quebec (Ibid.).

         She was in the census household of Jean Baptiste Brazeau dit Brassault and Marie Rose Villeneuve in 1852 Ste-Madeleine, Rigaud, Quebec (1852C Cdn Transcription Project, District 536, page 7d, 8a, (15), line 20-29.).

82. Simon Regis Villeneuve was born on 13 May 1803 Ste-Madeleine-de-Rigaud, Quebec (PRDH online, #2679160.). He was baptized on 14 May 1803 Ste-Madeleine-de-Rigaud, Quebec (Ibid.). He married **Marie Madeleine Belanger**, daughter of **Francois Belanger** and **Marie Madeleine Charlebois,** on 21 Nov 1825 Ste-Madeleine-de-Rigaud, Quebec (Ibid., #3459987.).

He and **Marie Madeleine Belanger** were enumerated in the census in 1852 Ste-Madeleine, Rigaud, Quebec. Also in the family: **Marie Sophie Villeneuve** and **Joseph Telesphore Villeneuve** *(Villeneuve, Simon, Cultivateur, Rigaud, Catholique, 48, M; Bélanger, Magdeleine, Rigaud, Catholique, 47, F; Villeneuve, Sophie, Rigaud, Catholique, 18, F; Villeneuve, Télesphore, Rigaud, Catholique, 11, M)* (1852C Cdn Transcription Project, District 536, page 26d, 27a, (53), line 27-30.).

Marie Madeleine Belanger was born on 20 May 1806 Ste-Madeleine-de-Rigaud, Quebec (PRDH online, #2679349.). She was baptized on 20 May 1806 Ste-Madeleine-de-Rigaud, Quebec *(father's occupation: agriculture)* (PRDH online, #2679349.).

Children of **Simon Regis Villeneuve** and **Marie Madeleine Belanger** all born Ste-Madeleine-de-Rigaud, Quebec, were as follows:

 i. Simon Regis Villeneuve was born on 8 May 1827 (Ibid., #4617534.). He was baptized on 9 May 1827 Ste-Madeleine-de-Rigaud, Quebec (Ibid.). He died on 12 Oct 1827 Ste-Madeleine-de-Rigaud, Quebec (Ibid., #4622856.). He was buried on 16 Oct 1827 Ste-Madeleine-de-Rigaud, Quebec *(age 5 months)* (PRDH online, #4622856.).

 ii. Elie Alfred Villeneuve was born on 30 Dec 1828 (Ibid., #4617858.). He was baptized on 1 Jan 1829 Ste-Madeleine-de-Rigaud, Quebec (Ibid.). He died on 21 Feb 1846 Ste-Madeleine-de-Rigaud, Quebec, at age 17 (Ibid., #4624535.). He was buried on 24 Feb 1846 Ste-Madeleine-de-Rigaud, Quebec *(age 17)* (PRDH online, #4624535.).

 iii. Marie Sophie Villeneuve was born on 2 Jan 1834 (Ibid., #4619032.). She was baptized on 2 Jan 1834 Ste-Madeleine-de-Rigaud, Quebec (Ibid.).

  She was in the census household of Simon Regis Villeneuve and Marie Madeleine Belanger in 1852 Ste-Madeleine, Rigaud, Quebec (1852C Cdn Transcription Project, District 536, page 26d, 27a, (53), line 27-30.).

 iv. Joseph Telesphore Villeneuve was born on 29 Jan 1841 (PRDH online, #4620805.). He was baptized on 30 Jan 1841 Ste-Madeleine-de-Rigaud, Quebec (Ibid.).

  He was in the census household of Simon Regis Villeneuve and Marie Madeleine Belanger in 1852 Ste-Madeleine, Rigaud, Quebec (1852C Cdn Transcription Project, District 536, page 26d, 27a, (53), line 27-30.).

83. **Antoine Theodore Villeneuve** was born on 14 May 1805 Ste-Madeleine-de-Rigaud, Quebec (PRDH online, #2679265.). He was baptized on 15 May 1805 Ste-Madeleine-de-Rigaud, Quebec *(father's occupation: agriculture)*. He married **Veronique Emilie Chevrier dit Lajeunesse**, daughter of **Francois Chevrier dit Lajeunesse** and **Marguerite Rouleau,** on 1 Feb 1830 Ste-Madeleine-de-Rigaud, Quebec (PRDH online, #3461657.).

Veronique Emilie Chevrier dit Lajeunesse was born on 28 Jun 1810 Ste-Madeleine-de-Rigaud, Quebec (Ibid., #2679688.). She was baptized on 28 Jun 1810 Ste-Madeleine-de-Rigaud, Quebec *(father's occupation: agriculture)* (PRDH online, #2679688.).

Children of **Antoine Theodore Villeneuve** and **Veronique Emilie Chevrier dit Lajeunesse** were as follows:

 i. Joseph Theodore Villeneuve was born on 19 Mar 1831 Ste-Madeleine-de-Rigaud, Quebec (Ibid., #4618318.). He was baptized on 19 Mar 1831 Ste-Madeleine-de-Rigaud, Quebec (Ibid.).

 ii. Thomas Clement Villeneuve was born on 13 Mar 1832 Ste-Madeleine-de-Rigaud, Quebec (Ibid., #4618568.). He was baptized on 14 Mar 1832 Ste-Madeleine-de-Rigaud, Quebec (Ibid.).

 iii. Hilaire Villeneuve was born on 21 Mar 1833 Ste-Madeleine-de-Rigaud, Quebec (Ibid., #4618843.). He was baptized on 22 Mar 1833 Ste-Madeleine-de-Rigaud, Quebec (Ibid.).

 iv. Francois Emelien Villeneuve was born on 10 Dec 1834 Ste-Madeleine-de-Rigaud, Quebec (Ibid., #4619261.). He was baptized on 10 Dec 1834 Ste-Madeleine-de-Rigaud, Quebec (Ibid.). He died on 9 Sep 1835 (Ibid., #4623628.). He was buried on 12 Sep 1835 Ste-Madeleine-de-Rigaud, Quebec (Ibid.).

 v. Marie Monique Villeneuve was born on 16 May 1836 Hawkesbury, Ontario (Ibid., #4619646.). She was baptized on 17 May 1836 Ste-Madeleine-de-Rigaud, Quebec (Ibid.).

 vi. Regis Emelien Villeneuve was born on 13 Nov 1837 (Ibid., #4620032.). He was baptized on 14 Nov 1837 Ste-Madeleine-de-Rigaud, Quebec (Ibid.).

 vii. Francois Xavier Villeneuve was born on 13 Jul 1839 Ste-Madeleine-de-Rigaud, Quebec (Ibid., #4620440.). He was baptized on 13 Jul 1839 Ste-Madeleine-de-Rigaud, Quebec (Ibid.). He died on 28 Aug 1839 (Ibid., #4623985.). He was buried on 30 Aug 1839 Ste-Madeleine-de-Rigaud, Quebec (Ibid.).

 viii. Francois Xavier Villeneuve was born on 17 Aug 1840 Ste-Madeleine-de-Rigaud, Quebec (Ibid., #4620697.). He was baptized on 17 Aug 1840 Ste-Madeleine-de-Rigaud, Quebec (Ibid.).

 ix. Marie Philomene Villeneuve was born on 26 May 1842 Ste-Madeleine-de-Rigaud, Quebec (Ibid., #4621142.). She was baptized on 27 May 1842 Ste-Madeleine-de-Rigaud, Quebec (Ibid.).

 x. Alphonse Villeneuve was born on 30 Aug 1843 (Ibid., #4621444.). He was baptized on 3 Sep 1843 Ste-Madeleine-de-Rigaud, Quebec (Ibid.).

     xi.   Julie Honorine Villeneuve was born on 14 Jan 1845 (Ibid., #4621740.). She was baptized on 15 Jan 1845 Ste-Madeleine-de-Rigaud, Quebec (Ibid.). She died on 5 Feb 1845 (Ibid., #4624481.). She was buried on 7 Feb 1845 Ste-Madeleine-de-Rigaud, Quebec *(age 22 days)* (PRDH online, #4624481.).

    xii.   Antoine Villeneuve was born on 8 May 1846 Hawkesbury, Ontario (Ibid., #4622038.). He was baptized on 9 May 1846 Ste-Madeleine-de-Rigaud, Quebec (Ibid.).

    xiii.   Sophie Villeneuve was born on 17 Jul 1847 Hawkesbury, Ontario (Ibid., #4622261.). She was baptized on 18 Jul 1847 Ste-Madeleine-de-Rigaud, Quebec (Ibid.). She died on 14 Sep 1847 (Ibid., #4624644.). She was buried on 16 Sep 1847 Ste-Madeleine-de-Rigaud, Quebec (Ibid.).

    xiv.   Sophie Villeneuve was born on 22 Oct 1848 Hawkesbury, Ontario (Ibid., #4622468.). She was baptized on 23 Oct 1848 Ste-Madeleine-de-Rigaud, Quebec (Ibid.).

84. **Francois Xavier Villeneuve** was born on 27 May 1807 Ste-Madeleine-de-Rigaud, Quebec (Ibid., #2679422.). He was baptized on 28 May 1807 Ste-Madeleine-de-Rigaud, Quebec *(father's occupation: agriculture)* (PRDH online, #2679422.). He married **Marguerite Rachelle Ranger**, daughter of **Thomas Ranger** and **Josephte Chevrier,** on 25 Nov 1833 Ste-Madeleine-de-Rigaud, Quebec (Ibid., #3462783.).

He and **Marguerite Rachelle Ranger** were enumerated in the census in 1852 Ste-Madeleine, Rigaud, Quebec. Also in the family: **Francois Xavier Villeneuve, Marie Tharsile Villeneuve, Arline Marine Villeneuve, Marie Solyma Villeneuve, Marie Adeline Villeneuve, Marie Alphonsine Villeneuve, Edmond Villeneuve, Francois Alphonse Villeneuve**, and **Joseph Villeneuve** *(Villeneuve, Frs. X, Cultivateur, Rigaud, Catholique, 46, M; Ranger, Marguerite, Rigaud, Catholique, 38, F; Villeneuve, Xavier, Rigaud, Catholique, 17, M; Villeneuve, Tharsile, Rigaud, Catholique, 16, F; Villeneuve, Marine, Rigaud, Catholique, 14, F; Villeneuve, Clorinthe, Rigaud, Catholique, 10, F; Villeneuve, Sélina, Rigaud, Catholique, 8, F; Villeneuve, Adeline, Rigaud, Catholique, 6, F; Villeneuve, Alphonsine, Rigaud, Catholique, 4, F; Villeneuve, Edmond, Rigaud, Catholique, 9, M; Villeneuve, Alphonse, Rigaud, Catholique, 7, M; Villeneuve, Joseph, Rigaud, Catholique, 1, M)* (1852C Cdn Transcription Project, District 536, page 61d, 62a, (123) & page 59d, 60a, (119), line 44-50, 1-5.).

Marguerite Rachelle Ranger was born on 8 Aug 1814 Ste-Madeleine-de-Rigaud, Quebec (PRDH online, #2680101.). She was baptized on 8 Aug 1814 Ste-Madeleine-de-Rigaud, Quebec (Ibid.).

Children of **Francois Xavier Villeneuve** and **Marguerite Rachelle Ranger** were as follows:

    i.   Francois Xavier Villeneuve was born on 18 Aug 1834 Ste-Madeleine-de-Rigaud, Quebec (Ibid., #4619183.). He was baptized on 18 Aug 1834 Ste-Madeleine-de-Rigaud, Quebec (Ibid.).
He was in the census household of Francois Xavier Villeneuve and Marguerite Rachelle Ranger in 1852 Ste-Madeleine, Rigaud, Quebec (1852C Cdn Transcription Project, District 536, page 61d, 62a, (123) & page 59d, 60a, (119), line 44-50, 1-5.).

    ii.   Marie Tharsile Villeneuve was born on 5 Oct 1835 Ste-Madeleine-de-Rigaud, Quebec (PRDH online, #4619483.). She was baptized on 6 Oct 1835 Ste-Madeleine-de-Rigaud, Quebec (Ibid.).
She was in the census household of Francois Xavier Villeneuve and Marguerite Rachelle Ranger in 1852 Ste-Madeleine, Rigaud, Quebec (1852C Cdn Transcription Project, District 536, page 61d, 62a, (123) & page 59d, 60a, (119), line 44-50, 1-5.).

    iii.   Arline Marine Villeneuve was born on 17 Apr 1837 Ste-Madeleine-de-Rigaud, Quebec (PRDH online, #4619913.). She was baptized on 17 Apr 1837 Ste-Madeleine-de-Rigaud, Quebec (Ibid.).
She was in the census household of Francois Xavier Villeneuve and Marguerite Rachelle Ranger in 1852 Ste-Madeleine, Rigaud, Quebec (1852C Cdn Transcription Project, District 536, page 61d, 62a, (123) & page 59d, 60a, (119), line 44-50, 1-5.).

    iv.   Edmond Villeneuve was born on 26 Nov 1838 Ste-Madeleine-de-Rigaud, Quebec (PRDH online, #4620270.). He was baptized on 27 Nov 1838 Ste-Madeleine-de-Rigaud, Quebec (Ibid.). He died on 16 Mar 1839 Ste-Madeleine-de-Rigaud, Quebec (Ibid., #4623950.). He was buried on 18 Mar 1839 Ste-Madeleine-de-Rigaud, Quebec *(age 4 months)* (PRDH online, #4623950.).
He was in the census household of Francois Xavier Villeneuve and Marguerite Rachelle Ranger in 1852 Ste-Madeleine, Rigaud, Quebec (1852C Cdn Transcription Project, District 536, page 61d, 62a, (123) & page 59d, 60a, (119), line 44-50, 1-5.).

    v.   Marie Elise Villeneuve was born on 15 Dec 1839 Ste-Madeleine-de-Rigaud, Quebec (PRDH online, #4620531.). She was baptized on 15 Dec 1839 Ste-Madeleine-de-Rigaud, Quebec (Ibid.).

    vi.   Benjamin Villeneuve was born on 1 Nov 1841 Ste-Madeleine-de-Rigaud, Quebec (Ibid., #4620997.). He was baptized on 2 Nov 1841 Ste-Madeleine-de-Rigaud, Quebec (Ibid.).

    vii.   Marie Solyma Villeneuve was born on 2 Aug 1843 Ste-Madeleine-de-Rigaud, Quebec (Ibid., #4621421.). She was baptized on 2 Aug 1843 Ste-Madeleine-de-Rigaud, Quebec (Ibid.).

> She was in the census household of Francois Xavier Villeneuve and Marguerite Rachelle Ranger in 1852 Ste-Madeleine, Rigaud, Quebec (1852C Cdn Transcription Project, District 536, page 61d, 62a, (123) & page 59d, 60a, (119), line 44-50, 1-5.).

viii. Francois Alphonse Villeneuve was born on 14 Feb 1845 Ste-Madeleine-de-Rigaud, Quebec (PRDH online, #4621764.). He was baptized on 14 Feb 1845 Ste-Madeleine-de-Rigaud, Quebec (Ibid.).

> He was in the census household of Francois Xavier Villeneuve and Marguerite Rachelle Ranger in 1852 Ste-Madeleine, Rigaud, Quebec (1852C Cdn Transcription Project, District 536, page 61d, 62a, (123) & page 59d, 60a, (119), line 44-50, 1-5.).

ix. Marie Adeline Villeneuve was born on 17 Mar 1847 Ste-Madeleine-de-Rigaud, Quebec (PRDH online, #4622199.). She was baptized on 17 Mar 1847 Ste-Madeleine-de-Rigaud, Quebec (Ibid.).

> She was in the census household of Francois Xavier Villeneuve and Marguerite Rachelle Ranger in 1852 Ste-Madeleine, Rigaud, Quebec (1852C Cdn Transcription Project, District 536, page 61d, 62a, (123) & page 59d, 60a, (119), line 44-50, 1-5.).

x. Marie Alphonsine Villeneuve was born on 30 Sep 1848 Ste-Madeleine-de-Rigaud, Quebec (PRDH online, #4622458.). She was baptized on 30 Sep 1848 Ste-Madeleine-de-Rigaud, Quebec (Ibid.).

> She was in the census household of Francois Xavier Villeneuve and Marguerite Rachelle Ranger in 1852 Ste-Madeleine, Rigaud, Quebec (1852C Cdn Transcription Project, District 536, page 61d, 62a, (123) & page 59d, 60a, (119), line 44-50, 1-5.).

xi. Joseph Villeneuve was born circa 1851 (Ibid.).

> He was in the census household of Francois Xavier Villeneuve and Marguerite Rachelle Ranger in 1852 Ste-Madeleine, Rigaud, Quebec (1852C Cdn Transcription Project, District 536, page 61d, 62a, (123) & page 59d, 60a, (119), line 44-50, 1-5.).

85. **Marie Angelique Villeneuve** was born on 7 May 1809 Vaudreuil, Quebec (PRDH online, #2590704.). She was baptized on 8 May 1809 Vaudreuil, Quebec (Ibid.). She married **Vincent Belanger**, son of **Francois Belanger** and **Marie Madeleine Charlebois,** on 21 Nov 1831 Ste-Madeleine-de-Rigaud, Quebec (Ibid., #3462151.).

Vincent Belanger was born on 28 May 1802 Ste-Madeleine-de-Rigaud, Quebec (Ibid., #2758340.). He was baptized on 28 May 1802 Ste-Madeleine-de-Rigaud, Quebec *(father's occupation: cultivator)* (PRDH online, #2758340.).

Children of **Marie Angelique Villeneuve** and **Vincent Belanger** were as follows:

i. Julie Belanger was born on 5 Feb 1833 Ste-Madeleine-de-Rigaud, Quebec (Ibid., #4618807.). She was baptized on 6 Feb 1833 Ste-Madeleine-de-Rigaud, Quebec (Ibid.).

ii. Francois Damase Belanger was born on 30 Jun 1834 Ste-Madeleine-de-Rigaud, Quebec (Ibid., #4619153.). He was baptized on 1 Jul 1834 Ste-Madeleine-de-Rigaud, Quebec (Ibid.).

iii. Francois Zephirin Belanger was born on 24 Aug 1835 Ste-Madeleine-de-Rigaud, Quebec (Ibid., #4619448.). He was baptized on 25 Aug 1835 Ste-Madeleine-de-Rigaud, Quebec (Ibid.).

iv. Marie Adeline Belanger was born on 9 Dec 1836 Ste-Madeleine-de-Rigaud, Quebec (Ibid., #4619811.). She was baptized on 10 Dec 1836 Ste-Madeleine-de-Rigaud, Quebec (Ibid.).

v. Marie Julienne Belanger was born on 21 Sep 1838 Ste-Madeleine-de-Rigaud, Quebec (Ibid., #4620229.). She was baptized on 23 Sep 1838 Ste-Madeleine-de-Rigaud, Quebec (Ibid.). She died on 30 Dec 1845 Notre-Dame-de-Montreal, Quebec, at age 7 (Ibid., #3324103.). She was buried on 2 Jan 1846 Notre-Dame-de-Montreal, Quebec (Ibid.).

vi. Marie Olympe Leocadie Belanger was born on 2 Dec 1840 Ste-Madeleine-de-Rigaud, Quebec (Ibid., #4620759.). She was baptized on 3 Dec 1840 Ste-Madeleine-de-Rigaud, Quebec (Ibid.). She died on 14 Jan 1846 Notre-Dame-de-Montreal, Quebec, at age 5 (Ibid., #3324217.). She was buried on 17 Jan 1846 Notre-Dame-de-Montreal, Quebec (Ibid.).

vii. Joseph Prosper Belanger was born on 6 Apr 1842 Ste-Madeleine-de-Rigaud, Quebec (Ibid., #4621098.). He was baptized on 6 Apr 1842 Ste-Madeleine-de-Rigaud, Quebec (Ibid.).

viii. Telesphore Belanger was born on 1 Oct 1843 Ste-Madeleine-de-Rigaud, Quebec (Ibid., #4621456.). He was baptized on 2 Oct 1843 Ste-Madeleine-de-Rigaud, Quebec (Ibid.). He died on 31 Dec 1846 Notre-Dame-de-Montreal, Quebec, at age 3 (Ibid., #3324104.). He was buried on 2 Jan 1846 Notre-Dame-de-Montreal, Quebec (Ibid.).

ix. Octavie Belanger was born on 11 Aug 1845 Notre-Dame-de-Montreal, Quebec (Ibid., #3314236.). She was baptized on 11 Aug 1845 Notre-Dame-de-Montreal, Quebec (Ibid.). She died on 30 Jun 1846 Notre-Dame-de-Montreal, Quebec (Ibid., #3325119.). She was buried on 2 Jul 1846 Notre-Dame-de-Montreal, Quebec (Ibid.).

86. Francois Villeneuve was born on 16 Feb 1812 Oka, Quebec (Ibid., #2752345.). He was baptized on 17 Feb 1812 Oka, Quebec *(father's occupation: cultivator)* (PRDH online, #2752345.). He married **Marie Madeleine Lalonde**, daughter of **Antoine Lalonde** and **Marie Marguerite Mondion,** on 6 Feb 1837 Ste-Madeleine-de-Rigaud, Quebec (Ibid., #3464214.).

He and **Marie Madeleine Lalonde** were enumerated in the census in 1852 Ste-Madeleine, Rigaud, Quebec. Also in the family: **Madeleine Josephine Villeneuve, Marguerite Valerie Villeneuve, Rose Aimee Villeneuve, Louise Villeneuve, Antoine Benjamin Villeneuve**, and **Joseph Alphonse Villeneuve** *(Villeneuve, François, Cultivateur, Rigaud, Catholique, 41, M; Lalonde, Magdeleine, Rigaud, Catholique, 33, F; Villeneuve, Joséphine, Rigaud, Catholique, 14, F; Villeneuve, Valeri, Rigaud, Catholique, 6, F; Villeneuve, Aimée, Rigaud, Catholique, 5, F; Villeneuve, Louise, Rigaud, Catholique, 9 mois, F; Villeneuve, Benjamin, Rigaud, Catholique, 10, M; Villeneuve, Joseph, Rigaud, Catholique, 3, M)* (1852C Cdn Transcription Project, District 536, page 40d, 41a, (81), line 16-23.).

Marie Madeleine Lalonde was born on 22 Jul 1818 Ste-Madeleine-de-Rigaud, Quebec (PRDH online, #2680517.). She was baptized on 24 Jul 1818 Ste-Madeleine-de-Rigaud, Quebec *(father's occupation: agriculture)* (PRDH online, #2680517.).

Children of **Francois Villeneuve** and **Marie Madeleine Lalonde** were as follows:

    i. Madeleine Josephine Villeneuve was born on 23 Nov 1837 Ste-Madeleine-de-Rigaud, Quebec (Ibid., #4620036.). She was baptized on 23 Nov 1837 Ste-Madeleine-de-Rigaud, Quebec (Ibid.). She was in the census household of Francois Villeneuve and Marie Madeleine Lalonde in 1852 Ste-Madeleine, Rigaud, Quebec (1852C Cdn Transcription Project, District 536, page 40d, 41a, (81), line 16-23.).

    ii. Louis Dosithee Villeneuve was born on 22 Oct 1838 Ste-Madeleine-de-Rigaud, Quebec (PRDH online, #4620249.). He was baptized on 23 Oct 1838 Ste-Madeleine-de-Rigaud, Quebec (Ibid.). He died on 3 Nov 1838 Ste-Madeleine-de-Rigaud, Quebec (Ibid., #4623902.). He was buried on 4 Nov 1838 Ste-Madeleine-de-Rigaud, Quebec *(age 12 days)* (PRDH online, #4623902.).

    iii. Marie Adele Villeneuve was born on 19 Jan 1840 Ste-Madeleine-de-Rigaud, Quebec (Ibid., #4620547.). She was baptized on 19 Jan 1840 Ste-Madeleine-de-Rigaud, Quebec (Ibid.). She died on 25 Aug 1840 Ste-Madeleine-de-Rigaud, Quebec (Ibid., #4624063.). She was buried on 27 Aug 1840 Ste-Madeleine-de-Rigaud, Quebec *(age 7 months)* (PRDH online, #4624063.).

    iv. Antoine Benjamin Villeneuve was born on 3 Mar 1841 Ste-Madeleine-de-Rigaud, Quebec (Ibid., #4620837.). He was baptized on 3 Mar 1841 Ste-Madeleine-de-Rigaud, Quebec (Ibid.). He was in the census household of Francois Villeneuve and Marie Madeleine Lalonde in 1852 Ste-Madeleine, Rigaud, Quebec (1852C Cdn Transcription Project, District 536, page 40d, 41a, (81), line 16-23.).

    v. Joseph Tancrede Villeneuve was born on 1 Apr 1843 Ste-Madeleine-de-Rigaud, Quebec (PRDH online, #4621339.). He was baptized on 2 Apr 1843 Ste-Madeleine-de-Rigaud, Quebec (Ibid.). He died on 18 Jun 1843 Ste-Madeleine-de-Rigaud, Quebec (Ibid., #4624352.). He was buried on 19 Jun 1843 Ste-Madeleine-de-Rigaud, Quebec (Ibid.).

    vi. Francois Xavier Villeneuve was born on 26 May 1844 Ste-Madeleine-de-Rigaud, Quebec (Ibid., #4621592.). He was baptized on 26 May 1844 Ste-Madeleine-de-Rigaud, Quebec (Ibid.). He died on 9 Jun 1844 Ste-Madeleine-de-Rigaud, Quebec (Ibid., #4624450.). He was buried on 11 Jun 1844 Ste-Madeleine-de-Rigaud, Quebec *(age 15 days)* (PRDH online, #4624450.).

    vii. Marguerite Valerie Villeneuve was born on 16 Jul 1845 Ste-Madeleine-de-Rigaud, Quebec (Ibid., #4621863.). She was baptized on 20 Jul 1845 Ste-Madeleine-de-Rigaud, Quebec (Ibid.). She was in the census household of Francois Villeneuve and Marie Madeleine Lalonde in 1852 Ste-Madeleine, Rigaud, Quebec (1852C Cdn Transcription Project, District 536, page 40d, 41a, (81), line 16-23.).

    viii. Rose Aimee Villeneuve was born on 4 Oct 1846 Ste-Madeleine-de-Rigaud, Quebec (PRDH online, #4622134.). She was baptized on 4 Oct 1846 Ste-Madeleine-de-Rigaud, Quebec (Ibid.). She was in the census household of Francois Villeneuve and Marie Madeleine Lalonde in 1852 Ste-Madeleine, Rigaud, Quebec (1852C Cdn Transcription Project, District 536, page 40d, 41a, (81), line 16-23.).

    ix. Angele Alphonsine Villeneuve was born on 6 Mar 1848 Ste-Madeleine-de-Rigaud, Quebec (PRDH online, #4622372.). She was baptized on 6 Mar 1848 Ste-Madeleine-de-Rigaud, Quebec (Ibid.). She died on 16 Jul 1848 Ste-Madeleine-de-Rigaud, Quebec (Ibid., #4624685.). She was buried on 18 Jul 1848 Ste-Madeleine-de-Rigaud, Quebec *(age 4 months)* (PRDH online, #4624685.).

      x.   Joseph Alphonse Villeneuve was born on 20 Feb 1849 Ste-Madeleine-de-Rigaud, Quebec (Ibid., #4622517.). He was baptized on 20 Feb 1849 Ste-Madeleine-de-Rigaud, Quebec (Ibid.).

        He was in the census household of Francois Villeneuve and Marie Madeleine Lalonde in 1852 Ste-Madeleine, Rigaud, Quebec (1852C Cdn Transcription Project, District 536, page 40d, 41a, (81), line 16-23.).

      xi.   Louise Villeneuve was born circa 1851 (Ibid.).

        She was in the census household of Francois Villeneuve and Marie Madeleine Lalonde in 1852 Ste-Madeleine, Rigaud, Quebec (1852C Cdn Transcription Project, District 536, page 40d, 41a, (81), line 16-23.).

87. Antoine Benjamin Villeneuve was born on 10 Jun 1814 Ste-Madeleine-de-Rigaud, Quebec (PRDH online, #2680081.). He was baptized on 11 Jun 1814 Ste-Madeleine-de-Rigaud, Quebec *(father's occupation: agriculture)* (PRDH online, #2680081.). He married **Marie Mathilde Thomas dit Tranchemontagne**, daughter of **Joseph Thomas dit Tranchemontagne** and **Josephte Sabourin,** on 23 Feb 1835 Ste-Madeleine-de-Rigaud, Quebec (Ibid., #3463416.).

Marie Mathilde Thomas dit Tranchemontagne was born on 13 Jun 1818 Ste-Madeleine-de-Rigaud, Quebec (Ibid., #2680502.). She was baptized on 13 Jun 1818 Ste-Madeleine-de-Rigaud, Quebec (Ibid.).

Children of **Antoine Benjamin Villeneuve** and **Marie Mathilde Thomas dit Tranchemontagne** were as follows:

      i.   Marie Sophie Villeneuve was born on 13 Apr 1836 Ste-Madeleine-de-Rigaud, Quebec (Ibid., #4619621.). She was baptized on 13 Apr 1836 Ste-Madeleine-de-Rigaud, Quebec (Ibid.).

      ii.   Philomene Villeneuve was born on 23 May 1837 Ste-Madeleine-de-Rigaud, Quebec (Ibid., #4619937.). She was baptized on 23 May 1837 Ste-Madeleine-de-Rigaud, Quebec (Ibid.).

      iii.   Marie Odile Villeneuve was born on 17 Sep 1838 Ste-Madeleine-de-Rigaud, Quebec (Ibid., #4620228.). She was baptized on 19 Sep 1838 Ste-Madeleine-de-Rigaud, Quebec (Ibid.).

      iv.   Josephine Villeneuve was born on 22 Nov 1839 Ste-Madeleine-de-Rigaud, Quebec (Ibid., #4620519.). She was baptized on 22 Nov 1839 Ste-Madeleine-de-Rigaud, Quebec (Ibid.).

      v.   Joseph Alphonse Villeneuve was born on 1 Aug 1841 Ste-Madeleine-de-Rigaud, Quebec (Ibid., #4620946.). He was baptized on 1 Aug 1841 Ste-Madeleine-de-Rigaud, Quebec (Ibid.). He died on 25 Nov 1842 Ste-Madeleine-de-Rigaud, Quebec, at age 1 (Ibid., #4624289.). He was buried on 26 Nov 1842 Ste-Madeleine-de-Rigaud, Quebec *(age 15 months)* (PRDH online, #4624289.).

      vi.   Cleophas Villeneuve was born circa Dec 1844 (Ibid., #3323350.). He died on 20 Jul 1845 Notre-Dame-de-Montreal, Quebec (Ibid.). He was buried on 22 Jul 1845 Notre-Dame-de-Montreal, Quebec *(age 7 months)* (PRDH online, #3323350.).

      vii.   Napoleon Villeneuve was born circa Jan 1845 (Ibid., #3323651.). He died on 1 Oct 1845 Notre-Dame-de-Montreal, Quebec (Ibid.). He was buried on 4 Oct 1845 Notre-Dame-de-Montreal, Quebec *(age 9 months)* (PRDH online, #3323651.).

      viii.   Marie Mathilde Villeneuve was born on 27 Aug 1846 Notre-Dame-de-Montreal, Quebec (Ibid., #3316887.). She was baptized on 27 Aug 1846 Notre-Dame-de-Montreal, Quebec (Ibid.). She died on 2 Jul 1849 Notre-Dame-de-Montreal, Quebec, at age 2 (Ibid., #4218545.). She was buried on 4 Jul 1849 Notre-Dame-de-Montreal, Quebec (Ibid.).

      ix.   Marie Eminie Villeneuve was born on 14 Dec 1848 Notre-Dame-de-Montreal, Quebec (Ibid., #3322369.). She was baptized on 15 Dec 1848 Notre-Dame-de-Montreal, Quebec (Ibid.).

88. **Veronique Villeneuve** was born on 9 Nov 1816 Ste-Madeleine-de-Rigaud, Quebec (Ibid., #2680337.). She was baptized on 10 Nov 1816 Ste-Madeleine-de-Rigaud, Quebec *(father's occupation: agriculture)* (PRDH online, #2680337.). She married **Francois Andre Sabourin**, son of **Francois Sabourin** and **Louise Seguin,** on 30 Jan 1849 Ste-Madeleine-de-Rigaud, Quebec (Ibid., #3467178.).

Question: *Called Louise in the 1852 census* (1852C Cdn Transcription Project, District 536, page 23d, 24a, (47), line 42-46.).

She and **Francois Andre Sabourin** were enumerated in the census in 1852 Ste.Madeleine, Rigaud, Vaudreuil, Quebec. Also in the family: **Louis Sabourin**, **Alphonse Sabourin**, and **Napoleon Sabourin** *(Sabourin, André, Cultivateur, Rigaud, Catholique, 35, M; Villneuve, Véronique, Rigaud, Catholique, 35, F; Sabourin, Louise, Rigaud, Catholique, 7, F; Sabourin, Alphonse, Rigaud, Catholique, 2, M; Sabourin, Napoléon, Rigaud, Catholique, 1, M)* (1852C Cdn Transcription Project, District 536, page 23d, 24a, (47), line 42-46.).

Francois Andre Sabourin was born on 15 Dec 1816 Ste-Madeleine-de-Rigaud, Quebec (PRDH online, #2680348.). He was baptized on 16 Dec 1816 Ste-Madeleine-de-Rigaud, Quebec (Ibid.). He married **Marie Agnes Edesse Vallee**, daughter of **Antoine Vallee** and **Genevieve Vinet,** on 1 Aug 1843 Ste-Madeleine-de-Rigaud, Quebec (Ibid., #3465783.).

Children of **Veronique Villeneuve** and **Francois Andre Sabourin** were as follows:
  i.   Alphonse Sabourin was born circa 1850 (1852C Cdn Transcription Project, District 536, page 23d, 24a, (47), line 42-46.).
       He was in the census household of Francois Andre Sabourin and Veronique Villeneuve in 1852 Ste.Madeleine, Rigaud, Vaudreuil, Quebec (1852C Cdn Transcription Project, District 536, page 23d, 24a, (47), line 42-46.).
  ii. Napoleon Sabourin was born circa 1851 (Ibid.).
       He was in the census household of Francois Andre Sabourin and Veronique Villeneuve in 1852 Ste.Madeleine, Rigaud, Vaudreuil, Quebec (1852C Cdn Transcription Project, District 536, page 23d, 24a, (47), line 42-46.).

89. Francois Israel Seguin was born on 8 Oct 1797 Vaudreuil, Quebec (PRDH online, No. 770957.). He was baptized on 9 Oct 1797 Vaudreuil, Quebec (Ibid.). He married **Marguerite Lecompte**, daughter of **Gabriel Lecompte** and **Marie Rose Lefaivre,** on 7 Feb 1825 Vaudreuil, Quebec (Ibid., #3472931.).

Children of **Francois Israel Seguin** and **Marguerite Lecompte** all born Ste-Madeleine-de-Rigaud, Quebec, were as follows:
  i.   Emilie Marguerite Seguin was born on 18 May 1827 (Ibid., #4617542.). She was baptized on 19 May 1827 Ste-Madeleine-de-Rigaud, Quebec (Ibid.). She married Joseph Gideon Ladurantaie dit Lacatte, son of Bonaventure Ladurente dit Locate and Josephte Robillard, on 16 Oct 1849 Vaudreuil, Quebec (Ibid., #3478370.).
       Joseph Gideon Ladurantaie dit Lacatte was born on 4 Feb 1828 (Ibid., #4087980.). He was baptized on 22 Jul 1828 Montebello, Quebec (Ibid.).
  ii. Marie Josephte Seguin was born on 15 Apr 1829 (Ibid., #4617923.). She was baptized on 16 Apr 1829 Ste-Madeleine-de-Rigaud, Quebec (Ibid.).
  iii. Mathilde Seguin was born on 7 Jul 1831 (Ibid., #4618399.). She was baptized on 8 Jul 1831 Ste-Madeleine-de-Rigaud, Quebec (Ibid.).
  iv. Francois Seguin was born on 9 May 1833 (Ibid., #4618875.). He was baptized on 12 May 1833 Ste-Madeleine-de-Rigaud, Quebec (Ibid.).

90. Antoine Seguin was born on 5 Oct 1798 Vaudreuil, Quebec (Ibid., No. 774130.). He was baptized on 6 Oct 1798 Oka, Quebec (Ibid.). He married **Theotiste St.Denis**, daughter of **Gabriel Denis dit St.Denis** and **Josephe Seguin dit Laderoute,** on 15 Feb 1830 Ste-Madeleine-de-Rigaud, Quebec *(Consanguinity: 4)* (PRDH online, #3461678.). He married **Marie Lecompte**, daughter of **Gabriel Lecompte** and **Marie Rose Lefebvre,** on 15 Aug 1836 Vaudreuil, Quebec (Ibid., #3475350.).

Theotiste St.Denis was born on 27 Oct 1801 Vaudreuil, Quebec (Ibid., #2589975.). She was baptized on 28 Oct 1801 Vaudreuil, Quebec (Ibid.). She died on 6 Mar 1836 Hawkesbury, Ontario, at age 34 (Ibid., #4623671.). She was buried on 8 Mar 1836 Ste-Madeleine-de-Riguad, Quebec (Ibid.).

Children of **Antoine Seguin** and **Theotiste St.Denis** were:
  i.   Marcelline Seguin was born on 9 Dec 1830 Ste-Madeleine-de-Riguad, Quebec (Ibid., #4618240.). She was baptized on 9 Dec 1830 Ste-Madeleine-de-Riguad, Quebec (Ibid.).

Children of **Antoine Seguin** and **Marie Lecompte** were as follows:
  i.   Marie Philomene Seguin was born on 7 Jun 1837 Hawkesbury, Ontario (Ibid., #4619948.). She was baptized on 7 Jun 1837 Ste-Madeleine-de-Riguad, Quebec (Ibid.).
  ii. Antoine Isidore Seguin was born on 30 Sep 1838 Hawkesbury, Ontario (Ibid., #4620235.). He was baptized on 30 Sep 1838 Ste-Madeleine-de-Riguad, Quebec (Ibid.).
  iii. Alphonse Jeremie Seguin was born on 7 Sep 1840 Hawkesbury, Ontario (Ibid., #4620706.). He was baptized on 7 Sep 1840 Ste-Madeleine-de-Riguad, Quebec (Ibid.).
  iv. Marie Henriette Seguin was born on 9 May 1842 (Ibid., #4621125.). She was baptized on 10 May 1842 Ste-Madeleine-de-Riguad, Quebec (Ibid.).
  v.   Antoine Napoleon Seguin was born on 23 Feb 1844 (Ibid., #4621535.). He was baptized on 23 Feb 1844 Ste-Madeleine-de-Riguad, Quebec (Ibid.).
  vi. Marie Rose Seguin was born on 7 Jan 1846 (Ibid., #4621966.). She was baptized on 9 Jan 1846 Ste-Madeleine-de-Riguad, Quebec (Ibid.). She died on 15 Jan 1846 (Ibid., #4624528.). She was buried on 17 Jan 1846 Ste-Madeleine-de-Riguad, Quebec (Ibid.).
  vii. Theodore Euclide Seguin was born on 19 Mar 1847 Hawkesbury, Ontario (Ibid., #4622201.). He was baptized on 20 Mar 1847 Ste-Madeleine-de-Riguad, Quebec (Ibid.).
       His telephone number was *Quebec Metis.*

91. **Theodore Seguin** was born on 28 Jun 1801 Oka, Quebec (Ibid., #2752207.). He was baptized on 29 Jun 1801 Oka, Quebec (Ibid.). He married **Marie Theotiste Brazeau**, daughter of **Andre Brazeau** and **Angelique Constance Rocbrune,** on 9 Jan 1832 Ste-Madeleine-de-Rigaud, Quebec (Ibid., #3462197.).

He and **Marie Theotiste Brazeau** were enumerated in the census in 1852 Ste-Madeleine, Vaudreuil, Quebec. Also in the family: **Andre Seguin, Francois Xavier Seguin, Alexandre Seguin, Marie Cecile Seguin, Marie Ostie Seguin, Napoleon Seguin, Rosalie Seguin, Theodore Seguin,** and **David Seguin** *(Séguin, Théodore, Journalier, Rigaud, Catholique, 50, M; Brazeau, Théotiste, Rigaud, Catholique, 35, F; Séguin, André, Rigaud, Catholique, 19, M; Séguin, François, Rigaud, Catholique, 17, M; Séguin, Théodore, Rigaud, Catholique, 15, M; Séguin, Alexdre, Rigaud, Catholique, 12, M; Séguin, Napoleon, Rigaud, Catholique, 5, M; Séguin, David, Rigaud, Catholique, 11 mois, M; Séguin, Tharsile, Rigaud, Catholique, 10, F; Séguin, Ostie, Rigaud, Catholique, 7, F; Séguin, Rosalie, Rigaud, Catholique, 3, F)* (1852C Cdn Transcription Project, District 536, page 13d, 14a, (27), line 28-38.).

Marie Theotiste Brazeau was born on 24 Oct 1815 St-Benoit, Quebec (PRDH online, #2514900.). She was baptized on 25 Oct 1815 St-Benoit, Quebec (Ibid.).

Children of **Theodore Seguin** and **Marie Theotiste Brazeau** were as follows:

    i.   Andre Seguin was born on 12 Dec 1832 Ste-Madeleine-de-Rigaud, Quebec (Ibid., #4618765.). He was baptized on 13 Dec 1832 Ste-Madeleine-de-Rigaud, Quebec (Ibid.).

        He was in the census household of Theodore Seguin and Marie Theotiste Brazeau in 1852 Ste-Madeleine, Vaudreuil, Quebec (1852C Cdn Transcription Project, District 536, page 13d, 14a, (27), line 28-38.).

    ii.   Francois Xavier Seguin was born on 18 Jun 1834 Ste-Madeleine-de-Rigaud, Quebec (PRDH online, #4619138.). He was baptized on 20 Jun 1834 Ste-Madeleine-de-Rigaud, Quebec (Ibid.).

        He was in the census household of Theodore Seguin and Marie Theotiste Brazeau in 1852 Ste-Madeleine, Vaudreuil, Quebec (1852C Cdn Transcription Project, District 536, page 13d, 14a, (27), line 28-38.).

    iii.   Theodore Seguin was born circa 1836 (Ibid.).

        He was in the census household of Theodore Seguin and Marie Theotiste Brazeau in 1852 Ste-Madeleine, Vaudreuil, Quebec (1852C Cdn Transcription Project, District 536, page 13d, 14a, (27), line 28-38.).

    iv.   Adeline Seguin was born on 18 Mar 1838 Ste-Madeleine-de-Rigaud, Quebec (PRDH online, #4620103.). She was baptized on 19 Mar 1838 Ste-Madeleine-de-Rigaud, Quebec (Ibid.). She died on 17 Jul 1838 Ste-Madeleine-de-Rigaud, Quebec *(age 4 months)* (PRDH online, #4623859.). She was buried on 18 Jul 1838 Ste-Madeleine-de-Rigaud, Quebec (Ibid.).

    v.   Alexandre Seguin was born on 26 Jun 1839 Ste-Madeleine-de-Rigaud, Quebec (Ibid., #4620467.). He was baptized on 26 Jun 1839 Ste-Madeleine-de-Rigaud, Quebec (Ibid.).

        He was in the census household of Theodore Seguin and Marie Theotiste Brazeau in 1852 Ste-Madeleine, Vaudreuil, Quebec (1852C Cdn Transcription Project, District 536, page 13d, 14a, (27), line 28-38.).

    vi.   Marie Cecile Seguin was born on 12 Dec 1841 Ste-Madeleine-de-Rigaud, Quebec (PRDH online, #4621029.). She was baptized on 13 Dec 1841 Ste-Madeleine-de-Rigaud, Quebec (Ibid.).

        She was in the census household of Theodore Seguin and Marie Theotiste Brazeau in 1852 Ste-Madeleine, Vaudreuil, Quebec (1852C Cdn Transcription Project, District 536, page 13d, 14a, (27), line 28-38.).

    vii.   Marie Ostie Seguin was born on 22 Jun 1844 Ste-Madeleine-de-Rigaud, Quebec (PRDH online, #4621613.). She was baptized on 22 Jun 1844 Ste-Madeleine-de-Rigaud, Quebec (Ibid.).

        She was in the census household of Theodore Seguin and Marie Theotiste Brazeau in 1852 Ste-Madeleine, Vaudreuil, Quebec (1852C Cdn Transcription Project, District 536, page 13d, 14a, (27), line 28-38.).

    viii.   Napoleon Seguin was born on 1 Jul 1846 Ste-Madeleine-de-Rigaud, Quebec (PRDH online, #4622069.). He was baptized on 3 Jul 1846 Ste-Madeleine-de-Rigaud, Quebec (Ibid.).

        He was in the census household of Theodore Seguin and Marie Theotiste Brazeau in 1852 Ste-Madeleine, Vaudreuil, Quebec (1852C Cdn Transcription Project, District 536, page 13d, 14a, (27), line 28-38.).

    ix.   Rosalie Seguin was born on 15 Jul 1848 Ste-Madeleine-de-Rigaud, Quebec (PRDH online, #4622429.). She was baptized on 15 Jul 1848 Ste-Madeleine-de-Rigaud, Quebec (Ibid.).

She was in the census household of Theodore Seguin and Marie Theotiste Brazeau in 1852 Ste-Madeleine, Vaudreuil, Quebec (1852C Cdn Transcription Project, District 536, page 13d, 14a, (27), line 28-38.).

    x. David Seguin was born circa 1851 (Ibid.).

He was in the census household of Theodore Seguin and Marie Theotiste Brazeau in 1852 Ste-Madeleine, Vaudreuil, Quebec (1852C Cdn Transcription Project, District 536, page 13d, 14a, (27), line 28-38.).

92. **Marie Theotiste Seguin** was born on 23 Apr 1803 Ste-Madeleine-de-Rigaud, Quebec (PRDH online, #2679154.). She was baptized on 24 Apr 1803 Ste-Madeleine-de-Rigaud, Quebec *(father's occupation: cultivator)* (PRDH online, #2679154.). She married **Michel Gelin St.Denis**, son of **Toussaint St.Denis** and **Suzanne Cadieux,** on 30 Jan 1826 Ste-Madeleine-de-Rigaud, Quebec (Ibid., #2590081.).

Michel Gelin St.Denis was born on 15 Oct 1802 Vaudreuil, Quebec (Ibid.). He was baptized on 15 Oct 1802 Vaudreuil, Quebec (Ibid.).

Children of **Marie Theotiste Seguin** and **Michel Gelin St.Denis** all born Ste-Madeleine-de-Rigaud, Quebec, were as follows:

    i. Michel St.Denis was born on 5 Nov 1826 (Ibid., #4617443.). He was baptized on 6 Nov 1826 Ste-Madeleine-de-Rigaud, Quebec (Ibid.).

    ii. Francois Hilaire St.Denis was born on 7 Mar 1828 (Ibid., #4617696.). He was baptized on 8 Mar 1828 Ste-Madeleine-de-Rigaud, Quebec (Ibid.).

    iii. Marie Marcelline St.Denis was born on 23 Apr 1830 (Ibid., #4618110.). She was baptized on 23 Apr 1830 Ste-Madeleine-de-Rigaud, Quebec (Ibid.).

    iv. Antoine Alexandre St.Denis was born on 19 Dec 1831 (Ibid., #4618495.). He was baptized on 23 Dec 1831 Ste-Madeleine-de-Rigaud, Quebec (Ibid.).

    v. Marguerite Olympe St.Denis was born on 19 Feb 1834 (Ibid., #4619063.). She was baptized on 20 Feb 1834 Ste-Madeleine-de-Rigaud, Quebec (Ibid.). She died on 30 Jul 1834 Ste-Madeleine-de-Rigaud, Quebec (Ibid., #4623518.). She was buried on 31 Jul 1834 Ste-Madeleine-de-Rigaud, Quebec *(Olympe, age 5 months)* (PRDH online, #4623518.).

    vi. Joseph Bertis St.Denis was born on 22 Nov 1835 (Ibid., #4619514.). He was baptized on 24 Nov 1835 Ste-Madeleine-de-Rigaud, Quebec (Ibid.).

    vii. Theophile St.Denis was born on 17 Mar 1838 (Ibid., #4620101.). He was baptized on 18 Mar 1838 Ste-Madeleine-de-Rigaud, Quebec (Ibid.).

    viii. Elzeard Pierre St.Denis was born on 28 Dec 1840 (Ibid., #4620775.). He was baptized on 29 Dec 1840 Ste-Madeleine-de-Rigaud, Quebec (Ibid.).

    ix. Olympe St.Denis was born on 15 May 1843 (Ibid., #4621368.). She was baptized on 15 May 1843 Ste-Madeleine-de-Rigaud, Quebec (Ibid.).

93. **Marie Clothilde Cleophee Seguin dit Laderoute** was born on 23 Mar 1809 Ste-Madeleine-de-Rigaud, Quebec (Ibid., #2679575.). She was baptized on 24 Mar 1809 Ste-Madeleine-de-Rigaud, Quebec *(father's occupation: agriculture)* (PRDH online, #2679575.). She married **Joseph Vallee**, son of **Pierre Vallee** and **Elisabeth Robillard,** on 10 Feb 1828 Ste-Madeleine-de-Rigaud, Quebec (Ibid., #3460832.).

Joseph Vallee was born on 15 Jul 1800 Ste-Anne-de-Bellevue, Quebec (Ibid., #2382754.). He was baptized on 16 Jul 1800 Ste-Anne-de-Bellevue, Quebec (Ibid.).

Children of **Marie Clothilde Cleophee Seguin dit Laderoute** and **Joseph Vallee** all born Ste-Madeleine-de-Rigaud, Quebec, were as follows:

  149   i. Emilie Vallee, b. 20 Nov 1828; m. Theodore Francois Xavier Mallette.

    ii. Joseph Hilaire Vallee was born on 6 Mar 1830 (Ibid., #4618079.). He was baptized on 6 Mar 1830 Ste-Madeleine-de-Rigaud, Quebec (Ibid.).

    iii. Pierre Isidore Vallee was born on 7 Jul 1831 (Ibid., #4618397.). He was baptized on 7 Jul 1831 Ste-Madeleine-de-Rigaud, Quebec (Ibid.).

    iv. Antoine Adlebert Vallee was born on 10 Mar 1833 (Ibid., #4618832.). He was baptized on 10 Mar 1833 Ste-Madeleine-de-Rigaud, Quebec (Ibid.). He died on 22 Mar 1840 Ste-Madeleine-de-Rigaud, Quebec, at age 7 (Ibid., #4624026.). He was buried on 24 Mar 1840 Ste-Madeleine-de-Rigaud, Quebec (Ibid.).

    v. Rose Chrysolithe Vallee was born on 19 Jun 1834 (Ibid., #4619139.). She was baptized on 20 Jun 1834 Ste-Madeleine-de-Rigaud, Quebec (Ibid.).

    vi. Romain Elie Hector Vallee was born on 8 Aug 1838 (Ibid., #4620203.). He was baptized on 9 Aug 1838 Ste-Madeleine-de-Rigaud, Quebec (Ibid.).

     vii.   Ostie Philomene Vallee was born on 10 Mar 1840 (Ibid., #4620585.). She was baptized on 10 Mar 1840 Ste-Madeleine-de-Rigaud, Quebec (Ibid.).

     viii.   Marie Julie Vallee was born on 11 Feb 1842 (Ibid., #4621066.). She was baptized on 12 Feb 1842 Ste-Madeleine-de-Rigaud, Quebec (Ibid.).

     ix.   Marie Delina Zenaide Vallee was born on 22 Feb 1844 (Ibid., #4621532.). She was baptized on 22 Feb 1844 Ste-Madeleine-de-Rigaud, Quebec (Ibid.).

     x.   Marie Cleophee Vallee was born on 5 Jan 1846 (Ibid., #4652162.). She was baptized on 6 Jan 1846 Ste-Madeleine-de-Rigaud, Quebec (Ibid.).

94. Jean Seguin dit Laderoute was born on 26 Mar 1811 (Ibid., #2679765.). He was baptized on 31 Mar 1811 Ste-Madeleine-de-Rigaud, Quebec *(father's occupation: agriculture)* (PRDH online, #2679765.). He married **Marie Louise Vallee**, daughter of **Jean Baptiste Vallee** and **Marguerite Dion,** on 28 Jul 1834 Ste-Madeleine-de-Riguad, Quebec (Ibid., #3463073.).

Marie Louise Vallee was born on 7 Feb 1814 (Ibid., #2680052.). She was baptized on 13 Feb 1814 Ste-Madeleine-de-Riguad, Quebec (Ibid.).

Children of **Jean Seguin dit Laderoute** and **Marie Louise Vallee** were as follows:

     i.   Louise Delphine Seguin was born circa Nov 1837 (Ibid., #4623886.). She died on 22 Sep 1838 Ste-Madeleine-de-Riguad, Quebec (Ibid.). She was buried on 24 Sep 1838 Ste-Madeleine-de-Riguad, Quebec *(age 10 months)* (PRDH online, #4623886.).

     ii.   Benjamin Seguin was born on 5 May 1848 (Beauharnois), St-Timothee, Quebec (Ibid., #4436414.). He was baptized on 6 May 1848 (Beauharnois), St-Timothee, Quebec (Ibid.).

95. Jeremie Seguin was born on 20 Jun 1816 Ste-Madeleine-de-Rigaud, Quebec (Ibid., #2680307.). He was baptized on 21 Jun 1816 Ste-Madeleine-de-Rigaud, Quebec *(father's occupation: agriculture)* (PRDH online, #2680307.). He married **Josephte Rousselle**, daughter of **Jean Baptiste Roussel dit Vocelle or Voicel** and **Marie Victoire Gauthier,** on 19 Oct 1835 Ste-Madeleine-de-Rigaud, Quebec (Ibid., #3463624.).

Josephte Rousselle was born on 25 Aug 1815 Ste-Madeleine-de-Rigaud, Quebec (Ibid., #2680213.). She was baptized on 26 Aug 1815 Ste-Madeleine-de-Rigaud, Quebec (Ibid.).

Children of **Jeremie Seguin** and **Josephte Rousselle** were as follows:

     i.   Julienne Seguin was born on 26 Jul 1836 (Ibid., #4619719.). She was baptized on 30 Jul 1836 Ste-Madeleine-de-Riguad, Quebec (Ibid.). She died on 29 Sep 1837 at age 1 (Ibid., #4623793.). She was buried on 30 Sep 1837 Ste-Madeleine-de-Riguad, Quebec *(age 14 months)* (PRDH online, #4623793.).

     ii.   Pie Gabelus Seguin was born on 3 May 1838 (Ibid., #4620134.). She was baptized on 5 May 1838 Ste-Madeleine-de-Riguad, Quebec (Ibid.).

     iii.   Marie Sophie Seguin was born on 29 Feb 1840 (Ibid., #4620572.). She was baptized on 29 Feb 1840 Ste-Madeleine-de-Riguad, Quebec (Ibid.).

     iv.   Charles Theophile Seguin was born on 11 Jul 1842 (Ibid., #4621172.). He was baptized on 15 Jul 1842 Ste-Madeleine-de-Riguad, Quebec (Ibid.).

     v.   Napoleon Seguin was born on 16 Jan 1844 (Ibid., #4621520.). He was baptized on 17 Jan 1844 Ste-Madeleine-de-Riguad, Quebec (Ibid.).

     vi.   Julienne Alphonsine Seguin was born on 21 Mar 1846 (Ibid., #4622009.). She was baptized on 22 Mar 1846 Ste-Madeleine-de-Riguad, Quebec (Ibid.).

     vii.   Pierre Elie Seguin was born on 17 Feb 1848 (Ibid., #4622363.). He was baptized on 18 Feb 1848 Ste-Madeleine-de-Riguad, Quebec (Ibid.).

96. Benjamin Seguin was born on 20 Sep 1818 Ste-Madeleine-de-Rigaud, Quebec (Ibid., #2680539.). He was baptized on 21 Sep 1818 Ste-Madeleine-de-Rigaud, Quebec *(father's occupation: agriculture)* (PRDH online, #2680539.). He married **Flavie Dion**, daughter of **Arsene Dion** and **Madeleine Leduc,** on 21 Jan 1840 Ste-Madeleine-de-Riguad, Quebec (Ibid., #3464974.).

Flavie Dion was born on 15 Jan 1824 (Ibid., #2681287.). She was baptized on 16 Jan 1824 Ste-Madeleine-de-Riguad, Quebec (Ibid.).

Children of **Benjamin Seguin** and **Flavie Dion** were as follows:

     i.   Arsene Seguin was born on 21 Oct 1840 (Ibid., #4620733.). He was baptized on 22 Oct 1840 Ste-Madeleine-de-Riguad, Quebec (Ibid.). He died on 28 Oct 1840 (Ibid., #4624075.). He was buried on 30 Oct 1840 Ste-Madeleine-de-Riguad, Quebec (Ibid.).

     ii.   Magdeleine Philomene Seguin was born on 21 Oct 1841 (Ibid., #4621006.). She was baptized on 23 Oct 1841 Ste-Madeleine-de-Riguad, Quebec (Ibid.). She died on 23 Apr 1842 (Ibid., #4624247.). She was buried on 25 Apr 1842 Ste-Madeleine-de-Riguad, Quebec (Ibid.).

iii. Joseph Seguin was born on 9 Nov 1843 (Ibid., #4621479.). He was baptized on 10 Nov 1843 Ste-Madeleine-de-Riguad, Quebec (Ibid.). He died on 11 Nov 1843 (Ibid., #4624406.). He was buried on 13 Nov 1843 Ste-Madeleine-de-Riguad, Quebec (Ibid.).

iv. Julie Melina Seguin was born on 8 May 1845 (Ibid., #4621817.). She was baptized on 9 May 1845 Ste-Madeleine-de-Riguad, Quebec (Ibid.).

v. Joseph Seguin was born on 7 Apr 1847 (Ibid., #4622217.). He was baptized on 8 Apr 1847 Ste-Madeleine-de-Riguad, Quebec (Ibid.).

97. Monique Seguin was born on 13 Mar 1820 Ste-Madeleine-de-Rigaud, Quebec (Ibid., #2680729.). She was baptized on 14 Mar 1820 Ste-Madeleine-de-Rigaud, Quebec *(father's occupation: cultivator)* (PRDH online, #2680729.). She married **Alexandre Emery Rousselle**, son of **Jean Baptiste Roussel dit Vocelle or Voicel** and **Marie Victoire Gauthier,** on 22 Sep 1840 Ste-Madeleine-de-Rigaud, Quebec (Ibid., #3465152.).

Alexandre Emery Rousselle was born on 16 Oct 1817 Ste-Madeleine-de-Riguad, Quebec (Ibid., #2680423.). He was baptized on 16 Oct 1817 Ste-Madeleine-de-Riguad, Quebec (Ibid.).

Children of **Monique Seguin** and **Alexandre Emery Rousselle** were as follows:

i. Marie Josephine Rousselle was born on 29 Nov 1841 (Ibid., #4621019.). She was baptized on 30 Nov 1841 Ste-Madeleine-de-Riguad, Quebec (Ibid.).

ii. Paul Leon Rousselle was born on 26 Jan 1843 (Ibid., #4621303.). He was baptized on 26 Jan 1843 Ste-Madeleine-de-Riguad, Quebec (Ibid.). He died on 2 Sep 1843 (Ibid., #4624377.). He was buried on 4 Sep 1843 Ste-Madeleine-de-Riguad, Quebec (Ibid.).

98. Marie Elisabeth Sophie Villeneuve was born on 3 Oct 1805 Ste-Madeleine-de-Riguad, Quebec (Ibid., #2679299.). She was baptized on 3 Oct 1805 Ste-Madeleine-de-Riguad, Quebec (Ibid.). She married **Hyacinthe Seguin**, son of **Andre Seguin** and **Marie Louise Robillard,** on 19 Sep 1825 Ste-Madeleine-de-Riguad, Quebec *(Consanguinity: 6)* (PRDH online, #3459773.). She died on 25 Jul 1843 Ste-Madeleine-de-Riguad, Quebec, at age 37 (Ibid., #4624364.). She was buried on 27 Jul 1843 Ste-Madeleine-de-Riguad, Quebec (Ibid.).

Hyacinthe Seguin was baptized on 23 Oct 1795 Vaudreuil, Quebec (Ibid., #770757.).

Children of **Marie Elisabeth Sophie Villeneuve** and **Hyacinthe Seguin** were as follows:

150 i. Joseph Hyacinthe Seguin, b. 12 Jul 1826 Ste-Madeleine-de-Riguad, Quebec; m. Sophie Sauve.

ii. Jean Adolphe Seguin was born on 11 Aug 1827 Ste-Madeleine-de-Riguad, Quebec (Ibid., #4617589.). He was baptized on 11 Aug 1827 Ste-Madeleine-de-Riguad, Quebec (Ibid.).

iii. Marie Adele Seguin was born on 14 Jan 1829 Ste-Madeleine-de-Riguad, Quebec (Ibid., #4617868.). She was baptized on 15 Jan 1829 Ste-Madeleine-de-Riguad, Quebec (Ibid.).

iv. Magloire Benjamin Seguin was born on 2 Aug 1830 (Ibid., #4618167.). He was baptized on 7 Aug 1830 Ste-Madeleine-de-Riguad, Quebec (Ibid.). He died on 24 Mar 1833 Ste-Madeleine-de-Riguad, Quebec, at age 2 (Ibid., #4623386.). He was buried on 25 Mar 1833 Ste-Madeleine-de-Riguad, Quebec (Ibid.).

v. Emery Seguin was born on 11 Feb 1832 Ste-Madeleine-de-Riguad, Quebec (Ibid., #4618539.). He was baptized on 11 Feb 1832 Ste-Madeleine-de-Riguad, Quebec (Ibid.).

vi. Joseph Theophile Seguin was born on 25 Feb 1833 Ste-Madeleine-de-Riguad, Quebec (Ibid., #4618817.). He was baptized on 25 Feb 1833 Ste-Madeleine-de-Riguad, Quebec (Ibid.).

vii. Veronique Seguin was born on 7 Dec 1834 Ste-Madeleine-de-Riguad, Quebec (Ibid., #4619260.). She was baptized on 7 Dec 1834 Ste-Madeleine-de-Riguad, Quebec (Ibid.).

viii. Marie Philomene Seguin was born on 25 Dec 1836 Ste-Madeleine-de-Riguad, Quebec (Ibid., #4619806.). She was baptized on 26 Dec 1836 Ste-Madeleine-de-Riguad, Quebec (Ibid.).

ix. Marie Josephine Seguin was born on 11 Dec 1838 Ste-Madeleine-de-Riguad, Quebec (Ibid., #4620280.). She was baptized on 13 Dec 1838 Ste-Madeleine-de-Riguad, Quebec (Ibid.).

x. Amelie Seguin was born on 26 Aug 1840 Ste-Madeleine-de-Riguad, Quebec (Ibid., #4620701.). She was baptized on 27 Aug 1840 Ste-Madeleine-de-Riguad, Quebec (Ibid.).

xi. Elizabeth Seguin was born on 25 Jul 1843 Ste-Madeleine-de-Riguad, Quebec (Ibid., #4621413.). She was baptized on 27 Jul 1843 Ste-Madeleine-de-Riguad, Quebec (Ibid.). She died on 6 Aug 1843 Ste-Madeleine-de-Riguad, Quebec (Ibid., #4624369.). She was buried on 7 Aug 1843 Ste-Madeleine-de-Riguad, Quebec (Ibid.).

99. Pierre Louis Xavier Villeneuve was born on 25 Feb 1808 Ste-Madeleine-de-Riguad, Quebec (Ibid., #2679485.). He was baptized on 25 Feb 1808 Ste-Madeleine-de-Riguad, Quebec (Ibid.). He married **Marie Sophie Sabourin**, daughter of **Paul Eusebe Sabourin** and **Hippolyte Sauve,** on 9 Jan 1832 Ste-Madeleine-de-Riguad, Quebec (Ibid., #3462103.).

Marie Sophie Sabourin was born on 25 Apr 1810 Ste-Madeleine-de-Rigaud, Quebec (Ibid., #2679667.). She was baptized on 26 Apr 1810 Ste-Madeleine-de-Rigaud, Quebec *(father's occupation: agriculture)* (PRDH online, #2679667.).

Children of **Pierre Louis Xavier Villeneuve** and **Marie Sophie Sabourin** were as follows:

    i.   Pierre Guillaume Villeneuve was born on 11 Mar 1833 Hawkesbury, Ontario (Ibid., #4618833.). He was baptized on 12 Mar 1833 Ste-Madeleine-de-Riguad, Quebec (Ibid.).

    ii.   Camille Villeneuve was born on 18 Jul 1835 Hawkesbury, Ontario (Ibid., #4619417.). He was baptized on 19 Jul 1835 Ste-Madeleine-de-Riguad, Quebec (Ibid.).

    iii.   Francois Xavier Villeneuve was born on 11 Apr 1837 Hawkesbury, Ontario (Ibid., #4619911.). He was baptized on 15 Apr 1837 Ste-Madeleine-de-Riguad, Quebec (Ibid.).

    iv.   Marie Madeleine Villeneuve was born on 15 Apr 1839 Hawkesbury, Ontario (Ibid., #4620387.). She was baptized on 15 Apr 1839 Ste-Madeleine-de-Riguad, Quebec (Ibid.).

    v.   Eusebe Villeneuve was born on 30 Oct 1841 (Ibid., #4620995.). He was baptized on 30 Oct 1841 Ste-Madeleine-de-Riguad, Quebec (Ibid.). He died on 26 Nov 1845 Montreal, Quebec, at age 4 (Ibid., #4652653.). He was buried on 28 Nov 1845 Ste-Anne-de-Bellevue, Quebec (Ibid.).

    vi.   Hyacinthe Villeneuve was born on 10 Aug 1843 (Ibid., #4621427.). He was baptized on 11 Aug 1843 Ste-Madeleine-de-Riguad, Quebec (Ibid.). He died on 18 Apr 1846 at age 2 (Ibid., #4652660.). He was buried on 20 Apr 1846 Ste-Anne-de-Bellevue, Quebec (Ibid.).

    vii.   Napoleon Villeneuve was born on 13 Nov 1845 (Ibid., #3314883.). He was baptized on 14 Nov 1845 Ste-Madeleine-de-Riguad, Quebec (Ibid.). He died on 22 Aug 1846 (Ibid., #4652668.). He was buried on 23 Aug 1846 Ste-Anne-de-Bellevue, Quebec (Ibid.).

    viii.   Marie Seraphie Villeneuve was born on 14 Jul 1847 (Ibid., #3319133.). She was baptized on 18 Jul 1847 Notre-Dame, Montreal, Quebec (Ibid.). She died on 29 Jul 1847 (Ibid., #4652679.). She was buried on 30 Jul 1847 Ste-Anne-de-Bellevue, Quebec (Ibid.).

    ix.   Marie Villeneuve was born on 24 Aug 1849 (Bonsecours), Stukely-Nord, Quebec (Ibid., #2962960.). She was baptized on 24 Aug 1849 (Bonsecours), Stukely-Nord, Quebec (Ibid.).

100. Pierre Emery Villeneuve was born on 19 Nov 1809 Ste-Madeleine-de-Riguad, Quebec (Ibid., #2679630.). He was baptized on 19 Nov 1809 Ste-Madeleine-de-Riguad, Quebec (Ibid.). He married **Marguerite Scholastique Lavallee**, daughter of **Pierre Lavallee dit Menon** and **Marie Genevieve Citoleux,** on 18 Jan 1842 Ste-Madeleine-de-Riguad, Quebec (Ibid., #3465412.).

Marguerite Scholastique Lavallee was born on 9 Feb 1820 Ste-Madeleine-de-Riguad, Quebec (Ibid., #2680712.). She was baptized on 9 Feb 1820 Ste-Madeleine-de-Riguad, Quebec (Ibid.).

Children of **Pierre Emery Villeneuve** and **Marguerite Scholastique Lavallee** were as follows:

    i.   Marie Philomene Villeneuve was born on 8 Nov 1842 (Ibid., #4621236.). She was baptized on 12 Nov 1842 Ste-Madeleine-de-Riguad, Quebec (Ibid.).

    ii.   Emery Noel Villeneuve was born on 25 Dec 1843 Ste-Madeleine-de-Riguad, Quebec (Ibid., #4621505.). He was baptized on 25 Dec 1843 Ste-Madeleine-de-Riguad, Quebec (Ibid.). He died on 29 Apr 1844 Ste-Madeleine-de-Riguad, Quebec (Ibid., #4624440.). He was buried on 1 May 1844 Ste-Madeleine-de-Riguad, Quebec (Ibid.).

    iii.   Joseph Emery Villeneuve was born on 26 Apr 1845 Ste-Madeleine-de-Riguad, Quebec (Ibid., #4621806.). He was baptized on 27 Apr 1845 Ste-Madeleine-de-Riguad, Quebec (Ibid.).

    iv.   Hedwige Villeneuve was born circa Jan 1847 (Ibid., #3330163.). She died on 26 Dec 1848 Notre-Dame, Montreal, Quebec (Ibid.). She was buried on 28 Dec 1848 Notre-Dame, Montreal, Quebec *(age 23 months)* (PRDH online, #3330163.).

    v.   Marie Aimee Villeneuve was born on 23 Nov 1848 (Ibid., #3322280.). She was baptized on 26 Nov 1848 Notre-Dame, Montreal, Quebec (Ibid.).

101. Marie Louise Madeleine Villeneuve was born on 2 Feb 1812 Ste-Madeleine-de-Riguad, Quebec (Ibid., #2679850.). She was baptized on 3 Feb 1812 Ste-Madeleine-de-Riguad, Quebec (Ibid.). She married **Jean Baptiste Bertrand**, son of **Antoine Bertrand** and **Marie Josephe Cholet dit Laviolette,** on 16 May 1836 Ste-Madeleine-de-Riguad, Quebec (Ibid., #3463890.).

Jean Baptiste Bertrand was born on 4 Apr 1811 Vaudreuil, Quebec (Ibid., #2590852.). He was baptized on 4 Apr 1811 Vaudreuil, Quebec (Ibid.).

Children of **Marie Louise Madeleine Villeneuve** and **Jean Baptiste Bertrand** were:

    i.   Marie Madeleine Bertrand was born on 22 Jul 1838 Ste-Madeleine-de-Riguad, Quebec (Ibid., #4620190.). She was baptized on 23 Jul 1838 Ste-Madeleine-de-Riguad, Quebec (Ibid.).

102. **Vincent Hermenegilde Villeneuve** was born on 22 Jan 1814 Ste-Madeleine-de-Riguad, Quebec (Ibid., #2680046.). He was baptized on 23 Jan 1814 Ste-Madeleine-de-Riguad, Quebec (Ibid.). He married **Marguerite Sophie Bertrand**, daughter of **Antoine Bertrand** and **Marie Josephe Cholet dit Laviolette,** on 8 Aug 1836 Ste-Madeleine-de-Riguad, Quebec (Ibid., #3463953.).

Marguerite Sophie Bertrand was born on 8 Aug 1816 Ste-Madeleine-de-Riguad, Quebec (Ibid., #2680318.). She was baptized on 9 Aug 1816 Ste-Madeleine-de-Riguad, Quebec (Ibid.).

Children of **Vincent Hermenegilde Villeneuve** and **Marguerite Sophie Bertrand** were as follows:

    i.   Marie Clarinte Villeneuve was born on 15 Aug 1837 Ste-Madeleine-de-Riguad, Quebec (Ibid., #4619990.). She was baptized on 15 Aug 1837 Ste-Madeleine-de-Riguad, Quebec (Ibid.).

    ii.   Joseph Theophile Villeneuve was born on 3 Mar 1839 Ste-Madeleine-de-Riguad, Quebec (Ibid., #4620352.). He was baptized on 4 Mar 1839 Ste-Madeleine-de-Riguad, Quebec (Ibid.).

    iii.   Adelina Villeneuve was born on 15 Dec 1847 (Ibid., #4089401.). She was baptized on 25 Dec 1847 Montebello, Quebec (Ibid.).

103. **Marie Luce Alice Villeneuve** was born on 12 Dec 1815 Ste-Madeleine-de-Riguad, Quebec (Ibid., #2680239.). She was baptized on 13 Dec 1815 Ste-Madeleine-de-Riguad, Quebec *(father's occupation: agriculture)* (PRDH online, #2680239.). She married **Benjamin Patrice Belanger**, son of **Francois Belanger** and **Marie Madeleine Charlebois,** on 1 Oct 1838 Ste-Madeleine-de-Riguad, Quebec (Ibid., #3464618.).

Benjamin Patrice Belanger was born on 17 Mar 1813 Ste-Madeleine-de-Riguad, Quebec (Ibid., #2679970.). He was baptized on 17 Mar 1813 Ste-Madeleine-de-Riguad, Quebec (Ibid.).

Children of **Marie Luce Alice Villeneuve** and **Benjamin Patrice Belanger** were as follows:

    i.   Marie Madeleine Belanger was born on 3 Aug 1839 Ste-Madeleine-de-Riguad, Quebec (Ibid., #4620455.). She was baptized on 3 Aug 1839 Ste-Madeleine-de-Riguad, Quebec (Ibid.).

    ii.   Marie Olympe Belanger was born on 5 Dec 1840 Ste-Madeleine-de-Riguad, Quebec (Ibid., #4620761.). She was baptized on 6 Dec 1840 Ste-Madeleine-de-Riguad, Quebec (Ibid.). She died on 22 Dec 1847 Notre-Dame, Montreal, Quebec, at age 7 (Ibid., #3328480.). She was buried on 24 Dec 1847 Notre-Dame, Montreal, Quebec (Ibid.).

    iii.   Francois Xavier Belanger was born on 19 Apr 1842 Ste-Madeleine-de-Riguad, Quebec (Ibid., #4621106.). He was baptized on 19 Apr 1842 Ste-Madeleine-de-Riguad, Quebec (Ibid.). He died on 26 Apr 1842 Ste-Madeleine-de-Riguad, Quebec (Ibid., #4624249.). He was buried on 28 Apr 1842 Ste-Madeleine-de-Riguad, Quebec (Ibid.).

    iv.   Joseph Alphonse Belanger was born on 3 May 1843 Ste-Madeleine-de-Riguad, Quebec (Ibid., #4621363.). He was baptized on 5 May 1843 Ste-Madeleine-de-Riguad, Quebec (Ibid.). He died on 10 Sep 1843 Ste-Madeleine-de-Riguad, Quebec (Ibid., #4624381.). He was buried on 11 Sep 1843 Ste-Madeleine-de-Riguad, Quebec (Ibid.).

    v.   Marie Philomene Belanger was born on 1 Aug 1844 Ste-Madeleine-de-Riguad, Quebec (Ibid., #4621641.). She was baptized on 1 Aug 1844 Ste-Madeleine-de-Riguad, Quebec (Ibid.). She died on 15 Jan 1845 (Ibid., #4624480.). She was buried on 18 Jan 1845 Ste-Madeleine-de-Riguad, Quebec (Ibid.).

    vi.   Philomene Belanger was born on 7 Dec 1845 Notre-Dame, Montreal, Quebec (Ibid., #3315045.). She was baptized on 7 Dec 1845 Notre-Dame, Montreal, Quebec (Ibid.). She died on 16 Sep 1846 Notre-Dame, Montreal, Quebec (Ibid., #3325540.). She was buried on 18 Sep 1846 Notre-Dame, Montreal, Quebec (Ibid.).

    vii.   Elie Belanger was born on 26 Apr 1848 Notre-Dame, Montreal, Quebec (Ibid., #3320852.). He was baptized on 27 Apr 1848 Notre-Dame, Montreal, Quebec (Ibid.). He died on 23 Mar 1849 Notre-Dame, Montreal, Quebec (Ibid., #4218167.). He was buried on 26 Mar 1849 Notre-Dame, Montreal, Quebec (Ibid.).

104. **Paul Regis Seguin** was born on 30 Sep 1814 Ste-Madeleine-de-Riguad, Quebec (Ibid., #2680113.). He was baptized on 30 Sep 1814 Ste-Madeleine-de-Riguad, Quebec *(father's occupation: day laborer)* (PRDH online, #2680113.). He married **Julie Aurelie Tessier**, daughter of **Nicolas Tessier** and **Julie Beaudry,** on 25 Jan 1842 Ste-Madeleine-de-Riguad, Quebec (Ibid., #3465422.).

Julie Aurelie Tessier was born on 14 Jan 1823 Vaudreuil, Quebec (Ibid., #2591995.). She was baptized on 15 Jan 1823 Vaudreuil, Quebec (Ibid.).

Children of **Paul Regis Seguin** and **Julie Aurelie Tessier** were:

    i.   Flavien Seguin was born on 19 Jan 1845 Hawkesbury, Ontario (Ibid., #4621752.). He was baptized on 27 Jan 1845 Ste-Madeleine-de-Riguad, Quebec (Ibid.).

105. **Anthime Seguin** was born on 14 Sep 1824 Ste-Madeleine-de-Riguad, Quebec (Ibid., #2681406.). He was baptized on 15 Sep 1824 Ste-Madeleine-de-Riguad, Quebec (Ibid.). He married **Marie Louise Seguin**, daughter of **Etienne Seguin** and **Charlotte Jouin or Joint or Lemire,** on 21 Jun 1847 Grenville, Quebec *(Consanguinity: 2)* (PRDH online, #3464953.).

As of 21 Jun 1847, he was also known as **Antoine Villeneuve** (Ibid.).

Marie Louise Seguin was born on 17 Feb 1830 (Ibid., #4618075.). She was baptized on 20 Feb 1830 Ste-Madeleine-de-Riguad, Quebec (Ibid.).

Children of **Anthime Seguin** and **Marie Louise Seguin** were:

    i.   Zoe Seguin was born on 1 Feb 1849 Hawkesbury, Ontario (Ibid., #4682911.). She was baptized on 25 Feb 1849 St-André-d'Argenteuil, Quebec (Ibid.).

106. **Simon Francois Regis Lefaivre** was born on 15 Jul 1810 Vaudreuil, Quebec (Ibid., #2590787.). He was baptized on 15 Jul 1810 Vaudreuil, Quebec (Ibid.). He married **Sophie Robillard**, daughter of **Amable Robillard** and **Charlotte Legros,** on 3 Oct 1836 Vaudreuil, Quebec (Ibid., #3475362.).

He and **Sophie Robillard** were enumerated in the census in 1852 St.Michel, Vaudreuil, Quebec. Also in the family: **Marie Louise Sophie Lefaivre**, **Rose Lefaivre**, **Marie Virginie Lefaivre**, **Francois Xavier Lefaivre**, **Marie Selima Lefaivre**, and **M. E. Lefaivre** *(Lefaivre, Regis, Journalier, Vaudreuil F, Catholique romaine, 41, M; Robillard, Sophie, Vaudreuil F, Catholique romaine, 31, F; Lefaivre, Louise, Vaudreuil F, Catholique romaine, 14, F; Lefaivre, Rose, Vaudreuil F, Catholique romaine, 12, F; Lefaivre, Virginie, Vaudreuil F, Catholique romaine, 9, F; Lefaivre, Xavier, Vaudreuil F, Catholique romaine, 7, M; Lefaivre, Sélima, Vaudreuil F, Catholique romaine, 4, F; Lefaivre, M. E., Vaudreuil F, Catholique romaine, F)* (1852C Cdn Transcription Project, District 534, page 26d, 27a, (53), page 27d, 28a, (55), line 47-50, 1-4.).

Sophie Robillard was born on 16 Dec 1817 Oka, Quebec (PRDH online, #2752414.). She was baptized on 16 Dec 1817 Oka, Quebec (Ibid.).

Children of **Simon Francois Regis Lefaivre** and **Sophie Robillard** were as follows:

    i.   Francois Regis Lefaivre was born on 6 Aug 1837 Vaudreuil, Quebec (Ibid., #4179361.). He was baptized on 7 Aug 1837 Vaudreuil, Quebec (Ibid.). He died on 27 May 1838 Vaudreuil, Quebec (Ibid., #4181959.). He was buried on 28 May 1838 Vaudreuil, Quebec (Ibid.).

    ii.   Marie Louise Sophie Lefaivre was born on 23 Apr 1839 Vaudreuil, Quebec (Ibid., #4179592.). She was baptized on 24 Apr 1839 Vaudreuil, Quebec (Ibid.).

       She was in the census household of Simon Francois Regis Lefaivre and Sophie Robillard in 1852 St.Michel, Vaudreuil, Quebec (1852C Cdn Transcription Project, District 534, page 26d, 27a, (53), page 27d, 28a, (55), line 47-50, 1-4.).

    iii.   Rose Lefaivre was born on 25 Sep 1841 Vaudreuil, Quebec (PRDH online, #4179913.). She was baptized on 27 Sep 1841 Vaudreuil, Quebec (Ibid.).

       She was in the census household of Simon Francois Regis Lefaivre and Sophie Robillard in 1852 St.Michel, Vaudreuil, Quebec (1852C Cdn Transcription Project, District 534, page 26d, 27a, (53), page 27d, 28a, (55), line 47-50, 1-4.).

    iv.   Marie Virginie Lefaivre was born on 14 Jul 1843 Vaudreuil, Quebec (PRDH online, #4180175.). She was baptized on 14 Jul 1843 Vaudreuil, Quebec (Ibid.).

       She was in the census household of Simon Francois Regis Lefaivre and Sophie Robillard in 1852 St.Michel, Vaudreuil, Quebec (1852C Cdn Transcription Project, District 534, page 26d, 27a, (53), page 27d, 28a, (55), line 47-50, 1-4.).

    v.   Francois Xavier Lefaivre was born on 19 Aug 1845 Vaudreuil, Quebec (PRDH online, #4180470.). He was baptized on 20 Aug 1845 Vaudreuil, Quebec (Ibid.).

       He was in the census household of Simon Francois Regis Lefaivre and Sophie Robillard in 1852 St.Michel, Vaudreuil, Quebec (1852C Cdn Transcription Project, District 534, page 26d, 27a, (53), page 27d, 28a, (55), line 47-50, 1-4.).

    vi.   Marie Selima Lefaivre was born on 27 Jun 1848 Vaudreuil, Quebec (PRDH online, #4180897.). She was baptized on 28 Jun 1848 Vaudreuil, Quebec (Ibid.).

       She was in the census household of Simon Francois Regis Lefaivre and Sophie Robillard in 1852 St.Michel, Vaudreuil, Quebec (1852C Cdn Transcription Project, District 534, page 26d, 27a, (53), page 27d, 28a, (55), line 47-50, 1-4.).

    vii.   M. E. Lefaivre was born circa 1852 (Ibid.).

       She was in the census household of Simon Francois Regis Lefaivre and Sophie Robillard in 1852 St.Michel, Vaudreuil, Quebec (1852C Cdn Transcription Project, District 534, page 26d, 27a, (53), page 27d, 28a, (55), line 47-50, 1-4.).

107. Elisabeth Cecile Lefebvre was born on 11 Nov 1816 Vaudreuil, Quebec (PRDH online, #2591353.). She was baptized on 12 Nov 1816 Vaudreuil, Quebec (Ibid.). She married **Jean Evangeliste Gauthier**, son of **Pierre Gauthier** and **Victoire Marguerite Leger,** on 23 Aug 1841 Vaudreuil, Quebec (Ibid., #3476562.).

She and **Jean Evangeliste Gauthier** were enumerated in the census in 1852 St.Michel, Vaudreuil, Quebec. Also in the family: **Marie Louise Gauthier, Jean Evangeliste Alain Gauthier, Pierre Suplicien Gauthier, Louis Edmond Gauthier**, and **Honore Gauthier** *(Gauthier, Evangeliste, Journalier, Vaudreuil F, Catholique romaine, 34, M; Lefaivre, Elisabeth, Vaudreuil F, Catholique romaine, 36, F; Gauthier, Louise, Vaudreuil F, Catholique romaine, 10, M; Gauthier, Allain, Vaudreuil F, Catholique romaine, 8, M; Gauthier, Pre, Vaudreuil F, Catholique romaine, 7, M; Gauthier, Edmond, Vaudreuil F, Catholique romaine, 3, M; Gauthier, Honoré, Vaudreuil F, Catholique romaine, 10 mois, M)* (1852C Cdn Transcription Project, District 534, page 19d, 20a, (39), line 27-33.).

Jean Evangeliste Gauthier was born on 2 Oct 1818 Vaudreuil, Quebec (PRDH online, #2591543.). He was baptized on 2 Oct 1818 Vaudreuil, Quebec (Ibid.).

Children of **Elisabeth Cecile Lefebvre** and **Jean Evangeliste Gauthier** were as follows:

    i. Marie Louise Gauthier was born on 28 Jun 1842 Vaudreuil, Quebec (Ibid., #4180021.). She was baptized on 29 Jun 1842 Vaudreuil, Quebec (Ibid.).
    She was in the census household of Jean Evangeliste Gauthier and Elisabeth Cecile Lefebvre in 1852 St.Michel, Vaudreuil, Quebec (1852C Cdn Transcription Project, District 534, page 19d, 20a, (39), line 27-33.).

    ii. Jean Evangeliste Alain Gauthier was born on 19 Jul 1844 Vaudreuil, Quebec (PRDH online, #4180318.). He was baptized on 20 Jul 1844 Vaudreuil, Quebec (Ibid.).
    He was in the census household of Jean Evangeliste Gauthier and Elisabeth Cecile Lefebvre in 1852 St.Michel, Vaudreuil, Quebec (1852C Cdn Transcription Project, District 534, page 19d, 20a, (39), line 27-33.).

    iii. Pierre Suplicien Gauthier was born on 24 Feb 1846 Vaudreuil, Quebec (PRDH online, #4180549.). He was baptized on 24 Feb 1846 Vaudreuil, Quebec (Ibid.).
    He was in the census household of Jean Evangeliste Gauthier and Elisabeth Cecile Lefebvre in 1852 St.Michel, Vaudreuil, Quebec (1852C Cdn Transcription Project, District 534, page 19d, 20a, (39), line 27-33.).

    iv. Louis Edmond Gauthier was born on 14 Apr 1849 Vaudreuil, Quebec (PRDH online, #4181034.). He was baptized on 14 Apr 1849 Vaudreuil, Quebec (Ibid.).
    He was in the census household of Jean Evangeliste Gauthier and Elisabeth Cecile Lefebvre in 1852 St.Michel, Vaudreuil, Quebec (1852C Cdn Transcription Project, District 534, page 19d, 20a, (39), line 27-33.).

    v. Honore Gauthier was born circa 1851 (Ibid.).
    He was in the census household of Jean Evangeliste Gauthier and Elisabeth Cecile Lefebvre in 1852 St.Michel, Vaudreuil, Quebec (1852C Cdn Transcription Project, District 534, page 19d, 20a, (39), line 27-33.).

108. Marie Ostie Lefebvre was born on 1 Apr 1819 Vaudreuil, Quebec (PRDH online, #2591588.). She was baptized on 2 Apr 1819 Vaudreuil, Quebec (Ibid.). She married **Jules Leger**, son of **Jean Baptiste Antoine Leger dit Parisien** and **Rose Rapin,** on 16 Feb 1846 Vaudreuil, Quebec (Ibid., #3477353.).

She and **Jules Leger** were enumerated in the census in 1852 St.Michel, Vaudreuil, Quebec *(Léger, Jules, Cultivateur, Vaudreuil F, Catholique romaine, 36, M; Lefaivre, Marie O., Vaudreuil F, Catholique romaine, 33, F)* (1852C Cdn Transcription Project, District 534, page 17d, 18a, (35), line 18-19.).

Jules Leger was born on 8 Aug 1816 Vaudreuil, Quebec (PRDH online, #2591329.). He was baptized on 8 Aug 1816 Vaudreuil, Quebec *(father's occupation: cultivator)* (PRDH online, #2591329.).

Children of **Marie Ostie Lefebvre** and **Jules Leger** both born Vaudreuil, Quebec, were as follows:

    i. Jean Baptiste Jules Leger was born on 4 Dec 1846 (Ibid., #4180659.). He was baptized on 4 Dec 1846 Vaudreuil, Quebec (Ibid.).

    ii. Antoine Napoleon Leger was born on 3 Oct 1848 (Ibid., #4180942.). He was baptized on 3 Oct 1848 Vaudreuil, Quebec (Ibid.).

109. Marie Rose Lefaivre was born on 29 Jun 1822 Vaudreuil, Quebec (Ibid., #2591927.). She was baptized on 30 Jun 1822 Vaudreuil, Quebec (Ibid.). She married **Cyprien Daout**, son of **Charles Daoust dit Daut** and **Genevieve Leduc,** on 17 Nov 1846 Vaudreuil, Quebec (Ibid., #3477572.).

Cyprien Daout was born on 16 Sep 1816 (Ste-Jeanne-de-Chantal), L'Ile Perrot, Quebec (Ibid., #842554.). He was baptized on 16 Sep 1816 (Ste-Jeanne-de-Chantal), L'Ile Perrot, Quebec (Ibid.).

Children of **Marie Rose Lefaivre** and **Cyprien Daout** both born Vaudreuil, Quebec, were as follows:

     i.   Joseph Cyprien Daout was born on 17 Jun 1847 (Ibid., #4180740.). He was baptized on 17 Jun 1847 Vaudreuil, Quebec (Ibid.).

     ii.   Marie Louise Daout was born on 19 Oct 1848 (Ibid., #4180957.). She was baptized on 20 Oct 1848 Vaudreuil, Quebec (Ibid.).

110. Marie Marine Lefaivre was born circa 1828 (1852C Cdn Transcription Project, District 535, page 2d, 3a, (5), line 14-17.). She married **Antoine Charlebois**, son of **Louis Charlebois** and **Marie Charles (--?--),** on 31 Jul 1843 Vaudreuil, Quebec (PRDH online, #3476919.).

She and **Antoine Charlebois** were enumerated in the census in 1852 St.Michel, Vaudreuil, Quebec. Also in the family: **Marie Henriette Hermine Charlebois** and **Marie Louise Almais Charlebois** *(Lefaivre, Marina, Vaudreuil F, Catholique romaine, 24, F; Charlebois, Elbina, Vaudreuil F, Catholique romaine, 5, F; Charlebois, Elmaige, Vaudreuil F, Catholique romaine, 2, F; Charlebois, Antoine, Voyageur, Vaudreuil F, Catholique romaine, 34, M)* (1852C Cdn Transcription Project, District 535, page 2d, 3a, (5), line 14-17.).

Antoine Charlebois was born on 2 Aug 1815 Vaudreuil, Quebec (PRDH online, #2591251.). He was baptized on 3 Aug 1815 Vaudreuil, Quebec (Ibid.). He was *a voyageur* in 1852 (1852C Cdn Transcription Project, District 535, page 2d, 3a, (5), line 14-17.).

Children of **Marie Marine Lefaivre** and **Antoine Charlebois** all born Vaudreuil, Quebec, were as follows:

     i.   Antoine Charlebois was born on 17 Nov 1843 (PRDH online, #4180219.). He was baptized on 18 Nov 1843 Vaudreuil, Quebec (Ibid.).

     ii.   Marie Henriette Hermine Charlebois was born on 26 Jul 1846 (Ibid., #4180603.). She was baptized on 27 Jul 1846 Vaudreuil, Quebec (Ibid.).

        She was in the census household of Antoine Charlebois and Marie Marine Lefaivre in 1852 St.Michel, Vaudreuil, Quebec (1852C Cdn Transcription Project, District 535, page 2d, 3a, (5), line 14-17.).

     iii.   Marie Louise Almais Charlebois was born on 2 May 1849 (PRDH online, #4181041.). She was baptized on 3 May 1849 Vaudreuil, Quebec (Ibid.).

        She was in the census household of Antoine Charlebois and Marie Marine Lefaivre in 1852 St.Michel, Vaudreuil, Quebec (1852C Cdn Transcription Project, District 535, page 2d, 3a, (5), line 14-17.).

111. Simon Timineur dit Laflamme was born on 13 Mar 1814 Ste-Madeleine-de-Riguad, Quebec (PRDH online, #2680061.). He was baptized on 13 Mar 1814 Ste-Madeleine-de-Riguad, Quebec *(father's occupation: day laborer)* (PRDH online, #2680061.). He married **Mathilde St.Denis**, daughter of **Antoine St.Denis** and **Pelagie Marie Gauthier,** on 14 Nov 1836 Ste-Madeleine-de-Riguad, Quebec (Ibid., #3464098.).

He was also known as **Simon Kemner** (Ibid., #2680061.).

Mathilde St.Denis was born on 20 Oct 1815 Ste-Madeleine-de-Riguad, Quebec (Ibid., #756948.). She was baptized on 21 Oct 1815 Ste-Madeleine-de-Riguad, Quebec (Ibid.).

Children of **Simon Timineur dit Laflamme** and **Mathilde St.Denis** were as follows:

     i.   Joseph Honore Timineur was born on 26 May 1837 Hawkesbury, Ontario (Ibid., #4619940.). He was baptized on 29 May 1837 Ste-Madeleine-de-Riguad, Quebec (Ibid.).

     ii.   Michel Timineur was born on 28 Jan 1839 Hawkesbury, Ontario (Ibid., #4620312.). He was baptized on 29 Jan 1839 Ste-Madeleine-de-Riguad, Quebec (Ibid.).

     iii.   Marie Odile Timineur dit Laflamme was born on 30 Dec 1840 (Ibid., #4620776.). She was baptized on 31 Dec 1840 Ste-Madeleine-de-Riguad, Quebec (Ibid.).

     iv.   Pierre Quimineur was born on 4 Dec 1842 (Ibid., #4621253.). He was baptized on 5 Dec 1842 Ste-Madeleine-de-Riguad, Quebec (Ibid.). He died on 16 Jul 1843 (Ibid., #4624358.). He was buried on 19 Jul 1843 Ste-Madeleine-de-Riguad, Quebec (Ibid.).

     v.   Marie Julie Laflamme was born on 13 Aug 1844 (Ibid., #4621647.). She was baptized on 13 Aug 1844 Ste-Madeleine-de-Riguad, Quebec (Ibid.).

     vi.   Marie Marcelline Timineur was born on 9 Jul 1846 (Ibid., #4622075.). She was baptized on 9 Jul 1846 Ste-Madeleine-de-Riguad, Quebec (Ibid.).

     vii.   Theodore Timineur was born on 27 Apr 1848 Hawkesbury, Ontario (Ibid., #4622394.). He was baptized on 30 Apr 1848 Ste-Madeleine-de-Riguad, Quebec (Ibid.).

112. Marie Julienne Cadieux was born on 30 Jul 1814 Ste-Madeleine-de-Riguad, Quebec (Ibid., #2680098.). She was baptized on 31 Jul 1814 Ste-Madeleine-de-Riguad, Quebec (Ibid.). She married **Laurent Girouard**, son of **Joseph Girouard** and **Josephte Bleau dit Blo,** on 24 Feb 1835 Ste-Madeleine-de-Riguad, Quebec (Ibid., #3463378.).

She and **Laurent Girouard** were enumerated in the census in 1852 St.Michel, Vaudreuil, Quebec. Also in the family: **Marie Julienne Caroline Girouard, Jean Marie Laurent Girouard, Honore Adeodat Girouard, Damien**

Candide Girouard, **George Edouard Girouard**, and **Louise Girouard** *(Girouard, Laurent, Cultivateur, St. Laurent F, Catholique romaine, 47, M; Cadeux, Julienne, Rigaud F, Catholique romaine, 38, F; Girouard, Selima, Vaudreuil F, Catholique romaine, 15, F; Girouard, Laurent, Vaudreuil F, Catholique romaine, 12, M; Girouard, Honoré, Ecolier, Vaudreuil F, Catholique romaine, 11, M; Girouard, Candide, Vaudreuil F, Catholique romaine, 7, M; Girouard, George, Vaudreuil F, Catholique romaine, 5, M; Girouard, Louise, Vaudreuil F, Catholique romaine, 2, F)* (1852C Cdn Transcription Project, District 534, page 19d, 20a, (39), page 20d, 21a, (41), line 46-50, 1-3.).

  Laurent Girouard was born on 12 Dec 1805 (St.Laurent), Montreal, Quebec (PRDH online, #2466371.). He was baptized on 13 Dec 1805 (St.Laurent), Montreal, Quebec (Ibid.).

Children of **Marie Julienne Cadieux** and **Laurent Girouard** were as follows:

  i. Francois Joseph Girouard was born on 26 Nov 1835 Ste-Madeleine-de-Riguad, Quebec (Ibid., #4619516.). He was baptized on 27 Nov 1835 Ste-Madeleine-de-Riguad, Quebec (Ibid.).

  ii. Marie Julienne Caroline Girouard was born on 25 Feb 1837 Ste-Madeleine-de-Riguad, Quebec (Ibid., #4619871.). She was baptized on 26 Feb 1837 Ste-Madeleine-de-Riguad, Quebec (Ibid.).
      She was in the census household of Laurent Girouard and Marie Julienne Cadieux in 1852 St.Michel, Vaudreuil, Quebec (1852C Cdn Transcription Project, District 534, page 19d, 20a, (39), page 20d, 21a, (41), line 46-50, 1-3.).

  iii. Jean Marie Laurent Girouard was born on 21 Apr 1839 Ste-Madeleine-de-Riguad, Quebec (PRDH online, #4620389.). He was baptized on 22 Apr 1839 Ste-Madeleine-de-Riguad, Quebec (Ibid.).
      He was in the census household of Laurent Girouard and Marie Julienne Cadieux in 1852 St.Michel, Vaudreuil, Quebec (1852C Cdn Transcription Project, District 534, page 19d, 20a, (39), page 20d, 21a, (41), line 46-50, 1-3.).

  iv. Honore Adeodat Girouard was born on 5 Jan 1841 Ste-Madeleine-de-Riguad, Quebec (PRDH online, #4620787.). He was baptized on 7 Jan 1841 Ste-Madeleine-de-Riguad, Quebec (Ibid.).
      He was in the census household of Laurent Girouard and Marie Julienne Cadieux in 1852 St.Michel, Vaudreuil, Quebec (1852C Cdn Transcription Project, District 534, page 19d, 20a, (39), page 20d, 21a, (41), line 46-50, 1-3.).

  v. Scholastique Girouard was born on 7 Nov 1842 Vaudreuil, Quebec (PRDH online, #4180072.). She was baptized on 8 Nov 1842 Vaudreuil, Quebec (Ibid.).

  vi. Damien Candide Girouard was born on 21 Feb 1845 Vaudreuil, Quebec (Ibid., #4180397.). He was baptized on 23 Feb 1845 Vaudreuil, Quebec (Ibid.).
      He was in the census household of Laurent Girouard and Marie Julienne Cadieux in 1852 St.Michel, Vaudreuil, Quebec (1852C Cdn Transcription Project, District 534, page 19d, 20a, (39), page 20d, 21a, (41), line 46-50, 1-3.).

  vii. George Edouard Girouard was born on 7 Sep 1846 Vaudreuil, Quebec (PRDH online, #4180623.). He was baptized on 8 Sep 1846 Vaudreuil, Quebec (Ibid.).
      He was in the census household of Laurent Girouard and Marie Julienne Cadieux in 1852 St.Michel, Vaudreuil, Quebec (1852C Cdn Transcription Project, District 534, page 19d, 20a, (39), page 20d, 21a, (41), line 46-50, 1-3.).

  viii. Joseph Francois Bolivar Girouard was born on 14 Apr 1848 Vaudreuil, Quebec (PRDH online, #4180860.). He was baptized on 14 Apr 1848 Vaudreuil, Quebec (Ibid.). He died on 3 Sep 1849 Vaudreuil, Quebec, at age 1 (Ibid., #4182668.). He was buried on 4 Sep 1849 Vaudreuil, Quebec (Ibid.).

  ix. Louise Girouard was born circa 1850 (1852C Cdn Transcription Project, District 534, page 19d, 20a, (39), page 20d, 21a, (41), line 46-50, 1-3.).
      She was in the census household of Laurent Girouard and Marie Julienne Cadieux in 1852 St.Michel, Vaudreuil, Quebec (1852C Cdn Transcription Project, District 534, page 19d, 20a, (39), page 20d, 21a, (41), line 46-50, 1-3.).

113. Marie Sophie Cadieux was born on 18 Dec 1815 Ste-Madeleine-de-Riguad, Quebec (PRDH online, #2680247.). She was baptized on 19 Dec 1815 Ste-Madeleine-de-Riguad, Quebec *(father's occupation: agriculture)* (PRDH online, #2680247.). She married **Vincent Xavier Villeneuve**, son of **Vincent Xavier Villeneuve** and **Euphrosine Marie Quesnel,** on 23 Nov 1835 Ste-Madeleine-de-Riguad, Quebec *(Consanguinity: 4)* (PRDH online, #3463675.).

  Vincent Xavier Villeneuve was born on 4 Apr 1813 Ste-Madeleine-de-Riguad, Quebec (Ibid., #2679976.). He was baptized on 4 Apr 1813 Ste-Madeleine-de-Riguad, Quebec (Ibid.). As of 23 Nov 1835, he was also known as **Francois Xavier Villeneuve** (Ibid., #3463675.).

Children of **Marie Sophie Cadieux** and **Vincent Xavier Villeneuve** all born Ste-Madeleine-de-Riguad, Quebec, were as follows:

     i.   Francois Barnabe Villeneuve, b. 31 Aug 1836. (see previous).

     ii.   Antoine Villeneuve, b. 20 Apr 1838. (see previous).

     iii. Alphonse Villeneuve, b. 23 Dec 1839. (see previous).

     iv. Joseph Michel Villeneuve, b. 2 Jun 1841; d. 27 Oct 1844; bur. 30 Oct 1844. (see previous).

     v.   Paul Villeneuve, b. 28 May 1842; d. 1 Mar 1844; bur. 3 Mar 1844. (see previous).

     vi. Anastasie Villeneuve, b. 26 Aug 1843. (see previous).

     vii. Joseph Edmond Villeneuve, b. 19 Apr 1845. (see previous).

     viii. Marie Louise Villeneuve, b. 12 Nov 1846. (see previous).

     ix. Eleonore Villeneuve, b. 19 Sep 1848; d. 1 Aug 1849; bur. 2 Aug 1849. (see previous).

114. Jean Marie Cadieux was born on 10 May 1817 Ste-Madeleine-de-Riguad, Quebec (Ibid., #2680393.). He was baptized on 11 May 1817 Ste-Madeleine-de-Riguad, Quebec *(father's occupation: agriculture)* (PRDH online, #2680393.). He married **Julienne Villeneuve**, daughter of **Vincent Xavier Villeneuve** and **Euphrosine Marie Quesnel**, on 13 Feb 1844 Ste-Madeleine-de-Riguad, Quebec *(Consanguinity: 4)* (PRDH online, #3465916.).

He and **Julienne Villeneuve** were enumerated in the census in 1852 Ste.Madeleine, Rigaud, Vaudreuil, Quebec. Also in the family: **Francois Xavier Cadieux**, **Napoleon Cadieux**, **Marie Sophie Cadieux**, **Honore Cadieux**, and **Marguerite Villeneuve** *(Cadieux, J. Marie, Cultivateur, Rigaud, Catholique, 35, M; Villeneuve, Julienne, Rigaud, Catholique, 31, F; Cadieux, Xavier, Rigaud, Catholique, 6, M; Cadieux, Napoléon, Rigaud, Catholique, 5, M; Cadieux, Sophie, Rigaud, Catholique, 2, F; Cadieux, Honoré, Rigaud, Catholique, 5 mois, M; Villeneuve, Marguerite, Servante, Rigaud, Catholique, 19, F; Cadieux, Benj, Voyageur, Rigaud, Catholique, 19, M)* (1852C Cdn Transcription Project, District 536, page 35d, 36a, (71), line 27-34.).

Julienne Villeneuve was born on 4 Aug 1820 Ste-Madeleine-de-Riguad, Quebec (PRDH online, #2680784.). She was baptized on 4 Aug 1820 Ste-Madeleine-de-Riguad, Quebec (Ibid.).

Children of **Jean Marie Cadieux** and **Julienne Villeneuve** all born Ste-Madeleine-de-Riguad, Quebec, were as follows:

     i.   Francois Xavier Cadieux, b. 20 Apr 1845. (see previous).

     ii.   Napoleon Cadieux, b. 9 Aug 1846. (see previous).

     iii. Marie Eleonore Cadieux, b. 9 Jun 1848. (see previous).

     iv. Marie Sophie Cadieux, b. 22 Nov 1849. (see previous).

115. Josephte Caroline Cadieux was born on 19 Mar 1820 Ste-Madeleine-de-Riguad, Quebec (Ibid., #2680731.). She was baptized on 19 Mar 1820 Ste-Madeleine-de-Riguad, Quebec (Ibid.). She married **Michel Lefebvre**, son of **Hyacinthe Lefebvre dit Lasiseraie** and **Marie Madeleine Neveu dit Nepveu**, on 15 Jan 1839 Ste-Madeleine-de-Riguad, Quebec (Ibid., #3464739.).

She and **Michel Lefebvre** were enumerated in the census in 1852 Ste.Madeleine, Rigaud, Vaudreuil, Quebec. Also in the family: **Marie Scholastique Villeneuve**, **Marcelline Boucher**, **Marie Narsee Louise Lefebvre**, **Hyacinthe Napoleon Lefebvre**, **Hyacinthe Lefebvre**, and **Honore Lefebvre** *(Lefebvre, Michel, Cultivateur, Pte Claire, Catholique, 44, M; Cadieux, Caroline, Rigaud, Catholique, 34, F; Villeneuve, Scolastique, Rigaud, Catholique, 60, F; Boucher, Marceline, Rigaud, Catholique, 22, F; Cadieux, Louise, Rigaud, Catholique, 11, F; Cadieux, Napoléon, Rigaud, Catholique, 10, M; Cadieux, Hythe, Rigaud, Catholique, 6, M; Cadieux, Honoré, Rigaud, Catholique, 10 mois, M)* (1852C Cdn Transcription Project, District 536, page 35d, 36a, (71), line 38-45.).

Michel Lefebvre was born on 16 Jul 1807 Pointe-Claire, Quebec (PRDH online, #2800897.). He was baptized on 16 Jul 1807 Pointe-Claire, Quebec (Ibid.).

Children of **Josephte Caroline Cadieux** and **Michel Lefebvre** were as follows:

     i.   Marie Narsee Louise Lefebvre was born on 3 Jan 1841 Ste-Madeleine-de-Riguad, Quebec (Ibid., #4620784.). She was baptized on 5 Jan 1841 Ste-Madeleine-de-Riguad, Quebec (Ibid.).

         She was in the census household of Michel Lefebvre and Josephte Caroline Cadieux in 1852 Ste.Madeleine, Rigaud, Vaudreuil, Quebec (1852C Cdn Transcription Project, District 536, page 35d, 36a, (71), line 38-45.).

     ii.   Hyacinthe Napoleon Lefebvre was born on 12 Feb 1842 Ste-Madeleine-de-Riguad, Quebec (PRDH online, #4621067.). He was baptized on 13 Feb 1842 Ste-Madeleine-de-Riguad, Quebec (Ibid.).

         He was in the census household of Michel Lefebvre and Josephte Caroline Cadieux in 1852 Ste.Madeleine, Rigaud, Vaudreuil, Quebec (1852C Cdn Transcription Project, District 536, page 35d, 36a, (71), line 38-45.).

    iii.   Marie Priscille Lefebvre was born on 3 May 1843 Ste-Madeleine-de-Riguad, Quebec (PRDH online, #4621362.). She was baptized on 4 May 1843 Ste-Madeleine-de-Riguad, Quebec (Ibid.).

    iv.   Hyacinthe Lefebvre was born on 31 Jan 1846 Ste-Madeleine-de-Riguad, Quebec (Ibid., #4621981.). He was baptized on 31 Jan 1846 Ste-Madeleine-de-Riguad, Quebec (Ibid.).

       He was in the census household of Michel Lefebvre and Josephte Caroline Cadieux in 1852 Ste.Madeleine, Rigaud, Vaudreuil, Quebec (1852C Cdn Transcription Project, District 536, page 35d, 36a, (71), line 38-45.).

    v.   Joseph Louis Lefebvre was born on 4 May 1847 Ste-Madeleine-de-Riguad, Quebec (PRDH online, #4622227.). He was baptized on 5 May 1847 Ste-Madeleine-de-Riguad, Quebec (Ibid.).

    vi.   Joseph Honore Lefebvre was born on 21 May 1849 Ste-Madeleine-de-Riguad, Quebec (Ibid., #4622553.). He was baptized on 25 May 1849 Ste-Madeleine-de-Riguad, Quebec (Ibid.).

    vii.   Honore Lefebvre was born circa 1851 (1852C Cdn Transcription Project, District 536, page 35d, 36a, (71), line 38-45.).

       He was in the census household of Michel Lefebvre and Josephte Caroline Cadieux in 1852 Ste.Madeleine, Rigaud, Vaudreuil, Quebec (1852C Cdn Transcription Project, District 536, page 35d, 36a, (71), line 38-45.).

116. Marie Denise Cadieux was born on 22 Dec 1826 Ste-Madeleine-de-Riguad, Quebec (PRDH online, #4617459.). She was baptized on 22 Dec 1826 Ste-Madeleine-de-Riguad, Quebec (Ibid.). She married **Nicolas Emery Bertrand**, son of **Francois Vital Bertrand** and **Marie Hippolyte Apolline St.Julien dit Daragon,** on 14 Jul 1845 Ste-Madeleine-de-Riguad, Quebec (Ibid., #3466383.).

She and **Nicolas Emery Bertrand** were enumerated in the census in 1852 Ste.Madeleine, Rigaud, Vaudreuil, Quebec. Also in the family: **Marie Priscille Bertrand**, **Marie Eloise Bertrand**, **Francois Emery Bertrand**, and **Eleonore Bertrand** *(Bertrand, Emery, Cultivateur, Vaudreuil, Catholique, 36, M; Cadieux, Denise, Rigaud, Catholique, 24, F; Bertrand, Pressile, Rigaud, Catholique, 5, F; Bertrand, Eloise, Rigaud, Catholique, 4, F; Bertrand, Emery, Rigaud, Catholique, 2, M; Bertrand, Eleonard, Rigaud, Catholique, 1, F)* (1852C Cdn Transcription Project, District 536, page 8d, 9a, (17), line 11-16.).

Nicolas Emery Bertrand was born on 6 Sep 1816 Vaudreuil, Quebec (PRDH online, #2591339.). He was baptized on 6 Sep 1816 Vaudreuil, Quebec (Ibid.).

Children of **Marie Denise Cadieux** and **Nicolas Emery Bertrand** were as follows:

    i.   Marie Priscille Bertrand was born on 31 May 1846 Ste-Madeleine-de-Riguad, Quebec (Ibid., #4622048.). She was baptized on 1 Jun 1846 Ste-Madeleine-de-Riguad, Quebec (Ibid.).

       She was in the census household of Nicolas Emery Bertrand and Marie Denise Cadieux in 1852 Ste.Madeleine, Rigaud, Vaudreuil, Quebec (1852C Cdn Transcription Project, District 536, page 8d, 9a, (17), line 11-16.).

    ii.   Marie Eloise Bertrand was born on 29 May 1847 Ste-Madeleine-de-Riguad, Quebec (PRDH online, #4622243.). She was baptized on 30 May 1847 Ste-Madeleine-de-Riguad, Quebec (Ibid.).

       She was in the census household of Nicolas Emery Bertrand and Marie Denise Cadieux in 1852 Ste.Madeleine, Rigaud, Vaudreuil, Quebec (1852C Cdn Transcription Project, District 536, page 8d, 9a, (17), line 11-16.).

    iii.   Francois Emery Bertrand was born on 13 Mar 1849 Ste-Madeleine-de-Riguad, Quebec (PRDH online, #4622527.). He was baptized on 14 Mar 1849 Ste-Madeleine-de-Riguad, Quebec (Ibid.).

       He was in the census household of Nicolas Emery Bertrand and Marie Denise Cadieux in 1852 Ste.Madeleine, Rigaud, Vaudreuil, Quebec (1852C Cdn Transcription Project, District 536, page 8d, 9a, (17), line 11-16.).

    iv.   Eleonore Bertrand was born circa 1851 (Ibid.).

       She was in the census household of Nicolas Emery Bertrand and Marie Denise Cadieux in 1852 Ste.Madeleine, Rigaud, Vaudreuil, Quebec (1852C Cdn Transcription Project, District 536, page 8d, 9a, (17), line 11-16.).

117. Hyacinthe Seguin was born on 16 Aug 1821 Ste-Madeleine-de-Riguad, Quebec (PRDH online, #2680906.). He was baptized on 16 Aug 1821 Ste-Madeleine-de-Riguad, Quebec *(father's occupation: day laborer)* (PRDH online, #2680906.). He married **Marie Anne Charron**, daughter of **Jean Louis Charron** and **Venerande Tremblay,** on 7 Jan 1846 Montebello, Quebec (Ibid., #3987668.).

He and **Marie Anne Charron** were enumerated in the census in 1852 Notre-Dame, Petite Nation, Ottawa County, Ontario. Also in the family: **Adeline Seguin, Isabelle Seguin,** and **Hyacinthe Seguin** *(Seguin, Hyacinthe Jr, Farmer, Canada West, Roman Catholic, 30, M; Seguin, Mad Hyacinthe, ditto, ditto, 23, F; Seguin, Daline, ditto, ditto, 5, F;*

Seguin, Elisabeth, ditto, ditto, 3, F; Seguin, Hyacinthe, ditto, ditto, 2, M) (1852C Cdn Transcription Project, District 274, page 39d, 30a, (79), line 33-37.).

Marie Anne Charron was born circa 1829 (Ibid.).

Children of **Hyacinthe Seguin** and **Marie Anne Charron** were as follows:

    i. Adeline Seguin was born on 9 Oct 1846 Montebello, Quebec (PRDH online, #4089252.). She was baptized on 9 Oct 1846 Montebello, Quebec (Ibid.).

       She was in the census household of Hyacinthe Seguin and Marie Anne Charron in 1852 Notre-Dame, Petite Nation, Ottawa County, Ontario (1852C Cdn Transcription Project, District 274, page 39d, 30a, (79), line 33-37.).

    ii. Isabelle Seguin was born on 17 May 1848 (PRDH online, #4089425.). She was baptized on 30 Jun 1848 Montebello, Quebec (Ibid.).

       She was in the census household of Hyacinthe Seguin and Marie Anne Charron in 1852 Notre-Dame, Petite Nation, Ottawa County, Ontario (1852C Cdn Transcription Project, District 274, page 39d, 30a, (79), line 33-37.).

    iii. Hyacinthe Seguin was born circa 1850 (Ibid.).

       He was in the census household of Hyacinthe Seguin and Marie Anne Charron in 1852 Notre-Dame, Petite Nation, Ottawa County, Ontario (1852C Cdn Transcription Project, District 274, page 39d, 30a, (79), line 33-37.).

118. Francois Regis Emilien Villeneuve was born on 10 Feb 1819 Ste-Madeleine-de-Riguad, Quebec (PRDH online, #2680596.). He was baptized on 10 Feb 1819 Ste-Madeleine-de-Riguad, Quebec *(father's occupation: cultivator)* (PRDH online, #2680596.). He married **Marie Domitille Mathilde Cadieux**, daughter of **Joseph Cadieux** and **Marie Suzanne Villeneuve,** on 15 Aug 1842 Ste-Madeleine-de-Riguad, Quebec (Ibid., #3465536.).

Marie Domitille Mathilde Cadieux was born on 9 May 1819 Ste-Madeleine-de-Riguad, Quebec (Ibid., #2680625.). She was baptized on 9 May 1819 Ste-Madeleine-de-Riguad, Quebec (Ibid.).

Children of **Francois Regis Emilien Villeneuve** and **Marie Domitille Mathilde Cadieux** all born Ste-Madeleine-de-Riguad, Quebec, were as follows:

    i. Marie Angelique Villeneuve was born on 26 May 1843 (Ibid., #4621378.). She was baptized on 26 May 1843 Ste-Madeleine-de-Riguad, Quebec (Ibid.).

    ii. Marie Suzanne Villeneuve was born on 30 Jun 1844 (Ibid., #4621619.). She was baptized on 30 Jun 1844 Ste-Madeleine-de-Riguad, Quebec (Ibid.).

    iii. Regis Dositee Villeneuve was born on 20 Jul 1845 (Ibid., #4621866.). He was baptized on 21 Jul 1845 Ste-Madeleine-de-Riguad, Quebec (Ibid.).

    iv. Cleophas Ovila Villeneuve was born on 7 Mar 1847 (Ibid., #4622196.). He was baptized on 8 Mar 1847 Ste-Madeleine-de-Riguad, Quebec (Ibid.).

    v. Bazile Procul Villeneuve was born on 29 May 1848 (Ibid., #4622407.). He was baptized on 29 May 1848 Ste-Madeleine-de-Riguad, Quebec (Ibid.).

    vi. Elzire Sophie Villeneuve was born on 25 Aug 1849 (Ibid., #4622589.). She was baptized on 25 Aug 1849 Ste-Madeleine-de-Riguad, Quebec (Ibid.).

119. Judith Villeneuve was born in Aug 1838 St.Boniface, (Manitoba). She married **Jean Baptiste Regis Perreault**, son of **Pierre Perreault** and **Angelique Richard,** on 23 Nov 1858 St.Norbert, (Manitoba) *(M-15, Regis Perreau, adult son of Pierre Perreau and Angelique Richard, born in Canada, married 23 November 1858 Judith Villeneuve, adult daughter of Michel Villeneuve and Josephte Genthon in the presence of Amable Gaudry and Joseph Charrette. Lestanc C. of St. Norbert O.M.I. (page 7-8))* (SN1, page 7-8, M-15.).

She witnessed the baptism of **Elise Genthon** on 31 Aug 1858 St.Norbert, (Manitoba) *(B-21, Elise Genthon baptized 21 August 1858, born yesterday, legitimate daughter of Michel Genthon and Marie Gragrey [Gregoritz], Godfather: Joseph Gragrey [Gregoritz], Godmother: Judith Villeneuve. Lestanc o.m.i)* (SN1, B-21.).

She witnessed the baptism of **William Ladouceur** on 26 Sep 1858 St.Norbert, (Manitoba) *(B-26, William Ladouceur baptized 26 September 1858, born today, legitimate son of Augustin Ladouceur and Magdeleine Lambert, Godfather: Isaie Ladouceur, Godmother: Judith Villeneuve. Moulin O.M.I. (page 6))* (SN1, page 6, B-26.).

She witnessed the baptism of **Jean Baptiste Rivard** on 23 May 1862 St.Norbert, (Manitoba) *(B-12, Jean Baptiste Rivard, bt. 23 May 1862, born day before yesterday, of Baptiste Rivard and Marie Ouellette, Godfather: Regis Perreault, Godmother: Judith Villeneuve, Chs. M. Meny o.m.i. (page 57))* (SN1, page 57, B-12.).

She witnessed the baptism of **Veronique Frederic dit Paul** on 3 Sep 1862 St.Norbert, (Manitoba) *(B-21, Veronique Frippe (Frederic), baptized 3 September 1862, born this morning, of the legitimate marriage of Louis Frippe (Frederic) and Catherine Genthon, Godfather: Regis Perreault, Godmother: Judith Villeneuve, Ritchot priest. (page 61))* (MBS, C-14928.) (SN1, pabe 61, B-21.).

She witnessed the baptism of **Marie Lizotte** on 1 Jan 1863 St.Norbert, (Manitoba) *(B 45, Marie Lizotte, baptized 1 January 1863, born 29 December of the legitimate marriage of Pierre Lizotte and Catherine Magdelaine, Godfather: Regis Perrault, Godmother: Judith Villeneuve. N. J. Ritchot ptre. (page 69))* (SN1, page 69, B-45.).

She witnessed the baptism of **Jean Baptiste Regis Tourond** on 24 Dec 1866 St.Norbert, (Manitoba) *(B-70, Jean Baptiste Regis Tourond, baptized 24 December 1866, born yesterday, of the legitimate marriage of Jean Baptiste Tourond and Angelique Delorme, Godparents: Regis Perrault and Judith Villeneuve, N. J. Ritchot priest. (page 90))* (SN1, page 90, B-70.).

She witnessed the baptism of **Marie Celina Marchand** on 16 Mar 1867 St.Norbert, (Manitoba) *(B-14, Marie Celina Marchand, baptized 16 March 1867, born 14 March, of the legitimate marriage of Cyrille Marchand and Sophie Villeneuve, Godfather: Joseph Marchand, Godmother: Judith Villeneuve, L. Camper p.omi)* (MBS, C-14930.) (SN1, B-14.).

She witnessed the baptism of **Judith Lepine** on 18 Feb 1868 St.Norbert, (Manitoba) *(B-5, Judith Lepine, baptized 18 February 1868, born in the evening, of the legitimate marriage of Baptiste Lepine and Judith Parenteau, Godfather: Regis Perreault, Godmother: Judith Villeneuve, Decorby p.o.m.i)* (SN1, B-5.).

She witnessed the baptism of **Julienne Jolibois** on 9 Aug 1868 St.Norbert, (Manitoba) *(B-33, Julienne Jolibois, baptized 9 August 1868, born yesterday, of the legitimate marriage of Jean Baptiste Jolibois and Marguerite Robillard, Godfather: Regis Perrault, Godmother: Judith Villeneuve, N. J. Ritchot priest)* (MBS, C-14929.) (SN1, B-33.).

She and **Jean Baptiste Regis Perreault** were enumerated in the census on 15 Jul 1870 St.Norbert, Manitoba. Also in the family: **Julie P. Perreault** and **Gregoire Frederic** *(#1068-1071; Regis Perreault, St.Norbert, born Red River, age 40, son of Pierre Perreault, Metis, married, British Subject, French Metis, Catholic, Adopted by P. Perreault; Judith, 33, daughter of __ Villeneuve; Julie P., 11, daughter of __, single, Adopted by Regis Pereault; Gregoire Frederick, 5, son of Louis Frederick. (page 35))* (1870C-MB, #1068-1071, page 35.).

She witnessed the baptism of **Francois Gregoire Delorme** on 29 Jan 1875 St.Norbert, Manitoba *(B-5, Francois Gregoire Delorme, baptized 29 January 1875, born yesterday, of the legitimate marriage of Louis Delorme and Suzanne Jeanthon, Godfather: Regis Perrault (signed), Godmother: Judith Villeneuve, N. J. Ritchot priest)* (SN2, B-5.).

She had a scrip application: on 26 Nov 1875 St.Norbert, Provencher, Manitoba *(Judith Perreault; St.Norbert; Provencher; wife of Regis Perreault; farmer; HB Head: myself and husband; Born: Aug 1838; St.Boniface; Father: Michel Villeneuve (French Cdn) [was]; Mother: Josephte Dauphinais (HB) [is]; French; Judith Perreault (x); 26 Nov 1875; Regis Perreault; farmer; F. A. Med. Foucher; St.Boniface)* (MBS, C-14932.).

She witnessed the baptism of **Marie Rosalie Hamel** on 2 Apr 1880 St.Norbert, Manitoba *(B-17, Marie Rosalie Hamel, baptized 2 April 1880, born yesterday, legitimate child of Octave Hamel and Adeline Perreault. Godparents Regis Perreault (signed) and Judith Villeneuve, N. J. Ritchot, priest)* (SN2, B-17.).

She and **Jean Baptiste Regis Perreault** were enumerated in the census on 4 Apr 1881 Cartier, Provencher, Manitoba. Also in the family: **Gregoire Frederic** *(Regis PERRAULT, M, Male, French, 49, Quebec, Cultivateur, Catholique; Jullie PERRAULT, M, Female, French, 45, Manitoba, Catholique; Gregorie FREDERIC, Male, French, 16, Manitoba, Catholique)* (1881 Church of Latter Day Saints Census Transcription Project of Census Images from the National Archives of Canada, Ottawa, Canada, http://www.familysearch.org, Film #C-13283, District 184, Sub-district F, page 20, household 109+.).

She witnessed the baptism of **Francois Xavier Henry** on 20 Nov 1884 St.Norbert, Manitoba *(B-62, Francois Xavier Henry, baptized 20 November 1884, born yesterday, of the legitimate marriage of Francois Xavier Henry and Esther Marchand, Godfather: Regis Perreault, Godmother: Judith Villeneuve, N. J. Ritchot priest)* (SN2, B-62.).

She witnessed the baptism of **Marie Julienne Delorme** on 1 Jul 1885 St.Norbert, Manitoba *(B-25, Marie Julienne Delorme, baptized 1 July 1885, born yesterday, legitimate child of Magloire Delorme and Veronique Marchand, Godfather: Francois Xavier Henry. Godmother: Judith Villeneuve, both who did not sign. N. J. Ritchot)* (SN2, B-25.).

She and **Jean Baptiste Regis Perreault** were enumerated in the census on 31 Mar 1901 Ritchot, Provencher, Manitoba. Also in the family: **Gregoire Frederic** *(Perrault Regis, M, Head, M, Oct 15 1831, 70; Perrault Judith, F, Wife, M, ?, 1835, 64; Dauphinais Marie, F, Aunt, W , ?, ?, 66?; Grégoire Frederic, M, Employee??, M, Mar 4 1864, 36)* (Automated Genealogy 1901 Census Transcription Project and Census Images from the National Archives of Canada, http://www.automatedgenealogy.com, District 10-h-2, page 3, family 18, line 4-7.).

Jean Baptiste Regis Perreault was born on 15 Oct 1831 St.Jude, St.Hyacinthe, Quebec (1881 Canada, Film #C-13283, District 184, Sub-district F, page 20, household 109+.) (Rod MacQuarrie Research, 24 Oct 2009.). He was baptized on 16 Oct 1831 St.Jude, St.Hyacinthe, Quebec *(Oct 16, 1831 Baptism at St. Jude, St. Hyacinthe Co: B-, Régis Pérault: Le seise d'Octobre mil huit cent trente et un, je prêtre sousigné curé ai baptisé Régis né hier du légitime mariage de Pierre Pérault, cultivateur en cette paroisse, et d'Angélique Richard, parain Jean Marie Richard, maraine*

Rose Jared dite Vincent qui n'ont su signer ainsi que le père présent. M. CUSSON ptre. (Oct 16, 1831, I, priest undersigned, curate, have baptized Régis, born yesterday of the legitimate marriage of Pierre Pérault, farmer in this parish, and Angélique Richard, godfather Jean Marie Richard, godmother Rose Jared dite Vincent who as well as the father, don't know how to sign.)) (Rod Mac Quarrie, 24 Oct 2009.). He died on 8 Jan 1912 RM of Richot, Manitoba, at age 80 (Ibid.) (MB Vital Statistics, Death Reg. #1912,001663.). As of 12 Sep 1860, he was also known as **Regis Perreault** (SN1, page 33, B-32.).

He witnessed the baptism of **Rosalie St.Denis** on 12 Sep 1860 St.Norbert, (Manitoba) *(B-32, Rosalie St. Denys, baptized 12 September 1860, born yesterday morning of the legitimate marriage of Pierre St. Denys and Adelaide Genthon, Godfather: Regis Perrault, Godmother: Caroline Genthon, E. A. Gaste priest. (page 33))* (SN1, page 33, B-32.).

He witnessed the baptism of **Jean Baptiste Rivard** on 23 May 1862 St.Norbert, (Manitoba) *(B-12, Jean Baptiste Rivard, bt. 23 May 1862, born day before yesterday, of Baptiste Rivard and Marie Ouellette, Godfather: Regis Perreault, Godmother: Judith Villeneuve, Chs. M. Meny o.m.i. (page 57))* (SN1, page 57, B-12.).

He witnessed the baptism of **Veronique Frederic dit Paul** on 3 Sep 1862 St.Norbert, (Manitoba) *(B-21, Veronique Frippe (Frederic), baptized 3 September 1862, born this morning, of the legitimate marriage of Louis Frippe (Frederic) and Catherine Genthon, Godfather: Regis Perreault, Godmother: Judith Villeneuve, Ritchot priest. (page 61))* (MBS, C-14928.) (SN1, pabe 61, B-21.).

He witnessed the baptism of **Marie Lizotte** on 1 Jan 1863 St.Norbert, (Manitoba) *(B 45, Marie Lizotte, baptized 1 January 1863, born 29 December of the legitimate marriage of Pierre Lizotte and Catherine Magdelaine, Godfather: Regis Perrault, Godmother: Judith Villeneuve. N. J. Ritchot ptre. (page 69))* (SN1, page 69, B-45.).

He witnessed the burial of **Joseph Tourond** on 4 Mar 1865 St.Norbert, (Manitoba) *(S-5, Joseph Tourond, buried 4 March 1865, died last night, age one year and a few months, legitimate son of Baptiste Tourond and Angelique Delorme, Present: Alexis Delorme, Regis Perreault, St.Germain priest. (page 125))* (SN1, page 125, S-5.).

He witnessed the baptism of **Jean Baptiste Regis Tourond** on 24 Dec 1866 St.Norbert, (Manitoba) *(B-70, Jean Baptiste Regis Tourond, baptized 24 December 1866, born yesterday, of the legitimate marriage of Jean Baptiste Tourond and Angelique Delorme, Godparents: Regis Perrault and Judith Villeneuve, N. J. Ritchot priest. (page 90))* (SN1, page 90, B-70.).

He witnessed the marriage of **Jean Baptiste Huppe** and **Anargile Perreault dit Morin** on 28 Jan 1868 (Ste.Anne), St.Boniface, (Manitoba) *(M-6, Jean Huppe, son of Baptise Huppe and Elisabeth Charbonneau, married 28 January 1868 at Ste.Anne, Marie Anargile Perreault, daughter of Jean Baptiste Perreault and Marie Ducharme, Witnesses: Jean Baptiste Perreault dit Morin and Jeremie Berard, Lefloch priest. (page 106))* (SB-Rozyk St. Boniface Roman Catholic Church, Manitoba, Canada, Baptisms, Marriages and Burials 1860-1875 Extractions, Compiled by Rosemary Rozyk, page 106, M-6.).

He witnessed the baptism of **Judith Lepine** on 18 Feb 1868 St.Norbert, (Manitoba) *(B-5, Judith Lepine, baptized 18 February 1868, born in the evening, of the legitimate marriage of Baptiste Lepine and Judith Parenteau, Godfather: Regis Perreault, Godmother: Judith Villeneuve, Decorby p.o.m.i)* (SN1, B-5.).

He witnessed the marriage of **Charles Nault** and **Marie Louise Morin** on 12 May 1868 St.Boniface, (Manitoba) *(M-15, Charles Nault, widower of Marie Hamelin, married 12 May 1868, Louise Comtois dit Morin, daughter of Baptiste Morin and Marie Lafournaise, Witnesses: Baptiste Perreault dit Morin and Baptiste Nault, Lefloch priest. (page 117))* (SB-Rozyk, page 117, M-15.).

He witnessed the burial of **Charles Jolibois** on 26 Jul 1868 St.Norbert, (Manitoba) *(S-5, Charles Jolibois, buried 26 July 1868, died today, age 6 years, legitimate child of J. Baptiste Jolibois and Marguerite Robillard, Present: J. Bte. Tourond and Regis Perrault, N. J. Ritchot priest)* (SN1, S-5.).

He witnessed the baptism of **Julienne Jolibois** on 9 Aug 1868 St.Norbert, (Manitoba) *(B-33, Julienne Jolibois, baptized 9 August 1868, born yesterday, of the legitimate marriage of Jean Baptiste Jolibois and Marguerite Robillard, Godfather: Regis Perrault, Godmother: Judith Villeneuve, N. J. Ritchot priest)* (MBS, C-14929.) (SN1, B-33.).

He witnessed the baptism of **Marie Huppe** on 26 Mar 1869 (Ste.Anne), St.Boniface, (Manitoba) *(B-30, Marie Huppe, born 16 Mar 1869, bt. 26 Mar 1869 at the mission of Ste. Anne, daughter of Jean Huppe and Anagile Perreault, Godfather: Jean Baptiste Perreault, Godmother: Alphonsine Atkinson, Giroux ptre. (page 149))* (SB-Rozyk, page 149, B-30.).

He witnessed the marriage of **Godfroy Lagimoniere** and **Rosalie Lepine** on 15 Feb 1870 St.Norbert, (Manitoba) *(M-5, Godfrois Lagimoniere, minor son of Romain Lagimoniere and Marie Vaudry, married 15 February 1870, Rosalie Lepine, minor daughter of Jean Baptiste Lepine and Isabelle Parenteau in the presence of Romain Lagimoniere, father of the groom, J. Bte. Lepine, father of the bride, Regyse Perrault and others who did not sign. N. J. Ritchot, priest)* (SN1, M-5.).

He witnessed the burial of **Julie P. Perreault** on 6 Jul 1872 St.Norbert, Manitoba *(S-10, Julie Perreault, buried 6 July 1872, died yesterday, age around fourteen years, adopted child of Regis Perreault and Judith Villeneuve, born to La Roch Blanc and Mag. Piche, Present: Jean Baptiste Dauphinais, Regis Perreault and others, N. J. Ritchot priest)* (SN1, S-10.).

He witnessed the burial of **Julienne Jolibois** on 17 Apr 1873 St.Norbert, Manitoba *(S-19, Julienne Jolibois, buried 17 April 1873, child of J. B. Jolibois and Marguerite Robillard, died on the 15 th of this month, age around five years, Present: J. B. Jolibois and J. B. Perreault, J. B. Proulx priest)* (MBS, C-14929.) (SN1, S-19.).

He witnessed the burial of **Marie Natalie Marchand** on 22 Jun 1874 St.Norbert, Manitoba *(S-14, Marie Natalie Marchand, buried 21 June 1874, died day before yesterday, age sixteen months, legitimate infant of Cyrille Marchand and Sophie Villeneuve, Present: Regisse Perreault and Louis Frederic, N. J. Ritchot priest)* (SN2, S-14.).

He witnessed the baptism of **Francois Gregoire Delorme** on 29 Jan 1875 St.Norbert, Manitoba *(B-5, Francois Gregoire Delorme, baptized 29 January 1875, born yesterday, of the legitimate marriage of Louis Delorme and Suzanne Jeanthon, Godfather: Regis Perrault (signed), Godmother: Judith Villeneuve, N. J. Ritchot priest)* (SN2, B-5.).

He witnessed the baptism of **Marie Rosalie Hamel** on 2 Apr 1880 St.Norbert, Manitoba *(B-17, Marie Rosalie Hamel, baptized 2 April 1880, born yesterday, legitimate child of Octave Hamel and Adeline Perreault. Godparents Regis Perreault (signed) and Judith Villeneuve, N. J. Ritchot, priest)* (SN2, B-17.).

He witnessed the marriage of **Anaclet Lepine** and **Elise Tourond** on 27 Apr 1880 St.Norbert, Manitoba *(M-5, Anaclet Lepine, minor son of Jean Baptiste Lepine and Isabelle Parenteau, married 27 April 1880, Elise Tourond (signed), minor daughter of Jean Baptiste Tourond and Angelique Delorme, Present: Jean Baptiste Tourond (signed) father of the bride and Regis Perreault (signed), N. J. Ritchot priest)* (SN2, M-5.).

He witnessed the burial of **Ferdinand Paquin** on 2 Aug 1882 St.Norbert, Manitoba *(S-18, Ferdinand Paquin, buried 2 August 1882, died day before yesterday, age six years, legitimate child of Jean Paquin and Emelie Perreault, Present: Regis Perreault and Joseph Paquin, N. J. Ritchot priest)* (SN2, S-18.).

He witnessed the burial of **Paul Paquin** on 19 Aug 1882 St.Norbert, Manitoba *(S-19, Paul Paquin, buried 19 August 1882, died yesterday, age 4 years, legitimate child of Jean Paquin and Emilie Perreault, Present: Regis Perreault and Joseph Paquin, N. J. Ritchot priest)* (SN2, S-19.).

He witnessed the burial of **Joseph Paquin** on 8 Aug 1883 St.Norbert, Manitoba *(S-22, Joseph Paquin, buried 8 August 1883, died day before yesterday, age 17 years, legitimate son of Jean Paquin and Emilie Perreault, Present: Regis Perreault and Jean Baptiste Jolibois, N. J. Ritchot priest)* (SN2, S-22.).

He witnessed the baptism of **Francois Xavier Henry** on 20 Nov 1884 St.Norbert, Manitoba *(B-62, Francois Xavier Henry, baptized 20 November 1884, born yesterday, of the legitimate marriage of Francois Xavier Henry and Esther Marchand, Godfather: Regis Perreault, Godmother: Judith Villeneuve, N. J. Ritchot priest)* (SN2, B-62.).

He witnessed the marriage of **Pierre Laramee** and **Francoise Courchene** on 8 Jan 1885 St.Norbert, Caritier, Manitoba *(M-2, Pierre Laramee, widower of Marie Hamel, married 8 January 1885, Francoise Courchene adult daughter of Antoine Courchene and Brigette Delorme in the presence of Antoine Courchene, father of the bride, Regis Perreault, who did not sign and others who did not sign. N. J. Ritchot.)* (MM *Manitoba Marriages in Publication 45*, Volumes 1-3, compiled and edited by: Paul J. Lareau, Fr. Julien Hamelin, (240 Avenue Daly, Ottawa, Ontario K1N 6G2: Le Centre de Genealogie S.C., 1984), page 725.) (SN2, M-2.) (MB Vital Statistics, Marriage Reg. #1885,001735.).

He witnessed the burial of **Josephte Genthon dit Dauphinais** on 16 May 1885 St.Norbert, Manitoba *(S-14, Josephte Dauphinais, buried 16 May 1885, died the day before yesterday, age around sixty-two years, widow of the deceased Michel Villeneuve, Present: Regis Perreault, Louis Delorme, Jean Baptiste Jolibois, N. J. Ritchot)* (SN2, S-14.).

He witnessed the marriage of **Simon Marchand** and **Malvina Paquin** on 2 Mar 1886 St.Norbert, Manitoba *(M-5, Simon Marchand (signed), adult widower of Philomene Lambert, married 2 March 1886, Melvina Paquin (signed), adult daughter of Jean Paquin and Emilie Perreault, Present: Cyrille Marchand, father of the groom, Regis Perreault (signed), Rosalie Henry (signed), Adalard Seguin (signed), I. F. ? Pitt (signed), N. J. Ritchot priest)* (SN2, M-5.).

He witnessed the burial of **Isabelle Parenteau** on 14 Jan 1889 St.Norbert, Manitoba *(S-4, Isabelle Parenteau, buried 14 January 1889, died 11 January 1889, age 59 years, wife of second husband Jacques Saint-Denis, Present: Louis Delorme, Athanase Lepine, Cyrille Marchand, Anaclet Lepine, Regis Perrau, A. Dabaudes priest)* (SN2, S-4.).

Children of **Judith Villeneuve** and **Jean Baptiste Regis Perreault** were:

    i.   Julie P. Perreault (adopted) was born circa 1859 (1870C-MB, #1068-1071, page 35.). She died on 5 Jul 1872 St.Norbert, Manitoba (SN1, S-10.). She was buried on 6 Jul 1872 St.Norbert, Manitoba *(S-10, Julie Perreault, buried 6 July 1872, died yesterday, age around fourteen years, adopted child of Regis Perreault and Judith Villeneuve, born to La Roch Blanc and Mag. Piche, Present: Jean Baptiste Dauphinais, Regis Perreault and others, N. J. Ritchot priest)* (SN1, S-10.).

She was in the census household of Jean Baptiste Regis Perreault and Judith Villeneuve on 15 Jul 1870 St.Norbert, Manitoba (1870C-MB, #1068-1071, page 35.).

120. **Marie Reine Sabourin** was born on 5 May 1820 Ste-Madeleine-de-Riguad, Quebec (PRDH online, #2680754.). She was baptized on 6 May 1820 Ste-Madeleine-de-Riguad, Quebec *(father's occupation: cultivator)* (PRDH online, #2680754.). She married **Hyacinthe Evangeliste Leduc**, son of **Hyacinthe Leduc** and **Veronique Chevrier,** on 14 Jan 1839 Ste-Madeleine-de-Riguad, Quebec (Ibid., #3464731.).

She and **Hyacinthe Evangeliste Leduc** were enumerated in the census in 1852 Ste.Madeleine, Rigaud, Vaudreuil, Quebec. Also in the family: **Octavie Alodie Leduc**, **Jean Evangeliste Napoleon Appolinaire Leduc**, **Joseph Esdras Elzear Leduc**, and **Evangeliste Leduc** *(Leduc, Hythe fils, Cultivateur, Rigaud, Catholique, 38, M; Sabourin, Reine, Rigaud, Catholique, 31, F; Leduc, Odile, Rigaud, Catholique, 9, F; Leduc, Appolinaire, Rigaud, Catholique, 4, M; Leduc, Elzéar, Rigaud, Catholique, 2, M; Leduc, Evangéliste, Rigaud, Catholique, 6 mois, M)* (1852C Cdn Transcription Project, District 536, page 33d, 34a, (67), line 15-20.).

Hyacinthe Evangeliste Leduc was born on 27 Oct 1814 Ste-Madeleine-de-Riguad, Quebec (PRDH online, #2680118.). He was baptized on 27 Oct 1814 Ste-Madeleine-de-Riguad, Quebec *(father's occupation: agriculture)* (PRDH online, #2680118.).

Children of **Marie Reine Sabourin** and **Hyacinthe Evangeliste Leduc** were as follows:

    i.   Jude Evangeliste Leduc was born on 27 Oct 1839 Ste-Madeleine-de-Riguad, Quebec (Ibid., #4620507.). He was baptized on 28 Oct 1839 Ste-Madeleine-de-Riguad, Quebec (Ibid.). He died on 8 Oct 1842 Ste-Madeleine-de-Riguad, Quebec, at age 2 (Ibid., #4624280.). He was buried on 10 Oct 1842 Ste-Madeleine-de-Riguad, Quebec (Ibid.).

    ii.   Marie Mathilde Leocadie Leduc was born on 10 Feb 1841 Ste-Madeleine-de-Riguad, Quebec (Ibid., #4620814.). She was baptized on 11 Feb 1841 Ste-Madeleine-de-Riguad, Quebec (Ibid.). She died on 22 Jul 1841 Ste-Madeleine-de-Riguad, Quebec (Ibid., #4624166.). She was buried on 24 Jul 1841 Ste-Madeleine-de-Riguad, Quebec *(age 5 months)* (PRDH online, #4624166.).

    iii.   Octavie Alodie Leduc was born on 15 Aug 1842 Ste-Madeleine-de-Riguad, Quebec (Ibid., #4621189.). She was baptized on 16 Aug 1842 Ste-Madeleine-de-Riguad, Quebec (Ibid.).

       She was in the census household of Hyacinthe Evangeliste Leduc and Marie Reine Sabourin in 1852 Ste.Madeleine, Rigaud, Vaudreuil, Quebec (1852C Cdn Transcription Project, District 536, page 33d, 34a, (67), line 15-20.).

    iv.   Joseph Leopold Napoleon Leduc was born on 29 Mar 1844 Ste-Madeleine-de-Riguad, Quebec (PRDH online, #4621555.). He was baptized on 31 Mar 1844 Ste-Madeleine-de-Riguad, Quebec (Ibid.). He died on 12 Apr 1845 Ste-Madeleine-de-Riguad, Quebec, at age 1 (Ibid., #4624488.). He was buried on 14 Apr 1845 Ste-Madeleine-de-Riguad, Quebec (Ibid.).

    v.   Joseph Leopold Leduc was born on 14 May 1846 Ste-Madeleine-de-Riguad, Quebec (Ibid., #4622041.). He was baptized on 15 May 1846 Ste-Madeleine-de-Riguad, Quebec (Ibid.). He died on 25 May 1846 Ste-Madeleine-de-Riguad, Quebec (Ibid., #4624550.). He was buried on 26 May 1846 Ste-Madeleine-de-Riguad, Quebec *(age 10 days)* (PRDH online, #4624550.).

    vi.   Jean Evangeliste Napoleon Appolinaire Leduc was born on 22 Jul 1847 Ste-Madeleine-de-Riguad, Quebec (Ibid., #4622263.). He was baptized on 23 Jul 1847 Ste-Madeleine-de-Riguad, Quebec (Ibid.).

       He was in the census household of Hyacinthe Evangeliste Leduc and Marie Reine Sabourin in 1852 Ste.Madeleine, Rigaud, Vaudreuil, Quebec (1852C Cdn Transcription Project, District 536, page 33d, 34a, (67), line 15-20.).

    vii.   Joseph Esdras Elzear Leduc was born on 7 Sep 1849 Ste-Madeleine-de-Riguad, Quebec (PRDH online, #4622597.). He was baptized on 8 Sep 1849 Ste-Madeleine-de-Riguad, Quebec (Ibid.).

       He was in the census household of Hyacinthe Evangeliste Leduc and Marie Reine Sabourin in 1852 Ste.Madeleine, Rigaud, Vaudreuil, Quebec (1852C Cdn Transcription Project, District 536, page 33d, 34a, (67), line 15-20.).

    viii.   Evangeliste Leduc was born circa 1851 (Ibid.).

       He was in the census household of Hyacinthe Evangeliste Leduc and Marie Reine Sabourin in 1852 Ste.Madeleine, Rigaud, Vaudreuil, Quebec (1852C Cdn Transcription Project, District 536, page 33d, 34a, (67), line 15-20.).

121. **Marie Scholastique Sabourin** was born on 15 Jan 1824 Ste-Madeleine-de-Riguad, Quebec (PRDH online, #2681286.). She was baptized on 15 Jan 1824 Ste-Madeleine-de-Riguad, Quebec *(father's occupation: cultivator)* (PRDH online, #2681286.). She married **Joseph Vital Bertrand**, son of **Joseph Benjamin Bertrand** and **Marie**

Adelaide Gauthier, on 19 Feb 1844 Ste-Madeleine-de-Rigaud, Quebec *(Consganuinity: 5)* (PRDH online, #3465926.).

Joseph Vital Bertrand was born on 31 Jan 1820 Oka, Quebec (Ibid., #2752438.). He was baptized on 1 Feb 1820 Oka, Quebec *(father's occupation: cultivator)* (PRDH online, #2752438.).

Children of **Marie Scholastique Sabourin** and **Joseph Vital Bertrand** all born Ste-Marthe, Quebec, were as follows:

    i.   Scholastique Bertrand was born on 21 Dec 1844 (Ibid., #4723620.). She was baptized on 22 Dec 1844 Ste-Marthe, Quebec (Ibid.).

    ii.   Joseph Vital Bertrand was born on 7 Feb 1847 (Ibid., #4727864.). He was baptized on 8 Feb 1847 Ste-Marthe, Quebec (Ibid.). He died on 5 Jan 1848 Ste-Marthe, Quebec (Ibid., #4728158.). He was buried on 7 Jan 1848 Ste-Marthe, Quebec *(age 11 months)* (PRDH online, #4728158.).

    iii.   Emerance Bertrand was born on 4 Dec 1848 (Ibid., #4728017.). She was baptized on 5 Dec 1848 Ste-Marthe, Quebec (Ibid.).

122. Francois Andre Sabourin was born on 15 Dec 1816 Ste-Madeleine-de-Rigaud, Quebec (Ibid., #2680348.). He was baptized on 16 Dec 1816 Ste-Madeleine-de-Rigaud, Quebec (Ibid.). He married **Marie Agnes Edesse Vallee**, daughter of **Antoine Vallee** and **Genevieve Vinet,** on 1 Aug 1843 Ste-Madeleine-de-Rigaud, Quebec (Ibid., #3465783.). He married **Veronique Villeneuve**, daughter of **Regis Villeneuve** and **Ursule Seguin,** on 30 Jan 1849 Ste-Madeleine-de-Rigaud, Quebec (Ibid., #3467178.).

He and **Veronique Villeneuve** were enumerated in the census in 1852 Ste.Madeleine, Rigaud, Vaudreuil, Quebec. Also in the family: **Louis Sabourin**, **Alphonse Sabourin**, and **Napoleon Sabourin** *(Sabourin, André, Cultivateur, Rigaud, Catholique, 35, M; Villneuve, Véronique, Rigaud, Catholique, 35, F; Sabourin, Louise, Rigaud, Catholique, 7, F; Sabourin, Alphonse, Rigaud, Catholique, 2, M; Sabourin, Napoléon, Rigaud, Catholique, 1, M)* (1852C Cdn Transcription Project, District 536, page 23d, 24a, (47), line 42-46.).

Marie Agnes Edesse Vallee was born on 3 Mar 1821 Ste-Madeleine-de-Riguad, Quebec (PRDH online, #2680847.). She was baptized on 4 Mar 1821 Ste-Madeleine-de-Riguad, Quebec (Ibid.). She died on 8 Jan 1847 Ste-Madeleine-de-Riguad, Quebec, at age 25 (Ibid., #4624593.). She was buried on 11 Jan 1847 Ste-Madeleine-de-Riguad, Quebec *(age 25, wife of Andre Sabourin)* (PRDH online, #4624593.).

Children of **Francois Andre Sabourin** and **Marie Agnes Edesse Vallee** all born Ste-Madeleine-de-Riguad, Quebec, were as follows:

    i.   Louis Sabourin was born on 23 May 1844 (Ibid., #4621590.). He was baptized on 24 May 1844 Ste-Madeleine-de-Riguad, Quebec (Ibid.).
Question: *Called Louise in the 1852 census* (1852C Cdn Transcription Project, District 536, page 23d, 24a, (47), line 42-46.).
He was in the census household of Francois Andre Sabourin and Veronique Villeneuve in 1852 Ste.Madeleine, Rigaud, Vaudreuil, Quebec (1852C Cdn Transcription Project, District 536, page 23d, 24a, (47), line 42-46.).

    ii.   Andre Sabourin was born on 6 Aug 1845 (PRDH online, #4621877.). He was baptized on 6 Aug 1845 Ste-Madeleine-de-Riguad, Quebec (Ibid.). He died on 21 Feb 1847 Ste-Madeleine-de-Riguad, Quebec, at age 1 (Ibid., #4624598.). He was buried on 23 Feb 1847 Ste-Madeleine-de-Riguad, Quebec (Ibid.).

    iii.   Joseph Didime Sabourin was born on 6 Sep 1846 (Ibid., #4622116.). He was baptized on 7 Sep 1846 Ste-Madeleine-de-Riguad, Quebec (Ibid.). He died on 14 Oct 1846 Ste-Madeleine-de-Riguad, Quebec (Ibid., #4624580.). He was buried on 16 Oct 1846 Ste-Madeleine-de-Riguad, Quebec *(age one month)* (PRDH online, #4624580.).

Veronique Villeneuve was born on 9 Nov 1816 Ste-Madeleine-de-Rigaud, Quebec (Ibid., #2680337.). She was baptized on 10 Nov 1816 Ste-Madeleine-de-Rigaud, Quebec *(father's occupation: agriculture)* (PRDH online, #2680337.). Question: *Called Louise in the 1852 census* (1852C Cdn Transcription Project, District 536, page 23d, 24a, (47), line 42-46.).

Children of **Francois Andre Sabourin** and **Veronique Villeneuve** were as follows:

    i.   Alphonse Sabourin, b. circa 1850. (see previous).

    ii.   Napoleon Sabourin, b. circa 1851. (see previous).

123. Madeleine Sabourin was born on 25 Jun 1820 Ste-Madeleine-de-Riguad, Quebec (PRDH online, #2680772.). She was baptized on 26 Jun 1820 Ste-Madeleine-de-Riguad, Quebec *(father's occupation: cultivator)* (PRDH online, #2680772.). She married **Pierre Portelance**, son of **Henry Portelance** and **Suzanne Vachon,** on 22 Feb 1841 Ste-Madeleine-de-Riguad, Quebec (Ibid., #3465285.).

She and **Pierre Portelance** were enumerated in the census in 1852 Ste.Madeleine, Rigaud, Vaudreuil, Quebec. Also in the family: **Joseph Portelance**, **Alexandre Portelance**, **Andre Portelance**, **Pierre Portelance**, and **Marguerite Portelance** *(Portelance, Pierre, Cultivateur, Rigaud, Catholique, 34, M; Sabourin, Magdeleine, Rigaud, Catholique, 31, F; Portelance, Joseph, Rigaud, Catholique, 8, M; Portelance, Alexdre, Rigaud, Catholique, 7, M; Portelance, André, Rigaud, Catholique, 6, M; Portelance, Pierre, Rigaud, Catholique, 3 mois, M; Portelance, Marguerite, Rigaud, Catholique, 14 mois, F)* (1852C Cdn Transcription Project, District 536, page 25d, 26a, (51), line 25-31.).

Pierre Portelance was born on 30 Sep 1817 Ste-Madeleine-de-Riguad, Quebec (PRDH online, #2680421.). He was baptized on 2 Oct 1817 Ste-Madeleine-de-Riguad, Quebec (Ibid.).

Children of **Madeleine Sabourin** and **Pierre Portelance** were as follows:

    i. Francois Xavier Portelance was born on 22 Feb 1842 Ste-Madeleine-de-Riguad, Quebec (Ibid., #4621072.). He was baptized on 23 Feb 1842 Ste-Madeleine-de-Riguad, Quebec (Ibid.). He died on 4 Sep 1842 Ste-Madeleine-de-Riguad, Quebec (Ibid., #4624274.). He was buried on 5 Sep 1842 Ste-Madeleine-de-Riguad, Quebec *(age 6 months)* (PRDH online, #4624274.).

    ii. Joseph Portelance was born on 31 Jan 1843 Ste-Madeleine-de-Riguad, Quebec (Ibid., #4621309.). He was baptized on 1 Feb 1843 Ste-Madeleine-de-Riguad, Quebec (Ibid.).

      He was in the census household of Pierre Portelance and Madeleine Sabourin in 1852 Ste.Madeleine, Rigaud, Vaudreuil, Quebec (1852C Cdn Transcription Project, District 536, page 25d, 26a, (51), line 25-31.).

    iii. Alexandre Portelance was born on 24 Feb 1844 Ste-Marthe, Quebec (PRDH online, #4621536.). He was baptized on 25 Feb 1844 Ste-Madeleine-de-Riguad, Quebec (Ibid.).

      He was in the census household of Pierre Portelance and Madeleine Sabourin in 1852 Ste.Madeleine, Rigaud, Vaudreuil, Quebec (1852C Cdn Transcription Project, District 536, page 25d, 26a, (51), line 25-31.).

    iv. Andre Portelance was born on 14 Apr 1845 Ste-Madeleine-de-Riguad, Quebec (PRDH online, #4621793.). He was baptized on 14 Apr 1845 Ste-Madeleine-de-Riguad, Quebec (Ibid.).

      He was in the census household of Pierre Portelance and Madeleine Sabourin in 1852 Ste.Madeleine, Rigaud, Vaudreuil, Quebec (1852C Cdn Transcription Project, District 536, page 25d, 26a, (51), line 25-31.).

    v. Anonyme Portelance was born on 12 Mar 1846 Ste-Marthe, Quebec (PRDH online, #4728121.). He/she died on 12 Mar 1846 Ste-Marthe, Quebec (Ibid.). He/she was buried on 25 Mar 1846 Ste-Marthe, Quebec (Ibid.).

    vi. Napoleon Portelance was born on 14 May 1847 Ste-Madeleine-de-Riguad, Quebec (Ibid., #4622235.). He was baptized on 15 May 1847 Ste-Madeleine-de-Riguad, Quebec (Ibid.). He died on 19 Feb 1848 Ste-Madeleine-de-Riguad, Quebec (Ibid., #4624661.). He was buried on 21 Feb 1848 Ste-Madeleine-de-Riguad, Quebec *(age 8 months)* (PRDH online, #4624661.).

    vii. Marie Magdeleine Leocadie Portelance was born on 5 Dec 1848 Ste-Madeleine-de-Riguad, Quebec (Ibid., #4622488.). She was baptized on 5 Dec 1848 Ste-Madeleine-de-Riguad, Quebec (Ibid.). She died on 28 Jul 1849 Ste-Madeleine-de-Riguad, Quebec (Ibid., #4624741.). She was buried on 30 Jul 1849 Ste-Madeleine-de-Riguad, Quebec *(age 8 months)* (PRDH online, #4624741.).

    viii. Pierre Portelance was born circa 1850 (1852C Cdn Transcription Project, District 536, page 25d, 26a, (51), line 25-31.).

      He was in the census household of Pierre Portelance and Madeleine Sabourin in 1852 Ste.Madeleine, Rigaud, Vaudreuil, Quebec (1852C Cdn Transcription Project, District 536, page 25d, 26a, (51), line 25-31.).

    ix. Marguerite Portelance was born circa 1851 (Ibid.).

      She was in the census household of Pierre Portelance and Madeleine Sabourin in 1852 Ste.Madeleine, Rigaud, Vaudreuil, Quebec (1852C Cdn Transcription Project, District 536, page 25d, 26a, (51), line 25-31.).

124. Paul Sabourin was born on 4 Aug 1822 Ste-Madeleine-de-Riguad, Quebec (PRDH online, #4621502.). He was baptized on 4 Aug 1822 Ste-Madeleine-de-Riguad, Quebec (Ibid.). He married **Marie Angelique Brazeau dit Brassault**, daughter of **Jean Baptiste Brazeau dit Brassault** and **Marie Rose Villeneuve**, on 6 Feb 1849 Ste-Madeleine-de-Riguad, Quebec (Ibid., #3467198.).

He was in the census household of **Francois Sabourin** and **Louise Seguin** circa 1852 Ste.Madeleine, Rigaud, Vaudreuil, Quebec (1852C Cdn Transcription Project, District 536, page 8d, 9a, (17), line 19-27.).

Marie Angelique Brazeau dit Brassault was born on 5 Dec 1823 Ste-Madeleine-de-Rigaud, Quebec (PRDH online, #2681273.). She was baptized on 6 Dec 1823 Ste-Madeleine-de-Rigaud, Quebec *(father's occupation: cultivator)* (PRDH online, #2681273.).

She was in the census household of **Francois Sabourin** and **Louise Seguin** circa 1852 Ste.Madeleine, Rigaud, Vaudreuil, Quebec (1852C Cdn Transcription Project, District 536, page 8d, 9a, (17), line 19-27.).

Children of **Paul Sabourin** and **Marie Angelique Brazeau dit Brassault** were:

    i.   Treffle Sabourin was born circa 1851 (Ibid.).

       He was in the census household of Francois Sabourin and Louise Seguin circa 1852 Ste.Madeleine, Rigaud, Vaudreuil, Quebec (1852C Cdn Transcription Project, District 536, page 8d, 9a, (17), line 19-27.).

125. Justine Sabourin was born on 17 May 1824 Ste-Madeleine-de-Riguad, Quebec (PRDH online, #2681351.). She was baptized on 17 May 1824 Ste-Madeleine-de-Riguad, Quebec (Ibid.). She married **Joseph Vallee**, son of **Antoine Vallee** and **Genevieve Vinet,** on 3 Nov 1846 Ste-Madeleine-de-Riguad, Quebec (Ibid., #3466835.).

She and **Joseph Vallee** were enumerated in the census in 1852 Ste.Madeleine, Rigaud, Vaudreuil, Quebec. Also in the family: **Marie Aglaee Vallee, Hilaire Vallee**, and **Dozithe Vallee** *(Vallée, Joseph, Cultivateur, Rigaud, Catholique, 26, M; Sabourin, Justine, Rigaud, Catholique, 27, F; Sabourin, Aldebert, Rigaud, Catholique, 13, M; Vallée, Aglaé, Rigaud, Catholique, 4, F; Vallée, Hilaire, Rigaud, Catholique, 3, M; Vallée, Dozithé, Rigaud, Catholique, 2, F)* (1852C Cdn Transcription Project, District 536, page 60d, 61a, (121), line 44-49.).

Joseph Vallee was born on 9 Jun 1825 Ste-Madeleine-de-Riguad, Quebec (PRDH online, #4617213.). He was baptized on 9 Jun 1825 Ste-Madeleine-de-Riguad, Quebec (Ibid.).

Children of **Justine Sabourin** and **Joseph Vallee** were as follows:

    i.   Marie Aglaee Vallee was born on 24 Apr 1848 Ste-Madeleine-de-Riguad, Quebec (Ibid., #4622392.). She was baptized on 25 Apr 1848 Ste-Madeleine-de-Riguad, Quebec (Ibid.).

       She was in the census household of Joseph Vallee and Justine Sabourin in 1852 Ste.Madeleine, Rigaud, Vaudreuil, Quebec (1852C Cdn Transcription Project, District 536, page 60d, 61a, (121), line 44-49.).

    ii. Hilaire Vallee was born on 16 Jun 1849 Ste-Madeleine-de-Riguad, Quebec (PRDH online, #4622570.). He was baptized on 17 Jun 1849 Ste-Madeleine-de-Riguad, Quebec (Ibid.).

       He was in the census household of Joseph Vallee and Justine Sabourin in 1852 Ste.Madeleine, Rigaud, Vaudreuil, Quebec (1852C Cdn Transcription Project, District 536, page 60d, 61a, (121), line 44-49.).

    iii. Dozithe Vallee was born circa 1850 (Ibid.).

       She was in the census household of Joseph Vallee and Justine Sabourin in 1852 Ste.Madeleine, Rigaud, Vaudreuil, Quebec (1852C Cdn Transcription Project, District 536, page 60d, 61a, (121), line 44-49.).

126. Joseph Sabourin was born on 8 May 1826 Ste-Madeleine-de-Riguad, Quebec (PRDH online, #4617354.). He was baptized on 9 May 1826 Ste-Madeleine-de-Riguad, Quebec (Ibid.). He married **Marie Louise Brazeau**, daughter of **Jean Baptiste Brazeau dit Brassault** and **Marie Rose Villeneuve,** on 22 Feb 1848 Oka, Quebec (Ibid., #3467041.).

He and **Marie Louise Brazeau** were enumerated in the census in 1852 Ste.Madeleine, Rigaud, Vaudreuil, Quebec. Also in the family: **Francois Joseph Sabourin, Marie Louise Zenobe Sabourin,** and **Josephine Sabourin** *(Sabourin, Joseph, Cultivateur, Rigaud, Catholique, 25, M; Brazeau, Louise, Rigaud, Catholique, 24, F; Sabourin, Joseph, Rigaud, Catholique, 3, M; Sabourin, Louise, Rigaud, Catholique, 2, F; Sabourin, Joséphine, Rigaud, Catholique, 1 jour, F)* (1852C Cdn Transcription Project, District 536, page 23d, 24a, (47), line 37-41.).

Marie Louise Brazeau was born on 30 Jul 1827 Ste-Madeleine-de-Rigaud, Quebec (PRDH online, #4617581.). She was baptized on 30 Jul 1827 Ste-Madeleine-de-Rigaud, Quebec (Ibid.).

Children of **Joseph Sabourin** and **Marie Louise Brazeau** were as follows:

    i.   Francois Joseph Sabourin was born on 1 Dec 1848 Ste-Madeleine-de-Riguad, Quebec (Ibid., #4622483.). He was baptized on 1 Dec 1848 Ste-Madeleine-de-Riguad, Quebec (Ibid.).

       He was in the census household of Joseph Sabourin and Marie Louise Brazeau in 1852 Ste.Madeleine, Rigaud, Vaudreuil, Quebec (1852C Cdn Transcription Project, District 536, page 23d, 24a, (47), line 37-41.).

    ii. Marie Louise Zenobe Sabourin was born on 23 Nov 1849 Ste-Madeleine-de-Riguad, Quebec (PRDH online, #4622634.). She was baptized on 23 Nov 1849 Ste-Madeleine-de-Riguad, Quebec (Ibid.).

> She was in the census household of Joseph Sabourin and Marie Louise Brazeau in 1852 Ste.Madeleine, Rigaud, Vaudreuil, Quebec (1852C Cdn Transcription Project, District 536, page 23d, 24a, (47), line 37-41.).
>
> iii. Josephine Sabourin was born circa 1852 (Ibid.).
>> She was in the census household of Joseph Sabourin and Marie Louise Brazeau in 1852 Ste.Madeleine, Rigaud, Vaudreuil, Quebec (1852C Cdn Transcription Project, District 536, page 23d, 24a, (47), line 37-41.).

127. Louise Justine Sabourin was born on 18 Jul 1825 Ste-Madeleine-de-Riguad, Quebec (PRDH online, #4617228.). She was baptized on 19 Jul 1825 Ste-Madeleine-de-Riguad, Quebec (Ibid.). She married **Louis Seguin**, son of **Joseph Charles Seguin** and **Marie Augustine Ruth Kingsley,** on 21 Sep 1847 Ste-Madeleine-de-Riguad, Quebec *(Consanguinity)* (PRDH online, #3466967.).

Louis Seguin was born on 24 May 1820 Ste-Madeleine-de-Riguad, Quebec (Ibid., #2680761.). He was baptized on 24 May 1820 Ste-Madeleine-de-Riguad, Quebec *(father's occupation: cultivator)* (PRDH online, #2680761.).

Children of **Louise Justine Sabourin** and **Louis Seguin** were:

> i. Louis Joseph Seguin was born on 18 Sep 1848 Ste-Madeleine-de-Riguad, Quebec (Ibid., #4622452.). He was baptized on 19 Sep 1848 Ste-Madeleine-de-Riguad, Quebec (Ibid.).

128. Joseph Paul Seguin was born on 11 Oct 1821 Ste-Madeleine-de-Riguad, Quebec (Ibid., #2680937.). He was baptized on 12 Oct 1821 Ste-Madeleine-de-Riguad, Quebec *(father's occupation: cultivator)* (PRDH online, #2680937.). He married **Marie Rachel Denys**, daughter of **Michel Denis dit St.Denis** and **Marie Rose St.Julien,** on 15 Feb 1847 Vaudreuil, Quebec (Ibid., #3477646.).

Marie Rachel Denys was born on 17 Mar 1827 Vaudreuil, Quebec (Ibid., #4177929.). She was baptized on 19 Mar 1827 Vaudreuil, Quebec (Ibid.).

Children of **Joseph Paul Seguin** and **Marie Rachel Denys** were:

> i. Paul Amedee Seguin was born on 14 Feb 1848 Ste-Madeleine-de-Riguad, Quebec (Ibid., #4622362.). He was baptized on 15 Feb 1848 Ste-Madeleine-de-Riguad, Quebec (Ibid.).

129. Marie Ostie Sauve was born on 19 Feb 1810 Vaudreuil, Quebec (Ibid., #2590767.). She was baptized on 19 Feb 1810 Vaudreuil, Quebec (Ibid.). She married **Pierre Francois Sauve dit Laplante**, son of **Louis Sauve dit Laplante** and **Charlotte Bedard**, on 19 Aug 1833 Ste-Madeleine-de-Riguad, Quebec (Ibid., #3462728.).

Pierre Francois Sauve dit Laplante was born on 27 Aug 1806 Ste-Madeleine-de-Riguad, Quebec (Ibid., #2679366.). He was baptized on 28 Aug 1806 Ste-Madeleine-de-Riguad, Quebec *(father's occupation: agriculture)* (PRDH online, #2679366.).

Children of **Marie Ostie Sauve** and **Pierre Francois Sauve dit Laplante** were as follows:

> i. Damase Sauve was born on 6 Nov 1833 Ste-Madeleine-de-Riguad, Quebec (Ibid., #4618999.). He was baptized on 8 Nov 1833 Ste-Madeleine-de-Riguad, Quebec (Ibid.).
> ii. Venant Benjmain Sauve was born on 18 May 1836 Ste-Madeleine-de-Riguad, Quebec (Ibid., #4619647.). He was baptized on 19 May 1836 Ste-Madeleine-de-Riguad, Quebec (Ibid.).
> iii. Amedee Sauve was born on 4 May 1838 Ste-Madeleine-de-Riguad, Quebec (Ibid., #4620133.). He was baptized on 5 May 1838 Ste-Madeleine-de-Riguad, Quebec (Ibid.).
> iv. Joseph Napoleon Sauve was born on 28 Dec 1845 (Ibid., #4621964.). He was baptized on 7 Jan 1846 Ste-Madeleine-de-Riguad, Quebec (Ibid.).

130. Archange Sauve was born on 4 Apr 1812 Vaudreuil, Quebec (Ibid., #2590948.). She was baptized on 5 Apr 1812 Vaudreuil, Quebec (Ibid.). She married **Joachim Ranger**, son of **Henri Ranger** and **Josephe Poirier dit Desloges,** on 15 Feb 1836 Ste-Madeleine-de-Riguad, Quebec (Ibid., #3463807.).

Joachim Ranger was born on 10 Oct 1807 Ste-Madeleine-de-Riguad, Quebec (Ibid., #2679462.). He was baptized on 11 Oct 1807 Ste-Madeleine-de-Riguad, Quebec *(father's occupation: day laborer)* (PRDH online, #2679462.).

Children of **Archange Sauve** and **Joachim Ranger** were:

> i. Philomene Ranger was born on 6 Feb 1837 Hawkesbury, Ontario (Ibid., #4619887.). She was baptized on 17 Mar 1837 Ste-Madeleine-de-Riguad, Quebec (Ibid.).

131. Charles Norbert Sabourin was born on 21 Jun 1816 Ste-Madeleine-de-Riguad, Quebec (Ibid., #2680308.). He was baptized on 21 Jun 1816 Ste-Madeleine-de-Riguad, Quebec (Ibid.). He married **Marguerite Jeanne Franche**, daughter of **Pierre Franche dit Laframboise** and **Marie Louise Larocque dit Rocbrune,** on 12 Jan 1835 Ste-Madeleine-de-Riguad, Quebec (Ibid., #3463245.).

He and **Marguerite Jeanne Franche** were enumerated in the census in 1852 Ste.Madeleine, Rigaud, Vaudreuil, Quebec. Also in the family: **Joseph Charles Sabourin, Olive Sabourin, Isidore Sabourin, Alphonse Sabourin, Joseph Chrysologue Sabourin, Dozite Sabourin, Isaac Sabourin, Marie Eulalie Sabourin,** and **Joseph Sabourin** *(Sabourin, Charles, Journalier, Rigaud, Catholique, 34, M; Franche, Marguerite, St Benoit, Catholique, 40, F;*

Sabourin, Baramée, Rigaud, Catholique, 16, M; Sabourin, Olive, Rigaud, Catholique, 14, F; Sabourin, Isidore, Rigaud, Catholique, 12, M; Sabourin, Alphonse, Rigaud, Catholique, 10, M; Sabourin, Chrisologie, Rigaud, Catholique, 8, M; Sabourin, Dozité, Rigaud, Catholique, 6, M; Sabourin, Isaac, Rigaud, Catholique, 4, M; Sabourin, Joseph, Rigaud, Catholique, 5 mois, M; Sabourin, Eulalie, Rigaud, Catholique, 3, F) (1852C Cdn Transcription Project, District 536, page 15d, 16a, (31), line 44-50, page 50d, 51a, (10), line 1-4.).

Marguerite Jeanne Franche was born on 12 Mar 1812 St-Benoit, Quebec (PRDH online, #2514009.). She was baptized on 13 Mar 1812 St-Benoit, Quebec (Ibid.).

Children of **Charles Norbert Sabourin** and **Marguerite Jeanne Franche** were as follows:

    i.   Joseph Charles Sabourin was born on 25 Mar 1836 Ste-Madeleine-de-Riguad, Quebec (Ibid., #4619602.). He was baptized on 26 Mar 1836 Ste-Madeleine-de-Riguad, Quebec (Ibid.).
       He was in the census household of Charles Norbert Sabourin and Marguerite Jeanne Franche in 1852 Ste.Madeleine, Rigaud, Vaudreuil, Quebec (1852C Cdn Transcription Project, District 536, page 15d, 16a, (31), line 44-50, page 50d, 51a, (10), line 1-4.).

    ii. Olive Sabourin was born on 6 Nov 1837 Ste-Madeleine-de-Riguad, Quebec (PRDH online, #4620030.). She was baptized on 6 Nov 1837 Ste-Madeleine-de-Riguad, Quebec (Ibid.).
       She was in the census household of Charles Norbert Sabourin and Marguerite Jeanne Franche in 1852 Ste.Madeleine, Rigaud, Vaudreuil, Quebec (1852C Cdn Transcription Project, District 536, page 15d, 16a, (31), line 44-50, page 50d, 51a, (10), line 1-4.).

    iii. Isidore Sabourin was born on 7 Sep 1839 Ste-Madeleine-de-Riguad, Quebec (PRDH online, #4620478.). He was baptized on 7 Sep 1839 Ste-Madeleine-de-Riguad, Quebec (Ibid.).
       He was in the census household of Charles Norbert Sabourin and Marguerite Jeanne Franche in 1852 Ste.Madeleine, Rigaud, Vaudreuil, Quebec (1852C Cdn Transcription Project, District 536, page 15d, 16a, (31), line 44-50, page 50d, 51a, (10), line 1-4.).

    iv. Alphonse Sabourin was born on 4 Sep 1841 Ste-Madeleine-de-Riguad, Quebec (PRDH online, #4620966.). He was baptized on 5 Sep 1841 Ste-Madeleine-de-Riguad, Quebec (Ibid.).
       He was in the census household of Charles Norbert Sabourin and Marguerite Jeanne Franche in 1852 Ste.Madeleine, Rigaud, Vaudreuil, Quebec (1852C Cdn Transcription Project, District 536, page 15d, 16a, (31), line 44-50, page 50d, 51a, (10), line 1-4.).

    v.   Joseph Chrysologue Sabourin was born on 5 Sep 1843 Ste-Madeleine-de-Riguad, Quebec (PRDH online, #4621448.). He was baptized on 7 Sep 1843 Ste-Madeleine-de-Riguad, Quebec (Ibid.).
       He was in the census household of Charles Norbert Sabourin and Marguerite Jeanne Franche in 1852 Ste.Madeleine, Rigaud, Vaudreuil, Quebec (1852C Cdn Transcription Project, District 536, page 15d, 16a, (31), line 44-50, page 50d, 51a, (10), line 1-4.).

    vi. Dozite Sabourin was born on 11 Jul 1845 Ste-Madeleine-de-Riguad, Quebec (PRDH online, #4621857.). He was baptized on 11 Jul 1845 Ste-Madeleine-de-Riguad, Quebec (Ibid.).
       He was in the census household of Charles Norbert Sabourin and Marguerite Jeanne Franche in 1852 Ste.Madeleine, Rigaud, Vaudreuil, Quebec (1852C Cdn Transcription Project, District 536, page 15d, 16a, (31), line 44-50, page 50d, 51a, (10), line 1-4.).

    vii. Isaac Sabourin was born on 20 Oct 1847 Ste-Madeleine-de-Riguad, Quebec (PRDH online, #4622303.). He was baptized on 23 Oct 1847 Ste-Madeleine-de-Riguad, Quebec (Ibid.).
       He was in the census household of Charles Norbert Sabourin and Marguerite Jeanne Franche in 1852 Ste.Madeleine, Rigaud, Vaudreuil, Quebec (1852C Cdn Transcription Project, District 536, page 15d, 16a, (31), line 44-50, page 50d, 51a, (10), line 1-4.).

    viii. Marie Eulalie Sabourin was born on 23 Sep 1849 Ste-Madeleine-de-Riguad, Quebec (PRDH online, #4622607.). She was baptized on 24 Sep 1849 Ste-Madeleine-de-Riguad, Quebec (Ibid.).
       She was in the census household of Charles Norbert Sabourin and Marguerite Jeanne Franche in 1852 Ste.Madeleine, Rigaud, Vaudreuil, Quebec (1852C Cdn Transcription Project, District 536, page 15d, 16a, (31), line 44-50, page 50d, 51a, (10), line 1-4.).

    ix. Joseph Sabourin was born circa 1851 (Ibid.).
       He was in the census household of Charles Norbert Sabourin and Marguerite Jeanne Franche in 1852 Ste.Madeleine, Rigaud, Vaudreuil, Quebec (1852C Cdn Transcription Project, District 536, page 15d, 16a, (31), line 44-50, page 50d, 51a, (10), line 1-4.).

132. **Arsene Clement Sabourin** was born on 14 Aug 1821 Ste-Madeleine-de-Riguad, Quebec (PRDH online, #2680905.). He was baptized on 14 Aug 1821 Ste-Madeleine-de-Riguad, Quebec *(father's occupation: day laborer)* (PRDH online, #2680905.). He married **Mare Adelaide Patry or Patrice**, daughter of **Andre Patry** and **Louise Sabourin,** on 25 Nov 1845 Ste-Madeleine-de-Riguad, Quebec (Ibid., #3466533.).

Mare Adelaide Patry or Patrice was born on 11 Aug 1826 Ste-Madeleine-de-Riguad, Quebec (Ibid., #4617409.). She was baptized on 11 Aug 1826 Ste-Madeleine-de-Riguad, Quebec (Ibid.).

Children of **Arsene Clement Sabourin** and **Mare Adelaide Patry or Patrice** were:

> i. Josephine Sabourin was born on 27 Sep 1846 Ste-Madeleine-de-Riguad, Quebec (Ibid., #4622130.). She was baptized on 27 Sep 1846 Ste-Madeleine-de-Riguad, Quebec (Ibid.). She died on 27 Aug 1847 Ste-Madeleine-de-Riguad, Quebec (Ibid., #4624643.). She was buried on 28 Aug 1847 Ste-Madeleine-de-Riguad, Quebec (Ibid.).

133. **Benjamin Luc Charbonneau** was born on 24 Apr 1822 St-Benoit, Quebec (Ibid., #2516747.). He was baptized on 24 Apr 1822 St-Benoit, Quebec *(father's occupation: laborer)* (PRDH online, #2516747.). He married **Virginie Belec**, daughter of **Joseph Belec** and **Marguerite Langevin,** on 29 Aug 1843 (Mirabel), Ste-Scholastique, Quebec (Ibid., #3481889.).

He was enumerated in the census in 1852 Ste.Madeleine, Rigaud, Vaudreuil, Quebec. Also in the family: **Benjamin Charbonneau** and **Marie Anne Sabourin** *(Charbonneau, Benjamin, Journalier, Ste Scholastique F, Catholique, 27, M; Charbonneau, Benjamin, Journalier, Ste Scholastique F, Catholique, 4, M; Sabourin, Marianne, Journalier, Rivière à la g? F, Catholique, 60, F)* (1852C Cdn Transcription Project, District 536, page 9d, 10a, (19), line 31-33.).

Virginie Belec was born circa 1825.

Children of **Benjamin Luc Charbonneau** and **Virginie Belec** all born (Mirabel), Ste-Scholastique, Quebec, were as follows:

> i. Virginie Charbonneau was born on 15 Apr 1844 (PRDH online, #4559023.). She was baptized on 15 Apr 1844 (Mirabel), Ste-Scholastique, Quebec (Ibid.). She died on 4 Aug 1844 (Mirabel), Ste-Scholastique, Quebec (Ibid., #4562383.). She was buried on 6 Aug 1844 (Mirabel), Ste-Scholastique, Quebec *(age 4 months)* (PRDH online, #4562383.).
>
> ii. Anonyme Charbonneau was born on 22 Apr 1845 (Ibid., #4562435.). He/she died on 22 Apr 1845 (Mirabel), Ste-Scholastique, Quebec (Ibid.). He/she was buried on 23 Apr 1845 (Mirabel), Ste-Scholastique, Quebec (Ibid.).
>
> iii. Benjamin Charbonneau was born on 19 Jul 1846 (Ibid., #4559531.). He was baptized on 19 Jul 1846 (Mirabel), Ste-Scholastique, Quebec (Ibid.).
> He was in the census household of Benjamin Luc Charbonneau in 1852 Ste.Madeleine, Rigaud, Vaudreuil, Quebec (1852C Cdn Transcription Project, District 536, page 9d, 10a, (19), line 31-33.).
>
> iv. Virginie Charbonneau was born on 22 May 1848 (PRDH online, #4559960.). She was baptized on 22 May 1848 (Mirabel), Ste-Scholastique, Quebec (Ibid.).

134. **Virginie Charbonneau** was born on 12 Oct 1829 (Mirabel), Ste-Scholastique, Quebec (Ibid., #4555018.). She was baptized on 12 Oct 1829 (Mirabel), Ste-Scholastique, Quebec (Ibid.). She married **Francois Xavier Rouleau**, son of **Antoine Rouleau** and **Marie Giguere,** on 6 Mar 1848 Ste-Anne-du-Grand-Calumet, Quebec (Ibid., #3959957.). She died on 2 Jan 1849 Ste-Anne-du-Grand-Calumet, Quebec, at age 19 (Ibid., #4727368.). She was buried on 4 Jan 1849 Ste-Anne-du-Grand-Calumet, Quebec *(age 19, wife of Francois Xavier Rouleau)* (PRDH online, #4727368.).

Francois Xavier Rouleau was born on 9 May 1821 Berthierville, Quebec (Ibid., #2375202.). He was baptized on 10 May 1821 Berthierville, Quebec *(father's occupation: agriculture)* (PRDH online, #2375202.).

Children of **Virginie Charbonneau** and **Francois Xavier Rouleau** both born Ste-Anne-du-Grand-Calumet, Quebec, were as follows:

> i. Anonyme Rouleau was born on 2 Jan 1849 (Ibid., #4727369.). He/she died on 2 Jan 1849 Ste-Anne-du-Grand-Calumet, Quebec (Ibid.). He/she was buried on 4 Jan 1849 Ste-Anne-du-Grand-Calumet, Quebec (Ibid.).
>
> ii. Anonyme Rouleau was born on 2 Jan 1849 (Ibid., #4727370.). He/she died on 2 Jan 1849 Ste-Anne-du-Grand-Calumet, Quebec (Ibid.). He/she was buried on 4 Jan 1849 Ste-Anne-du-Grand-Calumet, Quebec (Ibid.).

135. **Marie Julienne Sabourin** was born on 21 Jul 1820 Ste-Madeleine-de-Riguad, Quebec (Ibid., #2680781.). She was baptized on 21 Jul 1820 Ste-Madeleine-de-Riguad, Quebec *(father's occuation: day laborer)* (PRDH online, #2680781.). She married **Antoine Gagnon**, son of **Charles Gagnon** and **Marie Anne Chaille dit Chagne,** on 28 Aug 1837 Ste-Madeleine-de-Riguad, Quebec (Ibid., #3464319.).

Antoine Gagnon was born on 20 Jan 1812 Notre-Dame-de-Montreal, Quebec (Ibid., #2488165.). He was baptized on 20 Jan 1812 Notre-Dame-de-Montreal, Quebec *(father's occuation: carpenter)* (PRDH online, #2488165.).

Children of **Marie Julienne Sabourin** and **Antoine Gagnon** all born Ste-Madeleine-de-Riguad, Quebec, were as follows:

    i.   Julie Gagnon was born on 6 Sep 1838 (Ibid., #4620216.). She was baptized on 6 Sep 1838 Ste-Madeleine-de-Riguad, Quebec (Ibid.). She died on 22 Sep 1838 Ste-Madeleine-de-Riguad, Quebec (Ibid., #4623885.). She was buried on 24 Sep 1838 Ste-Madeleine-de-Riguad, Quebec *(age 2 weeks)* (PRDH online, #4623885.).

    ii.   Marie Julie Gagnon was born on 9 Oct 1839 (Ibid., #4620498.). She was baptized on 9 Oct 1839 Ste-Madeleine-de-Riguad, Quebec (Ibid.).

    iii.   Anonyme Gagnon was born on 23 Jul 1841 (Ibid., #4624164.). He died on 23 Jul 1841 Ste-Madeleine-de-Riguad, Quebec (Ibid.). He was buried on 23 Jul 1841 Ste-Madeleine-de-Riguad, Quebec (Ibid.).

    iv.   Cyrille Onesime Gagnon was born on 10 Aug 1842 (Ibid., #4621182.). He was baptized on 12 Aug 1842 Ste-Madeleine-de-Riguad, Quebec (Ibid.).

    v.   Marie Philomene Gagnon was born on 14 Mar 1844 (Ibid., #4621545.). She was baptized on 14 Mar 1844 Ste-Madeleine-de-Riguad, Quebec (Ibid.).

    vi.   Virginie Gagnon was born on 21 Sep 1846 (Ibid., #4622128.). She was baptized on 22 Sep 1846 Ste-Madeleine-de-Riguad, Quebec (Ibid.).

    vii.   Joseph Aimee Gagnon was born on 1 May 1848 (Ibid., #4622396.). He was baptized on 5 May 1848 Ste-Madeleine-de-Riguad, Quebec (Ibid.).

136. Paul Desire Sabourin was born on 21 Jul 1821 Ste-Madeleine-de-Riguad, Quebec (Ibid., #2680898.). He was baptized on 21 Jul 1821 Ste-Madeleine-de-Riguad, Quebec *(father's occuation: day laborer)* (PRDH online, #2680898.). He married **Marie Julie Brunet**, daughter of **Jean Baptiste Brunet** and **Marie Rose Bedard,** on 12 Jan 1846 Ste-Madeleine-de-Riguad, Quebec (Ibid., #3466554.).

He was in the census household of **Paul Sabourin** and **Marie Anne Leblanc** in 1852 Ste.Madeleine, Rigaud, Vaudreuil, Quebec (1852C Cdn Transcription Project, District 536, page 50d, 51a, (101), line 5-17.).

Marie Julie Brunet was born on 26 Feb 1828 Ste-Madeleine-de-Riguad, Quebec (PRDH online, #4617686.). She was baptized on 26 Feb 1828 Ste-Madeleine-de-Riguad, Quebec (Ibid.).

She was in the census household of **Paul Sabourin** and **Marie Anne Leblanc** in 1852 Ste.Madeleine, Rigaud, Vaudreuil, Quebec (1852C Cdn Transcription Project, District 536, page 50d, 51a, (101), line 5-17.).

Children of **Paul Desire Sabourin** and **Marie Julie Brunet** were as follows:

    i.   Theophile Sabourin was born on 13 Dec 1846 Ste-Madeleine-de-Riguad, Quebec (PRDH online, #4622161.). He was baptized on 13 Dec 1846 Ste-Madeleine-de-Riguad, Quebec (Ibid.).
He was in the census household of Paul Sabourin and Marie Anne Leblanc in 1852 Ste.Madeleine, Rigaud, Vaudreuil, Quebec (1852C Cdn Transcription Project, District 536, page 50d, 51a, (101), line 5-17.).

    ii.   Julie Sabourin was born on 25 Dec 1848 Ste-Madeleine-de-Riguad, Quebec (PRDH online, #4622496.). She was baptized on 26 Dec 1848 Ste-Madeleine-de-Riguad, Quebec (Ibid.).
She was in the census household of Paul Sabourin and Marie Anne Leblanc in 1852 Ste.Madeleine, Rigaud, Vaudreuil, Quebec (1852C Cdn Transcription Project, District 536, page 50d, 51a, (101), line 5-17.).

    iii.   Josephine Sabourin was born circa 1851 (Ibid.).
She was in the census household of Paul Sabourin and Marie Anne Leblanc in 1852 Ste.Madeleine, Rigaud, Vaudreuil, Quebec (1852C Cdn Transcription Project, District 536, page 50d, 51a, (101), line 5-17.).

137. Edouard Sabourin was born on 6 Feb 1823 Ste-Madeleine-de-Riguad, Quebec (PRDH online, #2681144.). He was baptized on 7 Feb 1823 Ste-Madeleine-de-Riguad, Quebec *(father's occuation: day laborer)* (PRDH online, #2681144.). He married **Marie Arline Brunet dit Letang**, daughter of **Jean Baptiste Brunet** and **Marie Rose Bedard,** on 30 Jul 1844 Ste-Madeleine-de-Riguad, Quebec (Ibid., #3466010.).

Marie Arline Brunet dit Letang was born on 3 May 1824 Ste-Madeleine-de-Riguad, Quebec (Ibid., #2681348.). She was baptized on 4 May 1824 Ste-Madeleine-de-Riguad, Quebec (Ibid.).

Children of **Edouard Sabourin** and **Marie Arline Brunet dit Letang** all born Ste-Madeleine-de-Riguad, Quebec, were as follows:

    i.   Amedee Sabourin was born on 31 Jul 1845 (Ibid., #4621875.). He was baptized on 1 Aug 1845 Ste-Madeleine-de-Riguad, Quebec (Ibid.).

    ii.   Marie Arline Sabourin was born on 17 Feb 1847 (Ibid., #4622188.). She was baptized on 19 Feb 1847 Ste-Madeleine-de-Riguad, Quebec (Ibid.).

    iii.   Alfred Sabourin was born on 24 Jun 1849 (Ibid., #4622573.). He was baptized on 25 Jun 1849 Ste-Madeleine-de-Riguad, Quebec (Ibid.).

138. **Marie Rose Adele Sabourin** was born on 21 Mar 1825 Ste-Madeleine-de-Riguad, Quebec (Ibid., #4617178.). She was baptized on 21 Mar 1825 Ste-Madeleine-de-Riguad, Quebec (Ibid.). She married **Louis Millet**, son of **Charles Millet** and **Marie Marguerite Depos**, on 20 Feb 1843 Ste-Madeleine-de-Riguad, Quebec (Ibid., #3465692.).

She and **Louis Millet** were enumerated in the census in 1852 Ste.Madeleine, Rigaud, Vaudreuil, Quebec. Also in the family: **Eleonore Millet**, **Adele Millet**, **Marie Eugenie Millet**, and **Mathilde Millet** *(Millet, Louis, Journalier, Rigaud, Catholique, 32, M; Sabourin, Adèle, Rigaud, Catholique, 28, F; Millet, Leonard, Rigaud, Catholique, 8, F; Millet, Adèle, Rigaud, Catholique, 6, F; Millet, Eugenie, Rigaud, Catholique, 4, F; Millet, Mathilde, Rigaud, Catholique, 2, F)* (1852C Cdn Transcription Project, District 536, page 56d, 57a, (113), line 22-27.).

Louis Millet was born on 21 Oct 1814 St-Sulpice, Quebec (PRDH online, #2918176.). He was baptized on 21 Oct 1814 St-Sulpice, Quebec *(father's occuation: day laborer)* (PRDH online, #2918176.).

Children of **Marie Rose Adele Sabourin** and **Louis Millet** all born Ste-Madeleine-de-Riguad, Quebec, were as follows:

i. Eleonore Millet was born on 9 Oct 1844 (Ibid., #4621513.). She was baptized on 10 Oct 1844 Ste-Madeleine-de-Riguad, Quebec (Ibid.).

    She was in the census household of Louis Millet and Marie Rose Adele Sabourin in 1852 Ste.Madeleine, Rigaud, Vaudreuil, Quebec (1852C Cdn Transcription Project, District 536, page 56d, 57a, (113), line 22-27.).

ii. Adele Millet was born on 21 Dec 1845 (PRDH online, #4621951.). She was baptized on 22 Dec 1845 Ste-Madeleine-de-Riguad, Quebec (Ibid.).

    She was in the census household of Louis Millet and Marie Rose Adele Sabourin in 1852 Ste.Madeleine, Rigaud, Vaudreuil, Quebec (1852C Cdn Transcription Project, District 536, page 56d, 57a, (113), line 22-27.).

iii. Marie Eugenie Millet was born on 26 Sep 1847 (PRDH online, #4622295.). She was baptized on 27 Sep 1847 Ste-Madeleine-de-Riguad, Quebec (Ibid.).

    She was in the census household of Louis Millet and Marie Rose Adele Sabourin in 1852 Ste.Madeleine, Rigaud, Vaudreuil, Quebec (1852C Cdn Transcription Project, District 536, page 56d, 57a, (113), line 22-27.).

iv. Mathilde Millet was born on 31 Oct 1849 (PRDH online, #4622625.). She was baptized on 1 Nov 1849 Ste-Madeleine-de-Riguad, Quebec (Ibid.).

    She was in the census household of Louis Millet and Marie Rose Adele Sabourin in 1852 Ste.Madeleine, Rigaud, Vaudreuil, Quebec (1852C Cdn Transcription Project, District 536, page 56d, 57a, (113), line 22-27.).

139. **Francois Charles Sabourin** was born on 27 Sep 1819 Ste-Madeleine-de-Riguad, Quebec (PRDH online, #2680667.). He was baptized on 27 Sep 1819 Ste-Madeleine-de-Riguad, Quebec (Ibid.). He married **Marie Marguerite Hamelin**, daughter of **Francois Xavier Hamelin** and **Francoise Devoyeaux dit Laframboise,** on 12 Nov 1839 Ste-Madeleine-de-Riguad, Quebec (Ibid., #3464913.).

Marie Marguerite Hamelin was born on 4 Dec 1822 St-Benoit, Quebec (Ibid., #2516947.). She was baptized on 6 Dec 1822 St-Benoit, Quebec (Ibid.).

Children of **Francois Charles Sabourin** and **Marie Marguerite Hamelin** all born Ste-Madeleine-de-Riguad, Quebec, were as follows:

i. Olympe Sabourin was born on 8 Sep 1840 (Ibid., #4620709.). She was baptized on 9 Sep 1840 Ste-Madeleine-de-Riguad, Quebec (Ibid.). She died on 27 Aug 1841 Ste-Madeleine-de-Riguad, Quebec (Ibid., #4624182.). She was buried on 29 Aug 1841 Ste-Madeleine-de-Riguad, Quebec (Ibid.).

ii. Alphonse Sabourin was born on 5 Jan 1843 (Ibid., #4621286.). He was baptized on 6 Jan 1843 Ste-Madeleine-de-Riguad, Quebec (Ibid.).

iii. George Sabourin was born on 6 Jul 1845 (Ibid., #4621853.). He was baptized on 7 Jul 1845 Ste-Madeleine-de-Riguad, Quebec (Ibid.).

iv. Francois Xavier Sabourin was born on 28 Jul 1847 (Ibid., #4622265.). He was baptized on 28 Jul 1847 Ste-Madeleine-de-Riguad, Quebec (Ibid.). He died on 29 Jul 1847 Ste-Madeleine-de-Riguad, Quebec (Ibid., #4624633.). He was buried on 30 Jul 1847 Ste-Madeleine-de-Riguad, Quebec (Ibid.).

140. **Pierre Clement Sabourin** was born on 16 Apr 1821 Ste-Madeleine-de-Riguad, Quebec (Ibid., #2680862.). He was baptized on 16 Apr 1821 Ste-Madeleine-de-Riguad, Quebec (Ibid.). He married **Marguerite Deguire**, daughter of **Jerome Deguire** and **Charlotte Calve,** on 17 Oct 1843 Ste-Madeleine-de-Riguad, Quebec (Ibid., #3465834.).

Marguerite Deguire was born on 26 Mar 1818 St-Benoit, Quebec (Ibid.). She was baptized on 26 Mar 1818 St-Benoit, Quebec *(father's occupation: day laborer)* (PRDH online, #3465834.).
Children of **Pierre Clement Sabourin** and **Marguerite Deguire** all born Ste-Madeleine-de-Riguad, Quebec, were as follows:

> i. Marguerite Sabourin was born on 14 Aug 1844 (Ibid., #4621648.). She was baptized on 14 Aug 1844 Ste-Madeleine-de-Riguad, Quebec (Ibid.).
> ii. Marie Arline Sabourin was born on 25 Oct 1845 (Ibid., #4621922.). She was baptized on 25 Oct 1845 Ste-Madeleine-de-Riguad, Quebec (Ibid.).
> iii. Marie Auxilie Sabourin was born on 16 Mar 1848 (Ibid., #4622375.). She was baptized on 16 Mar 1848 Ste-Madeleine-de-Riguad, Quebec (Ibid.).

141. Josephte Seguin was born on 2 Aug 1828 Ste-Madeleine-de-Riguad, Quebec (Ibid., #4617778.). She was baptized on 2 Aug 1828 Ste-Madeleine-de-Riguad, Quebec (Ibid.). She married **Pierre Poitras**, son of **Joseph Poitras dit Turenne** and **Marie Houle,** on 9 Feb 1847 Ste-Madeleine-de-Riguad, Quebec (Ibid., #3466921.).
She and **Pierre Poitras** were enumerated in the census in 1852 Ste.Madeleine, Rigaud, Vaudreuil, Quebec. Also in the family: **Jean Baptiste Ronald Poitras**, **Joseph Poitras**, and **Marguerite Poitras** *(Poitras, Pierre, Batelier, Assomption, Catholique, 38, M; Séguin, Josephte, Rigaud, Catholique, 22, F; Poitra, J B Rouell(?), Rigaud, Catholique, 3, M; Poitra, Joseph, Rigaud, Catholique, 2, M; Séguin [?], Marg., Rigaud, Catholique, 2M, F)* (1852C Cdn Transcription Project, District 536, page 1a, (1), line 42-46.).
Pierre Poitras was born on 19 Dec 1814 L'Assomption, Quebec (PRDH online, #2439911.). He was baptized on 19 Dec 1814 L'Assomption, Quebec *(father's occupation: cultivator)* (PRDH online, #2439911.).
Children of **Josephte Seguin** and **Pierre Poitras** were as follows:

> i. Anonyme Poitras was born on 9 Jul 1847 Ste-Madeleine-de-Riguad, Quebec (Ibid., #4624623.). He/she died on 9 Jul 1847 Ste-Madeleine-de-Riguad, Quebec (Ibid.). He/she was buried on 11 Jul 1847 Ste-Madeleine-de-Riguad, Quebec (Ibid.).
> ii. Jean Baptiste Ronald Poitras was born on 3 Aug 1848 Ste-Madeleine-de-Riguad, Quebec (Ibid., #4622436.). He was baptized on 4 Aug 1848 Ste-Madeleine-de-Riguad, Quebec (Ibid.).
> He was in the census household of Pierre Poitras and Josephte Seguin in 1852 Ste.Madeleine, Rigaud, Vaudreuil, Quebec (1852C Cdn Transcription Project, District 536, page 1a, (1), line 42-46.).
> iii. Joseph Poitras was born circa 1850 (Ibid.).
> He was in the census household of Pierre Poitras and Josephte Seguin in 1852 Ste.Madeleine, Rigaud, Vaudreuil, Quebec (1852C Cdn Transcription Project, District 536, page 1a, (1), line 42-46.).
> iv. Marguerite Poitras was born circa 1852 (Ibid.).
> She was in the census household of Pierre Poitras and Josephte Seguin in 1852 Ste.Madeleine, Rigaud, Vaudreuil, Quebec (1852C Cdn Transcription Project, District 536, page 1a, (1), line 42-46.).

142. Joseph Edouard Sauve was born on 16 Oct 1822 Vaudreuil, Quebec (PRDH online, #2591970.). He was baptized on 17 Oct 1822 Vaudreuil, Quebec *(father's occupation: cultivator)* (PRDH online, #2591970.). He married **Marcelline Denys dit St.Denys**, daughter of **Hyacinthe Denis dit St.Denis** and **Marie Rose Cholet,** on 22 Oct 1844 Vaudreuil, Quebec (Ibid., #3477087.).
He and **Marcelline Denys dit St.Denys** were enumerated in the census in 1852 Ste-Madeleine-de-Rigaud, Vaudreuil, Quebec. Also in the family: **Joseph Oliivier Sauve**, **Marie Henriette Sauve**, and **Marguerite Sauve** *(Sauvé, Edouard, Rigaud, Catholique, 29, M; St Denis, Marceline, Cultivateur, Vaudreuil, Catholique, 25, F; St Denis, Joseph, Rigaud, Catholique, 3, M; St Denis, Henriette, Rigaud, Catholique, 3, F; St Denis, Marguerite, Rigaud, Catholique, 1, F)* (1852C Cdn Transcription Project, District 536, page 27d, 28a, (55), line 40-44.).
Marcelline Denys dit St.Denys was born on 19 Sep 1824 Vaudreuil, Quebec (PRDH online, #2592184.). She was baptized on 19 Sep 1824 Vaudreuil, Quebec *(father's occupation: cultivator)* (PRDH online, #2592184.).
Children of **Joseph Edouard Sauve** and **Marcelline Denys dit St.Denys** all born Ste-Madeleine-de-Rigaud, Quebec, were as follows:

> i. Aurelie Sauve was born on 11 May 1846 (Ibid., #4622039.). She was baptized on 12 May 1846 Ste-Madeleine-de-Rigaud, Quebec (Ibid.). She died on 29 Mar 1849 Ste-Madeleine-de-Rigaud, Quebec, at age 2 (Ibid., #4624716.). She was buried on 31 Mar 1849 Ste-Madeleine-de-Rigaud, Quebec (Ibid.).
> ii. Louise Sauve was born on 1 Jul 1847 (Ibid., #4622254.). She was baptized on 1 Jul 1847 Ste-Madeleine-de-Rigaud, Quebec (Ibid.). She died on 22 Jul 1847 Ste-Madeleine-de-Rigaud,

Quebec (Ibid., #4624628.). She was buried on 24 Jul 1847 Ste-Madeleine-de-Rigaud, Quebec *(age 3 weeks)* (PRDH online, #4624628.).

iii. Joseph Oliivier Sauve was born on 15 Jun 1848 (Ibid., #4622414.). He was baptized on 15 Jun 1848 Ste-Madeleine-de-Rigaud, Quebec (Ibid.).

He was in the census household of Joseph Edouard Sauve and Marcelline Denys dit St.Denys in 1852 Ste-Madeleine-de-Rigaud, Vaudreuil, Quebec (1852C Cdn Transcription Project, District 536, page 27d, 28a, (55), line 40-44.).

iv. Marie Henriette Sauve was born on 15 Jun 1848 (PRDH online, #4622415.). She was baptized on 15 Jun 1848 Ste-Madeleine-de-Rigaud, Quebec (Ibid.).

She was in the census household of Joseph Edouard Sauve and Marcelline Denys dit St.Denys in 1852 Ste-Madeleine-de-Rigaud, Vaudreuil, Quebec (1852C Cdn Transcription Project, District 536, page 27d, 28a, (55), line 40-44.).

v. Marguerite Sauve was born circa 1850 (Ibid.).

She was in the census household of Joseph Edouard Sauve and Marcelline Denys dit St.Denys in 1852 Ste-Madeleine-de-Rigaud, Vaudreuil, Quebec (1852C Cdn Transcription Project, District 536, page 27d, 28a, (55), line 40-44.).

143. Suzanne Vachon was born on 1 Dec 1822 Ste-Madeleine-de-Rigaud, Quebec (PRDH online, #2681123.). She was baptized on 3 Dec 1822 Ste-Madeleine-de-Rigaud, Quebec *(father's occupation: cultivator)* (PRDH online, #2681123.). She married **Felix Duchesne**, son of **Joseph Isidore Gatignon dit Duchene** and **Marie Genevieve Masson,** on 11 Feb 1840 Ste-Madeleine-de-Rigaud, Quebec (Ibid., #3465021.). She died on 4 Feb 1842 Ste-Madeleine-de-Rigaud, Quebec, at age 19 (Ibid., #4624227.). She was buried on 6 Feb 1842 Ste-Madeleine-de-Rigaud, Quebec *(age 19, wife of Felix Duchesne)* (PRDH online, #4624227.).

Felix Duchesne was born on 2 Nov 1818 St-Benoit, Quebec (Ibid., #2515686.). He was baptized on 2 Nov 1818 St-Benoit, Quebec *(father's occupation: laborer)* (PRDH online, #2515686.). He married **Rose Benard**, daughter of **Jean Baptiste Benard** and **Hyppolite Sauve,** on 7 Feb 1843 Ste-Madeleine-de-Rigaud, Quebec *(consanguinity: 4)* (PRDH online, #3465667.).

Children of **Suzanne Vachon** and **Felix Duchesne** were:

i. Marie Soulange Duchaine was born on 16 Dec 1840 Ste-Madeleine-de-Rigaud, Quebec (Ibid., #4620771.). She was baptized on 17 Dec 1840 Ste-Madeleine-de-Rigaud, Quebec (Ibid.).

144. Jean Baptiste Vachon was born on 5 Sep 1824 Ste-Madeleine-de-Rigaud, Quebec (Ibid., #2681398.). He was baptized on 6 Sep 1824 Ste-Madeleine-de-Rigaud, Quebec *(father's occupation: cultivator)* (PRDH online, #2681398.). He married **Marie Elisabeth Cardinal**, daughter of **Arsene Cardinal** and **Geenvieve Devoyau dit Laframboise,** on 15 Nov 1844 Ste-Madeleine-de-Rigaud, Quebec (Ibid., #3466132.).

He and **Marie Elisabeth Cardinal** were enumerated in the census in 1852 Ste-Madeleine-de-Rigaud, Vaudreuil, Quebec. Also in the family: **Edwidge Vachon**, **Anne Vachon**, **Jean Baptiste Vachon**, **Marie Domitille Vachon**, and **Dozithee Vachon** *(Vachon, J B, Cultivateur, Rigaud, Catholique, 27, M; Cardinal, Elisabethe, Rigaud, Catholique, 27, F; Vachon, Eduidge, Rigaud, Catholique, 6, F; Vachon, Nansy, Rigaud, Catholique, 5, F; Vachon, J B, Rigaud, Catholique, 3, M; Vachon, Domithilde, Rigaud, Catholiquem 3, F; Vachon, Dozithée, Rigaud, Catholique, 1, M)* (1852C Cdn Transcription Project, District 536, page 24d, 25a, (49), line 10-16.).

Marie Elisabeth Cardinal was born circa 1825 (Ibid.).

Children of **Jean Baptiste Vachon** and **Marie Elisabeth Cardinal** were as follows:

i. Edwidge Vachon was born on 22 Jul 1845 (PRDH online, #4621871.). She was baptized on 27 Jul 1845 Ste-Madeleine-de-Rigaud, Quebec (Ibid.).

She was in the census household of Jean Baptiste Vachon and Marie Elisabeth Cardinal in 1852 Ste-Madeleine-de-Rigaud, Vaudreuil, Quebec (1852C Cdn Transcription Project, District 536, page 24d, 25a, (49), line 10-16.).

ii. Anne Vachon was born on 4 Jan 1847 Ste-Madeleine-de-Rigaud, Quebec (PRDH online, #4622168.). She was baptized on 6 Jan 1847 Ste-Madeleine-de-Rigaud, Quebec (Ibid.).

She was in the census household of Jean Baptiste Vachon and Marie Elisabeth Cardinal in 1852 Ste-Madeleine-de-Rigaud, Vaudreuil, Quebec (1852C Cdn Transcription Project, District 536, page 24d, 25a, (49), line 10-16.).

iii. Jean Baptiste Vachon was born on 17 Sep 1848 Ste-Madeleine-de-Rigaud, Quebec *(twin)* (PRDH online, #4622453.). He was baptized on 19 Sep 1848 Ste-Madeleine-de-Rigaud, Quebec (Ibid.).

He was in the census household of Jean Baptiste Vachon and Marie Elisabeth Cardinal in 1852 Ste-Madeleine-de-Rigaud, Vaudreuil, Quebec (1852C Cdn Transcription Project, District 536, page 24d, 25a, (49), line 10-16.).

    iv. Marie Domitille Vachon was born on 17 Sep 1848 Ste-Madeleine-de-Rigaud, Quebec *(twin)* (PRDH online, #4622454.). She was baptized on 19 Sep 1848 Ste-Madeleine-de-Rigaud, Quebec (Ibid.).

        She was in the census household of Jean Baptiste Vachon and Marie Elisabeth Cardinal in 1852 Ste-Madeleine-de-Rigaud, Vaudreuil, Quebec (1852C Cdn Transcription Project, District 536, page 24d, 25a, (49), line 10-16.).

    v. Dozithee Vachon was born circa 1850 (Ibid.).

        He was in the census household of Jean Baptiste Vachon and Marie Elisabeth Cardinal in 1852 Ste-Madeleine-de-Rigaud, Vaudreuil, Quebec (1852C Cdn Transcription Project, District 536, page 24d, 25a, (49), line 10-16.).

145. Joseph Alexandre Berlinguet was born on 19 Jun 1825 Ste-Madeleine-de-Rigaud, Quebec (PRDH online, #4617217.). He was baptized on 19 Jun 1825 Ste-Madeleine-de-Rigaud, Quebec (Ibid.). He married **Justine Normand**, daughter of **Felix Normand** and **Marie Josephte Gauthier,** on 18 Oct 1847 Vaudreuil, Quebec (Ibid., #3477801.).

He and **Justine Normand** were enumerated in the census in 1852 St.Michel, Vaudreuil, Vaudreuil, Quebec. Also in the family: **Marie Olympe Berlinguet** and **Normantine Berlinguette** *(Berlinguette, Alexandre, Journalier, Rigaud F, Catholique romaine, 24, M; Norman, Justine, Rigaud F, Catholique romaine, 25, F; Berlinguette, Olypme, Vaudreuil F, Catholique romaine, 4, F; Berlinguette, Normantine, Vaudreuil F, Catholique romaine, 2, F)* (1852C Cdn Transcription Project, District 534, page 54d, 55a, (109), line 28-31.).

Justine Normand was born on 9 May 1827 Ste-Madeleine-de-Rigaud, Quebec (PRDH online, #4617536.). She was baptized on 11 May 1827 Ste-Madeleine-de-Rigaud, Quebec (Ibid.).

Children of **Joseph Alexandre Berlinguet** and **Justine Normand** were as follows:

    i. Marie Olympe Berlinguet was born on 28 Jun 1848 Vaudreuil, Quebec (Ibid., #4180898.). She was baptized on 29 Jun 1848 Vaudreuil, Quebec (Ibid.).

        She was in the census household of Joseph Alexandre Berlinguet and Justine Normand in 1852 St.Michel, Vaudreuil, Vaudreuil, Quebec (1852C Cdn Transcription Project, District 534, page 54d, 55a, (109), line 28-31.).

    ii. Normantine Berlinguette was born circa 1850 (Ibid.).

        She was in the census household of Joseph Alexandre Berlinguet and Justine Normand in 1852 St.Michel, Vaudreuil, Vaudreuil, Quebec (1852C Cdn Transcription Project, District 534, page 54d, 55a, (109), line 28-31.).

146. Marie Angelique Berlinguet was born on 21 Jul 1827 Ste-Madeleine-de-Rigaud, Quebec (PRDH online, #4617576.). She was baptized on 22 Jul 1827 Ste-Madeleine-de-Rigaud, Quebec (Ibid.). She married **Leandre Legault dit Deslauriers**, son of **Etienne Legault dit Deslauriers** and **Lucie Lalonde,** on 26 Jan 1847 Vaudreuil, Quebec (Ibid., #3477608.).

She and **Leandre Legault dit Deslauriers** were enumerated in the census in 1852 St.Michel, Vaudreuil, Vaudreuil, Quebec. Also in the family: **Leandre Legault dit Deslauriers, Henriette Legault,** and **Marie Reine Narcisse Villeneuve** *(Legault, Léandre, Journalier, Vaudreuil F, Catholique romaine, 30, M; Berlinguette, Angelique, Vaudreuil F, Catholique romaine, 23, F; Legault, Leandre, Vaudreuil F, Catholique romaine, 4, M; Legault, Henriette, Vaudreuil F, Catholique romaine, 4 mois, F; Villeneuve, Reine, Vaudreuil F, Catholique romaine, 50, F)* (1852C Cdn Transcription Project, District 534, page 25d, 26a, (51), line 43-47.).

Leandre Legault dit Deslauriers was born on 8 Jun 1822 Les Cedres, Quebec (PRDH online, #2676210.). He was baptized on 9 Jun 1822 Les Cedres, Quebec *(father's occupation: cultivator)* (PRDH online, #2676210.).

Children of **Marie Angelique Berlinguet** and **Leandre Legault dit Deslauriers** were as follows:

    i. Leandre Legault dit Deslauriers was born on 26 Mar 1848 Oka, Quebec (Ibid., #4722413.). He was baptized on 27 Mar 1848 Oka, Quebec (Ibid.).

        He was in the census household of Leandre Legault dit Deslauriers and Marie Angelique Berlinguet in 1852 St.Michel, Vaudreuil, Vaudreuil, Quebec (1852C Cdn Transcription Project, District 534, page 25d, 26a, (51), line 43-47.).

    ii. Henriette Legault was born circa 1851 (Ibid.).

        She was in the census household of Leandre Legault dit Deslauriers and Marie Angelique Berlinguet in 1852 St.Michel, Vaudreuil, Vaudreuil, Quebec (1852C Cdn Transcription Project, District 534, page 25d, 26a, (51), line 43-47.).

Generation Six

147. **Marie Angelique Brazeau dit Brassault** was born on 5 Dec 1823 Ste-Madeleine-de-Rigaud, Quebec (PRDH online, #2681273.). She was baptized on 6 Dec 1823 Ste-Madeleine-de-Rigaud, Quebec *(father's occupation: cultivator)* (PRDH online, #2681273.). She married **Paul Sabourin**, son of **Francois Sabourin** and **Louise Seguin,** on 6 Feb 1849 Ste-Madeleine-de-Rigaud, Quebec (Ibid., #3467198.).

She was in the census household of **Francois Sabourin** and **Louise Seguin** circa 1852 Ste.Madeleine, Rigaud, Vaudreuil, Quebec (1852C Cdn Transcription Project, District 536, page 8d, 9a, (17), line 19-27.).

Paul Sabourin was born on 4 Aug 1822 Ste-Madeleine-de-Rigaud, Quebec (PRDH online, #4621502.). He was baptized on 4 Aug 1822 Ste-Madeleine-de-Rigaud, Quebec (Ibid.).

He was in the census household of **Francois Sabourin** and **Louise Seguin** circa 1852 Ste.Madeleine, Rigaud, Vaudreuil, Quebec (1852C Cdn Transcription Project, District 536, page 8d, 9a, (17), line 19-27.).

Children of **Marie Angelique Brazeau dit Brassault** and **Paul Sabourin** were:

      i.   Treffle Sabourin, b. circa 1851. (see previous).

148. **Marie Louise Brazeau** was born on 30 Jul 1827 Ste-Madeleine-de-Rigaud, Quebec (PRDH online, #4617581.). She was baptized on 30 Jul 1827 Ste-Madeleine-de-Rigaud, Quebec (Ibid.). She married **Joseph Sabourin**, son of **Francois Sabourin** and **Louise Seguin,** on 22 Feb 1848 Oka, Quebec (Ibid., #3467041.).

She and **Joseph Sabourin** were enumerated in the census in 1852 Ste.Madeleine, Rigaud, Vaudreuil, Quebec. Also in the family: **Francois Joseph Sabourin**, **Marie Louise Zenobe Sabourin**, and **Josephine Sabourin** *(Sabourin, Joseph, Cultivateur, Rigaud, Catholique, 25, M; Brazeau, Louise, Rigaud, Catholique, 24, F; Sabourin, Joseph, Rigaud, Catholique, 3, M; Sabourin, Louise, Rigaud, Catholique, 2, F; Sabourin, Joséphine, Rigaud, Catholique, 1 jour, F)* (1852C Cdn Transcription Project, District 536, page 23d, 24a, (47), line 37-41.).

Joseph Sabourin was born on 8 May 1826 Ste-Madeleine-de-Riguad, Quebec (PRDH online, #4617354.). He was baptized on 9 May 1826 Ste-Madeleine-de-Riguad, Quebec (Ibid.).

Children of **Marie Louise Brazeau** and **Joseph Sabourin** were as follows:

      i.   Francois Joseph Sabourin, b. 1 Dec 1848 Ste-Madeleine-de-Riguad, Quebec. (see previous).

      ii. Marie Louise Zenobe Sabourin, b. 23 Nov 1849 Ste-Madeleine-de-Riguad, Quebec. (see previous).

      iii. Josephine Sabourin, b. circa 1852. (see previous).

149. **Emilie Vallee** was born on 20 Nov 1828 Ste-Madeleine-de-Rigaud, Quebec (Ibid., #4617840.). She was baptized on 20 Nov 1828 Ste-Madeleine-de-Rigaud, Quebec (Ibid.). She married **Theodore Francois Xavier Mallette**, son of **Hyacinthe Mallette** and **Marguerite Chevrier**, on 19 Feb 1849 Ste-Madeleine-de-Rigaud, Quebec (Ibid., #3467226.).

She and **Theodore Francois Xavier Mallette** were enumerated in the census in 1852 Ste-Madeleine, Rigaud, Quebec. Also in the family: **Octavie Mallette** and **Octave Mallette** *(Malette, ThéaDore, institeur, Rigaud F, Catholique romaine, 24, M; Vallé, Emelie, Rigaud F, Catholique romaine, 22, F; Mallette, Octavie, Rigaud F, Catholique romaine, 2, F; Mallette, Octave, Rigaud F, Catholique romaine, 8 mois, M)* (1852C Cdn Transcription Project, District 537, page 15d, 16a, (31), line 20-23.).

Theodore Francois Xavier Mallette was born on 3 Jan 1827 Ste-Madeleine-de-Rigaud, Quebec (PRDH online, #4617463.). He was baptized on 4 Jan 1827 Ste-Madeleine-de-Rigaud, Quebec (Ibid.).

Children of **Emilie Vallee** and **Theodore Francois Xavier Mallette** were as follows:

      i.   Octavie Mallette was born circa 1850 (1852C Cdn Transcription Project, District 537, page 15d, 16a, (31), line 20-23.).

          She was in the census household of Theodore Francois Xavier Mallette and Emilie Vallee in 1852 Ste-Madeleine, Rigaud, Quebec (1852C Cdn Transcription Project, District 537, page 15d, 16a, (31), line 20-23.).

      ii. Octave Mallette was born circa 1851 (Ibid.).

          He was in the census household of Theodore Francois Xavier Mallette and Emilie Vallee in 1852 Ste-Madeleine, Rigaud, Quebec (1852C Cdn Transcription Project, District 537, page 15d, 16a, (31), line 20-23.).

150. **Joseph Hyacinthe Seguin** was born on 12 Jul 1826 Ste-Madeleine-de-Riguad, Quebec (PRDH online, #4617387.). He was baptized on 13 Jul 1826 Ste-Madeleine-de-Riguad, Quebec (Ibid.). He married **Sophie Sauve**, daughter of **Hyacinthe Sauve** and **Judith Seguin dit Laderoute**, on 29 Jul 1848 Ste-Madeleine-de-Riguad, Quebec *(Consanguinity: 4)* (PRDH online, #3467055.).

Sophie Sauve was born on 14 Feb 1827 Ste-Madeleine-de-Riguad, Quebec (Ibid., #4617480.). She was baptized on 15 Feb 1827 Ste-Madeleine-de-Riguad, Quebec (Ibid.).

Children of **Joseph Hyacinthe Seguin** and **Sophie Sauve** were:

i. Julie Rosalie Seguin was born on 16 Jun 1849 Ste-Madeleine-de-Riguad, Quebec (Ibid., #4622569.). She was baptized on 16 Jun 1849 Ste-Madeleine-de-Riguad, Quebec (Ibid.).

Bibliography

1835C RRS HBCA E5/8 1835 Census of the Red River Settlement, HBCA E5/8, Hudson's Bay Company Archives, Provincial Archives, 200 Vaughan Street, Winnipeg, MB R3C 1T5, Canada.

1870C-MB 1870 Manitoba Census, National Archives of Canada, Ottawa, Ontario, Microfilm Reel Number C-2170.

1881 Church of Latter Day Saints Census Transcription Project of Census Images from the National Archives of Canada, Ottawa, Canada, http://www.familysearch.org.

Automated Genealogy 1852 Census Transcription Project and Census Images from the National Archives of Canada, http://www.automatedgenealogy.com.

Automated Genealogy 1901 Census Transcription Project and Census Images from the National Archives of Canada, http://www.automatedgenealogy.com.

DGFC Tanguay, Cyprien, *Dictionnaire Genealogique des Familles Canadiennes* (28 Felsmere Avenue, Pawtucket, Rhode Island 02861-2903: Quintin Publications, 1996 reprint).

DGFQ Jette, Rene, *Dictionnaire Genealogique des Familles du Quebec des Origines a 1730* (Montreal, Quebec, Canada: University of Montreal Press, 1983).

Manitoba Vital Statistics online, http://web2.gov.mb.ca.

MBS   Scrip Applications, Original White Settlers & Halfbreeds residing in Manitoba on 15 July 1870, RG15-19, Volume 1319 through 1324, 2128, Microfilm Reel Number C-14925 through C-14934, National Archives of Canada, Ottawa, Ontario.

MM *Manitoba Marriages* in *Publication 45*, Volumes 1-3, compiled and edited by: Paul J. Lareau, Fr. Julien Hamelin, (240 Avenue Daly, Ottawa, Ontario K1N 6G2: Le Centre de Genealogie S.C., 1984).

PRDH online index, http://www.genealogic.umontreal.ca.

Rod MacQuarrie Research.

SB-Rozyk St. Boniface Roman Catholic Church, Manitoba, Canada, Baptisms, Marriages and Burials 1860-1875 Extractions, Compiled by Rosemary Rozyk.

SN1 Catholic Parish Register of St.Norbert 1857-1873.

SN2 Catholic Parish Register of St.Norbert.

(--?--): Marie Charles, 77

Arel: Marie Suzanne, 4

Armstrong: Adelaide (b. 1843, d. 1843), 39; Francois Thomas (b. 1827, d. 1829), 39; Jean Narcisse (b. 1841,   ), 39; Joseph (b. 1845, d. 1845), 39; Louis Thomas (b. 1825, d. 1826), 39; Louis Thomas (b. 1835, d. 1836), 39; Marie Catherine (b. 1828, d. 1830), 39; Marie Josephte (b. 1831,   ), 39; Marie Louise (b. 1837,   ), 39; Marie Marguerite (b. 1830, d. 1830), 39; Mathilde (b. 1839,   ), 39; Thomas, 39; Thomas (b. 1800,   ), 7, 39

Aubry: Antoine (b. 1802,   ), 9; Audre dit Thecle, 9

Barbary: Pierre dit Grandmaison, 33; Rosalie dit Grandmaison (b. 1816,   ), 33

Beauchamp: Scholastique, 55

Beaudry: Julie, 74

Beaupre: Francois Xavier (b. 1837,   ), 58; Joseph (b. 1833,   ), 58; Julienne (b. 1836, d. 1842), 58; Marie Marcelline (b. 1839,   ), 58; Pierre, 57; Pierre (b. 1790, d. 1841), 13, 57

Bedard: Antoine, 7; Charlotte, 89; Hippolyte (b. 1801,   ), 4, 24; Jean (b. 1775,   ), 24, 28; Marie Anne (b. 1769), 2, 7; Marie Colombe (b. 1808,   ), 6, 28, 29; Marie Madeleine, 3, 4; Marie Rose, 58, 92

Belanger: Benjamin Patrice (b. 1813,   ), 16, 74; Elie (b. 1848, d. 1849), 74; Francois, 62, 65, 74; Francois (b. 1790,   ), 11; Francois Damase (b. 1834,   ), 65; Francois Xavier (b. 1842, d. 1842), 74; Francois Zephirin (b. 1835,   ), 65; Joseph Alphonse (b. 1843, d. 1843), 74; Joseph Prosper (b. 1842,   ), 65; Julie (b. 1833,   ), 65; Marie Adeline (b. 1836,   ), 65; Marie Julienne (b. 1838, d. 1845), 65; Marie Madeleine (b. 1806,   ), 15, 62, 63; Marie Madeleine (b. 1839,   ), 74; Marie Olympe (b. 1840, d. 1847), 74; Marie Olympe Leocadie (b. 1840, d. 1846), 65; Marie Philomene (b. 1844, d. 1845), 74; Octavie (b. 1845, d. 1846), 65; Philomene (b. 1845, d. 1846), 74; Telesphore (b. 1843, d. 1846), 65; Vincent (b. 1802,   ), 15, 65

Belec: Joseph, 91; Virginie (b. 1825,   ), 36, 91

Bellefeuille: Marguerite, 57

Benard: Jean Baptiste, 95; Rose, 95

Benoit: Francois, 38; Francois dit Laguerre, 38

Berlinguet: Francois Xavier, 54; Francois Xavier (b. 1793, d. 1832), 11, 54, 55; Francois Xavier (b. 1824, d. 1824), 55; Henriette (b. 1830, d. 1842), 55; Joseph Alexandre (b. 1825,   ), 55, 96; Marie, 41; Marie Angelique (b. 1827,   ), 55, 96; Marie Olympe (b. 1848,   ), 96

Berlinguette: Normantine (b. 1850,   ), 96

Bernesse: Archange (b. 1810,   ), 6; Guillaume, 6

Bertrand: Antoine, 73, 74; Eleonore (b. 1851,   ), 80; Emerance (b. 1848,   ), 86; Francois Emery (b. 1849,   ), 80; Francois Vital (b. 1780), 80; Jean Baptiste (b. 1811,   ), 16, 73; Joseph Benjamin (b. 1796,   ), 85; Joseph Vital (b. 1820,   ), 85, 86; Joseph Vital (b. 1847, d. 1848), 86; Marguerite Sophie (b. 1816,   ), 16, 74; Marie Eloise (b. 1847,   ), 80; Marie Madeleine (b. 1838,   ), 73; Marie Priscille (b. 1846,   ), 80; Nicolas Emery (b. 1816,   ), 20, 80; Scholastique (b. 1844,   ), 86

Bleau: Josephte dit Blo, 77

Bonhomme: Marie Madeleine, 12

Boucher: Marcelline (b. 1830,   ), 79

Bourbonnais: Angele (b. 1823,   ), 12, 57

Boyer: Antoine dit Germain (b. 1804,   ), 11, 54; Antoine Marcel (b. 1849,   ), 54; Julie (b. 1847, d. 1848), 54; Marguerite Caroline (b. 1837,   ), 54; Narcisse Godfroi (b. 1845,   ), 54; Philomene (b. 1843,   ), 54; Pierre dit Fontaine (b. 1765,   ), 54; Sarah Anne (b. 1840,   ), 54

Brabant: Marie Amable dit Lamothe (b. 1751,   ), 7; Marie Marguerite (b. 1787,   ), 14; Marie Rose dit Lamothe (b. 1765, d. 1833), 30

Brassault: Jean Baptiste (b. 1822, d. 1822), 61; Marie Elisabeth (b. 1821, d. 1821), 61

Brasseur: Francois, 4, 5; Marie Angelique (bt. 1770, d. 1845), 2, 4, 5; Marie Madeleine (b. 1774, d. 1820), 5

Bray: Guillaume, 38; Marie Angele (b. 1821, d. 1845), 38

Brazault: Marie Sophie (b. 1826, d. 1827), 61

Brazeau: Andre (bt. 1791, d. 1835), 69; Bernard Benjamin Treffle (b. 1838,   ), 61, 62; Emily Rose (b. 1840,   ), 61, 62; Francois Xavier (b. 1836,   ), 61, 62; Jean Baptiste (b. 1834,   ), 61, 62; Jean Baptiste dit Brassault (bt. 1793,   ), 15, 61, 62, 87, 88; Jean-Baptiste (bt. 1767,   ), 61; Marie Angelique dit Brassault (b. 1823,   ), 26, 27, 61, 87, 88, 97; Marie Edesse (b. 1832,   ), 61, 62; Marie Helene (b. 1831, d. 1832), 62; Marie Josephine (b. 1842,   ), 61, 62; Marie Louise (b. 1827,   ), 27, 62, 88, 89, 97; Marie Sophie (b. 1829,   ), 61, 62; Marie Theotiste (b. 1815,   ), 15, 69, 70; Rose Gertrude (b. 1843,   ), 61, 62

Brouillard: Edouard (b. 1808,   ), 5, 26; Elie Napoleon (b. 1847, d. 1848), 26; Marie Onesime (b. 1845,   ), 26; Pierre (bt. 1756,   ), 26

Brunet: Alexandre (b. 1834, d. 1838), 36; Francoise Amable dit Bourbonnais, 11; Jean Baptiste, 92; Jean Baptiste dit Bourbonnais or Payant, 57; Jean Baptiste dit Letang (b. 1788,   ), 58; Louis (b. 1780,   ), 7, 35, 36; Marie Arline dit Letang (b. 1824,   ), 37, 92; Marie Julie (b. 1828,   ), 36, 37, 92; Michel, 35; Rose Emelie dit Letang (b. 1820,   ), 13, 58

Cadieux: Alexis Noel (bt. 1799,   ), 5, 26; Benjamin (b. 1832,   ), 20; Clothilde Arline Adeline (b. 1823, d. 1841), 20; Francois (b. 1766,   ), 19, 26; Francois Barnabe (b. 1828,   ), 20; Francois Dosithee (b. 1843, d. 1843), 26; Francois Xavier (b. 1790, d. 1834), 4, 19, 59, 60; Francois Xavier (b. 1811, d. 1814), 19; Francois Xavier (b. 1825,   ), 20; Francois Xavier (b. 1845,   ), 60, 61, 79; Honore (b. 1851,   ), 20, 60, 79; Jean Marie (b. 1817,   ), 14, 19, 20, 60, 61, 79; Joseph (b. 1791,   ), 81; Joseph Alexandre (b. 1831, d. 1844), 26; Josephte Caroline (b.